VISUAL QUICKSTART GUIDE

WINDOWS XP

Second Edition

Chris Fehily

 Peachpit Press

Visual QuickStart Guide
Windows XP, Second Edition
Chris Fehily

Peachpit Press

1249 Eighth Street
Berkeley, CA 94710
510/524-2178
800/283-9444
510/524-2221 (fax)
Find us on the World Wide Web at: http://www.peachpit.com
Peachpit Press is a division of Pearson Education
To report errors, please send a note to errata@peachpit.com

Editor: Kathy Simpson
Production Coordinator: Pat Christenson
Compositor: Owen Wolfson
Indexer: Rebecca Plunkett
Cover Production: George Mattingly/GMD
Cover Design: The Visual Group

Notice of rights

Notice of liability

Trademarks

ISBN 0-321-33584-8

9 8 7 6 5 4 3 2

Printed and bound in the United States of America

Dedication

For Diane Yee

Special thanks to...

Kathy Simpson, my unflappable editor.

Cliff Colby at Peachpit for getting the ball rolling.

Pat Christenson and Owen Wolfson for producing a great-looking book.

Rebecca Plunkett for indexing.

TABLE OF CONTENTS

Chapter 4: Personalizing Your Work Environment   95

Chapter 5: Organizing Files and Folders   155

TABLE OF CONTENTS

INTRODUCTION

Windows XP is the latest Microsoft operating system for personal computers and the biggest overhaul of Windows since Windows 95. XP inherits its core from Windows 2000, Microsoft's corporate operating system, but its improved interface and new features make it a fit for everyone at home, school, or work.

Windows XP debuted in 2001, and Microsoft has since released improvements to make XP more reliable and secure. This edition of *Windows XP: Visual QuickStart Guide* covers Service Pack 2 (released in August 2004) and Windows Media Player 10 (released a month later). I also give new security and privacy tips; recommend third-party add-ins, utilities, and programs; and describe recent updates to the free XP programs.

✔ Tip

- See "What's New in Windows XP" later in this introduction for an overview of the new features in Service Pack 2 (SP2). See "Updating Windows XP" in Chapter 19 for information about installing SP2.

What Windows Does

Windows—like every operating system, Microsoft or otherwise—is software that controls:

The user interface. Windows manages the appearance, behavior, and interaction of the windows, buttons, icons, folders, menus, and other visual elements on your computer screen, either directly or indirectly through another program.

Storage. Windows' file system allocates space for and gives access to files—programs and documents—stored on disk or in memory.

Other software. Windows is a launching platform for programs. When you run Microsoft Word, Adobe Photoshop, The Sims, or any other Windows program, it relies on the services and building blocks that Windows provides for basic operations such as drawing a user interface, saving files, and sharing hardware.

Peripheral devices. Windows controls peripheral hardware such as your mouse, keyboard, monitor, printer, drives, digital camera, and MP3 player.

Networks and security. Windows controls the interaction of a group of computers and peripheral devices connected by a communications link such as Ethernet or Wi-Fi. Windows also protects your system and data from harm or loss.

System resources. Windows handles the allocation and use of your computer's low-level hardware resources such as memory (RAM) and central processing unit (CPU) time.

Task scheduling. Windows acts like a traffic cop, setting priorities and allocating time slices to the processes running on your PC.

Shareware

Many of the third-party programs that I recommend in this book are shareware. *Shareware* is software that you download from the internet without paying for ahead of time (as you do for proprietary or shrink-wrapped software). After a free tryout period, usually 30 days, you're expected to pay for the program if you keep using it. You can copy shareware and pass it along to others, but they too are expected to pay a fee if they use the product. Sometimes, paying the fee gets you a key code that unlocks expanded features or turns off nag messages.

Shareware is inexpensive because usually only one programmer writes it and offers it directly to customers, bypassing middleman markups and packaging expenses. Some programs are free. If a popular free program—particularly a file-sharing program—isn't labeled "public domain" or "open source" (www.opensource.org), you should check it for spyware. See "Securing Your Computer" in Chapter 12.

I give the shareware programs' home web sites, but you also can download them from www.download.com or www.tucows.com. To keep up to date with the latest software releases, I read www.betanews.com (or www.microsoft-watch.com for Microsoft products).

Figure i.1 This PC is running Windows XP Professional Edition with Service Pack 2 installed; CPU and memory information also appear.

The Editions of Windows XP

Table i.1 lists the editions of Windows XP (so far); this book covers the Home and Professional editions.

PRO In general XP Home and Pro look and work alike, so most discussions apply to both editions equally. You'll see this symbol wherever I discuss a Pro feature not offered in Home (**Table i.2** on the next page).

To find out which edition you're running, choose Start > Control Panel > Performance and Maintenance > System > General tab (or press Windows logo key+Break) (**Figure i.1**).

Table i.1

Windows XP Editions

EDITION	DESCRIPTION
Home	Minimal budget edition usually bundled with home and small-business PCs
Professional	Includes everything in Home Edition, plus components for power users and network administrators
Media Center	Pro Edition plus digital-media support for video, audio, pictures, movies, and recorded TV (meant more for living rooms than offices)
Tablet PC	Pro Edition plus digital-ink support that lets you use a stylus to write on Tablet PC screens directly
64-Bit	Pro Edition plus support for high-end systems using Intel or AMD 64-bit processors

THE EDITIONS OF WINDOWS XP

Table i.2

Features Unique to XP Pro	
PRO FEATURE	LETS YOU DO THIS
Domain membership	Join a large group of networked computers that's administered as a unit. (Home Edition PCs can use domain servers and printers but can't be domain members themselves.)
Dynamic disks	Treat multiple hard disks as a single large disk.
Encrypting file system	Encrypt files and folders to keep them safe from intruders.
Internet Information Services	Host and manage simple web sites.
Multilingual support	Dynamically change the language used for input, spell checking, help files, user-interface elements, and other text.
Multiprocessor support	Recognize and use a second processor automatically. (Home Edition will run on a two-processor system but will use only one processor.)
Offline files	Make network files available offline by storing shared files on your laptop so that they're accessible when you're not connected to the network. Reconnecting to the network updates your changes to the network files.
Remote Desktop	Control a remote computer, via internet or LAN, from another computer. Use your home PC to work with all your work PC's data and programs remotely, for example.
Roaming user profiles	Have your personal settings and desktop appear on any networked computer you log on to (not just your personal PC).
User management	Use Group Policy to define and enforce complex disk-, folder-, and file-level security policies by user. (Home Edition has only two simple security levels.)

What's New in Windows XP

If you're familiar with earlier versions of Windows, the following new XP features are the ones that you'll find notable.

Interface

Windows XP's updated user interface includes a redesigned Start menu and Control Panel, as well as cosmetic changes.

Cleaner desktop. The default desktop is austere (**Figure i.2**). You can add other icons or run Desktop Cleanup Wizard to remove rarely used ones.

Figure i.2 The Recycle Bin keeps a lonely vigil on the default desktop. If you upgraded to XP, your desktop retained its old personality. On a new PC, the manufacturer may have changed the background and scattered extra icons.

Redesigned Start menu. The new Start menu (**Figure i.3**) has two columns: programs on the left and system features such as Help and Support, My Documents, and Control Panel on the right. You can let it manage itself or customize it to your liking. See Chapter 2.

Uncluttered taskbar. The Windows XP taskbar is dynamic. An overflow of buttons is redistributed to hidden rows, which can be scrolled. If you have several documents open in the same program, button grouping lets you control all the documents with one menulike button. Icons in the system tray, now called the *notification area,* hide themselves if you haven't used them recently, preventing the tray from becoming comically crowded. See Chapter 2.

Simplified theme selection. You can customize Windows XP's look by using *themes*—style-coordinated groups of controls and backgrounds. Like before, you can download new themes and change individual elements such as colors, and save the edited theme under a new name.

Categorized Control Panel. Control Panel presents a new category view (**Figure i.4**) that groups control utility programs by what they do. This view reduces clutter but makes you click through an extra layer to get where you're going. Veterans can choose classic view to display all the programs individually.

Visual effects. Windows XP's graphical user interface adds animation, shadows, fades, slides, translucence, and other effects. You can turn these effects off if they distract you or slow your computer.

Relive the past. Windows XP has vivid icons, windows, buttons, and colors, but you can restore the less fashionable look of Windows 2000/98/Me (**Figure i.5**).

Figure i.3 The new Start menu centralizes commands in two columns, not one.

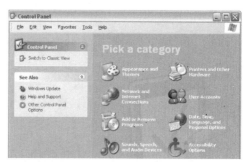

Figure i.4 Control Panel's new Category view groups items by function. See "Using Control Panel" in Chapter 4.

Figure i.5 Feeling nostalgic? Revert to the classic Windows interface. See "Restoring the Old Windows Look" in Chapter 4.

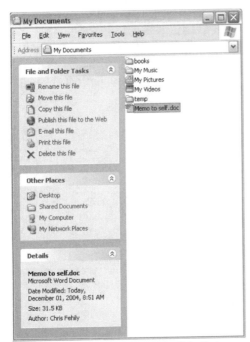

Figure i.6 The new task pane provides links that are relevant to the selection or current folder's contents.

Figure i.7 Windows Media Player plays and manages your digital music and movies.

Files and folders

Windows XP's file and folder tools let you organize your stuff efficiently. See Chapter 5.

Task pane. The new task pane (**Figure i.6**) provides shortcuts to related folders and locations, lets you perform common tasks easily, and displays details about the selected icon(s). See "Displaying Links to Common Tasks" in Chapter 5.

Compressed folders. Windows XP can Zip- or NTFS-compress folders, conserving disk space. Windows Explorer displays the contents of compressed folders just as it does normal folders. See "Compressing Files and Folders" in Chapter 5.

Offline files. You can store copies of your network files on your laptop's local disk and continue to work with them when you're disconnected from the network. Windows resynchronizes the files automatically when you reconnect. See "Making Network Files and Folders Available Offline" in Chapter 5.

Digital media

Microsoft has tried to make Windows XP a one-stop multimedia operating system.

Music, photos, and movies. Windows Media Player (Chapter 10) plays CDs and DVDs; copies files to portable music players; receives internet radio; helps you organize media files; and lets you shop at online music, audio, and video stores (**Figure i.7**). The Scanner and Camera Wizard (Chapter 9) links your scanner or digital camera to your PC and its hard drive. Windows Movie Maker (Chapter 11) lets you transfer and edit recorded video from your analog camcorder or digital video camera.

Rip and burn. Windows Explorer and Windows Media Player let you compile and create (*burn*) recordable data and music CDs.

Internet and communications

Windows XP comes with a suite of programs that you'll need after you connect to the internet (Chapter 12).

Web and email. Updated versions of Internet Explorer (Chapter 13) and Outlook Express (Chapter 14) improve your privacy and security.

Windows Messenger. Use Windows Messenger (Chapter 15) to see who's online, chat with instant messages, play games, and send and receive files (**Figure i.8**).

Connection security and sharing. Windows XP's built-in firewall establishes a barrier between your machine or network and the outside world, with no need for third-party software (Chapter 12). If you've set up a home or small-office network, you can use Internet Connection Sharing to let all the computers in that network share one connection (Chapter 17).

Stability

Windows XP inherits Windows 2000's stability and adds a few new tricks and bug fixes.

Protected memory. Windows XP prevents poorly written programs from invading or overwriting memory. An errant program may crash, but it won't bring down other programs or freeze your computer, which was common for Windows 95/98/Me.

Windows File Protection. Windows File Protection keeps crucial system files safe from being overwritten by outdated or unstable versions. This feature is familiar to users of Windows 2000/NT but a vast improvement over the internal recklessness of 95/98/Me.

Figure i.8 Windows Messenger lets you chat online.

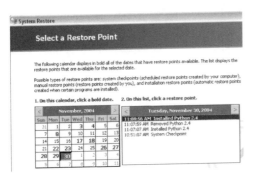

Figure i.9 System Restore restores your computer to a previous state without losing your personal files.

System Restore. System Restore (**Figure i.9**) records the state of your system both periodically and when you make changes such as installing programs or changing device drivers. If a change causes a severe system problem such as inability to boot your computer, you can roll back to a previous state without losing your personal data. The Windows 2000 version of this feature, called Last Known Good, was hard to use correctly; System Restore is easier. See "Restoring Your System" in Chapter 19.

Networking and user accounts

Windows XP is a true multiuser OS system with built-in privacy and security measures.

Automated network configuration. Windows XP makes it easy—much easier than in previous versions—to set up your own Ethernet or wireless network or to join an existing one. The Network Setup Wizard walks you through the steps that configure your internet connection and local network settings automatically. See Chapter 17.

Welcome screen. The Welcome screen lists the account of each authorized user. Each user can click his or her name, type a password, and start a session with a personalized desktop and access to private files. See "Logging On and Logging Off" in Chapter 1.

Fast User Switching. You can switch to another user account without actually logging off yourself—to, say, let someone check email—and then get back on quickly. See "Logging On and Logging Off" in Chapter 1.

Security features. Password-protected user accounts and file and folder permissions let you share your computer while you protect your personal files and prevent unwelcome software installation or viral infection. (And you can't press Esc to bypass logon, the way you could in Windows 95/98/Me.) See Chapter 16.

Forgotten-password recovery. Use the Forgotten Password Wizard to recover (or change) a forgotten password and create a password reset disk. See "Setting up User Accounts" in Chapter 16.

PRO **Remote Desktop.** Use your home computer to control your office computer (or vice versa) over a network or the internet. You can control the remote computer as though you were sitting at it (**Figure i.10**).

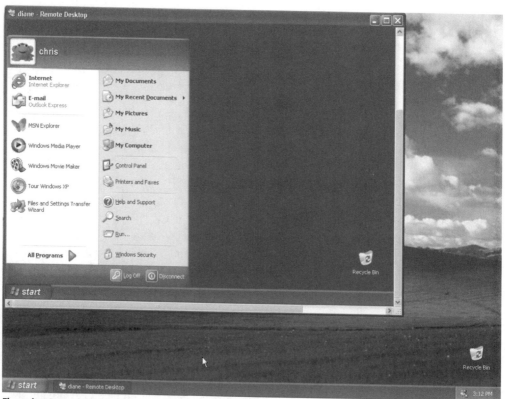

Figure i.10 Remote Desktop lets you control your computer from another computer. This screen shows the desktop of a remote computer on the desktop of a local one. See "Controlling a Computer with Remote Desktop" in Chapter 18.

Figure i.11 Windows product activation is a controversial new "feature" designed to enforce Microsoft's licensing policies and reduce piracy.

Installation and update

Several new features make Windows XP easier to install and keep up to date.

Product activation. Windows XP includes an invasive copy-protection scheme that prevents you from installing one copy of the OS on more than one machine at a time (**Figure i.11**). Bulk-purchased corporate copies of Windows XP are exempt from activation, and many new PCs come with a preactivated copy. See "Activating Windows XP" in the appendix.

Files and Settings Transfer Wizard. This wizard streamlines the process of moving selected files and personal settings from your old PC to your new one. See "Transferring Existing Files and Settings" in the appendix.

Device-driver library. XP's vast collection of built-in drivers increases the chance that a new Plug and Play device—say, a printer, scanner, or camera—will work out of the box.

Automatic updating. Windows Update uses your internet connection periodically to deliver and install the latest bug fixes, device drivers, and enhancements that are stored on Microsoft's web site. You can control this process. See "Updating Windows XP" in Chapter 19.

Uninstall Windows XP. If you decide to scrap Windows XP after installation, you can revert to your previous Windows 98/Me installation. You *can't* roll back to a Windows NT/2000 installation, however. See "Uninstalling Windows XP" in the appendix.

No more DOS. Windows XP, unlike Windows 95/98/Me, isn't stacked on top of rickety DOS. You can't boot into DOS directly, even by using a DOS boot floppy.

WHAT'S NEW IN WINDOWS XP

Help and support

Windows XP offers more help—and more types of help—than its predecessors. You can use the expanded help system to search the help files stored on your disk or use it as a gateway to find help online.

Help and Support Center. Use online tutorials, tours, and troubleshooting guides to learn about Windows XP (**Figure i.12**). Use your internet connection to search Microsoft's support web site or participate in Windows newsgroups. See Chapter 3.

Remote Assistance. Get live help from a friend or colleague who can view your screen or even take control of your computer (**Figure i.13**). See Chapter 3.

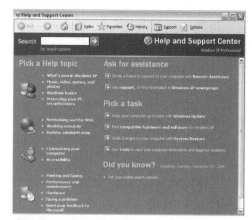

Figure i.12 Help and Support Center is a comprehensive source of local and online information about Windows XP.

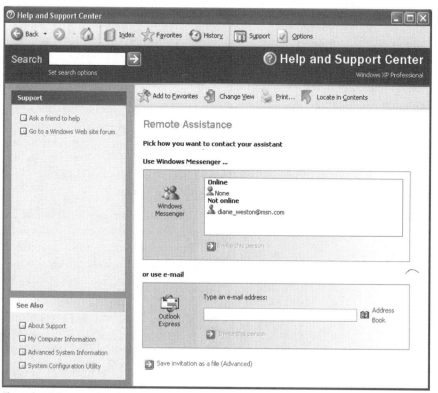

Figure i.13 Remote Assistance lets you invite someone you trust to view your screen or even work on your computer.

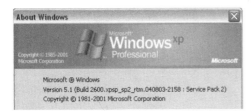

Figure i.14 The About Windows message box tells you if Service Pack 2 is installed.

Service Pack 2

Over time, Microsoft releases major updates to Windows XP. These updates, called *Service Packs*, contain fixes and enhancements, and the latest one—Service Pack 2—is all about security and privacy. SP2:

◆ Provides convenient, all-in-one access to the most up-to-date drivers, tools, security updates, patches, and other changes, including the Service Pack 1 changes

◆ Protects you from viruses, spyware, spam, crackers, and your own ignorance

◆ Attempts to reduce the bad press that Microsoft gets for releasing operating systems riddled with security holes

To find out if you have SP2, click Start; choose My Computer; then choose Help > About Windows (**Figure i.14**). If you need to install SP2, see "Updating Windows XP" in Chapter 19.

WHAT'S NEW IN WINDOWS XP

"Hackers"

When computer insiders call someone a *hacker,* it's not an insult. Though the term has negative connotations in the mainstream press and common usage, it actually acknowledges the person's advanced computer skills and ethos. Hackers generally aren't malicious, though some practice "electronic civil disobedience" to, say, expose flaws in electronic voting machines. In fact, hackers who discover security holes often report them quietly to software makers to be fixed before becoming common knowledge.

Cracker is the correct term for someone who breaks into systems to steal data and passwords, cause trouble, or turn a profit.

For more information, search for *"hacker vs cracker"* in Google. Look especially at Eric Raymond's *The Jargon File* (www.catb.org/~esr/jargon/html).

Security Center. Security Center monitors your settings for three important security components: Firewall, Automatic Updates, and Virus Protection (**Figure i.15**). See "Securing Your Computer" in Chapter 12.

Windows Firewall. XP's original firewall—Internet Connection Firewall—was not only weak, but also turned off by default. SP2 renames ICF to Windows Firewall, gives it a significant upgrade, and turns it on by default (**Figure i.16**). See "Securing Your Computer" in Chapter 12.

Automatic Updates. The new default settings for Control Panel's Automatic Updates program make it less likely that you'll miss or skip a critical security update from Microsoft and risk infection (**Figure i.17**). See "Updating Windows XP" in Chapter 19.

Figure i.15 Security Center posts startup and notification-area warnings if a security feature is turned off or misconfigured.

Figure i.16 A firewall helps protect your computer against viruses, intruders, and other security threats. Don't go online without one.

Figure i.17 Automatic Updates lets Windows check for the latest critical updates periodically and install them automatically.

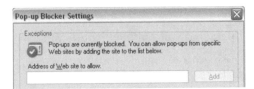

Figure i.18 Internet Explorer finally gets a pop-up blocker.

Figure i.19 Use this wizard to set up or connect to your wireless network at home, or to connect to an existing one elsewhere.

Internet Explorer enhancements.
Internet Explorer now includes a pop-up blocker that lets you suppress uninvited pop-up ads (**Figure i.18**), an add-on manager for controlling browser plug-ins, an information bar that appears when you do something dangerous, and other new security features. See Chapter 13.

Email privacy update. The new default settings for Outlook Express are designed to help protect your computer against viruses and worms and to reduce the amount of spam that you receive. See Chapter 14.

Wireless networking. The new Wireless Network Setup Wizard improves wireless support. It also simplifies the process of discovering and connecting to wireless networks in your home or on the road (**Figure i.19**). See Chapter 17.

Under-the-hood improvements. SP2 also includes features of lesser renown (such as easier Bluetooth connections and the latest DirectX updates for gamers), but it's the invisible fixes—like buffer-overflow protection—that offer strong, low-level security. If you're inclined to geekiness, read *Changes to Functionality in Microsoft Windows XP Service Pack 2* at http://go.microsoft.com/fwlink/?LinkId=28022.

Many bug fixes. If a particular bug has been bothering you, check whether Microsoft has squashed it: Go to http://support.microsoft.com/?kbid=811113, "List of Fixes Included in Windows XP Service Pack 2."

✔ Tip

- SP2 doesn't have an anti-spyware component; see "Securing Your Computer" in Chapter 12.

WHAT'S NEW IN WINDOWS XP

Upgrading to Windows XP

In the preceding section you saw that Windows XP offers many new features, but if you're jumping to XP from Windows 98 or Me, the biggest improvement is increased stability: The blue screens of death seldom appear. If you're switching from Windows 2000 Pro, XP will seem like an incremental upgrade (the NTFS file system stays the same), but take a look at Remote Desktop Connection, System Restore, Roll Back Driver, Wireless Network Setup Wizard, Fast User Switching, and Simple file sharing.

A Windows XP version upgrade costs much less than the full version. **Table i.3** tells you which Windows versions qualify for an upgrade to XP Home or Pro.

✔ Tip

- Windows 95, Windows 3.1, and Windows NT 3.51 don't qualify for an upgrade. Neither does any evaluation or server version. If you want to upgrade from a Windows server, Microsoft says to look at Windows Server 2003.

Table i.3

Upgrading from Earlier Windows Versions		
CURRENT VERSION	TO XP HOME	TO XP PRO
Windows 98/Windows 98 SE	✓	✓
Windows Me	✓	✓
Windows NT Workstation 4.0	✗	✓
Windows 2000 Professional	✗	✓
Windows XP Home		✓
Windows XP Professional	✗	

Not Eligible to Upgrade?

If you don't qualify for an upgrade because you're a first-time Windows customer or you own an ancient Windows version (Windows 95 or 3.1, for example), Microsoft suggests that you buy the full version, either shrink-wrapped or with a new PC.

Don't.

Instead, buy the XP *upgrade* version *and* get an older qualifying Windows version (one of the first four entries in Table i.3). So many unused copies of Windows 98, Me, NT 4, and 2000 are lying around that you shouldn't have trouble finding someone to *give* you one, but you can buy one at a computer swap meet or through online classified ads such as www.craigslist.org. Don't pay more than $10 (U.S.).

Install the qualifying version on your PC and then apply the XP upgrade, first making sure that your hardware meets XP's system requirements (see the appendix). Don't throw out the qualifying version; you may need it to reinstall XP someday.

Switching from a Mac

If you're a Mac OS 8/9/10 user moving to Windows, don't worry—the disorientation won't last long. Many of the differences between Windows and Mac OS are superficial. To get started, see **Table i.4** for some analogous features and programs. Some substitutes aren't equivalent but are XP's closest approximations.

✔ Tip

■ If you're a longtime Mac user switching to Windows, try David Coursey's *Mac OS X for Windows Users: A Switchers' Guide* (Peachpit Press, 2003) or David Pogue's *Switching to the Mac: The Missing Manual* (Pogue Press, 2003). These books actually were written for Windows users switching to Macs, but you can read them "backward."

Table i.4

Switching from Mac OS?

MAC FEATURE	XP EQUIVALENT	MAC PROGRAM	XP EQUIVALENT
Alias	Shortcut	Address Book	Address Book
Apple menu	Start menu	Adium X	Trillian
Application menu	Taskbar (or Alt+Tab)	Adobe Creative Suite	Adobe Creative Suite
Command key	Ctrl key (usually)	Apple Preview	Adobe Reader
Control Panel	Start > Control Panel	DVD Player	Windows Media Player
Dock	Taskbar (or Alt+Tab)	Fax	Fax
Drive (HD) icons	Start > My Computer	iCal	Microsoft Outlook
Eject Disk	Pushbutton on drive	iChat	Windows Messenger
Fast User Switching	Fast User Switching	iMovie	Windows Movie Maker
Find	Start > Search	iTunes	Windows Media Player or iTunes
Finder	Desktop/Windows Explorer		
Folders	Folders or directories	Key Caps	Character Map
Force Quit (Command+Option+Esc)	Task Manager (Ctrl+Alt+Delete)	Macromedia Dreamweaver	Macromedia Dreamweaver
Get Info	Right-click icon > Properties	Mail	Microsoft Outlook Express
Network	Start > My Computer > My Network Places	Microsoft Entourage	Microsoft Outlook
		Microsoft Office 2004	Microsoft Office 2003
One-button mouse	Two-button mouse (left button for normal clicks, right button for a shortcut menu)	Safari	Microsoft Internet Explorer
		Sherlock	Start > Search
		SimpleText/TextEdit	Notepad/WordPad
Option key	Alt key (usually)	StuffIt	WinZip
Printers	Start > Control Panel > Printers and Faxes	Terminal	Command Prompt
		Transmit	CuteFTP
Quit (Command+Q)	File > Exit (Alt+F4)	Unison	Forte Agent Newsreader
Restart	Start > Turn Off Computer		
Shut Down	Start > Turn Off Computer		
System Preferences	Start > Control Panel		
Trash	Recycle Bin		

About This Book

This book is for you if you're new to Windows, upgrading to XP from a previous Windows version, or need a quick reference at hand. My audience is beginning and intermediate Windows XP users, including people who are purchasing XP along with their first computers. Windows veterans can look up specific tasks quickly and find tricks, short-cuts, and secret lore. Wherever possible, I give step-by-step instructions for using features and programs.

If you're new to Windows, start with Chapters 1 and 2 to learn the basics of logging on, looking around, and making it work. After that I cover the material task by task, with plenty of screen shots.

✔ Tip

- Many of the tasks in this book require that you have an Administrator user account. If you're the only user, or if you installed Windows or maintain it, you're an administrator. Otherwise, see "Setting up User Accounts" in Chapter 16.

Conventions used in this book

Commands. I use shorthand instructions rather than list steps separately. Here's a command that opens a nested folder:

◆ Choose Start > My Computer > Local Disk (C:) > Documents and Settings > All Users.

This sequence means: Click the Start button (on the taskbar, in the bottom-left corner of the desktop) to reveal the Start menu; then click My Computer. Inside the window titled My Computer, double-click the drive icon labeled Local Disk (C:) to open it. Inside that window, double-click the icon Documents and Settings to open it. Inside *that* window, double-click the icon All Users to open it.

Each shorthand element (between the > symbols) refers to an icon, window, menu, button, check box, link, or some other user-interface component; just look for the component whose label matches the element name. Whenever a particular step is unclear or ambiguous, I spell it out rather than use shorthand.

Here's a command that launches the Notepad program:

◆ Choose Start > All Programs > Accessories > Notepad.

And one that shows filename extensions:

◆ Choose Start > Control Panel > Appearance and Themes > Folder Options > View tab > uncheck Hide Extensions for Known File Types > OK.

ABOUT THIS BOOK

Keyboard shortcuts. Use keyboard shortcuts so that you don't waste time moving your hand from keyboard to mouse repeatedly. These shortcuts involve the modifier keys that sit at the bottom corners of the keyboard's main section. Press these keys—Shift, Ctrl (Control), and Alt (Alternate)—together with other keys to change the action. The C key pressed by itself types a lowercase c; pressed along with the Shift key, it types an uppercase C; and pressed along with the Ctrl key, it issues the Copy command.

Modifier keys are joined to other keys with a plus sign. Ctrl+C, for example, means "Press the Ctrl key; hold it down while you press the C key; then release both keys." A three-key combination such as Ctrl+Alt+Delete means "Hold down the first two keys while you press the third one; then release all three." The modifiers always are listed first.

The *Windows logo key,* next to the Alt key on most PC keyboards, pulls up the Start menu when pressed by itself, but it also can be used as a modifier. Windows logo key+D, for example, minimizes all windows. When I give a Windows-logo-key shortcut, mentally add "if my keyboard has one," because not all keyboards do.

✔ Tip

- Use XP's Help and Support Center to view or print a list of keyboard shortcuts: Choose Start > Help and Support and then search for *Windows keyboard shortcuts overview*. Click a heading in the result page for a list of keyboard shortcuts.

Corrections and comments

I welcome email to fehily@pacbell.net with questions, suggestions, corrections, and gripes related to this book.

GETTING STARTED WITH WINDOWS XP

When you first meet Windows XP you might think that it's complicated—and you'd be right. But its interface is designed to let you wield a lot of power with a modest amount of learning. The secret is understanding the underlying consistency of the ways that Windows works. As you use Windows, techniques like switching programs, sizing windows, drag-and-drop, and cut-and-paste will become familiar.

This chapter and the next one get you up and running and introduce you to Windows fundamentals. Chapter 3 tells you how to get help with learning and configuring Windows, on or off the internet. After that you're on your way to becoming a power user.

Logging On and Logging Off

Logging on is the process of starting a session in Windows XP—the first thing you do after turning on your computer. After your computer powers up—or *boots*—you'll see a screen in which you enter your user name and (optional) password. Windows *user accounts* identify who has permission to use a particular computer (or network). User accounts are covered in Chapter 16, but for now you need to know only your user name and password, which depend on your installation:

◆ If you upgraded to Windows XP from Windows 98/Me with no user profile, there's no password.

◆ If you did a clean install of Windows XP, you set up at least one account during installation. Enter the user name and password you set for that account.

◆ If your PC came with Windows XP pre-installed, the Welcome screen that appears after booting lists the account name(s). Follow the manufacturer's instructions for logging on.

◆ If you upgraded to Windows XP from Windows 2000 Pro or NT 4.0, or from Windows 98/Me with user profiles turned on, your existing accounts migrated to the new installation. See "Setting up User Accounts" in Chapter 16.

◆ If you're on a large network at work or school, ask your network administrator.

Logging on Automatically

If your computer has only one user account with no password, Windows boots to that account's desktop directly. (XP comes with hidden Guest and Administrator accounts, but they don't apply here.)

You can set up your computer to log on automatically at startup even if it has more than one account or if your account is password-protected. You may like auto-logon if you're the main user but sometimes others log on or if you keep your own separate accounts for different tasks.

To log on automatically at startup:

1. Choose Start > Run; type control userpasswords2 and then press Enter.

   The Windows 2000-style User Accounts dialog box appears.

2. On the Users tab, uncheck Users Must Enter a User Name and Password to Use This Computer. (This check box won't appear if the computer doesn't support auto-logon, typically because it's on a network or domain.)

3. Click OK.

4. In the Automatically Log On dialog box, type the user name and password of the account that you want to log on to automatically; then click OK.

Now the system invisibly enters your user name and password at power-up. Anyone who turns on your computer can access the same resources that you do.

You can use the other accounts on the computer by using Fast User Switching or by logging off and then logging on to another account.

Figure 1.1 The Welcome screen is the easiest way to log on to a computer that only a few people use.

Figure 1.2 The classic (Windows 2000-style) logon prompt.

Figure 1.3 If you've set a password hint (see "Setting up User Accounts" in Chapter 16), you can click the ? button to display it.

Logging on

Logging on to a computer identifies you uniquely so that Windows can load your personal settings and grant you certain permissions. You have two ways to log on: the Welcome screen (**Figure 1.1**) and the classic logon prompt (**Figure 1.2**). If you're a home or small-business user, you'll probably log on via the Welcome screen. If you're on a large workplace network or using the classic prompt, see "Logging on to a Domain" in Chapter 16.

To use the Welcome screen:

1. Click your user name or picture.

2. If your account is password-protected, type your password in the Type Your Password box (**Figure 1.3**).

3. Press Enter or click the arrow button. Your personalized Windows desktop appears.

Hiding the Last User's Name

PRO The classic logon prompt (Figure 1.2) displays the name of the last user to log on—a security hole that lets anyone glean valid user names. To plug this hole, choose Start > Run; type `secpol.msc` and then press Enter. In Local Security Settings, open Local Policies > Security Options; then double-click and enable Interactive Logon: Do Not Display Last User Name.

LOGGING ON AND LOGGING OFF

Switching users

Fast User Switching lets more than one person log on at the same time. If you step away from your computer for a short time, you can leave your programs running *and* let someone else log on to, say, check email. When you log back on, Windows resumes your session where you left off.

Only one person at a time—the *active user*—actually can *use* the computer (type at the keyboard). People who are logged on but not active—*disconnected users*—can keep their programs running and files open in the background, invisible to the active user. To switch users, you must have Fast User Switching turned on. See "Controlling the Logon Process" in Chapter 16 to turn Fast User Switching on or off and find out which situations it won't work in.

To switch users without logging off:

1. Choose Start > Logoff.

2. Click Switch User or press Alt+S (**Figure 1.4**).

3. In the Welcome screen, click another account name or picture; then log on normally.

Figure 1.4 Choose Switch User to keep all your work running in background memory while someone else uses the computer.

Figure 1.5 The Users tab appears only if Fast User Switching is turned on.

Figure 1.6 This list is sorted by user name. Click any column heading to sort by that column.

Figure 1.7 This limited dialog box appears if you choose Start > Log Off when Fast User Switching is turned off.

To find out who else is logged on to your computer:

1. Right-click an empty area on the taskbar; then choose Task Manager.

   or

   Press Ctrl+Shift+Esc.

2. Click the Users tab to view users and their status (**Figure 1.5**).

If your computer is running slowly, use Task Manager to see the programs that other logged-on users are running and how much memory they're chewing up. Task Manager lists filenames rather than program names; *winword.exe* appears instead of *Microsoft Word*, for example.

To find out which programs other users are running:

1. Right-click an empty area on the taskbar; then click Task Manager.

   or

   Press Ctrl+Shift+Esc.

2. Click the Processes tab.

3. Check Show Processes from All Users (**Figure 1.6**).

✔ Tips

- To identify the active user quickly, click Start and read the user name at the top of the Start menu.

- To log off another user, see "Logging off" later in this section.

- Fast way to switch users: Right-click a user name in Task Manager's Users tab; then choose Connect or Disconnect from the shortcut menu (refer to Figure 1.10).

- If Fast User Switching is turned off, **Figure 1.7** appears instead of Figure 1.4.

- If Fast User Switching is turned on, press Windows logo key+L to switch users.

Locking your computer

You can *lock* your computer—that is, set it so that the keyboard and mouse won't change anything—to protect your programs and personal information while you're away from your PC. Locking prevents everyone except you (or an administrator) from unlocking your system and viewing your files or programs.

Figure 1.8 Your programs continue to run while your computer is locked.

To lock your computer:

◆ If the Welcome screen is turned on, press Ctrl+Shift+Esc; then choose Shut Down > Lock Computer (**Figure 1.8**).

 or

 If the Welcome screen is turned off, press Ctrl+Alt+Delete; then click Lock Computer (or press Enter).

Windows displays the Unlock Computer dialog box until you return.

To unlock your computer:

◆ In the Unlock Computer dialog box, type your password; then click OK (or press Enter).

✔ Tips

■ If more than one user account exists and Fast User Switching is turned on, you can't lock the computer.

■ If the Welcome screen is turned off, press Windows logo key+L to lock your computer.

Locking Subtleties

A locked computer still is subject to power-management settings; see "Conserving Power" in Chapter 4.

A locked computer doesn't interfere with shared printers or other network resources.

If an administrator unlocks your computer, Windows closes all your open programs (without saving any unsaved work) and logs you off.

Figure 1.9 Logging off is an option in the Start menu.

Figure 1.10 Logging other users off without warning is impolite because it kills their programs without saving their unsaved work.

Logging off

Logging off ends your session in Windows XP. When you log off your user account:

◆ Windows closes all your open programs and files. (Each program prompts you to save any unsaved work.)

◆ Windows disconnects your dial-up connections.

◆ You prevent curious or malicious passersby from using your user account to access your files or network.

◆ Your computer remains turned on.

◆ Windows displays a screen to let the next person log on.

To log off:

1. Choose Start > Log Off (**Figure 1.9**).

2. Click Log Off.

If Fast User Switching is turned on, and other users are logged on to your machine, you can use Task Manager to log them off.

To log someone else off:

1. Right-click an empty area on the taskbar; then click Task Manager.

   or

   Press Ctrl+Shift+Esc.

2. Click the Users tab to view logged-on users.

3. Select a user; then click Log Off.

   or

   Right-click a user; then choose Log Off from the shortcut menu (**Figure 1.10**).

4. In the confirmation dialog box that appears, click Yes to end the user's session.

Turning off your computer

Turning off your computer requires more than flipping the power switch absently. Windows prepares itself for shutdown by saving session and system information and by disconnecting network, dial-up, and other external connections.

To turn off your computer:

1. Choose Start > Turn Off Computer. (If you're on a network domain, choose Start > Shut Down.)

2. In the Turn Off Computer (or Shut Down Windows) dialog box (**Figures 1.11, 11.2,** and **1.13**), choose one of the options listed in **Table 1.1**.

✔ Tips

- To learn more about hibernate and standby, see "Conserving Power" in Chapter 4.

- Always save your work before putting your computer on standby. Standby saves your session in memory (not on hard disk), so a power interruption will trash your session.

- Hibernate saves everything in memory on your hard disk. If you have a lot of RAM, you need a lot of free disk space to hibernate.

- Hibernate's faster startup speed might tempt you to use it instead of Turn Off all the time. But use Turn Off occasionally to allow Windows to perform its background maintenance operations that require a clean startup. Also, Windows sometimes needs a clean startup to detect newly installed hardware.

- If the desktop is active, you can press Alt+F4 to show the Turn Off Computer dialog box.

Figure 1.11 The Turn Off Computer screen contains four choices. The fourth one, Hibernate, is hidden until...

Figure 1.12 ...you hold down the Shift key to see it.

Figure 1.13 If the Welcome screen is turned off or you're a network domain member, you'll see this screen instead of the one shown in Figure 1.11.

Emergency Shutdown

If the file-sharing police are pounding on your door and you need to shut down quickly, Windows lets you do so without scrambling under your desk to yank the plug: Press Ctrl+Shift+Esc to open Task Manager; hold down the Ctrl key; then choose Shut Down > Turn Off. (Alternatively, press Ctrl+Alt+Delete to open the Windows Security dialog box; then hold down Ctrl and click Shut Down.) The computer shuts down in a heartbeat, without saving any unsaved data. In some cases, Windows shows a last-resort warning to confirm shutdown.

This method also works if a frozen (*hung*) program prevents normal shutdown. See "Killing Unresponsive Programs" in Chapter 6.

■ When the Welcome screen is displayed you can click Turn Off Computer (or Turn Off *<computer name>*) in the bottom-left corner. Or, if you're logged on, use Task Manager: Press Ctrl+Shift+Esc; then choose a command from the Shut Down menu (refer to Figure 1.8).

■ Tweak UI's Logon options let you control who appears on the Welcome screen, modify parts of your log-on desktop, and suppress the unread-mail count on the Welcome screen. See the "Tweak UI" sidebar in "Using the Start Menu" in Chapter 2.

Table 1.1

Shutdown Options

Option	What It Does
Turn Off or Shut Down	Ends your session and shuts down Windows so that you can turn off the power safely. Many computers turn off the power automatically; if yours doesn't, push the power button after the "It's safe" message appears. This option quits your programs, prompting you to save any unsaved work. Use Turn Off/Shut Down when you're done for the day or when you need to muck around inside your computer.
Restart	Ends your session, shuts down Windows, and starts Windows again automatically. This option quits your programs, prompting you to save any unsaved work. Use Restart if you've installed hardware or software that requires a restart, or if Windows is acting erratically or sluggishly.
Stand By	Turns off hard disks, fans, the CPU, and other hardware but draws just enough power to maintain your session (your open programs and any work that you're doing in them) in memory. Use Stand By to stop using your computer for a short time and save power (especially useful for laptops). A computer on standby springs to life quickly—with your desktop exactly as you left it—when you use your mouse or keyboard, or press Ctrl+Alt+Delete.
Hibernate	Combines the safety of Turn Off with the convenience of Stand By. Hibernate saves your session to a file on your hard disk before turning off the power. When you restart the computer, your desktop is restored quickly and exactly as you left it. Older computers may not support this option.
Install Updates and Shut Down	This option appears only on computers with Service Pack 2 installed and Automatic Updates turned on (see "Updating Windows XP" in Chapter 19). When updates have been downloaded and are ready to install, Windows shows this option as the default choice and marks it with the Windows Security shield, which indicates that this is a security recommendation. This option ends your session, installs updates, and then shuts down Windows normally.

LOGGING ON AND LOGGING OFF

Exploring the Windows Interface

Figure 1.14 shows the basic elements that you'll find on the Windows XP desktop. Microsoft modeled Windows on a real-world office environment: You have a desktop, on which you work and use tools, and folders, in which you organize files.

Desktop. After you log on to Windows, the *desktop*—a work area that uses menus, icons, and windows to simulate the top of a desk—appears automatically.

Start menu. The *Start menu* is the central menu that lets you access the most useful folders, programs, and commands on your computer. Chapter 2 covers the Start menu.

EXPLORING THE WINDOWS INTERFACE

Figure 1.14 Basic elements of the Windows XP desktop. The desktop lets you move items and manage your tasks in vaguely the same way that you would on a physical desktop.

Taskbar. The *taskbar* lets you switch among open programs and documents. It also lets you launch programs and alerts you to certain events such as appointment reminders or incoming email. Chapter 2 covers the taskbar.

Mouse pointer. Use your mouse, stylus, trackball, touchpad, or a similar input device to move the *mouse pointer* to select items, drag icons, or choose commands onscreen.

Menus. A *menu* is a list of related commands. Most programs use menus to provide an easy-to-learn, easy-to-use alternative to memorizing instructions.

Toolbars. A *toolbar* is a row, column, or block of buttons or icons. When you click one of these buttons or icons, the program carries out a command or task.

Icons. An *icon* is a small image that represents an item to be opened, such as a file, folder, disk, program, or the Recycle Bin. An icon's picture is a visual cue designed to help you recall what the icon represents.

Windows. A *window* is a rectangular portion of your screen where a program runs. You can open many windows at the same time. Each window can be independently resized, moved, closed, maximized to occupy the entire screen, or minimized to a button on the taskbar.

Dialog boxes. A special type of window called a *dialog box* contains text boxes, buttons, tabs, scrolling lists, or drop-down lists that let you set preferences or run commands. Some dialog boxes—such as Open, Save As, and Print—are much the same in every Windows program. Others, such as the Properties dialog box shown in Figure 1.14, depend on the program or context.

The User Interface

You work with Windows through its *graphical user interface* (GUI, pronounced *gooey*), which offers pictures along with words to help you perform tasks. To make learning easier, Windows displays visual clues about how things work. Often these clues are analogous to those you see in the real world. If a door has a flat plate rather than a handle to grasp, it's a clue to push that door, not pull it. The three-dimensional (3D) look of buttons on your screen implies that you're supposed to push them (click them). You'll recognize similar hints throughout the user interface. This chapter and the next introduce Windows' standard GUI elements. Experienced Windows users may learn some new tricks from the sidebars and tips in these chapters.

EXPLORING THE WINDOWS INTERFACE

The Mouse

The mouse is one of two primary input devices in Windows (the other is the keyboard). Moving the mouse on your physical desk controls the motion of the mouse pointer on your screen. By moving the mouse pointer over an icon or control and then clicking, you can select an item, open or move a file, run a program, or throw something away, for example.

A mouse has a left and a right button. You'll use the left button for most actions, but skillful use of the right button, which displays a shortcut menu, is a key to working quickly.

✔ Tips

- Some mice have more than two buttons or a *scroll wheel* (a small wheel between the two main buttons) that you can program by following the instructions that came with the mouse.

- Instead of a mouse you may have a touchpad (used on laptops), trackball, or stylus (used on Tablet PCs).

- Lefties can swap the functions of the left and right mouse buttons. See "Configuring the Mouse" in Chapter 4.

- The pointer's shape changes depending on what it's pointing to. **Table 1.2** shows the default pointers that you'll see in Windows XP. To change the shapes, see "Configuring the Mouse" in Chapter 4.

- In text documents, don't confuse the cursor, which blinks steadily, with the mouse pointer, which never blinks. The *cursor* (also called the *insertion point*) indicates where text will be inserted when you type (**Figure 1.15**).

Figure 1.15 The cursor—the vertical bar at the end of the text—marks the insertion point for newly typed text. To move the insertion point, click the mouse pointer—the I-beam on the right—at a new insertion point or use the arrow keys.

Table 1.2

Mouse Pointers	
SHAPE	WHEN IT APPEARS
↖	The normal pointer. Click the area or item that you want to work with.
↖?	Appears when you click the question mark (?) in the top-right corner of a dialog box. Click any dialog-box item to get "What's This?" help.
↖⧖	Windows is doing something in the background—opening or saving a temporary file, for example. You can keep doing your own work but response time may be longer than usual.
⧖	Windows is busy with a task and will ignore you until it finishes. (Typically this pointer will appear in only one program window at a time; if it appears everywhere, your computer is indeed busy.)
↕ ↔ ↘	Appears when you point to a window's border (side or corner). Drag the border to resize the window. See "Windows" later in this chapter.
🖑	Appears when you point to a word or image linked to a help page, command, or web site. Click the link to jump to a related destination or display pop-up information.
⊘	The action that you're trying to perform is forbidden or the item that you're pointing at is unavailable.
I	The I-beam or I-bar appears where you can select or edit text. Click to set the insertion point, or click and drag to select (highlight) text.
+	Helps you move an item precisely. This pointer often appears in drawing programs.
✛	Appears when you choose Move or Size from a window's control menu. When it does, use the arrow keys to move or resize the window and then press Enter, or press Esc to cancel. See also "Windows" later in this chapter.

THE MOUSE

Figure 1.16 One tiny pixel is the pointer's hot spot, which you use to point precisely. For an arrow pointer, it's the tip of the arrow. In Microsoft's wilder alternative pointer schemes, finding the hot spot takes a little practice.

Figure 1.17 Click to select an icon...

Figure 1.18 ...or activate a dialog-box item.

Figure 1.19 Right-click an item to display its shortcut menu.

Figure 1.20 Drag to move items such as icons and folders. What this action actually accomplishes depends on where you drag to.

To point:

◆ Move the tip of the pointer over the item to which you want to point (**Figure 1.16**).

To click:

◆ Point to an item; then press and release the left mouse button without moving the mouse (**Figures 1.17** and **1.18**).

To double-click:

◆ Point to an item and click the left mouse button twice in rapid succession without moving the mouse.

✔ Tip

■ Double-click too slowly, and Windows interprets it as two single clicks, which isn't the same thing. To change the speed of what Windows recognizes as a double-click, see "Configuring the Mouse" in Chapter 4.

To right-click:

◆ Point to an item; then click the *right* mouse button without moving the mouse (**Figure 1.19**).

To drag:

◆ Point to an item; press *and hold* the left mouse button while you move the pointer to a new location; then release the button (**Figure 1.20**).

✔ Tips

■ Drag an object with the right mouse button to display a shortcut menu when you reach the new location.

■ Press Esc during a drag operation to cancel it.

■ Drag in a folder window or on the desktop to draw a rectangular *marquee* around icons. Releasing the mouse button selects the enclosed icons.

THE MOUSE

The Keyboard

The keyboard isn't just for typing text. Experienced Windows users use keystrokes instead of the mouse to issue commands. Windows provides hundreds of *keyboard shortcuts* that replicate almost every common mouse maneuver. You can use keyboard shortcuts to open, close, and navigate the Start menu, desktop, menus, windows, dialog boxes, programs, documents, and web pages.

In addition to keys for letters, numbers, and symbols, your keyboard has other types of keys:

Modifier keys alter the meaning of the other key(s) being pressed (**Table 1.3**).

Function keys are the keys along the keyboard's top or left side labeled F1, F2, and so on. Their functions depend on the program that you're using.

Navigation keys scroll windows and move things around (**Table 1.4**).

To use a keyboard shortcut:

1. Hold down the modifier key(s) Shift, Ctrl, or Alt.

2. Press the specified letter, number, symbol, or function key.

3. Release all the keys.

✔ Tips

■ For a complete list of keyboard shortcuts, choose Start > Help and Support; then search for *Windows keyboard shortcuts overview.*

■ Memorize all the keyboard shortcuts that you can. Using them is faster than moving the mouse to do the same thing.

Table 1.3

Modifier Keys	
KEY	PRESS TO
Shift	Type symbols or uppercase letters, or extend the selection when used with the mouse.
Ctrl	Modify the function of other keys. (Ctrl stands for Control.)
Alt	Access menus or modify the function of other keys. (Alt stands for Alternate.)

Table 1.4

Navigation Keys	
KEY	PRESS TO
Home	Scroll to the beginning
End	Scroll to the end
Page Up	Scroll up one page or window
Page Down	Scroll down one page or window
Arrow keys	Scroll in that direction or change the insertion point

The Esc Key

The Esc (for *Escape*) key, at the keyboard's top-left corner, usually means "Never mind" or "Stop what you're doing." Press it to cancel commands, interrupt long processes, cancel dialog boxes, close menus, and dismiss message boxes. Sometimes Esc does nothing. Its exact function depends on the context and the active program.

- Alt behaves a little differently from Shift and Ctrl. Shift or Ctrl does nothing when pressed by itself, but Alt pressed by itself activates the menu bar. (If you press Alt accidentally, press Alt again to get back to normal.)

- Newer keyboards have extra Windows-specific keys on either side of the spacebar. Press the Windows logo key alone to open the Start menu or press it in combination with letter keys for other actions, which I discuss where they're appropriate.

  The Application key displays the shortcut menu for the selected item (the same as right-clicking).

- Some keyboard shortcuts are consistent across all programs (F1 for help and Ctrl+C to copy, for example), but programs also define custom shortcuts.

- Some keyboard shortcuts won't work if StickyKeys is turned on in Accessibility Options. See "Accommodating Disabled Users" in Chapter 4.

Modifier keys also work with mouse clicks.

To Shift+click:

- Hold down Shift; then click before releasing the key.

To Shift+drag:

- Hold down Shift; then drag and drop before releasing the key.

✔ Tip

- Windows also has *Ctrl+click*, *Alt+click*, *Ctrl+drag*, and *Alt+drag* commands for file operations.

Keyboard Tricks

If you were raised on IBM 84-key, non-standard laptop, or ergonomic keyboards, you may be near madness from the placement of the Caps Lock, Ctrl, and Windows logo keys on standard 102-key keyboards.

PC Magazine's TradeKeys utility ($6 U.S.; www.pcmag.com) lets you change, swap, or disable keyboard keys (including modifier keys) in almost any way. Different users can switch among different mappings quickly.

A few keyboard utilities automate repetitive typing and reduce errors:

- ShortKeys ($20; www.shortkeys.com) lets you set up replacement text for keystrokes that you define. ShortKeys auto-replaces the keystrokes with the text as you type (like Word's AutoCorrect feature).

- Keyboard Express ($25; www.keyboardexpress.com) lets you define keyboard *macros,* which are keystroke sequences that run automatically.

- Microsoft's IntelliType Pro (free; www.microsoft.com/hardware/keyboard/download.asp) works with some non-Microsoft keyboards too. Use it to reassign or disable keys, issue common commands, open programs and web pages, and more.

Menus

Windows uses menus to list commands in groups (**Figure 1.21**). Menus are especially convenient when you're new to a program because they show you what commands are available and make experimenting easy.

Experienced users prefer to use keyboard shortcuts instead of the mouse to choose menu commands. Programs often provide a keyboard shortcut for a frequently used command, which appears to the right of the command on its menu line. To choose Copy, for example, press Ctrl+C. If no shortcut key is listed for the command, you can use Alt+ the menu's underlined letters instead.

Figure 1.21 Menus are located in the menu bar at the top of a program's window.

Figure 1.22 A checked command indicates an option that is turned on or selected.

Most menu commands take effect as soon as you choose them. If a command needs more information to complete, it's followed by an ellipsis (...), which lets you know that a dialog box will appear to let you enter more information. The Find command in Figure 1.21, for example, has an ellipsis because the command isn't complete until you specify what you want to find.

Some commands, such as Properties and Help > About, show a dialog box but have no ellipsis because no more information is needed to run the command.

✔ **Tips**

■ Commands with a triangular arrowhead next to them have additional choices listed in a *submenu*. To open a submenu, click or point to the command.

■ Checked commands (**Figure 1.22**) represent on/off options or mutually exclusive choices.

■ Dimmed commands are unavailable in the current context. Cut and Copy are unavailable if nothing is selected, for example.

■ Within individual menus, commands are grouped logically by horizontal lines called *command separators*.

■ Some menus are consistent across programs. The File menu almost always has the commands New, Open, Save, Save As, Print, and Exit; the Edit menu has the commands Undo, Cut, Copy, and Paste.

To choose a menu command:

1. Click the menu name.

   The menu appears, displaying its commands.

2. Point to the desired menu command.

3. Click to choose the command.

   The menu disappears.

MENUS

To choose a menu command by using the keyboard:

1. Hold down Alt; press the underlined letter in the menu name; then release both keys.

2. On the keyboard, press the underlined letter of a menu command.

3. If a submenu appears, press the underlined letter of a submenu command.

✔ Tips

■ By default menu letters aren't underlined until you hold down Alt. To always display underlines, choose Start > Control Panel > Appearance and Themes > Display > Appearance tab > Effects buttons > uncheck Hide Underlined Letters.

■ If two or more menu commands have the same underlined letter, press the letter repeatedly until you select the right command; then press Enter.

■ Another way to use the keyboard: Press F10 or Alt (by itself) to activate the menu bar; use the arrow keys to navigate to a command; then press Enter.

■ A shortcut menu will have one boldface command. You can simply press Enter to choose this default command.

■ To close a menu without choosing a command, press Esc twice (or click outside the menu).

■ To make menus appear faster, see the "Tweak UI" sidebar in "Using the Start Menu" in Chapter 2.

MENUS

Figure 1.23 The right mouse button's shortcut menus offer common commands quickly. Here are shortcut menus for Explorer, the Recycle Bin, and selected text in Notepad. Figure 1.19 shows the My Computer shortcut menu.

Shortcut menus

A *shortcut menu* (also called a *right-click menu* or *context menu*) is a context-sensitive menu that appears when you right-click an item (**Figure 1.23**). Windows provides shortcut menus for nearly all interface elements: icons, files, folders, disks, desktop, taskbar, Start button, the Recycle Bin, and so on. Shortcut menus are among the most useful features in Windows. Try right-clicking any item to see whether a shortcut menu pops up.

✔ Tips

- Shortcut-menu commands apply only to the item (or group of items) to which you point.

- Programs provide their own custom shortcut menus. Right-click a link in Internet Explorer or selected text in Notepad or Word, for example.

- Right-clicking a taskbar button or a title bar displays the control menu (sizing menu) for that program's window. See "Windows" later in this chapter.

To choose a shortcut-menu command:

1. Right-click an item.
   The shortcut menu appears, displaying its commands.

2. Point to the desired menu command.

3. Click to choose the command.
   The menu disappears.

MENUS

To choose a shortcut-menu command by using the keyboard:

1. Select (highlight) an item.

2. Hold down Shift; press F10; then release both keys.

3. Press the underlined letter of a menu command.

✔ Tips

- Press the Application key (if your keyboard has one) to display the shortcut menu for the selected item.

- To close a shortcut menu without choosing a command, press Esc or left-click outside the menu. (Right-clicking outside the menu only makes the menu jump to the pointer.)

- If multiple icons are selected, right-click any one of them to open the shortcut menu for the group.

Uninvited Menu Items

Utilities, shareware, and other programs often add their own entries to shortcut menus with or without your permission. If a right-click menu gets too crowded, you usually can remove items via the programs' Options or Preferences dialog boxes; look for options labeled *context menu*. WinZip, for example, adds Add to Zip File commands to Windows Explorer's shortcut menus. WinZip's Option > Configuration > Explorer Enhancements tab lets you show or hide these commands.

If no context-menu option is available, you can edit the registry (see "Editing the Registry" in Chapter 19). Many context-menu commands are in *HKEY_CLASSES_ROOT\Directory\ shell* and *HKEY_CLASSES_ROOT\Folder\shell*. Double-click *shell* to reveal the keys corresponding to each menu command. (You won't see and can't remove Windows' built-in commands.) Delete the keys that you don't want. In some cases, the keys are hidden elsewhere in *HKEY_CLASSES_ROOT*, and you'll have to hunt for the program's key (sometimes tricky— *Adobe.Acrobat.ContextMenu*, for example) or use Edit > Find to find the menu-item text (Scan for Viruses or whatever). Sometimes no keys are available, and you must live with the custom menu item. Back up your registry before you edit it.

Figure 1.24 Toolbars from Windows Explorer (top) and Adobe Photoshop (middle). The bottom toolbar shows Microsoft's standard icons, which many programs adopt for consistency. Left to right: New, Open, Save, Print, Print Preview, Spell Check, Cut, Copy, Paste, Format Painter, Undo, and Redo.

Figure 1.25 A word-processing tool tip.

Figure 1.26 In Internet Explorer, the Back button's menu lets you revisit sites that you've seen recently.

Figure 1.27 Toggle buttons stay pressed until they're clicked a second time. These pushed-in buttons boldface and left-align the selected text in a word processor.

Toolbars

A *toolbar* is a row, column, or block of buttons with icons that you click to perform some action, choose a tool, or change a setting (**Figure 1.24**). Toolbar buttons often duplicate menu functions, but they're more convenient because they're always visible—generally at one edge of the work area. Programs typically have several toolbars, each responsible for a group of tasks. In a word processor, for example, there's a toolbar for formatting text and paragraphs, and another for performing file operations.

✔ Tips

- Many programs display *tool tips*—short descriptions of toolbar buttons and icons that appear temporarily when the mouse pointer pauses on them (**Figure 1.25**).

- A toolbar button with a small triangular arrow pointing to the right or down will reveal its own small, self-contained menu when clicked (**Figure 1.26**).

- Often you can customize toolbars, create new ones, and move them around onscreen to suit your preferences. Experiment. Right-click a toolbar to see whether a shortcut menu appears. Click an empty area of a toolbar (usually its left side), and try dragging to dock it at an edge of the window or just let it float in the middle.

- Some toolbars have *toggle buttons* that push in (turn on) with one click and pop out (turn off) with the next. They can set global options or conditions that apply to only the current selection (**Figure 1.27**).

- Toolbars can appear and disappear automatically, depending on what you're doing in the program.

Icons

An *icon* is a small picture that represents an item you can manipulate. Windows uses icons on the desktop and in Windows Explorer to represent folders, files, disks, documents, programs, the Recycle Bin, and hardware devices (**Figure 1.28**).

You select (highlight) an icon or group of icons to perform an action. Left-click to select; right-click to open the shortcut menu.

What happens when you open an icon depends on the icon's type. A *folder* or *disk* icon opens in Windows Explorer. A *document* or *image* icon opens in its associated program, launching that program if it's not already open. A *program* icon launches the program. The *Recycle Bin* icon displays the items to be deleted when you empty the bin.

To select an icon:

◆ Click it (**Figure 1.29**).

or

Press the arrow keys until the icon is selected.

or

Press the first letter of the icon's name. If two or more icons have the same initial letter, press the letter repeatedly until you select the right icon.

✔ Tips

■ Selecting an icon deselects any other selected icons.

■ You can configure Windows to select an icon just by pointing at it. See "Using Alternative Mouse Behavior" in Chapter 4.

Figure 1.28 An icon's image depends on what it represents. System objects such as My Computer and the Recycle Bin have default images. All documents of the same type—Text (.txt) files, for example—have the same icon. Program (.exe) files such as Internet Explorer have icons that were created for and are part of the program.

Figure 1.29 Click an icon to select it.

Figure 1.30 Ctrl+click to select multiple (nonconsecutive) icons. This window shows icons in Details view.

Figure 1.31 You can drag across icons diagonally to create a selection. Icons within the rectangle darken to confirm that they're selected.

To select multiple icons:

◆ Ctrl+click each icon that you want to select (**Figure 1.30**).

or

Drag a selection rectangle around the icons (**Figure 1.31**). The area always is a rectangle; you can't surround an odd-shaped area.

or

Click the first icon that you want to select; then Shift+click the last icon. All icons in between are selected automatically—at least by Windows' definition of "in between."

✔ Tip

■ In Windows Explorer it's easiest to work with multiple icons in Details view, in which all icons appear in a single column. To use Details view, choose View > Details. See "Viewing Files and Folders in Different Ways" in Chapter 5.

To select all icons in a window:

◆ Choose Edit > Select All (or press Ctrl+A).

To deselect an icon:

◆ If the icon is the only one selected, click anywhere in the window or desktop other than the selected icon.

or

If the icon is part of a multiple selection, Ctrl+click it to remove it from the selection.

✔ Tips

■ To select *almost* all the icons in a window, press Ctrl+A; then Ctrl+click the icons you *don't* want.

■ Choose Edit > Invert Selection to reverse which icons are selected and which are not.

ICONS

To move an icon:

◆ Drag it to a new position (**Figures 1.32** and **1.33**).

✔ Tips

■ Use the View > Arrange Icons By submenu to control icon positions within a window.

■ You can drag icons to new positions within a window set to Thumbnails, Tiles, or Icons view but not within a window set to List or Details view.

■ You can move multiple icons at the same time by dragging any icon in a multiple selection.

To open an icon:

◆ Double-click it.

or

Select it; then press Enter or choose File > Open.

✔ Tips

■ To open multiple icons at the same time, select the icons; then press Enter or choose File > Open.

■ To open a document or image with something besides the associated (default) program, right-click its icon; then choose File > Open With > Choose Program.

■ You can configure Windows to open an icon with a single click. See "Using Alternative Mouse Behavior" in Chapter 4.

Figure 1.32 Drag and drop an icon to move it to...

Figure 1.33 ...a new position in the window (or on the desktop).

Close button

Maximize/
restore button

Title bar

Control menu

Minimize button

Border

Figure 1.34 Your basic window.

Windows

The Windows interface takes its trade-mark name from the rectangles on your screen—the windows—in which you work. **Figure 1.34** shows a typical window with its parts labeled. When you work with Windows XP you'll have multiple (overlapping) windows open at the same time so that you can, say, alternate working with a word processor, email program, and web browser.

You can identify a window by its *title bar*, which lists the name of the program, document, or folder. Each window has its own boundaries and can present different views of its contents. To manage multiple windows, you need to learn a few basic skills.

✔ Tips

■ The windows that you actually work with often are crowded with other items, such as menus, toolbars, status bars, and task panes.

■ Windows don't *have* to be rectangular. See "Changing Player Appearance with Skins" in Chapter 10, for example.

Activating a window

If you have multiple windows open, only one window is active at any time. The *active window* is the one that receives your keystrokes (text entry, navigational movements, or commands). You can identify the active window by its dark-colored title bar; inactive-window title bars are a washed-out color (**Figure 1.35**). (The default color is blue; to change it, see "Choosing a Desktop Theme" in Chapter 4.) An inactive window can be hidden partially or entirely behind another window, where it remains inactive until you bring it to the foreground.

To activate a window:

◆ Click anywhere on the window (but don't click a button or menu lest you activate it accidentally).

or

Click the window's taskbar icon.

or

Hold down Alt and press Esc repeatedly until the desired window appears; then release both keys.

or

Hold down Alt and press Tab repeatedly until the desired program icon is highlighted in the pop-up selection bar; then release both keys. (This technique is called *Alt+tabbing.*)

✔ Tips

■ Programs whose windows are inactive can still carry out tasks—called *background tasks*—such as downloading files or printing documents. *Inactive* means that *you* are ignoring the window, but Windows still gives it the resources to do its job.

Figure 1.35 You can tell which window is active by looking for the darker color of the title bar—the center one, in this case.

■ Generally the active window is in front of all other windows. But some windows, such as Task Manager and Help, can be set to stay on top—in the foreground—even when inactive.

■ Alt+Esc and Alt+Tab don't produce identical results. For details, see "Switching Programs" in Chapter 6.

WINDOWS

Figure 1.36 A maximized window reduces the need for scrolling but hides other windows. When a window is maximized, its Maximize button changes to the Restore button.

Figure 1.37 A minimized window reduces screen clutter and reveals other windows lurking in the background.

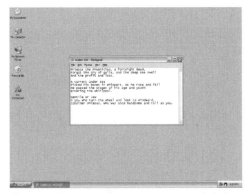

Figure 1.38 You can resize or move a restored window to work with multiple windows conveniently. When a window is restored, its Restore button changes to the Maximize button.

Figure 1.39 Right-clicking a taskbar icon displays its control menu.

Resizing, moving, and closing windows

You can *maximize* a window to the size of your whole screen (**Figure 1.36**), *minimize* it to a button on the taskbar (**Figure 1.37**), or *restore* it to a free-floating rectangle on your screen (**Figure 1.38**). To adjust the size of a restored window, drag its corners or edges.

To resize a window:

◆ Drag any window border (side or corner).

The pointer changes to a double-headed arrow when it's moved over a border. See "The Mouse" earlier in this chapter.

or

Activate the window; press Alt+spacebar; press S; use the arrow keys to resize the window; then press Enter.

To maximize a window:

◆ If the window is minimized, right-click its taskbar button; then choose Maximize (**Figure 1.39**).

or

If the window is restored, click its Maximize button (▣) or double-click its title bar.

or

If the window is restored, activate it; press Alt+spacebar; then press X.

To minimize a window:

◆ Click its Minimize button (▬).

or

Activate the window; press Alt+spacebar; then press N.

To restore a window:

◆ Right-click its taskbar button; then choose Restore.

or

If the window is maximized, click its Restore button ( ) or double-click its title bar.

or

If the window is maximized, press Alt+spacebar; then press R.

✔ Tips

■ If you use Alt+spacebar+(underlined letter) to maximize or restore a window, that window remains active; if you minimize it, it doesn't.

■ You can resize only restored windows, not maximized or minimized windows.

■ Many windows have resize handles in the bottom-right corner that are ridged and easy to grab.

■ To arrange multiple (restored) windows neatly on your desktop, see "Managing Windows by Using the Taskbar" in Chapter 2.

■ Some utility programs, such as Calculator and Character Map, can't be maximized or resized.

To move a window:

◆ Drag its title bar (**Figure 1.40**).

or

Activate the window; press Alt+spacebar; press M; use the arrow keys to move the window; then press Enter.

✔ Tips

■ You can move only restored windows, not maximized or minimized windows.

■ You can move a window so that a portion of it lies off the screen's edge.

Figure 1.40 The title bar provides convenient ways to move and resize a window: Drag it to move the window, or double-click it to alternate between restored and maximized states.

WINDOWS

Figure 1.41 If a document window is maximized, its window controls appear directly below the program's window controls.

To close a window:

◆ Click its Close button ( ).

or

Right-click its taskbar button; then click Close.

or

Double-click the icon at the far-left end of the title bar.

or

Press Alt+F4.

or

Activate the window; press Alt+spacebar; then press C.

or

Choose File > Close to close the file or File > Exit to quit the application, whichever is appropriate. (This distinction between Close and Exit isn't consistent across programs.)

You'll be prompted to save any unsaved work.

✔ Tips

■ In Windows Explorer, Internet Explorer, and some other programs, closing a window quits the program entirely.

■ The desktop itself is a window open under all other windows; you "close" it by logging off or shutting down.

■ Many programs, such as Word and Adobe Photoshop, let you have more than one document open at the same time. Each document window has its own title bar and dedicated controls, letting you work in it without affecting other windows (**Figure 1.41**).

WINDOWS

Scrolling

If a window is too small to display all its contents, scroll bars appear. A *scroll bar* is a vertical or horizontal bar at the side or bottom of a window that you can move with the mouse to slide that window's contents around.

A scroll bar has three components: *scroll arrows* at its ends for moving incrementally, a sliding *scroll box* for moving to an arbitrary location, and the scroll-bar *shaft* (gray background) for jumping by one window at a time (**Figure 1.42**).

To scroll a window's contents:

◆ To scroll up or down line by line, click the up or down scroll arrow.

or

To scroll up or down incrementally, press an arrow key.

or

To scroll up or down by a window, click the shaft above or below the vertical scroll box, or press Page Up or Page Down.

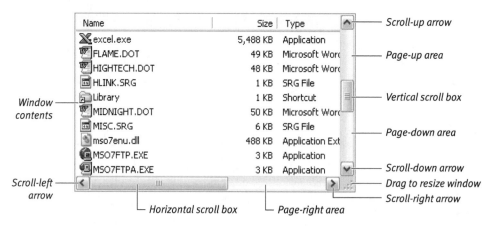

Figure 1.42 The size of a scroll box is proportional to the fraction of the window contents displayed, so the scroll box indicates visually how much you *can't* see, as well as showing you where you are.

or

To scroll left or right incrementally, click the left or right scroll arrow.

or

To scroll left or right by a window, click the shaft to the left or right of the horizontal scroll box.

or

To move to an arbitrary location, drag a scroll box to the place you want. (Some programs show the scrolling content or a location indicator while you drag so you know when to stop; other programs make you guess.)

✔ Tips

- If your mouse has a wheel, you often can scroll up or down by turning it.

- In many programs you can press Ctrl+Home and Ctrl+End to go to a document's beginning or end. If yours won't, the fastest way to scroll is to drag the scroll box to the top or bottom of the scroll bar.

- In Windows Explorer, Internet Explorer, Notepad, and some other programs, you can right-click anywhere on a scroll bar to show a navigation shortcut menu.

- Holding down the mouse button on a scroll arrow or shaft auto-repeats the scrolling behavior. (If you lean on the shaft for more than a few seconds, Windows can lose track of video memory, and the window contents will appear distorted or sliced up before Windows recovers.)

- You can use the mysterious Scroll Lock key for keyboard scrolling. When Scroll Lock is toggled on (its keyboard indicator is lit) and you press a navigation key, some programs scroll the view without affecting the cursor or selection.

Automatic Scrolling

Many programs scroll automatically in the following situations:

- ◆ When you drag highlighted text or graphics near the window's edge, the area scrolls in the direction of the drag.

- ◆ When you extend a highlighted selection by dragging past an edge, the area scrolls in the direction of the drag (sometimes at high velocities).

- ◆ When you drag an object past the edge of a scrollable window, the area auto-scrolls at a speed proportional to how far past the edge you drag.

- ◆ When you tab to a text box or type or paste text into a partially hidden text box, the form auto-scrolls to reveal the whole box.

- ◆ Using Find, Replace, or a similar command auto-scrolls to show the matching selection or new cursor location.

Dialog Boxes

Dialog boxes let you enter new information or view or change existing settings. A dialog box is a small temporary window that a program displays to respond to a command or event (**Figure 1.43**).

✔ Tip

■ Dialog boxes appear when you must enter more information to complete a command. See the sidebar in "Menus" earlier in this chapter.

OK, Cancel, Apply

Most dialog boxes have an OK button and a Cancel button, and many have an Apply button too. The differences are:

OK. Saves your changes and closes the dialog box (often equivalent to pressing Enter).

Cancel. Discards your changes and closes the dialog box (equivalent to pressing Esc).

Apply. Saves your changes and leaves the dialog box open for more changes. Apply is handy if you want to try out a change with the chance to change it right back.

The Apply button's behavior has a slight wrinkle: If you click Apply and then click Cancel, changes made *before* you click Apply are saved, but changes made *after* you click Apply are lost—usually, that is. Some programs behave differently.

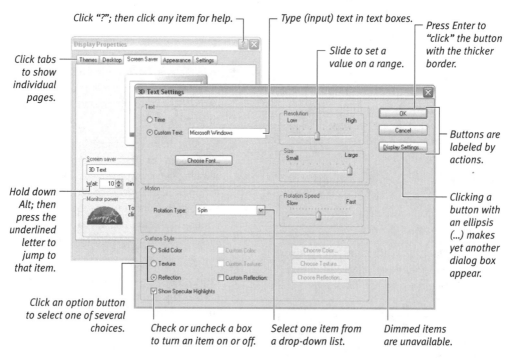

Click "?"; then click any item for help.

Click tabs to show individual pages.

Type (input) text in text boxes.

Slide to set a value on a range.

Press Enter to "click" the button with the thicker border.

Buttons are labeled by actions.

Clicking a button with an ellipsis (...) makes yet another dialog box appear.

Hold down Alt; then press the underlined letter to jump to that item.

Click an option button to select one of several choices.

Check or uncheck a box to turn an item on or off.

Select one item from a drop-down list.

Dimmed items are unavailable.

Figure 1.43 Dialog boxes let you change settings by using buttons, check boxes, text boxes, lists, and other controls.

Figure 1.44 Use the Back and Next buttons to step through a wizard. You can cancel a wizard to make your settings manually.

Figure 1.45 Message boxes bring your program to a halt. You must respond before the program can do anything further.

Table 1.5

Dialog-Box Keyboard Shortcuts

Press	To
Ctrl+Tab	Select the next tab
Ctrl+Shift+Tab	Select the previous tab
Tab	Select the next option
Shift+Tab	Select the previous option
Alt+underlined letter	Select the corresponding option or click the corresponding button
Spacebar	Click a button, toggle a check box, or choose an option button (if that option is active)
Arrow keys	Select an item in an option-button group or list, or move a slider
F1	Display Help
F4	Display list items
Enter	Click the selected button (with the dotted outline) or the default button (with the shadow)
Esc	Click the Cancel button

The differences between dialog boxes and normal windows are:

- File Open and File Save dialog boxes usually are resizable, to let you vary the number of files that they display. Most other dialog boxes aren't resizable.

- Some open dialog boxes won't let you keep working in their program until you close them. You still can use other programs, though.

- When you edit text in a dialog box, you can't use the Edit menu to cut, copy, and paste, but you can use keyboard shortcuts (Ctrl+X, Ctrl+C, and Ctrl+V) or right-click to use a shortcut menu.

- Use keyboard shortcuts to navigate dialog boxes quickly (**Table 1.5**).

- A *wizard* is a series of interactive dialog boxes that steps you through a complex task (**Figure 1.44**).

- Windows uses a *message box* to notify you of events or ask for a decision (**Figure 1.45**).

DIALOG BOXES

Properties

Almost every object in Windows has a
Properties dialog box full of information
about its contents and settings. Items with
properties include files, folders, disks, documents, programs, hardware devices, the
taskbar, the Start menu, the desktop, and
My Computer.

To display an item's properties:

◆ Right-click the item; then choose
Properties (**Figure 1.46**).

 or

 Select (highlight) the item; then press
Alt+Enter.

 or

 Hold down Alt; then double-click
the item.

Figure 1.46 You can choose an item's
properties from its shortcut (right-click)
menu. The Properties command usually is
bottommost on the menu.

Figure 1.47 The properties information shown is appropriate for the item you select. Here are properties for a Word document (top) and a hard disk (bottom).

Figure 1.47 shows Properties dialog boxes for a Word file and a hard disk. Windows lets you change some properties; you can rename the file or compress the hard disk. Many properties are *read-only,* however, meaning that Windows sets them and you can't change them. You can inspect—but not change—a hard disk's capacity or a file's creation date, for example.

✔ Tips

- A read-only property usually is shown as black text on a gray background; a modifiable (read-write) property is set in a text box, check box, list, or similar control. If it's not obvious whether you can change a property, try to click it or tab to it.

- Some dialog boxes have a button labeled Restore, Restore Defaults, Defaults, or Reset. Clicking this button changes your current settings back to Windows' factory-installed settings. Be careful, because you (or the programs that you've installed) have probably made more changes than you remember—or even know about.

- Some programs let you add file properties such as comments and custom name-value attributes. In the Properties dialog box of a Microsoft Word document, for example, click the Custom tab (or choose File > Properties inside Word itself).

- To see how much disk space a group of files or folders occupies, select their icons; then display the properties for the selected group.

PROPERTIES

Transferring Data

One of the regular things you'll do in Windows is move data around: copy web-page text to an email message, put graphics-editor images in a word-processing document, move paragraphs around in a text file, export spreadsheet rows to a database, embed a chart in a presentation, and so on. Windows gives you a few ways to do so.

Figure 1.48 If nothing is selected, the Cut and Copy commands are dimmed.

Cut, copy, and paste

Cut, copy, and paste, which are second nature to experienced Windows users, are used to organize documents, folders, and disks.

Cut and paste removes (cuts) information and places it on the clipboard so that it can be moved (pasted) elsewhere. Cutting deletes the data from its original location.

Copy and paste copies information to the clipboard so that it can be duplicated (pasted) elsewhere. Copying leaves the original data intact (nothing visible happens).

You'll find Cut, Copy, and Paste commands in a program's Edit menu (**Figure 1.48**), but each program may handle these operations differently. In Windows Explorer, for example, you can copy or move files and folders from one disk or folder to another. In Microsoft Word, you can copy or move text or graphics to another part of a document or to a different document. In Internet Explorer, you can only copy material from web pages, not cut it.

To cut:

1. Select (highlight) the material to remove.

2. Choose Edit > Cut.

   or

   Press Ctrl+X.

   or

   Right-click the section; then choose Cut from the shortcut menu.

Figure 1.49 In windows that have no Edit menu, such as this dialog box, you can cut, copy, and paste by using keyboard shortcuts or the shortcut (right-click) menu.

To copy:

1. Select (highlight) the material to copy.

2. Choose Edit > Copy.
   or
   Press Ctrl+C.
   or
   Right-click the selection; then choose Copy from the shortcut menu.

To paste:

1. Click the mouse (or move the cursor) to where you want to the material to appear.

2. Choose Edit > Paste.
   or
   Press Ctrl+V.
   or
   Right-click; then choose Paste from the shortcut menu.

If you mean to copy (Ctrl+C) something and accidentally cut (Ctrl+X) it instead, or if you paste something in the wrong place, you can recover by undoing your action.

To undo a cut or paste:

◆ Immediately after you cut or paste, choose Edit > Undo (Ctrl+Z).

✔ Tips

■ Keyboard shortcuts save time, but they're especially useful when the Edit menu is unavailable (**Figure 1.49**).

■ Many programs have an Edit > Paste Special command that pastes, links, or embeds the clipboard contents in a document in the format you specify. The Paste Special command in the Microsoft Word, for example, lets you strip all formatting from pasted text, for example.

TRANSFERRING DATA

The Clipboard

The *clipboard* is the invisible area of memory where Windows stores cut or copied data, where it remains until overwritten when you cut or copy something else. This scheme lets you paste the same thing multiple times in different places. You can transfer information from one program to another provided that the second program can read data generated by the first. A little experimenting shows that you often can combine dissimilar data—you can paste text from Notepad or Word into Photoshop, for example. Note that you can't paste something that you've *deleted* or *cleared* (as opposed to cut) because Windows doesn't place that something on the clipboard.

Use ClipBook Viewer to see what's on the clipboard: Choose Start > Run; type `clipbrd` and then press Enter (**Figure 1.50**). ClipBook Viewer has some handy features such as network clip-sharing and the ability to save clips as files, but if you're a writer, editor, researcher, or graphic artist, you'll want something more powerful. Try ClipCache Plus ($20 U.S.; `www.clipcache.com`) or ClipMate ($30; `www.thornsoft.com`), which let you save, organize, combine, preview, and control many persistent clips. (The Microsoft Office clipboard can stack a dozen clips, but that's nothing compared to these utilities.)

Figure 1.50 The first time that you open ClipBook Viewer, the clip appears in a minimized window in the viewer's lower-left corner. Click the maximize button on the minimized bar to see the clip.

Dolore quis aliquip dolore te velit ad, sed ut illum nibh autem vel. Minim nulla ex lobortis nulla odio qui tation eros dolor, duis qui adipiscing. Erat aliquip, consectetuer tation suscipit dignissim dolor praesent nulla ut vero ut dignissim, consequat ut commodo, dolore in ea vel iriure facilisi. WHAT COLOR IS AN ORANGE?

Dolore quis aliquip dolore te velit ad, sed ut illum nibh autem vel. WHAT COLOR IS AN ORANGE? Minim nulla ex lobortis nulla odio qui tation eros dolore, duis qui adipiscing. Erat aliquip, consectetuer tation suscipit dignissim dolor praesent nulla ut vero ut dignissim, consequat ut commodo, dolore in ea vel iriure facilisi.

Figure 1.51 Click in the middle of some highlighted text (top), and drag it elsewhere within the same document (bottom) or to a different window or program.

Figure 1.52 Dragging highlighted text to the desktop creates a reusable scrap file. The scrap's contents determine its filename, type, and icon. Treat a scrap file like any other file: Delete it, rename it, or double-click it to open it in its own window.

Drag and drop

WordPad, Outlook Express, Outlook, Word, Microsoft PowerPoint, and many other email and word-processing programs let you drag and drop as a faster alternative to cut and paste. **Figure 1.51** shows you how. Move any amount of text, from single character to epic poem. This technique doesn't involve the clipboard and won't change its contents.

✔ Tips

- Press Ctrl as you drag to *copy,* rather than move, the highlighted material.

- When you drag highlighted material near the window's edge, the document auto-scrolls until you move (usually jerk) away from the edge. See the "Automatic Scrolling" sidebar in "Windows" earlier in this chapter.

- If you drag highlighted text or graphics out of your document and onto the desktop, Windows creates a persistent *scrap* file, which remains there for future pasting (**Figure 1.52**). Drag a scrap icon from the desktop back into a document window, and the clip appears. You also can drag a scrap icon onto a taskbar button, pause until the document appears, and then drag and drop it in the document.

TRANSFERRING DATA

39

Intermediate formats

Another way to exchange data between programs is to save it in a format that both the source and target programs can read and write. To read a list of addresses into a mailing-list program from a spreadsheet or database, for example, save the addresses in a CSV-format file (a text file of comma-separated values); then open it in the mailing-list program. The source program's Save As dialog box lists the format types that you can save (**Figure 1.53**). The target program usually will auto-convert the CSV file when you open it with File > Open, but you may have to step through a wizard to organize the incoming data. Image-editing programs such as Paint and Photoshop can exchange files in JPEG, GIF, TIFF, PNG, and other popular graphic formats.

Import/export

Use import and export tools to transfer large amounts of data or data in incompatible formats. Most address-book, browser, email, spreadsheet, database, and statistical programs have Import and Export commands, typically on the File menu. The commands vary by program (they're not part of Windows), so read the documentation for both the source and target programs. Import/export operations can be routine—most database programs can skip the CSV step and export to the native Excel format directly, for example—but they're superlative when no standard exchange-format exists. If you want to try new email and browser programs, import/export is the only practical way to transfer all your addresses, messages, bookmarks, cookies, and other information (**Figure 1.54**).

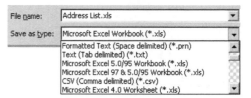

Figure 1.53 Excel's Save As dialog box lets you save a spreadsheet in formats other than the native Excel format.

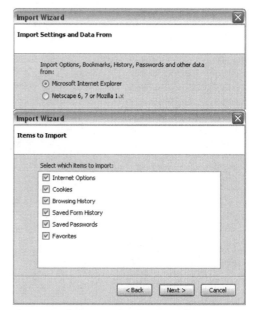

Figure 1.54 The Import Wizard in the Mozilla Firefox browser imports bookmarks (favorites), cookies, passwords, settings, and other items from Internet Explorer and other browsers.

Figure 1.55 Click the Create New tab to insert a new object; click the Create from File tab to insert an existing file. Check Link to File if you want the data to self-update when the source file is edited. The Result box explains the inserted object's behavior.

OLE

OLE (pronounced *oh-lay*), for Object Linking and Embedding, lets you insert self-updating material from a source document in one program into a target document running in another. If you insert an Excel spreadsheet as a linked object into a Word document, for example, any changes that you make to the spreadsheet separately in Excel appear in the Word document automatically.

To insert an OLE object:

1. Open or create a document in a program that supports OLE (WordPad, Word, Excel, or PowerPoint, for example).

2. Click or move the cursor to where you want the inserted object to appear.

3. Choose Insert > Object.

   This command may appear elsewhere in non-Microsoft programs.

4. In the Object dialog box, choose the object type and link type that you want to create (**Figure 1.55**).

5. Click OK.

✔ Tips

- You can cut, copy, and paste OLE objects. To delete one, click it and then press Delete.

- To edit an OLE object, double-click it. If it's linked to a file, the document opens in its own window. If it's not linked, the source program's menus appear in place of the current program's menus; click off the object or press Esc when you're done editing, and the original menus reappear.

- After editing a linked object, you may have to "encourage" it to update itself. Select it and then use the program's Update function (the F9 key in Microsoft Office programs).

TRANSFERRING DATA

THE START
MENU AND TASKBAR

After you log on, Windows displays the desktop and its components (**Figure 2.1**). The *desktop* sets the backdrop for your working environment and lets you organize the resources on your computer. The *Start menu* is the central location that lists the most useful folders, programs, and commands. The *taskbar* tells you what programs are running on your computer and lets you activate or close them.

Start menu ——

Desktop

Taskbar

Figure 2.1 Basic desktop elements. Your desktop may look a little different if you upgraded from a previous version of Windows or if your PC's manufacturer added icons and changed the desktop background.

Exploring the Start Menu

The Start menu lets you access useful software and services, including programs, documents, folders, and commands, while the majority of Windows XP's files run in the background quietly to support Windows itself and other programs.

If you've used a previous version of Windows, you'll notice that the redesigned Start menu has two columns instead of one. The left side lists programs, and the right side shows links to common Windows components and system folders.

To open the Start menu:

◆ Click Start, at the left end of the taskbar (or press Ctrl+Esc).

or

Press and release the Windows logo key.

Start menu left column

The left column of the Start menu has three parts, separated by horizontal lines (**Figure 2.2**):

Pinned Items list. Items in the top section of this column remain there, always available to open. You can select programs to appear here, as well as their order. Your web browser and email program are two appropriate choices. See "Adding items to the Start menu" in the next section.

Most Frequently Used Programs list. Windows maintains this list by appending programs as you use them. Each added program replaces one that you haven't used recently. You can delete items from this list and set the number of items displayed, but you can't reorder or add items manually.

All Programs menu. The All Programs menu displays all the programs that you've installed or that Windows Setup has installed. Click the right-pointing arrow (or press P) to see it; it's not displayed by default because it's big.

Start menu right column

The right column of the Start menu also is divided into three sections.

Files, drives, and network: My Documents, My Recent Documents, My Pictures, My Music, My Computer, My Network Places. This part of the Start menu lets you open your personal documents and other files, open Windows Explorer for all the drives in your computer, and reach places on your network.

Figure 2.2 The Start menu's icons vary by installation and regular use, but the overall layout stays the same.

Workplace and device management: Control Panel, Printers and Faxes. Control Panel lets you change your work environment and hardware settings (see Chapter 4). Printers and Faxes lets you change print settings such as page orientation, fineness (resolution) of printed copies, whether to print in color, and whether your fax should pick up automatically or wait for you to do it (see Chapter 7).

Everything else: Help and Support, Search, Run. Help and Support Center, a vast improvement over Windows Help, is connected to the internet whenever you are and can find much that can help you with Windows—from a small help file to an article in the vast Microsoft Knowledge Base (see Chapter 3). Search lets you find files, folders, objects, and text strings on any drive that you're permitted to access. Run lets you run a program or open a folder or document by typing its name.

To close the Start menu:

◆ Press and release the Windows logo key, or press Esc.

  or

  Click anywhere off the menu (on the desktop or in a program, for example).

Using the Start Menu

As in previous Windows versions, Start-menu commands are a click away. If you don't like the Start menu's default layout and behavior, it's susceptible to behavior-modification therapy.

To choose a Start-menu item:

◆ Click the item.

or

Use the arrow keys to navigate to the item; then press Enter.

or

Press the key of the item's first letter.

If two or more items share the same first letter, press that letter repeatedly until the desired item is highlighted; then press Enter.

✔ Tips

■ A menu item with a right-pointing arrow (such as All Programs in Figure 2.2) opens a submenu when you click or point to it.

■ If you prefer the old one-column Start menu, called the classic Start menu, see "Restoring the Old Windows Look" in Chapter 4.

Tweak UI

The easiest way to customize the Windows user interface is with the Tweak UI utility, one of the PowerToys described in "Using the Free Utility Programs" in Chapter 6. After installing Tweak UI, choose Start > All Programs > PowerToys for Windows XP > Tweak UI. Browse around the options in the Explorer-style tree in the left pane, and you'll find ways to change the desktop, Start menu, taskbar, icons, common dialog boxes, mouse behavior, Welcome screen, Windows Explorer, Control Panel, hard-drive letters, and much more. Most settings aren't available through the normal Windows interface.

One of the most useful tweaks makes menus snappier: Click the Mouse option in the left pane and then drag the Menu Speed slider left. If you drag it all the way left and click OK, you'll notice no delay between when you click a menu and when Windows displays it. I've scattered other Tweak UI tips throughout this book. (Some Tweak UI settings provides functions that are otherwise unavailable to XP Home users.)

When you change a setting, Tweak UI actually is changing a registry entry. Many of the registry hacks that you'll find on the web are replicated—more safely—by Tweak UI. See "Editing the Registry" in Chapter 19.

Adding items to the Start menu

Icons in the Start menu are *shortcuts*—links to computer or network items such as programs, files, folders, disks, web pages, printers, hardware devices, and other computers. You can add items to the Start menu by dragging and dropping or by pinning. You also can remove or reorder items.

✔ Tip

- Changing or deleting a shortcut has no effect on the item that it's linked to; removing a program's shortcut won't uninstall the actual program.

To pin an item to the Start menu:

1. Locate the item (icon) that you want to display at the top of the menu.

2. Right-click the icon; then choose Pin to Start Menu (**Figure 2.3**).

   or

   Drag the item to the Start button (**Figures 2.4** and **2.5**).

Figure 2.3 You can right-click a program in the Start menu, in Windows Explorer, in My Computer, or on the desktop. For documents, folder, and disks, use drag and drop.

Figure 2.4 You can pin a program, folder, file, or even a disk to the Start menu by dropping it on the Start button.

Figure 2.5 The Start menu pops open if you pause on the Start button while dragging, letting you drop the item in the desired position.

Figure 2.6 The horizontal black line shows where the item will land when it's dropped.

Figure 2.7 This technique works in both the Pinned Items and Most Frequently Used Programs lists. In the Pinned Items list, you also can choose Unpin from Start Menu.

Figure 2.8 Besides letting you configure the Start menu, this dialog box lets you choose the old-style, one-column Start menu.

✔ Tips

■ If you don't know the item's location, use the Search command in Windows Explorer to find it; then right-click it or drag it from the Search Results window.

■ If you can't drag icons onto the Start menu, or if right-clicking Start-menu items has no effect, turn on Start-menu dragging and dropping. See "Customizing the Start Menu" later in this chapter.

■ You can't pin items to the classic (one-column) Start menu.

To move a pinned item:

◆ Drag the item to a new position (**Figure 2.6**).

To remove a pinned item:

◆ Right-click the item; then choose Remove from This List (**Figure 2.7**).

To configure the program lists:

1. Right-click the Start button; then choose Properties to open the Taskbar and Start Menu Properties dialog box (**Figure 2.8**).

   or

   Choose Start > Control Panel > Appearance and Themes > Taskbar and Start Menu > Start Menu tab.

continues on next page

2. Make sure that Start Menu (not Classic Start Menu) is selected; then click Customize to open the Customize Start Menu dialog box (**Figure 2.9**).

3. Select an icon size for programs.

Choose Small Icons to make the Start menu's left column less cluttered or Large Icons to make the menu easier to read.

4. In the Programs section, type the number of programs to display in the menu's bottom-left section.

Using more programs gives you quicker access but takes up more vertical space.

5. Click Clear List to erase the menu's bottom-left section (if you don't want someone else to know what you've been running).

Windows will repopulate the list over time.

6. In the Show on Start Menu section, check the boxes if you want your web browser and email program pinned in the menu's top-left section.

7. Use the drop-down lists to choose among the installed browsers and email programs.

8. Click OK.

✔ Tips

■ You can't choose Large Icons for the menu's right column or for All Programs; that setting always is Small Icons.

■ Changes you make to the Start menu apply only to you, the logged-on user.

■ Tweak UI's Taskbar and Start Menu > Start Menu > Frequently Used Programs option lets you stop the programs of your choice from appearing on the Start menu.

Figure 2.9 The General tab of the Customize Start Menu dialog box affects what you see in the menu's left column, where programs are listed.

Figure 2.10 The All Programs menu superimposes itself over the right side of the Start menu.

Figure 2.11 Dragging an item to the All Programs menu requires patience.

Modifying the All Programs menu

The All Programs menu, which appears when you click or point to All Programs in the Start menu (**Figure 2.10**), displays all the programs that you, Windows Setup, and your PC manufacturer have installed on your computer. Program installers generally add program icons to the All Programs menu, but you can add, delete, or reorder them manually. The menu accepts not only program icons, but also document, folder, and disk icons.

To add an item to the All Programs menu:

1. Locate the item (icon) that you want to add.

2. Drag the icon over the Start button, and pause until the Start menu opens.

3. Continue to drag, and pause over All Programs until the submenu opens.
   The black horizontal line shows where the icon will appear when you drop it (**Figure 2.11**).

4. Drop the icon on the submenu.

✔ Tips

- Adding a folder to the All Programs menu creates a submenu that lists its contents.

- The default name for an item's shortcut starts with Shortcut To (Shortcut to Outlook Express, for example). To change the name, right-click the item; then choose Rename from the shortcut menu.

- If you can't drag icons to the All Programs menu, or if right-clicking icons has no effect, turn on Start-menu dragging and dropping. See "Customizing the Start Menu" later in this chapter.

- If you're using the classic (one-column) Start menu, you can manage icons with the Customize Classic Start Menu dialog box. Right-click Start; choose Properties; then click Customize.

To delete an item:

1. Right-click the item; then choose Delete (**Figure 2.12**).

2. If a confirmation message box appears, click Yes or Delete Shortcut.

✔ Tip

■ To undelete an item from the Recycle Bin, see "Deleting Files and Folders" in Chapter 5.

To move an item:

◆ Drag the item to a new position.
This technique works as shown in Figure 2.6.

To sort items alphabetically:

◆ Right-click any menu item; then choose Sort by Name.
Windows sorts folders in alphabetical order at the top, followed by other menu items in alphabetical order.

✔ Tip

■ You can sort any submenu this way, not only All Programs.

Managing All Programs items with folders

To keep your All Programs menu from growing wildly long, you can consolidate menu items into submenus (**Figure 2.13**). You add submenus by creating folders.

Every item that appears on the Start menu is contained in one of two folders: \Documents and Settings\<*your user name*>\Start Menu and \Documents and Settings\All Users\Start Menu. Only you, the logged-on user, can access items in the <*your user name*> folder; I cover those here. Everyone who has a user account can access the items in the All Users folder; I cover those in Chapter 16.

Figure 2.12 If your desktop is clear, you also can drag an item off the menu and drop it into the Recycle Bin to delete it.

Figure 2.13 A menu item with a right-pointing triangle spawns a submenu when you click or point to it.

Figure 2.14 You can add or delete items that are visible only to you (as shown here) or to all users.

To add or delete All Programs items:

1. Right-click the Start button; then choose Explore (**Figure 2.14**).

2. To add (or delete) menu items, drag icons into (or delete icons from) the Start Menu\Programs folder or any folder nested in the Programs folder (**Figures 2.15** and **2.16**).

Figure 2.15 The arrows indicate two Start Menu folders: one for all users (top arrow) and one for only you (bottom arrow). Click the plus sign (+) next to a folder to reveal its nested folders.

Figure 2.16 Icons placed inside the Start Menu folder itself appear above the horizontal line in the All Programs menu. (Note where the icons in the right pane of Figure 2.15 appear here.) Icons placed inside the Programs folder appear below the line. Subfolders inside the Programs folder appear as submenus.

To add a submenu:

1. Right-click the Start button; then choose Explore (refer to Figure 2.14).

2. Click the Start Menu\Programs folder in the window's left pane (refer to Figure 2.15, bottom arrow).

3. Choose File > New > Folder.

   or

   Right-click an empty area in the right pane; then choose New > Folder.

4. Type the name of the folder; then press Enter.

   You create an empty folder, which is an empty submenu (**Figure 2.17**).

5. To make a particular item appear in the new submenu, drop a shortcut to it on the new folder; then close the Explorer window.

6. Choose Start > All Programs to see the new submenu (**Figure 2.18**).

✔ Tip

■ To create a nested submenu, follow the same instructions, but in step 2, click the plus sign next to Programs; click the first folder you added; then continue with step 3.

Figure 2.17 A subfolder within the Programs folder appears as a submenu in the All Programs menu.

Figure 2.18 The new folder appears as an empty submenu at the bottom of the All Programs menu. You can drag the folder up or down the menu to reposition it.

Figure 2.19 If you rename a top-level menu item, you edit in the Start menu directly. If you rename a submenu item, you edit in a dialog box.

Customizing the Start Menu

The Start menu's Windows components and default behavior are easy to change. You can, for example, change the name of My Computer; decide which icons the menu displays; and highlight recently installed programs.

To rename a Start-menu item:

1. Right-click any menu item; then choose Rename.

2. Type a new name or edit the existing one; then press Enter (**Figure 2.19**).

✔ Tips

- It's okay to rename any folder in the Start menu, even My Documents, but *don't* rename the Startup folder. If you do, Windows won't launch programs automatically when the computer boots.

- The keyboard shortcuts for Cut, Copy, and Paste (Ctrl+X, Ctrl+C, and Ctrl+V) work in the edit box.

- To cancel renaming an item, press Esc while editing.

CUSTOMIZING THE START MENU

To configure the Start menu:

1. Right-click the Start button; then choose Properties.

2. Make sure that Start Menu (not Classic Start Menu) is selected; then click Customize.

3. Click the Advanced tab (**Figure 2.20**).

4. Choose the desired options in **Table 2.1**.

5. Click OK in each open dialog box.

✔ Tips

- You still can open Control Panel even if you've chosen Display As a Menu: Right-click Control Panel; then choose Open. If Control Panel spawns its submenu too quickly for you to right-click, right-click a nearby menu icon (such as My Computer); then, without choosing anything on the right-click menu, point back to Control Panel and right-click it. (This technique works for any Display As a Menu folder.)

- Right-click an individual document to delete it from the My Recent Documents list. The list still will contain 15 items.

- In the classic Start menu, My Recent Documents is named Documents.

Figure 2.20 The Advanced tab (which isn't that advanced) of the Customize Start Menu dialog box affects overall Start-menu behavior, including what you see in the menu's right column, where Windows components are listed.

Figure 2.21 Display As a Menu makes a Start-menu folder expand as a submenu that displays its contents (rather than open as a window).

Table 2.1

Start-Menu Advanced Tab Settings

OPTION/SETTING	DESCRIPTION
Open Submenus When I Pause on Them with My Mouse	Checked: Display a submenu when you point to it. Unchecked: Display a submenu when you click it.
Highlight Newly Installed Programs	Checked: Highlight new programs in orange for a few days. Unchecked: Don't distinguish new programs.
Control Panel, My Computer, My Documents, My Music, My Pictures, Network Connections	Display As a Link: Display a shortcut that opens that folder. Display As a Menu: Open a submenu (**Figure 2.21**). Don't Display This Item: Remove that folder from the Start menu.
Enable Dragging and Dropping	Checked: Lets you drag icons on, off, and within the Start menu and display their shortcut (right-click) menus. Unchecked: Lock Start-menu items in place.
Favorites Menu	Checked: Add a link to your Favorites folder, which contains shortcuts to web pages, documents, and folders that you've bookmarked. Unchecked: Favorites menu doesn't appear.
Help and Support, Run, Search	Checked: Item appears in bottom-right section of Start menu. Unchecked: Item doesn't appear on Start menu. (If you use these commands rarely or invoke them with keystrokes, uncheck them to save menu space.)
My Network Places	Checked: Show a link to shared resources on your network. Unchecked: Show this computer and its peripherals only.
Printers and Faxes	Checked: Add a link to the Printers and Faxes folder. Unchecked: Printers and Faxes appears only in Control Panel.
Scroll Programs	Checked: An overflow of items in the All Programs menu appears as a long one-column list with scroll arrows. Unchecked: An overflow of items appears in a big multicolumn submenu, classic-Windows style.
System Administration Tools	Display on the All Programs Menu: Tools appear in All Programs menu and in Control Panel. Display on the All Programs Menu and the Start Menu: Tools appear in All Programs menu, Start menu, and Control Panel. Don't Display This Item: Tools appear only in Control Panel.
List My Most Recently Opened Documents	Checked: Display shortcuts to your 15 most recently opened documents in the My Recent Documents submenu in the Start menu; reopen any document by clicking its name. Unchecked: Hide list. Click Clear List to empty the list without deleting the documents.

Exploring the Taskbar

The taskbar provides quick access to programs and the status of background processes. It appears by default at the bottom of your screen and is divided into segments with distinct functions (**Figure 2.22**):

Start button. Click this button to open the Start menu.

Quick Launch bar. A customizable toolbar that lets you display the desktop or launch a program with a single click. The taskbar has a few other toolbars that you can show or hide.

Taskbar buttons. Buttons on the taskbar represent all open windows. You can use these buttons to resize, switch among, or close programs.

Notification area (system tray). This area displays the clock and shows the status of programs and activities.

Empty area. The taskbar has its own short-cut menu, which you reach by right-clicking an empty area. If your taskbar is crowded, right-click just to the right of the Start button, where there's always an unoccupied sliver.

✔ Tip

■ Point (without clicking) to any icon on the taskbar to show a helpful tool tip.

Start-menu button   Quick Launch toolbar   Taskbar buttons   Empty area   Notification area (system tray)

Figure 2.22 The parts of the taskbar.

Figure 2.23 Clicking a window's toolbar button brings the window to the top of the pile, if it happens to be hidden by other windows.

Figure 2.24 Among other things, the control menu lets you close a window, sometimes without first restoring it.

■ To press taskbar buttons with the keyboard: Press Ctrl+Esc to open the Start menu; press Esc to close it; then tab to the first taskbar button. Next, use the arrow keys to highlight the desired button; then press the spacebar to activate the window or Shift+F10 to open its control menu.

Managing Windows by Using the Taskbar

The windows of multiple open programs tend to overlap or hide one another, making them hard to tell apart or find. When you launch a program, its button appears on the taskbar; you can use the taskbar to manage open programs and switch among windows easily.

To view several windows at the same time, you can drag and resize them or use taskbar controls to tile them on your desktop. To clear your desktop, you can minimize all windows to taskbar buttons.

To activate a window:

◆ Click the taskbar button representing that window (**Figure 2.23**).

✔ Tips

■ The active window's taskbar button appears pushed in; others appear normal.

■ If a window is active, clicking its taskbar button minimizes (hides) it.

■ An inactive program's taskbar button appears normal (popped out), whether its window is minimized, restored, or maximized.

■ If a program is busy, clicking its taskbar button may not activate the window.

■ Right-click a taskbar button to open the window's control (resizing) menu (**Figure 2.24**).

■ To switch windows without using the taskbar, press Alt+Tab, or see "Switching Programs" in Chapter 6.

■ Some programs—usually, programs that run all the time—have notification-area icons (covered later in this chapter) instead of taskbar buttons.

To minimize all windows:

◆ Right-click an empty area on the taskbar; then choose Show the Desktop.

or

If the Quick Launch toolbar is displayed, click the desktop icon (**Figure 2.25**).

or

Press Windows logo key+D or Windows logo key+M.

To restore minimized windows:

◆ Right-click an empty area on the taskbar; then choose Undo Minimize All.

or

Click the desktop icon on the Quick Launch toolbar.

or

Press Windows logo key+D or Windows logo key+Shift+M.

To arrange windows on your desktop:

1. Minimize the windows that you *don't* want arranged on the desktop.

2. Right-click an empty area on the taskbar; then choose Cascade Windows, Tile Windows Horizontally, or Tile Windows Vertically (**Figure 2.26**).

✔ Tips

■ To reverse this arrangement, right-click an empty area on the taskbar; then choose Undo Cascade or Undo Tile.

■ To display the Quick Launch toolbar, right-click an empty area on the taskbar; then choose Toolbars > Quick Launch.

Figure 2.25 Showing the desktop even minimizes dialog boxes (which don't appear as taskbar buttons).

Figure 2.26 Here, I chose Tile Windows Horizontally. Minimized windows aren't arranged, so your taskbar may have more buttons than are tiled on the desktop.

Figure 2.27 The Taskbar and Start Menu Properties dialog box lets you change the taskbar's appearance and behavior.

Figure 2.28 A group button displays a small arrow and the number of open documents for the program. Click the button to show the document that you want. Button grouping won't work in a taskbar docked to the screen's left or right edge.

Configuring the Taskbar

You can change many aspects of the taskbar. A space-saving feature groups similar windows in one menulike taskbar button rather than crowding the taskbar with one truncated button for each open window.

To configure the taskbar:

1. Right-click an empty area on the taskbar; then choose Properties (**Figure 2.27**).

2. Check Lock the Taskbar to keep the taskbar at its current size and position. Uncheck it if you want to resize or move the taskbar or any of its toolbars.

3. Check Auto-Hide the Taskbar to hide the taskbar when you don't need it.

    The taskbar disappears until you point to the edge of the screen where it's located.

4. Check Keep the Taskbar on Top of Other Windows to prevent other windows—even maximized windows—from covering the taskbar.

5. Check Group Similar Taskbar Buttons to reduce taskbar clutter.

    Windows rearranges taskbar buttons for each program so that all of them are adjacent. If the taskbar becomes so crowded that button text is truncated, buttons for the same program are consolidated into one button displaying the number of program sessions or documents (**Figure 2.28**).

6. Check Show Quick Launch to display the Quick Launch toolbar on the taskbar.

    Quick Launch lets you show the desktop or open a program with a single click. See "Adding Toolbars to the Taskbar" later in this chapter.

7. Click OK (or Apply).

✔ Tips

- To show an auto-hidden taskbar with the keyboard, press Ctrl+Esc or the Windows logo key.

- To lock or unlock the taskbar quickly, right-click an empty area on it; then choose Lock the Taskbar. A check mark will appear. Repeating this process toggles the lock on or off.

- To open taskbar properties via Control Panel, choose Start > Control Panel > Appearance and Themes > Taskbar and Start Menu > Taskbar tab.

- Right-click a group button to manage multiple windows as a group (**Figure 2.29**).

- If the taskbar becomes *too* crowded, Windows hides some taskbar buttons and displays scroll buttons (**Figure 2.30**).

- The taskbar won't group a program's windows into one button if there's enough room for a separate button for each window.

- Tweak UI's Taskbar and Start Menu > Grouping options lets you decide how programs are collapsed into groups. See the "Tweak UI" sidebar in "Using the Start Menu" earlier in this chapter.

Figure 2.29 A group button's shortcut menu lets you arrange all the group's windows, minimize them, or close them (without affecting other windows).

Figure 2.30 These scroll buttons let you access hidden buttons on a jam-packed taskbar.

Taskbar Recommendations

As the uniform command center for all your running programs, the taskbar is one of the most powerful features of Windows and among the ones that you'll use most often. Efficient taskbar settings can make using your computer more pleasant. Here are my recommendations for taskbar Properties settings:

Lock the Taskbar: On.

Auto-Hide the Taskbar: Off, unless you're working with a small screen or want to devote every pixel to a particular window.

Keep the Taskbar on Top of Other Windows: On.

Group Similar Taskbar Buttons: On, unless you work regularly with few open windows.

Show Quick Launch: On.

Figure 2.31 The taskbar widens automatically when you drag it to the left or right edge. Open windows self-adjust to accommodate the taskbar's new location.

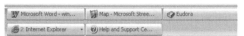

Figure 2.32 Taskbars at the screen's top or bottom resize in button-height increments. Taskbars to the left or right resize without constraints.

To move the taskbar:

1. If the taskbar is locked, unlock it (right-click an empty area on the taskbar; then uncheck Lock the Taskbar).

2. Point to an empty area on the taskbar; then drag to any edge of your screen (**Figure 2.31**).

✔ Tip

- Try docking the taskbar to the screen's left or right edge. It may feel awkward at first, but it reduces the amount of mousing needed for routine tasks.

To resize the taskbar:

1. If the taskbar is locked, unlock it (right-click an empty area on the taskbar; then uncheck Lock the Taskbar).

2. Point to the inside edge of the taskbar (the pointer becomes a double-headed arrow); then drag toward the desktop for a larger taskbar or toward the screen edge for a smaller one (**Figure 2.32**).

✔ Tips

- If you make your taskbar more than one line deep, truncated buttons and tool-bars will expand.

- If you shrink the taskbar until it disappears off an edge, drag the thin blue line at that edge to get it back. If you can't grab the blue line: Press Ctrl+Esc, Esc, Alt+spacebar, and S; press an arrow key repeatedly to resize the taskbar toward the middle of the screen; then press Enter.

CONFIGURING THE TASKBAR

Using the Notification Area

Windows XP changes the name of the *system tray* (or just *tray*) to the *notification area,* which lives at the right end of the taskbar, holding the clock and small icons that monitor activities on your computer or network (**Figure 2.33**).

Windows and other programs use icons here to let you know things—that you've received new email, for example. Some icons flash to get your attention, whereas others appear for the duration of an event (such as printing a document). Hover the pointer over an icon to find out what it represents (**Figure 2.34**).

These icons have no standard controls. Some, you click; others, you double- or right-click; and some ignore clicks.

✔ Tips

- Programs can display what they please in the notification area (and some abuse the privilege). You can dismiss some icons with a right-click, whereas others cling like barnacles. A program's options or preferences (usually found in the Edit or Tools menu) may let you control tray settings.

- If you hide the clock, you have more room for icons.

Figure 2.33 Notification-area icons give the status of background programs, tasks, and services. The number of icons grows as you install more programs.

Figure 2.34 The tool tip for this icon shows internet-connection statistics.

Figure 2.35 The Taskbar tab lets you change the notification area's appearance and behavior.

Figure 2.36 A tall or vertical taskbar displays the day, the date, and more icons.

Figure 2.37 A < button indicates that Windows has hidden some notification-area icons (refer to Figure 2.33). Click the button to expand the notification area and display all icons, as shown here. (Note that the button becomes a >.)

To show or hide the clock:

1. Right-click an empty area on the taskbar or notification area; then choose Properties (**Figure 2.35**).

2. Check Show the Clock to display the time, or uncheck this box to hide it.

3. Click OK (or Apply).

✔ Tips

■ Hover the pointer over the time to display the day and date.

■ A taskbar on the left or right screen edge (or a tall one at the top or bottom) displays the day and date automatically (**Figure 2.36**).

■ Double-click the clock to open the Date and Time Properties dialog box. See "Changing the Date and Time" in Chapter 4.

Windows manages the notification area by watching you work. If you don't use an icon regularly, Windows calls it inactive and hides it, but you can control icon display rather than accept the default behavior (**Figure 2.37**).

USING THE NOTIFICATION AREA

To control icon display in the notification area:

1. Right-click an empty area on the taskbar or notification area; then choose Properties.

2. To show all icons, uncheck Hide Inactive Icons; click OK; then skip the remaining steps.

3. To customize the behavior of icons, click Customize.

   The Name column shows the programs (**Figure 2.38**).

4. In the Behavior column, click each program that you want to customize; then choose Hide When Inactive, Always Hide, or Always Show in the list box.

   or

   Click Restore Defaults to restore the icons' standard behavior.

5. Click OK in each open dialog box.

✔ Tip

- If Hide Inactive Icons is checked, you can customize notifications directly. Right-click an empty area on the notification area; then choose Customize Notifications.

Figure 2.38 You can specify the notification behavior for items displayed currently as well as in the past.

Adding Toolbars to the Taskbar

Specialized toolbars are available on the taskbar (**Figure 2.39**):

Address. A text box that accepts any address on the web, on your network, or on your computer. Enter a web address (URL) to launch or activate Internet Explorer (or your default browser); a program name to launch the program; a document name and path to open the document in its associated program (launching the program if necessary); or a folder name to open a Windows Explorer window.

Desktop. Links to all desktop shortcuts, so that you don't have to minimize all windows to reach them.

Links. Links to Internet Explorer's Favorites folder. You can drag file or web-page shortcuts onto this toolbar or right-click to delete links.

Quick Launch. Provides one-click access—much quicker than the Start menu—to commonly used items. It also lets you minimize all windows to show the desktop.

Quick Launch toolbar   *Address toolbar*   *Desktop toolbar*   *Links toolbar*

Figure 2.39 Toolbars occupy a lot of taskbar space. Click the >> button that appears at the toolbar's right end to display a menu of items or commands that won't fit on the taskbar.

✔ Tips

- By default, only Quick Launch is displayed on the taskbar.

- Address and Links also appear in Windows Explorer and Internet Explorer.

- The Address toolbar auto-completes—that is, proposes matching entries that you've typed before. You can keep typing, or you can use the down-arrow key to select a match and then press Enter. If you type something that Windows doesn't understand, Windows searches and either finds what you want or displays an error message.

- Many tasks in this section require an unlocked taskbar. Right-click an empty area on the taskbar. If Lock the Taskbar is checked, uncheck it.

To show or hide taskbar toolbars:

- ◆ Right-click an empty area on the taskbar; point to Toolbars; then check or uncheck a name in the submenu to toggle that toolbar (**Figure 2.40**).

✔ Tips

- Drag the vertical rib at the toolbar's left end to resize or move the toolbar. A toolbar dragged onto the desktop can float freely or dock against any screen edge.

- To create a custom toolbar, right-click an empty area on the taskbar; choose Toolbars > New Toolbar; specify a folder whose contents you want to make into a toolbar; then click OK. Sadly, this toolbar vanishes when you close it or log off; you repeat the New Toolbar process to get it back.

- To create a custom toolbar quickly, drag a folder to the edge of the desktop and drop it.

Figure 2.40 You can show or hide each toolbar independently of the others.

Figure 2.41 The Open Folder command works with only the Links and Quick Launch toolbars (and with custom toolbars created with Toolbars > New Toolbar).

Figure 2.42 The left button launches Internet Explorer (Chapter 13). The Show Desktop button (center) minimizes all windows to make the desktop visible. The right button launches Windows Media Player (Chapter 10).

To customize a taskbar toolbar:

◆ Right-click an empty area on the toolbar; then choose one of these commands at the top of the shortcut menu (**Figure 2.41**):

View. Shows large (double-size) or small (default) toolbar icons.

Open Folder. Opens the folder that the toolbar represents. Adding, changing, and deleting shortcuts in the folder is easier than manipulating the toolbar's small icons.

Show Text. Displays a text label next to each toolbar icon, which takes a lot of space. This feature is on by default for Links but not for Quick Launch.

Show Title. Shows the toolbar name—generally a waste of space except as an extra empty area for right-clicking or dragging.

Close Toolbar. Closes the toolbar.

✔ Tips

■ Quick Launch begins with three Microsoft-supplied buttons (**Figure 2.42**). You can add buttons for instant access to favorite programs and documents or delete buttons that you don't need.

■ Click Show Desktop a second time to restore all windows to their original positions.

■ You can press Windows logo key+D once to show the desktop and twice to restore windows.

To add a button to Quick Launch:

1. Locate the item (icon) that you want to add, and drag it over the toolbar.

   When the icon hovers over the toolbar, a black I-bar appears where it will land.

2. Drop the icon where you want it (**Figure 2.43**).

✔ Tips

- You can add almost any item to Quick Launch: a program, document, folder, disk, hardware device, Control Panel program, and so on.

- Drag buttons within the toolbar to reorder them.

To delete a button from Quick Launch:

1. Right-click the button; then choose Delete.

2. If a confirmation message box appears, click Yes.

✔ Tips

- Deleting a shortcut doesn't remove the file that it represents.

- You can drag an unwanted button from the toolbar to the Recycle Bin.

- Don't delete the Show Desktop button; it's a command, not a shortcut. If you delete it accidentally, go to `http://support.microsoft.com/?kbid=190355`, "How to Re-Create the Show Desktop Icon on Quick Launch Toolbar."

Figure 2.43 When you drag over the Quick Launch bar, a vertical black line will appear to show where the item will land when it's dropped.

Shortcut to   mortgage.xls
mortgage.xls

Figure 2.44 You can distinguish a shortcut from the file to which it's linked by the small curved arrow.

Managing Shortcuts

I've covered creating, editing, and deleting shortcuts in the Start menu and Quick Launch toolbar. Shortcuts also can appear on the desktop and in folders. A shortcut can link to a program, document, folder, disk, printer or other device, web address (URL), or system folder (such as My Computer). When you double-click a shortcut, its linked file opens. You can create and modify a shortcut to any item and store it anywhere; it's a tiny file.

Windows offers two types of shortcut files: *Windows* shortcuts (.lnk files) and *internet* shortcuts (.url files). A shortcut shares the icon of the original but adds a small boxed arrow in one corner (**Figure 2.44**).

✔ Tips

- You can make several shortcuts to the same object and store them in different places.

- You can make shortcuts to network-accessible items, not just local items.

- Don't confuse a shortcut *icon,* which is a placeholder for an object, with a shortcut (right-click) *menu* or a *keyboard* shortcut, which is a command keystroke.

- Tweak UI's Explorer > Shortcut > Shortcut Overlay option lets you remove the little arrow from shortcut icons. Uncheck the Explorer > Prefix "Shortcut to" on New Shortcuts option to remove the *Shortcut to* text from new shortcuts. See the "Tweak UI" sidebar in "Using the Start Menu" earlier in this chapter.

To create a shortcut:

1. Locate the item (icon) that you want to create a shortcut to.

2. Right-drag the icon to a destination (typically, the desktop or a folder); then choose Create Shortcut(s) Here from the shortcut menu.

   or

   Right-click the icon; then choose Send To > Desktop (Create Shortcut) (**Figure 2.45**).

   or

   Right-click the icon; then choose Create Shortcut.

   This method creates a shortcut in the same location as the original. You can move the shortcut anywhere.

   or

   Alt+drag the icon to a destination.

   or

   Ctrl+Shift+drag the icon to a destination.

Figure 2.45 The shortcut menu lets you create a desktop shortcut quickly.

✔ Tips

■ If you want to create a shortcut to a program (.exe file), look for programs supplied with Windows—such as Notepad—in the \Windows or \Windows\System32 folder. (The Windows folder is named WINNT on some systems.) For other programs, look in a folder nested in \Program Files.

■ If you create a shortcut to a shortcut, the new shortcut points to the original target.

Figure 2.46 You can bring back the system-folder desktop shortcuts that Microsoft removed.

Figure 2.47 Getting rid of *Shortcut to* usually is the first objective in renaming.

To display system-folder shortcuts on the desktop:

1. Right-click an empty area on the desktop; then choose Properties.

2. Choose Desktop tab > Customize Desktop.

3. In the Desktop Icons section, check the boxes for the shortcuts that you want on the desktop (**Figure 2.46**); then click OK in each open dialog box.

✔ Tip

■ The Desktop Icons dialog box lets you change system icons. Select the icon; then click Change Icon to choose a new icon. (To restore the original icon, select the icon; then click Restore Default.)

To rename a shortcut:

1. Right-click the shortcut; then choose Rename.

   or

   Select (highlight) the shortcut; then press F2.

   or

   Click the shortcut's title (not its icon) twice slowly; don't double-click.

2. Retype or edit the name; then press Enter (**Figure 2.47**).

   You can use the Cut, Copy, and Paste keyboard shortcuts (Ctrl+X, Ctrl+C, and Ctrl+V) while editing.

✔ Tips

■ Shortcut names can include letters, numbers, spaces, and some punctuation marks but not these characters: \ : / * ? " > < |.

■ You can rename a shortcut in the General tab of the shortcut's Properties dialog box.

MANAGING SHORTCUTS

To delete a shortcut:

◆ Right-click the shortcut; then choose Delete.

or

Select (highlight) a shortcut or multiple shortcuts; then press Delete.

✔ Tip

■ To recover (undelete) a shortcut from the Recycle Bin, see "Deleting Files and Folders" in Chapter 5.

To view or change a shortcut's properties:

◆ Right-click the shortcut; then choose Properties.

or

Select (highlight) the shortcut; then press Alt+Enter (**Figures 2.48** and **2.49**).

✔ Tips

■ Privacy tip: An internet shortcut's Web Document tab (refer to Figure 2.49) shows the number of times that you've visited the page.

■ Some targets—printers and My Computer, for example—can't be modified.

■ Shortcut keys work only for desktop and Start-menu shortcuts, and they won't work at all if they conflict with program-defined or other shortcut keys.

■ Run Maximized is useful for programs that "forget" to run in full-screen mode when you start them from the shortcut.

■ If you use Run Minimized for Startup-folder icons, programs will start automatically as taskbar buttons, and your logon desktop won't be cluttered with windows.

■ You can update the target (path) of the object that a shortcut points to, but usually it's easier to create a new shortcut.

Figure 2.48 The Properties dialog box of Windows shortcuts (to documents and programs) has a Shortcut tab, whereas...

Figure 2.49 ...internet shortcuts (URLs) have a Web Document tab. For details, see the "Shortcut Properties" sidebar.

MANAGING SHORTCUTS

Shortcut Properties

Information in a shortcut's Properties dialog box depends on what the shortcut represents. Here are some common properties.

Target is the name of the item that the shortcut points to. A shortcut to a file needs the full path to its location (unless the file is in a Windows system folder).

Start In is the folder in which the program looks for files to open or save, by default.

Shortcut Key specifies the keyboard shortcut with which to open (or switch to) the program. Press any key to make Ctrl+Alt+key appear here. You can assign Ctrl+Alt+E to Windows Explorer, for example, to open it without hunting for its shortcut. A shortcut key requires at least two of Ctrl, Shift, and Alt but can't use Esc, Enter, Tab, spacebar, Delete, Backspace, or Print Screen.

Run tells the program to open in a normal (restored), minimized, or maximized window.

Comment provides the descriptive text (tool tip) that appears when your pointer hovers over the shortcut.

Find Target opens the folder containing the file that the shortcut points to. The file will be selected in the folder window that appears.

Change Icon allows you to change the default icon of a shortcut, which is the same as that of the target. Changing this icon doesn't change the target's icon.

URL displays the address (URL) of a web page in an internet shortcut as though it were the target of a Windows shortcut.

Make This Page Available Offline for Internet Shortcuts allows you to download the web page for offline viewing. See "Browsing Tips" in Chapter 13.

Tidying Your Desktop

Over time, shortcuts tend to accumulate on your desktop. Microsoft's productivity elves have provided cleanup tools.

To arrange desktop shortcuts:

◆ Right-click an empty area on the desktop; point to Arrange Icons By; then choose a command from the submenu (**Figure 2.50**):

Name. Sorts alphabetically by name.

Size. Sorts by file size, with the smallest first. If the shortcut points to a program, the size refers to the size of the shortcut file.

Type. Sorts by file type, which keeps files with the same file extension together (.doc for Word files or .exe for programs, for example).

Modified. Sorts by the date when the shortcut (not the original) was last modified, with the most recent first.

Show in Groups. See "Grouping Icons" in Chapter 5.

Auto Arrange. Places icons in neat columns, starting on the screen's left side. Uncheck this option to drag icons anywhere on your desktop. This option won't work if your desktop is full.

Align to Grid. Turns on an invisible grid that makes icons snap into equally spaced alignment when you move them. Uncheck this option to turn off the grid (useful only if Auto Arrange is turned off).

Show Desktop Icons. Uncheck this option to hide all desktop icons; check it to show them.

Run Desktop Cleanup Wizard. Removes unused desktop shortcuts, described next.

✔ Tip

■ If your icons look grainy or badly drawn, right-click an empty area on the desktop; then choose Refresh to redisplay icons.

Figure 2.50 This submenu lets you sort your desktop shortcuts, align them, or hide them temporarily.

Virtual Desktop Manager

If you work with a crowded desktop, try organizing it with Virtual Desktop Manager. It lets you manage up to four desktops from the taskbar (a bit like having four monitors on the cheap). VDM is one of the PowerToys described in "Using the Free Utility Programs" in Chapter 6.

After installing VDM, right-click an empty area on the taskbar; then choose Toolbars > Desktop Manager. A toolbar labeled MSVDM appears on your taskbar. Use a custom keyboard shortcut or click one of the blue 1, 2, 3, or 4 buttons to switch among four virtual desktops, each having its own background and set of open programs and windows. Or click the green button to preview all four desktops. Right-click the MSVDM toolbar, and you'll see a few new VDM-specific commands atop the shortcut menu. Choose MSVDM Help for a brief tutorial.

TIDYING YOUR DESKTOP

Figure 2.51 You can run the desktop cleanup program whenever you want or automatically, in two-month intervals.

Figure 2.52 The wizard lists each desktop shortcut, along with the last time you used it.

To remove unused shortcuts:

1. Right-click an empty area on the desktop; then choose Arrange Icons By > Run Desktop Cleanup Wizard.

   or

   Right-click an empty area on the desktop; then choose Properties > Desktop tab > Customize Desktop > Clean Desktop Now (**Figure 2.51**).

2. Click Next to skip the Welcome page.

3. On the Shortcuts page, check the boxes of the shortcuts to remove from your desktop; then click Next (**Figure 2.52**).

4. Click Finish to confirm your choices.

   The wizard doesn't actually delete the shortcuts but stores them in a folder named Unused Desktop Shortcuts on your desktop, where you can retrieve them if you need them or delete them for real.

✔ Tips

- The Desktop Cleanup Wizard removes not only your personal shortcuts, but also shortcuts that appear on all users' desktops. To check whether a shortcut is shared, right-click the icon; choose Properties; then check the Location property in the General tab. If the path contains *All Users* (rather than your user name), it's a shared shortcut.

- The Desktop Cleanup Wizard appears automatically every 60 days, with a list of shortcuts that you haven't used for the past two months. Uncheck Run Desktop Cleanup Wizard Every 60 Days (refer to Figure 2.51) if you don't want the wizard to run automatically.

TIDYING YOUR DESKTOP

GETTING HELP

If you're already a Windows user, don't yield to the temptation to skip this chapter because you've given up on Microsoft's anemic help system. A change of heart—driven by what Microsoft spends on telephone support—has spawned XP's Help and Support Center, a hybrid web portal and on-disk help system. With it you use web-style links and searches to access:

◆ Standard documentation

◆ Animated tutorials

◆ Troubleshooting wizards

◆ Diagnostic and repair utilities

◆ Up-to-date configuration information about your system's hardware, software, and services

◆ Knowledge Base articles at Microsoft's support site and Windows newsgroups (if you're connected to the internet)

Also, XP's new Remote Assistance program lets a remote user view your screen—or even control your PC—to help you solve problems.

Starting Help and Support Center

The first stop in Help and Support Center (Help Center for short) is the home page (**Figure 3.1**), which includes links to basic information, external help resources, and common system tasks. Your home page may differ slightly from the one pictured because this help system isn't a static collection of pages; Microsoft and third parties like PC manufacturers are free to modify it. The "Did you know?" section in the bottom-right corner is the usual target for such changes.

To start Help and Support Center:

◆ Choose Start > Help and Support.

or

Press Windows logo key+F1.

✔ Tips

■ If your desktop is active, press F1 to start Help Center.

■ You can have multiple Help Center windows open at the same time.

■ To get help for a specific Windows component, such as Internet Explorer or Solitaire, use that program's Help menu rather than Help Center.

■ Unlike earlier Windows versions, XP's Help Center font size is independent of Internet Explorer's font size. To change font size in Help Center, choose Options (on the toolbar) > Change Help and Support Center Options (on the left panel) > Font Size Used for Help Content (see Figure 3.3 later in this chapter).

■ The home page's left column replaces the Help Contents page of earlier Windows help systems.

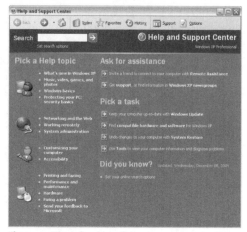

Figure 3.1 The left column lists common help topics. The green arrows in the right column mark links to support resources and system tools.

Figure 3.2 To get here from the home page, I clicked Windows Basics > Core Windows Tasks > Customizing Your Desktop. The hierarchy of choices lets me drill down into the help system until I find the relevant help page.

Help and Support Center options

Select from the options below to customize your Help and Support Center experience.

☑ Show Favorites on the navigation bar
☑ Show History on the navigation bar

Font size used for Help content:

○ Small
◉ Medium
○ Large

Options for icons in the navigation bar:

○ Show all text labels
◉ Show only default text labels
○ Do not show text labels

Figure 3.3 You can change the appearance of the navigation bar.

Navigating in Help Center

Find your way around Help Center by using web-like navigation. Help Center's toolbar, or *navigation bar*, looks and works like Internet Explorer's standard toolbar.

To navigate by clicking links:

1. On the Help Center home page, click a link below Pick a Help Topic.

   Help Center displays a subtopic list.

2. Keep clicking links to burrow to the topic you're looking for (**Figure 3.2**).

To navigate by using the navigation bar:

◆ On the navigation bar click the following buttons:

Back (or press Alt+left arrow) or **Forward** (Alt+right arrow) to move through recently viewed topics.

Home (Alt+H) to return to Help Center's home page.

Index (Alt+N) to search by keyword.

Favorites (Alt+A) to view help pages that you've saved. To save a help page, click Add to Favorites (just above the topic panel). These Favorites aren't the same ones as in Internet Explorer.

History (Alt+Y) to view pages that you've read during this help session.

Support (Alt+U) to launch Remote Assistance, contact a Microsoft support person, or visit Windows newsgroups.

Options (Alt+O) to set your own preferences for the help system (**Figure 3.3**).

Searching for Help Topics

When you tire of clicking and skimming Help Center's 10,000 pages, you can use the search function. It's fast, easy, and usually finds a wide range of related topics, which can acquaint you with features that you were unaware of.

To search for help topics:

1. In Help Center, type or paste a search phrase in the Search text box; then press Enter or click the green arrow (**Figure 3.4**). Help Center conducts the search and divides the results into three categories.

2. Click one of the categories listed in the Search Results panel (**Figure 3.5**):

   Suggested Topics lists pages with *keyword* matches. Microsoft assigns invisible keyword tags to help topics.

   Full-Text Search Matches lists pages that contain the literal phrase you entered.

   Microsoft Knowledge Base (on the internet) lists relevant articles that appear on Microsoft's massive support web site.

✔ Tips

- If your search phrase contains multiple words, Help Center searches for pages that contain all the words. A search for *keyboard shortcuts,* for example, yields pages that contain *keyboard* and *shortcuts,* though not necessarily adjacent in the text. To find an exact phrase, enclose it in quotes (*"keyboard shortcuts"*).

- The toolbar just above the topic panel lets you add the page to your help Favorites; shrink the Help Center window; print the topic; or locate the topic in the Help Center table of contents.

- Search terms aren't case-sensitive.

- Help Center ignores a long list of articles, prepositions, and other noise words: *a, the, of, like, from,* and so on.

Figure 3.4 If you choose a category in Pick a Help Topic on the home page before starting your search, Help Center displays a Search Only check box below the Search text box. Check this box to narrow your search; uncheck it to search the entire help system.

Figure 3.5 In a full-text search, the highlighted text shows matches for your search phrase.

Set search options

Find help and information from different sources. To change the scope of your search, select one or more providers from the following list.

Return up to 15 results per provider.

☑ Turn on search highlight.

☑ **Suggested Topics**
Displays results of the highest possible relevance. Search matches the terms you typed against terms that the author of a document defines as keywords for that document. Selecting this option makes it possible for you to limit your search to the specific Help category of the current topic.

☑ **Full-text Search Matches**
Displays documents whose text contains the term(s) you typed.
☐ Search in title only
☐ Match similar words

☑ **Microsoft Knowledge Base**
Displays relevant topics or articles from the Microsoft Knowledge Base Web site. The Knowledge Base is a source of technical support information and self-help tools for Microsoft products.
- All Microsoft Products - ▼

Search for:
All of the words ▼

☐ Search in Title only

Figure 3.6 Help Center shows up to 15 results per category by default. You may want to increase this limit and accept longer internet searches.

Customizing Help Center

Help Center's settings page lets you specify how to search and how to display results.

To set search options:

1. Click Options > Set Search Options (in the left panel) (**Figure 3.6**).

2. Set your choices in Set Search Options, working from **Table 3.1**.

✔ Tip

■ In Boolean searches, AND shows pages that contain both specified words; OR shows pages that contain either specified word; and AND NOT shows pages that don't contain the specified word. If you omit a Boolean operator, pages matching all specified words in any order are shown (same as AND).

Table 3.1

Help Center Search Options	
SET SEARCH OPTIONS	**SEARCH OPTION BEHAVIOR**
Return up to __ Results Per Provider	Type the number of results per category to show. The default is 15.
Turn on Search Highlight	Checked: Highlight search phrases in result pages (refer to Figure 3.5). Unchecked: Show results without highlighting.
Suggested Topics	Checked: Sort results by relevance by comparing your search phrase with a database of keywords. Unchecked: Sort results alphabetically.
Full-Text Search Matches	Checked: Show any document containing your search phrase. Unchecked: Searches are confined by other criteria (such as Suggested Topics).
Search in Title Only	Checked: Limit searches to topic titles and ignore body text. Unchecked: Search entire documents.
Match Similar Words	Checked: Search for alternative and approximate forms of words (network and networking). Unchecked: Searches for only the exact terms entered (not case-sensitive).
Microsoft Knowledge Base	Checked: Include a search of Microsoft's vast keyword-oriented database of technical articles. Unchecked: Don't search the Knowledge Base. Uncheck if you're not connected to the internet.
–All Microsoft Products–	Select a single Microsoft product to search on from a giant drop-down list or search on all Microsoft products (default).
Search for:	All of the Words: Show only documents that contain all your search terms. Any of the Words: Display all documents that contain any of your search terms. The Exact Phrase: Show all documents that contain your search terms in the order in which you give them (same as enclosing the phrase in quotes). The Boolean Phrase: Use the AND, OR, NOT, and NEAR operators in search phrases. (*internet NOT explorer* finds topics related to the internet but not to Microsoft's browser, for example.)
Search in Title Only	Checked: Ignore body text (within the Knowledge Base). Unchecked: Search body text (within the Knowledge Base).

CUSTOMIZING HELP CENTER

Using the Help Index

To search for help successfully you must speak Microsoft's dialect of English. If you want to snuff a file on your hard drive, do you search for *erase? delete? remove?* The official term is *delete*, but any of these will work thanks to Help Center's keyword searches, which include common synonyms. In other searches you may not be so lucky. The best way to learn the Windows vocabulary is to browse the Help Center index.

To use the Help index:

1. On the navigation bar, click Index (or press Alt+N).

   Help Center displays a list of keywords, sorted alphabetically (**Figure 3.7**).

2. In the keyword text box, type a word.

   As you type, the highlighted selection jumps to the keyword that's the closest match.

3. Double-click a list entry to see its matching help page in the right panel.

   If an entry has subentries, double-click an indented subentry rather than the top-level entry.

✔ Tip

- Type *troubleshooting* to see a list of Windows' Troubleshooters. Use these wizardlike tools to identify and resolve hardware, software, and networking problems (**Figure 3.8**).

Figure 3.7 You can scroll through the massive index to see help topics.

Figure 3.8 This troubleshooter steps you through help screens designed to help you fix network problems.

USING THE HELP INDEX

Figure 3.9 Here, I right-clicked the Screen Resolution slider for "What's This?" help. To dismiss the pop-up box, click it.

Getting Help in Dialog Boxes

Windows' designers describe the function of check boxes, options buttons, lists, and other dialog-box controls in a few words. This concision yields some obscurely worded labels in crowded dialog boxes. Fortunately, there's "What's This?" help for pop-up tips on individual controls.

To get pop-up help for a dialog-box element:

◆ Right-click an element; then click "What's This?" (**Figure 3.9**).

or

Click the question mark in the top-right corner of the dialog box; then click an element.

✔ Tip

■ Right-click inside the pop-up box to print it or copy its contents to the clipboard.

Allowing Others to Connect to Your Computer Remotely

You'll appreciate XP's Remote Assistance function if you've ever endured the friendship-dissolving stress of giving or receiving tech support over the phone. *Remote Assistance* lets you invite a friend or technical expert—anyone you trust who's running Windows XP—to help you by connecting to your PC over the internet or a network. That person can swap messages with you, view your screen, or (with your permission) use his mouse and keyboard to control your computer.

Remote Assistance relieves novices of having to explain problems in jargon they haven't learned and lets experts cut the chatter and work on the novice's machine directly. Experts can even install software, update hardware drivers, and edit the registry.

✔ Tip

- **PRO** Remote Assistance isn't the same as XP Pro's Remote Desktop (see Chapter 18). Among other differences, in Remote Assistance, both parties must be present at their PCs and agree to the connection.

Security Concerns

Like all remote-control technologies, Remote Assistance has security implications beyond the ordinary issues of strong passwords and firewalls. When you invite someone to take control of your PC you must balance your trust with others' inclinations toward malice. That person is free not only to fix your problem but also to, say, erase your hard drive or steal your files. You can view everything he's doing onscreen, and if you don't like what you see, press Esc to break the connection immediately. Still, damage done in a moment can take ages to undo. Even if that person can't control your PC, you could follow his bad advice and delete critical files or turn off security features yourself. Furthermore, you may not be able to confirm the identity of the other person.

Figure 3.10 If you're paranoid, uncheck this box to turn off Remote Assistance.

Figure 3.11 If you're concerned about security, you can shorten the maximum expiration period to a few minutes or hours. This setting affects the invitation-expiry choice in Figure 3.23.

Capturing Screen Shots

If you want to skip Remote Assistance, your expert may be able to solve your problem if you send him a screen shot via email. Press the Print Screen (PrntScrn) key to capture the entire screen or Alt+Print Screen to grab only the active window. The screen image is now stored on the invisible clipboard, ready for pasting into an email message (or a graphics program, if you want to edit, save, or print it). Serious screen-shooters use SnagIt ($40 U.S.; www.snagit.com), which captured all the shots in this book. Or try PrintScreen (free; www.gadwin.com).

Before starting a Remote Assistance session, set invitation and time limits.

To configure Remote Assistance:

1. Choose Start > Control Panel > Performance and Maintenance > System > Remote tab.

   or

   Press Windows logo key+Break; then click the Remote tab.

2. If it's unchecked, check Allow Remote Assistance Invitations to Be Sent from This Computer (**Figure 3.10**).

3. Click Advanced to open Remote Assistance Settings (**Figure 3.11**).

4. If you're the novice, and you don't want the expert to control your computer, uncheck Allow This Computer to Be Controlled Remotely.

   Even with this box checked, you must approve each request for control of your computer explicitly.

5. Use the two Invitations drop-down lists to specify the maximum duration of Remote Assistance invitations.

   The default setting is 30 days.

6. Click OK in each open dialog box.

In a Remote Assistance session the two connected parties—the *novice* and the *expert*—must:

◆ Be using Windows XP (either Home or Pro edition)

◆ Be on the same local area network (LAN) or have active internet connections

◆ Not be blocked by a firewall (see "Securing Your Computer" in Chapter 12)

The order of events in a Remote Assistance session is:

1. The novice sends the expert an invitation via email or Windows Messenger.

2. The expert accepts the invitation.

3. Remote Assistance opens a window that shows the novice's desktop to the expert.

4. The expert views the novice's desktop and exchanges messages with the novice or, with permission, takes control of the novice's computer.

5. Either party disconnects to end the session.

It's faster and easier to send an invitation via Windows Messenger, but you can use email instead. I'll describe both methods separately. Each step is marked by *Novice* or *Expert* to indicate who does what.

To get Remote Assistance by using Windows Messenger:

1. (**Novice**) Sign in to Messenger (choose Start > All Programs > Windows Messenger, or see Chapter 15).

2. (**Novice**) In Messenger, choose Actions > Ask for Remote Assistance (**Figure 3.12**).

3. (**Novice**) Specify the expert to invite; then click OK (**Figure 3.13**).

   Messenger invites the expert and opens a Conversation window (**Figure 3.14**).

Figure 3.12 Windows Messenger makes it easy to extend a Remote Assistance invitation.

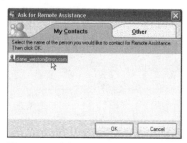

Figure 3.13 If the expert's email address isn't listed on the My Contacts tab, click the Other tab to enter it.

Figure 3.14 Wait for a response. If you change your mind or fix your problem while you're waiting, click Cancel (or press Alt+Q) to revoke the invitation.

Figure 3.15 When the expert receives an invitation, his Messenger taskbar button flashes and this invitation pops up on his screen.

Figure 3.16 To accept the invitation, the expert clicks Accept (or presses Alt+T) in Messenger.

Figure 3.17 Just to be sure, Remote Assistance makes you confirm the connection one last time.

4. (**Expert**) When an invitation pops up in your notification area (**Figure 3.15**), open Messenger and accept the invitation (**Figure 3.16**).

5. (**Novice**) Windows displays a message box when the expert accepts your invitation; click Yes (**Figure 3.17**).

6. (**Expert**) The novice's desktop appears in a Remote Assistance window (**Figure 3.18**).

continues on next page

Figure 3.18 To compensate for screen-size and resolution differences, the expert can click Actual Size or Scale to Window. Actual Size requires scrolling but usually displays a better image than Scale to Window, which distorts the novice's screen proportions to fit in the expert's Remote Assistance pane.

ALLOWING OTHERS TO CONNECT REMOTELY

7. (**Novice/Expert**) Both of you can communicate via Messenger (**Figure 3.19**).

8. (**Expert**) To ask permission to take control of the novice's computer (rather than just view the novice's desktop), click Take Control on the toolbar.

9. (**Novice**) To relinquish control of your PC to the expert, click Yes in the message box that appears (**Figure 3.20**).

10. (**Novice/Expert**) To cancel control, either of you can press Esc or click Stop Control.

Canceling control still lets the expert view the novice's desktop. To sever the connection (so that the expert can't see the novice's desktop), click Disconnect.

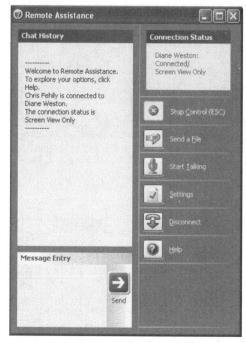

Figure 3.19 Novice and expert can use Messenger to communicate via instant messages, voice, files, or any of the methods described in Chapter 15. You also can bypass Messenger and just pick up the phone.

Figure 3.20 Click Yes to let the expert use *his* mouse and keyboard to control *your* computer. You'll see ghostly pointer movements, self-typing text, and self-opening windows as the expert fixes your problem.

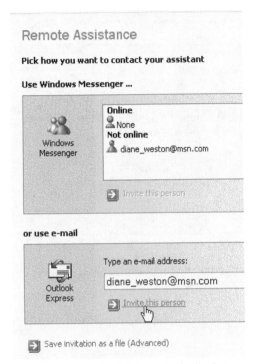

Figure 3.21 If you instead click Save Invitation As a File (Advanced), Windows saves the invitation as a .MsRcIncident file on your hard drive. You can transfer this invitation file over a network or via floppy disk or USB flash drive instead of emailing it.

To get Remote Assistance by using email:

1. (**Novice**) Choose Start > Help and Support.

2. (**Novice**) Click Invite a Friend to Connect to Your Computer with Remote Assistance. The Remote Assistance Wizard steps you through the process of inviting an expert via email.

3. (**Novice**) Click Invite Someone to Help You.

4. (**Novice**) Type the expert's email address in the Type an E-Mail Address box; then click Invite This Person (**Figure 3.21**).

5. (**Novice**) Type your name and a description of the problem; then click Continue (**Figure 3.22**).

6. (**Novice**) Set up your security options and make sure that you're online; then click Send Invitation (**Figure 3.23**).

continues on next page

Remote Assistance - E-mail an Invitation

Provide contact information

Instructions on how to use Remote Assistance are automatically attac the best way to contact you while the invitation is open, and a brief d

From (the name you would like to appear on the invitation):

Chris Fehily

Message:

How do I change my screen resolution?

Figure 3.22 Remote Assistance adds your message to the boilerplate text that it generates in the email invitation to be sent to the expert. Your name appears in the Subject line.

Remote Assistance - E-mail an Invitation

Set the invitation to expire

To lessen the chance that someone fraudulently gains access to your computer you can limit the time in which a recipient can accept a Remote Assistance invitation. Specify the duration that this invitation will remain open.

01 ▾ Hours ▾

☑ **Require the recipient to use a password**

For security reasons, it is strongly recommended that you set a password that the recipient must use to connect to your computer. Do not use your network or Windows logon password.

Type password: Confirm password:

●●●●●●●●   ●●●●●●●●

Important You must communicate the password to the recipient.

[Send Invitation]

Figure 3.23 If the expert doesn't respond to your invitation within the specified time period, the invitation expires. If you're unconcerned about security, you can specify a longer time limit. To set the maximum expiration period, see Figure 3.11.

7. (**Novice**) If a warning message appears, click Send.

   Remote Assistance tells you if your invitation was sent successfully.

8. (**Expert**) When the invitation arrives from the novice, open the attachment to accept the invitation (**Figure 3.24**).

9. (**Novice**) When the expert accepts the invitation, a message box like Figure 3.17 appears; click Yes to start a Remote Assistance session.

✔ Tips

- The expert can use (and reuse) an invitation until it expires (refer to Figure 3.23).

- The warning in step 7 protects you from worms—nasty programs that transmit copies of themselves secretly via email.

- If you, the expert, want the Remote Assistance window out of your way briefly while you're helping the novice, don't *close* it; you'll break the connection. *Minimize* it instead.

- When you invite an expert via email you're actually transmitting your IP address, which identifies you uniquely on the internet. If you have a *dynamic* (rather than *static*) IP address, which changes every time you connect to the internet, the expert won't be able to connect to your PC if you've broken your connection since sending the invitation or if you share an internet connection through a router (see Chapter 17). These issues don't arise for Messenger connections.

Figure 3.24 The file rcBuddy.MsRcIncident is attached to the email invitation. The expert opens (double-clicks) this file to accept the invitation, sending a message back to the novice.

Figure 3.25 Start on this page and follow this trail of clicks to get help from Microsoft: Support Services > Personal Support > More - Windows... > Microsoft Windows XP Home [or Professional] Edition. The page that you land on also has a Post Support Questions newsgroup link. Try posting a technical question and check back later to see if anyone answered.

Getting Help from Microsoft

When all else fails you can get help— free or paid—from Microsoft directly:

Microsoft Help and Support web site. Microsoft's online support pages at `http://support.microsoft.com` (**Figure 3.25**) let you:

◆ Get answers to frequently asked questions (FAQs)

◆ Download software updates, Service Packs, patches, and device drivers

◆ Ask nontechnical questions about pricing, training, and other Microsoft products

◆ Search the Microsoft Knowledge Base of more than 250,000 support articles, if you don't want to reach it through Help Center

Free telephone support. If you purchased your copy of Windows XP separately—that is, it didn't come on your computer—you can call Microsoft for unlimited help with installation. After XP is up and running, you can email or call for free (but not toll-free) help with two more problems. In the United States, the number is (425) 635-3311 (Redmond, Washington).

Paid telephone support. The meter starts running after you use up your free requests. Microsoft charges you $35 (U.S.) per request. (A single incident can span several phone calls.) The toll-free number is (800) 936-5700 (**Figure 3.26**).

✔ Tips

■ When you call, Microsoft will want your 20-digit product ID number. To look it up, choose Start > Control Panel > Performance and Maintenance > System > General tab. The ID number is in the Registered To section.

■ If you're outside the United States, click the International Support link in Figure 3.25.

■ If you refer to a particular Knowledge Base article frequently, you can create a Favorite or shortcut to the URL http://support.microsoft.com/?kbid=*article_id*, where *article_id* is the article's six-digit ID number (given in the article).

Phone Support
Wait Time: Will vary
Hours of Operation

2 support request(s)   (425) 635-3311
using e-mail or phone
(or chat if available)
are included at **no**
charge. Unlimited
installation support is
available by phone at
no charge.
Long Distance charges
may apply.

All additional support   (800) 936-5700
requests are $35.00 US
per request or use an
existing contract
Advanced Issues
$245.00 US

TTY/TDD help requests (800) 892-5234
- cost will vary

Figure 3.26 Here are the U.S. phone numbers for no-charge and paid Windows phone support.

PERSONALIZING YOUR WORK ENVIRONMENT

Each new version of Windows makes its designers assume more about the preferences and abilities of the "average" user. Because this user doesn't exist, Microsoft lets you change Windows XP's factory settings.

You can configure Windows in hundreds of ways ranging from superficial to meaningful. Changes to graphics, colors, and animation usually are cosmetic, whereas some other settings—the language used or adaptations for disabled users—change the way you work with Windows.

Using Control Panel

Control Panel is a central container of tools for changing preferences, configurations, and settings. These miniature programs commonly are called *applets* or *extensions*. Experienced Windows users are familiar with the interface in **Figure 4.1**, now called *classic view*. Windows XP's Control Panel defaults to a novice-friendly interface called *category view* (**Figures 4.2** and **4.3**).

To open Control Panel:

◆ Choose Start > Control Panel.

✔ Tips

■ To start Control Panel with a Start > Run command, type control and then press Enter.

■ To start Control Panel in the classic (one-column) Start menu, choose Start > Settings > Control Panel.

■ To show Control Panel in the My Computer folder, choose Start > Control Panel > Appearances and Themes > Folder Options > View tab > check Show Control Panel in My Computer (near the bottom).

To open an item in category view:

◆ Click its icon or category name.

In some cases, such as Add or Remove Programs, the item opens in its own window. In others, such as Appearance and Themes, the category opens to a list of tasks and icons that you can click.

Figure 4.1 Classic view consolidates all Control Panel tools in one window.

Figure 4.2 Category view groups Control Panel tools into functional categories. Click a category to...

Figure 4.3 ...open an item or (as here) display a list of related tasks and Control Panel tools.

Figure 4.4 Select this option to make the task pane appear on the left side of the Control Panel window (as in Figures 4.1 and 4.2).

Figure 4.5 The Switch View option toggles according to the current view. Windows veterans prefer classic view.

To open an item in classic view:

◆ Double-click the item.

or

Use the arrow keys to navigate to the desired item; then press Enter.

or

Press the key of the item's first letter; then press Enter.

If multiple items have the same first letter, press that letter repeatedly until the desired item is highlighted; then press Enter.

To switch Control Panel views:

1. If the Control Panel task pane isn't displayed, choose Tools > Folder Options > General tab > Show Common Tasks in Folders (**Figure 4.4**).

2. In the task pane, click Switch to Category View or Switch to Classic View (**Figure 4.5**).

✔ Tips

■ If you can't find the item you want in category view, click Other Control Panel Options in the task pane (or switch to classic view).

■ In either view, hold your pointer over a category or icon to see a pop-up description of it.

■ Working from Control Panel, you can create desktop shortcuts to its programs, which are handy if (for example) you're setting up a network or a printer and need to launch one program repeatedly. To create a shortcut, see "Managing Shortcuts" in Chapter 2.

■ Tweak UI's Control Panel options let you hide the Control Panel extensions of your choice. See the "Tweak UI" sidebar in "Using the Start Menu" in Chapter 2.

USING CONTROL PANEL

Changing Your Desktop Background

You can change the image, or *wallpaper*, that appears under the icons on your desktop. If you don't like the desktop backgrounds that Windows or your PC manufacturer provide, you can use a file of your own.

To change the desktop background:

1. Choose Start > Control Panel > Appearance and Themes > Display Properties > Desktop tab (**Figure 4.6**).

    or

    Right-click an empty area on the desktop; then choose Properties > Desktop tab.

2. Select an image from the Background list or click Browse to hunt for an image file on your computer or the network.

    Windows looks for Background files in the My Pictures, \Windows, and \Windows\Web\Wallpaper folders. (\Windows is named \WINNT on some systems.)

3. Select the file's icon in Windows Explorer; then click Set As Desktop Background in the Picture Tasks section of the task pane (**Figure 4.7**).

4. From the Position drop-down list, choose one of these options:

    Center to center the image on the desktop background.

    Tile to repeat the image over the entire screen. This option works best with small images.

    Stretch to resize the image to fit your screen (with some distortion). This option works best with large images and photos.

Figure 4.6 Use the Desktop tab to select an image or browse for an HTML page as your desktop background.

Figure 4.7 A picture folder is one for which the Pictures or Photo Album folder-type template has been applied on the Customize tab of the folder's Properties dialog box.

Resizing Desktop Images

The Stretch function of Display Properties is handy, although the results sometimes are amusing. But digital-camera photos can be larger than your screen—demonstrating the lack of a matching Squish function. Here's how to detect and deal with the problem:

1. Right-click an empty area of your desktop; then choose Properties > Settings tab.

2. In the Screen Resolution box (bottom left), note the number of pixels (for example, 1024 × 768).

3. Find the icon or thumbnail of the image that you want to use for wallpaper, and hover the pointer over it until its file-information tool tip appears. (Alternatively, right-click the icon and choose Properties > Summary tab > Advanced button.)

   Dimensions gives the image's width and height size in pixels (for example, 1600 × 1200).

If the image's dimensions exceed your computer's screen resolution, Windows fills your screen with the center portion of the image, and the edges go wherever leftover pixels go. This result will be fine with you if the image edges are uninteresting. But if you want the uncropped image to be your wallpaper, make a copy and use the Resize function of your favorite graphics program to shrink it to the same size as your screen (or close).

5. Select a desktop color to fill the space, if any, unoccupied by a picture.

   or

   Select a predefined color or click Other to specify a custom color.

6. Click OK (or Apply).

✔ Tips

■ To display a solid desktop color with no picture, select None in the Background list.

■ To use a web image as wallpaper, right-click the image in Internet Explorer; then choose Set As Background. The downloaded image appears as Internet Explorer Background in the Background list. Each new internet image you define as a background replaces the old one.

■ To use a web image as your *permanent* background, right-click the image in Internet Explorer; choose Save Picture As; save the image in My Pictures or a folder of your own; then proceed as described.

■ To place live web content on your desktop, see the next section.

CHANGING YOUR DESKTOP BACKGROUND

Displaying Web Content on Your Desktop

The desktop background isn't limited to static images; you can embed a browser window in your desktop to display self-updating web information such as weather reports, stock prices, and news (**Figure 4.8**). An always-on internet connection such as DSL or cable works best, but a regular dial-up modem works too, in a creaky sort of way.

You can work with desktop web content (called Active Desktop in earlier Windows versions) just as if you were working in a browser window. When you click a link Windows opens (or activates) a browser with the link's target displayed.

Web content is updated periodically or when you request it. You have several options that will keep web content current.

To add a web-content item:

1. Choose Start > Control Panel > Appearance and Themes > Display > Desktop tab > Customize Desktop > Web tab (**Figure 4.9**).

    or

    Right-click an empty area on the desktop; then choose Properties > Desktop tab > Customize Desktop > Web tab.

Figure 4.8 Some stock quotes, sports scores, and a weather map on the desktop.

Figure 4.9 Use the Web tab to display web pages on your desktop.

Figure 4.10 The live content's source can be a web page, local file, or network file.

Figure 4.11 This Microsoft web page contains live content designed especially for desktop display, including an investor ticker and weather map. Click Add to Active Desktop to add a particular item; then click Yes to confirm.

Figure 4.12 Click OK to accept the vendor's default update schedule. Click Customize to start the Offline Favorite Wizard and specify your own schedule for updating content.

2. Click New, and choose one of three options (**Figure 4.10**):

    Visit Gallery. Click Visit Gallery to visit Microsoft's Internet Explorer Desktop Gallery web page (**Figure 4.11**); then choose items on the page.

    Location. If you know the item's web address (URL), type it in the Location box.

    Browse. This option lets you access several standard locations—including My Recent Documents, My Network, and your Favorites folder—that may contain potential items for your desktop.

3. Click OK to confirm your choices (**Figure 4.12**).

4. Click OK in each open dialog box.

Wallpaper Image Formats

Any image to be used as wallpaper must be in one of these formats:

- ◆ .BMP or .DIB (Windows Bitmap)
- ◆ .JPEG or .JPG (Joint Photographic Experts Group)
- ◆ .GIF (Graphics Interchange Format, also called the CompuServe graphics format)
- ◆ .PNG (Portable Network Graphics)
- ◆ .HTM or .HTML (Hypertext Markup Language)

HTML is the language used to code web pages. Custom-design the .html file to fit your screen, because it won't have scroll bars and its text and links will have to contend with desktop icons. Position options aren't offered for HTML backgrounds; an HTML file always will display as full-screen and centered.

A wallpaper graphic can be any size on disk; the file-size limit of earlier Windows versions doesn't apply to XP.

To delete a web-content item:

1. Right-click an empty area on the desktop; then choose Properties > Desktop tab > Customize Desktop > Web tab.

2. Select the item that you want to delete; then click Delete.

✔ Tips

■ To display web content on the desktop quickly: Right-drag the link icon from Internet Explorer's Address bar to the desktop; then choose Create Active Desktop Items Here (**Figure 4.13**).

■ Windows stores web content in the folder \Windows\Offline Web Pages. (\Windows is named \WINNT on some systems.)

■ Some gallery items require you to download and install an ActiveX control, a module available from Microsoft that helps complex graphics display correctly.

To modify web content:

1. Right-click an empty area on the desktop; then choose Arrange Icons By > Lock Web Items on Desktop.

   If this box is checked, uncheck it. Now you can modify web content.

2. Point to the item's top edge until a border pops up from that edge (**Figure 4.14**).

3. To move the window, drag the top border.

   or

   To resize the window, drag the left, right, or bottom border.

   or

   Click an icon on the top border (**Figure 4.15**).

4. After you've set everything up, recheck Lock Web Items on Desktop to prevent accidental changes.

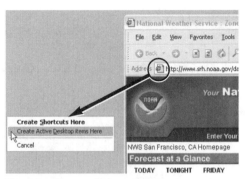

Figure 4.13 You can drag a web page onto your desktop directly from your browser.

Figure 4.14 Web-content items are displayed as (slightly nonstandard) windows.

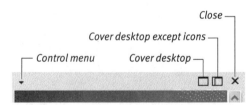

Figure 4.15 You can move, resize, close, or maximize (but not minimize) web-content windows. The Full Screen button becomes the Restore button when the window is maximized.

Figure 4.16 Check the items that you want to update (synchronize).

✔ **Tip**

■ To redisplay a web-content window that you've closed, check its box on the Web tab of the Desktop Items dialog box (refer to Figure 4.9).

To update web-content items manually:

◆ To update *all* items, right-click an empty area on the desktop; then choose Properties > Desktop tab > Customize Desktop > Web tab > Synchronize button (refer to Figure 4.9).

 or

 To update *some* items, choose Start > All Programs > Accessories > Synchronize; check one or more items; then click Synchronize (**Figure 4.16**).

 or

 To update *one* item, point to the item's top edge until a border pops up from that edge; click the down arrow in the top-left corner; then click Synchronize (refer to Figure 4.14).

To display a web-content item's properties:

◆ Point to the item's top edge until a border pops up from that edge; click the down arrow in the top-left corner; then click Properties.

 or

 Right-click an empty area on the desktop; choose Properties > Desktop tab > Customize Desktop > Web tab; select an item; then click Properties.

 or

 Choose Start > All Programs > Accessories > Synchronize; select an item; then click Properties.

To change a web-content item's update schedule:

1. Display the item's properties.

2. On the Schedule tab, set the item's update schedule (**Figure 4.17**).

✔ Tips

■ To see when an item was last updated, choose Start > Accessories > Synchronize; then inspect the Last Updated column (refer to Figure 4.16).

■ You can turn off updates of a web-content item if you want to keep the contents you have. Display the item's properties; then, on the Web Document tab, uncheck Make This Page Available Offline (**Figure 4.18**).

Figure 4.17 You can specify that updates occur manually or automatically and add, edit, or delete automatic schedules. Your computer can connect automatically at the times set for updating.

Figure 4.18 Unchecking this box hides the web document's summary information and suppresses the Schedule and Download tabs.

Figure 4.19 Each person with a user account can pick a distinct theme.

Choosing a Desktop Theme

If Windows' default appearance and colors aren't to your taste, you can change them with a different desktop *theme*—a stored set of colors, icons, fonts, sounds, and other elements that redecorate your desktop. You can pick a predefined theme or create your own.

To choose a theme:

1. Choose Start > Control Panel > Appearance and Themes > Display > Themes tab.

   or

   Right-click an empty area on the desktop; then choose Properties > Themes tab.

2. In the Theme list, select a new theme (**Figure 4.19**).

3. Click OK (or Apply).

✔ Tips

■ Windows comes with only two themes, but many others are freely available. Try www.themexp.org, www.topthemes.com, and the Themes section of www.download.com. Movie and game sites have them too. For an extreme makeover, try WindowBlinds ($20 U.S.; www.windowblinds.net).

■ Select the Windows Classic theme to restore the look of Windows 2000/98/Me.

■ The classic look of some windows (such as the command-prompt window) can't be changed with themes.

■ If you choose More Themes Online in Figure 4.19, you're taken to Microsoft's web site for a sales pitch for Microsoft Plus! ($30).

To create a custom theme:

1. Choose Start > Control Panel > Appearance and Themes > Display > Themes tab.

   or

   Right-click an empty area on the desktop; then choose Properties > Themes tab.

2. In the Theme list, select an existing theme as a starting point for creating a new one.

3. Set the relevant Control Panel options to change the theme (**Figures 4.20** and **4.21**).

4. When you're finished making changes, click Apply on the Themes tab (refer to Figure 4.19).

5. Click Save As; type a theme name; then click Save.

   Windows saves the theme in your My Documents folder.

6. Click OK (or Apply).

✔ Tips

- If you modify a theme without saving it, Windows saves your changes with the name *Previous-theme-name* (Modified). Your modified theme is discarded if you select a different theme. If you modify a theme and save it, you must use a new theme name.

- To populate the Theme list, Windows looks in your My Documents and \Windows\Resources\Themes folders. Click Browse on the Themes tab to open a theme located elsewhere. (\Windows is named \WINNT on some systems.)

Figure 4.20 The Appearance tab lets you select the overall window and button style, color scheme, and font size.

Figure 4.21 Click Advanced on the Appearance tab to fine-tune the font and color of individual interface elements.

To delete a custom theme:

1. Choose Start > Control Panel > Appearance and Themes > Display > Themes tab.

   or

   Right-click an empty area on the desktop; then choose Properties > Themes tab.

2. In the Theme list, select the theme that you want to delete; then click Delete.

✔ Tip

■ You can delete only the themes that you created or installed, not the ones that Windows provides.

Themes and Control Panel

You can tailor individual theme elements by changing Control Panel settings directly. The elements that you can change (with relevant Control Panel programs) are:

◆ Background (Display > Desktop tab)

◆ Desktop icons (Display > Desktop tab > Customize Desktop)

◆ Windows and buttons (Display > Appearance tab)

◆ Colors and fonts (Display > Appearance tab and Display > Appearance tab > Advanced)

◆ Screen saver (Display > Screen Saver tab)

◆ Mouse pointers (Mouse > Pointers tab)

◆ Sounds (Sounds and Audio Devices > Sounds tab)

CHOOSING A DESKTOP THEME

Setting a Screen Saver

A *screen saver* is a utility that causes a monitor to blank out or display images after a specified time passes without keyboard or mouse activity. (Pressing a key or moving the mouse deactivates the screen saver.) Screen savers were developed originally to prevent hardware damage to your monitor, but today's monitors don't need that, so modern screen savers provide decoration or entertainment instead. A screen saver also can password-protect your computer and hide your screen when it takes effect.

To set a screen saver:

1. Choose Start > Control Panel > Appearance and Themes > Display > Screen Saver tab (**Figure 4.22**).

   or

   Right-click an empty area on the desktop; then choose Properties > Screen Saver tab.

2. Select a screen saver in the list.

   (To turn off the screen saver, select None, click OK, and skip the remaining steps.)

3. Specify how long your computer must be idle before the screen saver activates.

   Try 10 to 15 minutes.

4. Click Settings to see any options for the selected screen saver—to change color or animation style, for example.

5. (Optional) Check On Resume, Password Protect (or On Resume, Display Welcome Screen) to display a logon window when you begin using your computer after screen-saver activation.

Figure 4.22 Set your screen saver's wait time carefully so your boss won't realize how long it's been since you did anything.

Figure 4.23 My Pictures Slideshow scrolls through all the pictures in the selected folder.

6. Click Preview to see a full-screen preview of the screen saver.

   Press a key or move your mouse to end the test.

7. Click OK (or Apply).

✔ Tips

- Your screen-saver password is the same as your logon password. If you have no logon password, you can't set a screen-saver password.

- Appearances aside, screen savers—particularly complex ones such as 3D Flying Objects and 3D Pipes—waste energy and processor time. To save resources, turn off your monitor manually or automatically after a certain period of inactivity. See "Conserving Power" later in this chapter.

To use personal pictures as a screen saver:

1. Make sure you have two or more pictures in a folder on your computer (usually, your My Pictures folder).

2. On the Screen Saver tab (refer to Figure 4.22), choose My Pictures Slideshow from the Screen Saver drop-down list.

3. Click Settings to specify the folder containing your pictures, define picture size, and set other options (**Figure 4.23**).

4. Click OK in each open dialog box.

✔ Tip

- Tweak UI's Logon > Screen Saver option lets you dismiss a screen saver within a few-second grace period without prompting you for your password. See the "Tweak UI" sidebar in "Using the Start Menu" in Chapter 2.

Idly Folding Proteins

Forget screen savers. Instead, put your idle PC to work solving great math and science problems. By participating in *distributed*—or *grid*—*computing* projects you (and thousands of others) donate bits of your computer's spare processing power to large-scale, not-for-profit research projects. It's fascinating, free, and doesn't interfere with your normal computer use. Visit www.grid.org or http://gridcafe.web.cern.ch to learn about grid projects worldwide. You'll find projects for researching cancer, AIDS, anthrax, and smallpox; predicting climate change; searching for ETs; folding proteins; finding prime numbers; and more.

SETTING A SCREEN SAVER

Configuring the Monitor

Windows lets you get the most out of your display hardware with these settings:

Screen resolution is the amount (fineness) of detail in your screen's image, expressed in pixels wide by pixels high. (A *pixel* is the smallest building block of the display.) Conventional screens have resolutions of 640 × 480 (largely useless except in emergencies), 800 × 600, 1024 × 768, and 1152 × 864. High-end "cinema" monitors support much higher resolutions.

Color quality ranges from 16 ugly colors for archaic Standard VGA to 4 billion colors (32 bits per pixel) for the best monitors and video cards. The number of colors available correlates to your resolution setting—most video cards display fewer colors at higher resolutions—so you may have to reduce resolution to get higher color quality. The available resolution and color choices adjust automatically. If your digital photos look blotchy, increase color quality.

Refresh rate is the frequency at which the screen is redrawn to maintain a steady image. Higher refresh rates yield less flicker. A refresh rate below 72 hertz, or 72 times per second, can tire your eyes if you look at the screen too long.

Color matching ensures that colors are represented accurately and consistently across color printers, scanners, cameras, monitors, and programs. Without color management onscreen and printed colors can vary greatly: Orange can appear brown, green can appear blue, and so on. Graphic designers love color matching because it does away with trial and error in resolving color differences. Color matching requires a separate color profile (.icm file) for each device connected to your computer. This profile conveys the device's color characteristics to the color management system every time colors are scanned, displayed, or printed.

ClearType

ClearType is Microsoft's font-smoothing technology that makes words appear sharper on laptop and LCD screens. (Don't use ClearType on a normal desktop CRT monitor—it actually will make text blurrier.) Turn it on to see if you like the change in font resolution:

1. Choose Start > Control Panel > Display > Appearance tab > Effects button > check Use the Following Method to Smooth Edges of Screen Fonts.

2. Select ClearType in the drop-down list.

3. Click OK in each open dialog box.

More information about ClearType is at www.microsoft.com/typography/cleartype. Download the ClearType Tuner utility, and use it to fine-tune ClearType to your preferences.

CONFIGURING THE MONITOR

Figure 4.24 Better video cards have 64 MB or more of memory—overkill for word processing and email but barely enough for gaming and digital video. Some high-end video cards add extra tabs to the Display dialog box, as shown here.

✔ Tips

■ Changing these settings affects all users who log on to your computer.

■ Don't always choose the maximum resolution available. If you spend most of your time typing memos or reading email, you may find that medium resolution reduces eyestrain. For general use try 800 × 600 on a 15-inch monitor, 1024 × 768 on a 17-inch monitor, or 1152 × 864 on a 19-inch monitor.

■ Flat-panel screen (laptop or desktop) images may look fuzzy at less-than-maximum resolutions.

■ Video-card memory largely determines the maximum resolution and color quality that you can use. To see how much video memory you have, choose Start > Control Panel > Appearance and Themes > Display > Settings tab > Advanced > Adapter tab > Adapter Information section (**Figure 4.24**).

■ To adjust the monitor for vision impairments, see "Accommodating Disabled Users" later in this chapter.

■ For notes on installing and configuring peripherals, see Chapter 8.

CONFIGURING THE MONITOR

To set screen resolution and color quality:

1. Choose Start > Control Panel > Appearance and Themes > Display > Settings tab (**Figure 4.25**).

   or

   Right-click an empty area on the desktop; then choose Properties > Settings tab.

2. Drag the Screen Resolution slider to set the display size.

3. From the Color Quality drop-down list, choose the number of colors.

   Choose 16-bit or higher color, or photographic images will appear grainy (*dithered*).

4. Click Apply.

5. If Windows asks you to confirm settings, click OK.

   Your screen turns black briefly and refreshes with the new settings.

6. After your settings change, you have 15 seconds to accept the changes (**Figure 4.26**).

✔ Tips

- If you have more than one monitor (driven by multiple video cards or by a single card that supports multiple monitors), the Settings tab displays a monitor icon for each monitor. Click a monitor icon to activate it before choosing its resolution and color settings.

- If you need a 256-color display to run an old DOS game or program, don't set your entire system to 256 colors even if it's available. Instead, use the Compatibility feature; see "Running Older Programs" in Chapter 6.

Figure 4.25 Increasing the number of pixels displays more information on your screen, but icons and text get smaller.

Figure 4.26 If your new screen settings look good, click Yes; otherwise, click No or just wait to revert to your previous settings.

Figure 4.27 To reduce eyestrain, choose the highest refresh rate that your monitor and video card support, but check the documentation or the manufacturer's web site to find out what the hardware will accept.

- Click the Troubleshoot button to start Display Troubleshooter, which helps you resolve flicker, installation, video, multiple-monitor, resolution, and other problems.

- The Advanced button lets you view the hardware properties of your monitor and video card. You can adjust some settings, but you usually don't need to unless you're installing a new driver, setting color matching, or changing the refresh rate.

To set the refresh rate:

1. Choose Start > Control Panel > Appearance and Themes > Display > Settings tab > Advanced > Monitor tab (**Figure 4.27**).

   or

   Right-click an empty area on the desktop; then choose Properties > Monitor tab.

2. If you have multiple monitors, in the Monitor Type section, select the monitor that you're working with currently.

3. In the Monitor Settings section, choose a refresh rate from the drop-down list.

4. Click Apply.

5. If Windows asks you to confirm settings, click OK.

   Your screen turns black briefly.

6. After your refresh rate changes, you have 15 seconds to accept the change (refer to Figure 4.26).

✔ Tip

- Don't uncheck Hide Modes That This Monitor Cannot Display to choose a higher refresh rate. A refresh rate that exceeds the capabilities of your monitor or video card can distort images and damage hardware.

CONFIGURING THE MONITOR

To manage color profiles:

1. Choose Start > Control Panel > Appearance and Themes > Display > Settings tab > Advanced > Color Management tab (**Figure 4.28**).

   or

   Right-click an empty area on the desktop; then choose Properties > Color Management tab.

2. To add a color profile, click Add; then use the Add Profile Association dialog box to select a color profile to associate with the current monitor (**Figure 4.29**).

   or

   To remove a profile, select it; then click Remove.

   or

   To set a profile as the default for the current monitor, select it; then click Set As Default.

3. Click OK in each open dialog box.

✔ Tips

- I've only touched on color management here. To learn more, search for *color management* in Windows Help and Support Center.

- Right-click a color profile (.icm file) in Windows Explorer to install it or associate it with a device.

Figure 4.28 The Color Profiles list shows all color profiles associated with the current monitor and video card (none, in this case, which is fine for everyday use).

Figure 4.29 Color profiles installed with a monitor and video card are stored in the \Windows\System32\Spool\Drivers\Color folder. (\Windows is named \WINNT on some systems.)

Figure 4.30 ClickLock is a mercy for touchpad users.

Figure 4.31 This tab lets you select predefined pointer schemes (which range from cute to practical), create your own pointer schemes, or browse to select an individual pointer (rather than an entire scheme).

Configuring the Mouse

Use the Mouse utility in Control Panel to control settings such as button configuration, double-click speed, mouse pointers, responsiveness, and wheel behavior.

To configure the mouse:

1. Choose Start > Control Panel > Printers and Other Hardware > Mouse.

2. To swap the left and right mouse-button functions, Buttons tab > check Switch Primary and Secondary Buttons.

3. If Windows often interprets your double-clicks as two single clicks, Buttons > drag the Double-Click Speed slider toward Slow.

4. To make dragging easier, Buttons > check Turn on ClickLock (**Figure 4.30**); then you can select text or drag icons without holding down the mouse button continuously.

5. To customize mouse pointers, Pointers tab > Scheme to set or create a new pointer scheme (**Figure 4.31**).

   Use Customize to change individual pointers. For information about the default pointer scheme, see "The Mouse" in Chapter 1.

continues on next page

CONFIGURING THE MOUSE

6. On the Pointer Options tab, adjust how the pointer responds to the mouse's physical actions (**Figure 4.32**).

7. If your mouse or trackball has a wheel, on the Wheel tab, adjust its scroll behavior (**Figure 4.33**).

8. Click OK (or Apply).

✔ Tips

■ Fancy mice, such as Logitech mice, come with their own driver software. Installing these drivers adds new options and can change some default mouse settings. A cordless mouse may add a tab that indicates remaining battery life, for example.

■ A computer with a special default pointing device—such as a touchpad on a laptop—replaces the Wheel tab with a tab of controls for that device.

■ When you install an alternative pointing device such as a stylus or tablet, look for a Control Panel item devoted to that device.

■ To adjust the mouse and insertion point for mobility impairments, see "Accommodating Disabled Users" later in this chapter.

■ To drag an icon with ClickLock turned on, point to the icon; press the left mouse button for the ClickLock interval; release the button; drag the icon to a destination; then press the button again for the ClickLock interval.

■ Tweak UI's Mouse options let you adjust mouse double-click, drag, and hover sensitivity; specify how fast the mouse wheel scrolls; and activate windows just by pointing to them. See the "Tweak UI" sidebar in "Using the Start Menu" in Chapter 2.

Figure 4.32 If the pointer distracts you while you type, check Hide Pointer While Typing. If you need to keep track of the pointer as it moves, check Display Pointer Trails (useful for laptop screens). Adjust the pointer's speed to have it respond more quickly or slowly to mouse movements.

Figure 4.33 A mouse wheel can stand in for scroll bars; roll the wheel to scroll up or down a list, document, or web page. If your mouse has no wheel, these settings are ignored.

Figure 4.34 The Troubleshoot button connects you to Help and Support Center with step-by-step advice and tutorial.

- A few mouse utilities: Mouse Machine records mouse moves and clicks for automated playback (free; `www.pcsupport.dk/software/MouseMachine.html`). Cool Mouse assigns various actions to the mouse's middle button and wheel ($25 U.S.; `www.shelltoys.com`).

- The Hardware tab (**Figure 4.34**) lists the pointing devices attached to your computer and provides access to the Properties dialog box, which is the same as the one in Device Manager.

- For general information about installing and configuring peripherals, see Chapter 8.

To access the mouse's device driver:

1. Choose Start > Control Panel > Performance and Maintenance > System > Hardware tab > Device Manager (**Figure 4.35**).

2. Double-click Mice and Other Pointing Devices; then double-click the name of the mouse (**Figure 4.36**).

Figure 4.35 Like all peripherals, mice have device drivers that you may need to update or tweak from time to time.

Figure 4.36 If you're having trouble activating your mouse wheel, the Wheel Detection setting on the Advanced Settings tab may help. See also "Managing Device Drivers" in Chapter 8.

CONFIGURING THE MOUSE

Configuring the Keyboard

A keyboard should just work after you plug it in, with no adjustments in software. You can use Control Panel's Keyboard utility to change some settings after installation.

To configure the keyboard:

1. Choose Start > Control Panel > Printers and Other Hardware > Keyboard.

2. On the Speed tab (**Figure 4.37**), update the following settings:

   Repeat Delay controls the amount of time that elapses before a character begins to repeat when you hold down a key.

   Repeat Rate adjusts how quickly a character repeats when you hold down a key.

   Cursor Blink Rate controls the blink rate of the text cursor (insertion point). To stop the cursor from blinking, set the blink rate to None.

3. Click OK (or Apply).

✔ Tips

- Fancy keyboards with buttons for CD players and web browsers come with their own driver software. Installing these drivers adds new options and can change some default keyboard settings.

- The Hardware tab (**Figure 4.38**) provides access to the Properties dialog box, which is the same as the one in Device Manager.

- To adjust the keyboard for mobility impairments, see "Accommodating Disabled Users" later in this chapter.

- To choose an international keyboard layout, see "Localizing Your System" later in this chapter.

Figure 4.37 If you type rapidly, drag the Character Repeat sliders to the right to make your keyboard more responsive.

Figure 4.38 Keyboard malfunctions are rare, but the keyboard has its own Troubleshoot button to connect to Help and Support Center.

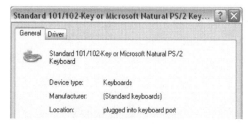

Figure 4.39 The keyboard installs a driver and claims system resources, like any other device. See also "Managing Device Drivers" in Chapter 8.

To access the keyboard's device driver:

1. Choose Start > Control Panel > Performance and Maintenance > System > Hardware tab > Device Manager.

2. Double-click Keyboards; then double-click the name of the keyboard (**Figure 4.39**).

CONFIGURING THE KEYBOARD

Configuring Sound and Audio Devices

Most computers have sound devices such as sound cards, microphones, and speakers, either built-in or external. Use Control Panel's Sounds and Audio Devices utility to configure the sounds and sound devices used in Windows.

✔ Tips

■ For general information about installing and configuring peripherals, see Chapter 8.

■ To adjust sounds for hearing impairments, see "Accommodating Disabled Users" later in this chapter.

Controlling Audio Hardware

When you choose Control Panel > Sounds and Audio Devices > Volume tab, the Device Volume Advanced controls are really a mini control panel for your audio hardware. You may see these controls in a typical installation:

CD Player controls the volume of audio CDs (if your CD drive is connected to the sound card directly with a three-conductor cable).

Line-In controls the volume of the sound card's Line-In or Aux input (usually used to record from a stereo or other external playback device).

Mic controls the sound card's microphone input volume (usually used with a microphone or dictation headset).

PC Speaker controls the volume of your PC's built-in speaker, which is connected to the motherboard, not the sound card.

SW Synth controls the volume of music produced by the sound card's MIDI synthesizer or wavetable.

Volume Control is the master control—the same one shown in Figure 4.40.

Wave sounds are generated by Windows, games, MP3s, Windows Media Player, and many other programs.

Depending on your computer's audio hardware, you may see all or some of these controls, or others not listed here. If you don't want to display all the available controls, turn them on or off individually (choose Options > Properties).

CONFIGURING SOUND AND AUDIO DEVICES

Figure 4.40 The slider in the Device Volume section is a master volume control for audio hardware.

Figure 4.41 The Volume Control dialog box lets you adjust volume and balance for playback and recording devices individually.

Sound volume

Windows lets you control the master volume level for all audio hardware or for each device individually.

To control sound volume:

1. Choose Start > Control Panel > Sounds, Speech, and Audio Devices > Sounds and Audio Devices > Volume tab (**Figure 4.40**).

2. Move the slider left to lower the sound level or right to increase it.

   or

   Check Mute to turn off sound.

3. Check Place Volume Icon in the Taskbar to show a notification-area icon that you can click to change the volume quickly.

4. Click OK (or Apply).

✔ Tip

■ To mute all sound quickly, click the volume icon in the taskbar's notification area (system tray); then check Mute in the panel that pops up.

To control sound volume for individual audio devices:

1. Choose Start > Control Panel > Sounds, Speech, and Audio Devices > Sounds and Audio Devices > Volume tab (refer to Figure 4.40).

2. In the Device Volume section, click Advanced to display the Volume Control dialog box (**Figure 4.41**).

3. Choose Options > Properties; check boxes to choose controls to show or hide audio devices; then click OK.

continues on next page

CONFIGURING SOUND AND AUDIO DEVICES

4. Drag the Balance and Volume sliders (or click Mute) to adjust each audio device individually.

5. Choose Options > Exit or click the window's Close button.

6. In the Sounds and Audio Devices Properties dialog box, click OK (or Apply).

✔ Tips

- In the Volume Control dialog box, choose Options > Advanced Controls; then click one of the Advanced buttons to control bass, treble, and other settings.

- To adjust *recording* volume levels, choose Options > Properties; then select Recording in the Adjust Volume For section. The Volume Control dialog box changes to the Recording Control dialog box.

Speaker settings

Your computer creates sound with several devices, including its own internal speaker, attached external speakers, headphones, and (less often) dedicated speech or synthesizer cards. These too are controlled by the Sounds and Audio Devices applet.

To configure speakers and headphones:

1. Choose Start > Control Panel > Sounds, Speech, and Audio Devices > Sounds and Audio Devices > Volume tab (refer to Figure 4.40).

2. In the Speaker Settings section, click Speaker Volume to adjust the volume of each speaker separately.

3. In the Speaker Settings section, click Advanced to select the speaker or headphone setup that you have on your computer (**Figure 4.42**).

4. In the Sounds and Audio Devices Properties dialog box, click OK (or Apply).

Figure 4.42 The Advanced Audio Properties dialog box lets you tell Windows about your speaker setup and orientation, stereo separation, and more.

Figure 4.43 You can choose (or mute) each sound individually or use a sound scheme to apply a group of sounds.

System sounds

The Sounds tab lets you customize system sound effects, which are audio clips (beeps, chords, or music snippets) associated with system events such as emptying the trash or error messages.

To configure system sound effects:

1. Choose Start > Control Panel > Sounds, Speech, and Audio Devices > Sounds and Audio Devices > Sounds tab (**Figure 4.43**).

2. To choose a predefined group of sound effects, choose a scheme from the Sound Scheme drop-down list.

3. To change a sound for a particular event, select the event in the Program Events list; then select the sound in the Sounds list.

   or

   Select the event and click Browse to select another sound file (in .wav audio format) on your system.

   or

   Select (None) in the Sounds list to remove a sound.

4. To preview a sound for a particular event, select the event in the Program Events list; then click the Play button (the button with the right-pointing triangle).

5. To save a changed sound scheme, click Save As; type a name; then click OK.

6. To delete a custom sound scheme, select the scheme; then click Delete.

   You can delete only the schemes that you created or installed, not the ones Windows provides.

7. Click OK (or Apply).

✔ Tip

■ Place .wav files in the \Windows\Media folder to have them appear in the Sounds list. (\Windows is named \WINNT on some systems.)

CONFIGURING SOUND AND AUDIO DEVICES

123

Recording and playback

If your system has multiple input or output audio devices, the Audio and Voice tabs let you pick which device to use for sound playback, sound recording, MIDI or voice playback, and voice recording.

To configure audio and voice settings:

1. Choose Start > Control Panel > Sounds, Speech, and Audio Devices > Sounds and Audio Devices.

2. On the Audio tab (**Figure 4.44**), select the default devices for audio playback and recording.

3. If your audio programs require the sound card selected in Default Device, check Use Only Default Devices; if your audio programs can use any sound card on your computer, uncheck the box.

4. On the Voice tab (**Figure 4.45**), select the default devices for voice playback and recording.

5. Click OK (or Apply).

✔ Tip

■ Some specialized multimedia devices, such as video-capture cards, may appear in the Default Device lists on the Audio or Sounds tabs. If you have such a device and you're getting no sound, check these two tabs.

Figure 4.44 MIDI is the sound source that games use normally; it also plays music nicely without grabbing lots of disk space.

Figure 4.45 Click Test Hardware to start the Sound Hardware Test Wizard, which helps you make sure that your PC can play sounds and capture your voice.

Figure 4.46 Audio and video devices are identified by make and model—crucial information when you're dealing with the manufacturer's web support.

Figure 4.47 The Driver tab lets you inspect, update, roll back, or uninstall a device's driver. See also "Managing Device Drivers" in Chapter 8.

Audio device drivers

Getting audio hardware to work in Windows can be a problem (especially if you have a lot of it). If you know who made a sound component that's giving you trouble, try the manufacturer's web site for updated drivers, patches, and tips.

To access an audio or video device's driver:

1. Choose Start > Control Panel > Sounds, Speech, and Audio Devices > Sounds and Audio Devices > Hardware tab (**Figure 4.46**).

2. Select an item in the Devices list; then click Properties (**Figure 4.47**).

✔ Tips

■ Click the Troubleshoot button (refer to Figure 4.46) to open Help and Support Center's step-by-step troubleshooting tutorial.

■ Each multimedia device on the Hardware tab has the same Properties dialog box that it does in Device Manager.

CONFIGURING SOUND AND AUDIO DEVICES

Changing the Date and Time

Keep your system time accurate, because Windows uses it to timestamp files and email, schedule tasks, and record events.

To set the date and time:

1. Choose Start > Control Panel > Date, Time, Language, and Regional Options > Date and Time, or double-click the clock in the taskbar.

2. On the Date & Time tab (**Figure 4.48**), adjust the date and time as needed.

3. On the Time Zone tab (**Figure 4.49**), select your time zone in the list.

   Windows assumes that you want to Automatically Adjust Clock for Daylight Saving Changes. Uncheck this box if you don't want to use daylight saving time.

4. On the Internet Time tab (**Figure 4.50**), check Automatically Synchronize with an Internet Time Server to synchronize your computer clock with a highly accurate clock. (Type any time-server address in the Server box.) Once a week is the only interval you get unless you click Update Now.

5. Click OK (or Apply).

✔ Tips

■ Internet-time synchronization occurs regularly only if you have a full-time internet connection such as DSL or cable. If you use dial-up, click Update Now while you're connected to the internet to synchronize your clock immediately.

■ A time server won't synchronize your system time if your date is incorrect.

Figure 4.48 To set the time in the Time box, type new numbers; press the up- and down-arrow keys; or click the small up and down arrows.

Figure 4.49 The map is decorative; you can't click your location to specify your time zone.

Figure 4.50 For hyperaccurate system time, use Tardis 2000 ($20 U.S.; www.kaska.demon.co.uk) or Dimension 4 (free; www.thinkman.com) to synchronize the clock at fine intervals. When your computer is shut down, the motherboard battery maintains the time.

Figure 4.51 The language that you choose affects how programs format numbers, currencies, times, and dates.

Figure 4.52 The Sample section shows how selected settings affect the appearance of quantities.

Localizing Your System

Windows supports many international standards, formats, and languages. Use Control Panel's Regional and Language Options utility to adjust country-specific settings such as unit of measurement; currency, number, and date formats; and keyboard and display language.

To choose formats for numbers, currencies, times, and dates:

1. Choose Start > Control Panel > Date, Time, Language, and Regional Options > Regional and Language Options > Regional Options tab (**Figure 4.51**).

2. In the Standards and Formats section, choose a language from the drop-down list.

3. To change individual settings, click Customize (**Figure 4.52**).

4. Click OK (or Apply).

✔ Tip

- You can't save customized regional settings as though they were themes. If you customize and then choose another language in the list, you lose customized settings.

To choose a keyboard layout for a different language:

1. Choose Start > Control Panel > Date, Time, Language, and Regional Options > Regional and Language Options > Languages tab > Details button (**Figure 4.53**).

2. Click Add; specify the language and keyboard layout to install; then click OK.

3. Repeat step 2 for each language that you want to add.

4. When you're done adding languages, click Apply.

5. In the Preferences section, click Language Bar; then check Show the Language Bar on the Desktop.

6. Click OK in each open dialog box.

7. On the taskbar, click the Language bar to choose a keyboard layout (**Figure 4.54**).

✔ Tip

■ Use the Character Map program to view the characters available on your keyboard; see "Using the Free Utility Programs" in Chapter 6.

Figure 4.53 Keyboard layouts rearrange the keys' character assignments. Pressing the [key on a U.S. keyboard with a German layout types the ü character, for example.

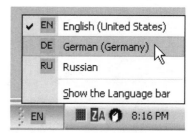

Figure 4.54 In the menu, choose the language or keyboard layout that you want to switch to, or switch by pressing the left Shift and left Alt keys at the same time.

Figure 4.55 If an older program is unable to recognize your preferred language, Windows can swap the character set.

To specify the preferred language for older programs:

1. Choose Start > Control Panel > Date, Time, Language, and Regional Options > Regional and Language Options > Advanced tab (**Figure 4.55**).

2. In the Language for Non-Unicode Programs section, choose your preferred language from the drop-down list.

3. If your word processor or web browser isn't displaying foreign-language content correctly, in the Code Page Conversion Tables section, check the languages to install.

4. To apply your Regional and Language Options settings to your user account and to all new user accounts, check the box in the Default User Account Settings section.

5. Click OK (or Apply).

LOCALIZING YOUR SYSTEM

Accommodating Disabled Users

Windows XP can be set up to assist disabled users. *Accessibility* is Microsoft's umbrella term for tools that make a computer easier to use for people with poor eyesight, hearing, or mobility. Accessibility tools are:

◆ Accessibility Wizard

◆ Accessibility Options

◆ Magnifier

◆ Narrator

◆ On-Screen Keyboard

◆ Utility Manager

✔ Tip

■ Accessibility tools are for everyone. Graphic designers and developers can use Magnifier for pixel-level design work. And On-Screen Keyboard is handy if you find yourself with a broken keyboard.

Accessibility Wizard

Accessibility Wizard helps you choose accessibility options step by step. Use it to learn about Windows' accessibility functions without exploring each setting individually.

To run the Accessibility Wizard:

1. Choose Start > All Programs > Accessories > Accessibility > Accessibility Wizard.

2. Click Next.

   Accessibility Wizard guides you through the available accessibility options (**Figure 4.56**).

✔ Tip

■ Settings in the Accessibility Wizard also are available in Control Panel's Accessibility Options utility.

Figure 4.56 The Accessibility Wizard asks questions and sets accessibility options appropriately. In this introductory screen, you set the size of onscreen text.

Figure 4.57 To toggle between high-contrast and standard colors, press Alt+left Shift+Print Screen.

Accessibility Options

Control Panel's Accessibility Options utility lets you adjust accessibility settings for vision-, hearing-, or mobility-impaired users.

To set accessibility options for vision-impaired users:

1. Choose Start > Control Panel > Accessibility Options > Accessibility Options > Display tab (**Figure 4.57**).

2. To make Windows and other programs use a color scheme that increases legibility, check Use High Contrast; then click Settings to pick the scheme.

3. To make the cursor (insertion point) blink faster or slower, drag the Blink Rate slider.

4. To make the cursor wider so that it's easier to see, drag the Width slider to the right.

5. Click OK (or Apply).

✔ Tips

■ Some high-contrast color schemes include large and extra-large fonts.

■ See also "Magnifier" and "Narrator" later in this section.

To set accessibility options for hearing-impaired users:

1. Choose Start > Control Panel > Accessibility Options > Accessibility Options > Sound tab (**Figure 4.58**).

2. To display a signal onscreen when Windows plays a system sound (such as a warning beep or incoming-mail beep), check Use SoundSentry.

3. If you turned on SoundSentry, select a visual signal, such as flashing the title bar or the entire screen.

4. To turn on captioning for programs that support it, check Use ShowSounds.

5. Click OK (or Apply).

To set accessibility options for mobility-impaired users:

1. Choose Start > Control Panel > Accessibility Options > Accessibility Options > Keyboard tab (**Figure 4.59**).

2. To make the Shift, Ctrl, Alt, and Windows logo keys toggle on or off by pressing and releasing them (rather than holding them down), check Use StickyKeys.

3. To have Windows ignore brief or repeated keystrokes, check Use FilterKeys.

4. To make the computer beep whenever you press Caps Lock, Num Lock, or Scroll Lock, check Use ToggleKeys.

5. To make programs display extra keyboard help (if available), check Show Extra Keyboard Help in Programs.

6. Click the Mouse tab (**Figure 4.60**).

7. To use the numeric keypad to move the mouse pointer and to click, double-click, or drag, check Use MouseKeys.

8. Click OK (or Apply).

Figure 4.58 ShowSounds, which works a little like TV closed-captioning, substitutes text captions for speech and other sounds. Programs labeled "Windows XP Compatible" generally support this feature.

Figure 4.59 StickyKeys is useful for people who have trouble pressing more than one key simultaneously FilterKeys is for people who have trouble pressing keys quickly or lightly. ToggleKeys is useful for everyone, disabled or not.

ACCOMMODATING DISABLED USERS

Figure 4.60 MouseKeys is designed for people who have trouble using the mouse, but it's also handy for making precise moves in graphics programs.

✔ Tips

- Click Settings to fine-tune the behavior of StickyKeys, FilterKeys, ToggleKeys, or MouseKeys; each utility has several functions that you can choose individually.

- StickyKeys lets you use keyboard shortcuts such as Ctrl+Z or Ctrl+Alt+Delete without having to hold down multiple keys simultaneously.

- FilterKeys prevents rrrrrrrepeated keystrokes when you hold down a key. See also "Configuring the Keyboard" earlier in this chapter.

- If you watch the keyboard (rather than the screen) when typing, you may find ToggleKeys useful for warning you that you've TURNED ON CAPS LOCK ACCIDENTALLY.

- In MouseKeys mode, press 2, 4, 6, or 8 on the numeric keypad to move the pointer. Press 5 to click, + to double-click, – to right-click, Insert to start dragging, or Delete to end dragging. Hold down Shift to move in small, precise increments or Ctrl to jump in large increments.

- The keyboard shortcuts for toggling Accessibility options on and off are:
  StickyKeys. Press Shift five times in a row.
  FilterKeys. Hold down the right Shift key for eight seconds.
  ToggleKeys. Hold down the Num Lock key for five seconds.
  MouseKeys. Press left Alt+left Shift+ Num Lock.

- See also "On-Screen Keyboard" later in this chapter.

To set general accessibility options:

1. Choose Start > Control Panel > Accessibility Options > Accessibility Options > General tab (**Figure 4.61**).

2. To make Windows turn off all accessibility features after a period of inactivity, check the box in the Automatic Reset section; then select a length of time.

3. To display a confirmation message or beep every time you use a shortcut key to turn an accessibility feature on or off, check the boxes in the Notification section.

4. To turn on support for special input devices (keyboard and mouse replacements attached to a serial port), check the box in the SerialKey Devices section; then click Settings to define the device's chosen port name and data rate.

5. To apply these accessibility settings to all future logons or new user profiles, check the boxes in the Administrative Options section.

6. Click OK (or Apply).

Figure 4.61 Automatic Reset is useful when several people use your computer but only some require accessibility options. Notification is useful to alert people who might turn on an accessibility feature accidentally. SerialKey is appropriate for people who can't use a standard keyboard or mouse.

Figure 4.62 Magnifier acts as a magnifying glass that follows the pointer or cursor around the screen.

Figure 4.63 Select Invert Colors for a high-contrast color scheme that improves visibility in the magnification window.

Magnifier

Magnifier is a magnification program for visually impaired users; it displays a special panel at the top of the screen that shows an enlarged version of the area of the screen near the pointer or cursor (**Figure 4.62**). When you first open Magnifier, the Magnifier Settings dialog box appears (**Figure 4.63**).

To open and configure Magnifier:

1. Choose Start > All Programs > Accessories > Accessibility > Magnifier.

2. In the Magnifier Settings dialog box, select the magnification level; specify whether the magnified area tracks the mouse pointer, highlighted area, or insertion point; or change the color scheme.

3. To hide the Magnifier Settings window, minimize it; to exit, click Close or Exit.

✔ Tips

■ The Magnifier window is docked to the top of the screen by default, but you can move it, resize it, or drag it to any screen edge to lock it in place.

■ Magnifier is a bare-bones utility, and even Microsoft suggests that you may need a more robust commercial program. Even so, Magnifier is helpful given its limits.

■ Taskbar Magnifier is a "mini" Magnifier that displays the magnified part of the screen in a small rectangle on the taskbar. Taskbar Magnifier is one of the PowerToys described in "Using the Free Utility Programs" in Chapter 6. After installing it, right-click an empty area on the taskbar; then choose Toolbars > Taskbar Magnifier.

ACCOMMODATING DISABLED USERS

Narrator

Narrator is a text-to-speech (TTS) program for visually impaired users; it uses a voice synthesizer and your system's audio hardware to read aloud the contents of the active window, menu options, text that you've typed, and text and captions of other screen elements. When you first open Narrator, the Narrator dialog box appears (**Figure 4.64**).

To open and configure Narrator:

1. Choose Start > All Programs > Accessories > Accessibility > Narrator.

2. In the Narrator dialog box, specify whether new windows, menus, or short-cut menus are read aloud when displayed; whether typed characters are read aloud; or whether the active item on your screen is read aloud.

3. Click Voice to adjust the synthesized voice's speed, volume, or pitch.

4. To hide the Narrator window, minimize it; to exit, click Close or Exit.

✔ Tips

- Only the English version of Windows XP supports Narrator.

- For fun, have Narrator read your email.

- See also "Configuring Speech Recognition and Translation" later in this chapter.

- Narrator, like Magnifier, is less capable than full-featured commercial alternatives. If you need a TTS program to use a computer, buy a third-party program or find a charitable cause or government program that donates such software. Try TextAloud ($30 U.S.; www.nextup.com) with AT&T Natural Voices (www.naturalvoices.att.com).

Figure 4.64 Narrator is designed to work with Notepad, WordPad, Control Panel programs, Internet Explorer, the Windows desktop, and Windows Setup; it may not read words aloud correctly in other programs.

Figure 4.65 On-Screen Keyboard displays a facsimile of a full keyboard that floats atop the active program.

On-Screen Keyboard

This virtual keyboard lets mobility-impaired users click the mouse (or other pointing device) to type. The program that's accepting your typed characters must be active while you're using On-Screen Keyboard.

To open and configure On-Screen Keyboard:

1. Choose Start > All Programs > Accessories > Accessibility > On-Screen Keyboard (**Figure 4.65**).

2. Use the Keyboard menu to choose the onscreen keyboard's layout.

3. Use the Settings menu to add a click when you select a key; choose a font; or set the typing mode.

4. To close On-Screen Keyboard, choose File > Exit (or click Close).

ACCOMMODATING DISABLED USERS

Utility Manager

Utility Manager manages Magnifier, Narrator, and On-Screen Keyboard from a central location.

To open and configure Utility Manager:

1. Choose Start > All Programs > Accessories > Accessibility > Utility Manager (**Figure 4.66**).

or

Press Windows logo key+U.

2. Select an accessibility tool; then click Start or Stop.

3. Use the check boxes to tell Windows to start any or all tools when you log on, lock your desktop, or start Utility Manager.

4. Click OK (or Apply).

✔ Tip

■ If your keyboard has no Windows logo key, use On-Screen Keyboard to open Utility Manager with the keyboard shortcut. This maneuver turns on features that are otherwise unavailable.

Figure 4.66 The first time that you open Utility Manager from the Start menu, a warning message tells you that some of Utility Manager's features are available only if you start it by pressing Windows logo key+U.

Configuring Speech Recognition and Translation

Control Panel's Speech utility controls Windows' speech-recognition and text-to-speech (speech synthesizer) features.

The Speech Recognition tab is visible only if you've installed a program that supports speech-recognition features such as voice dictation. Microsoft Word 2002 and later versions, for example, let you speak commands and dictate text.

The Text-to-Speech tab controls the text-to-speech translation of the Windows speech synthesizer. The only built-in program that reads to you is Narrator, which has its own voice controls (see "Accommodating Disabled Users" earlier in this chapter).

✔ Tips

■ Depending on the hardware installed on your computer, Speech can appear in Control Panel as its own extension or as part of Sounds, Speech and Audio Devices.

■ Windows XP's speech tools are immature. Try an established product such as Dragon Naturally Speaking (www.scansoft.com).

CONFIGURING SPEECH AND TRANSLATION

To configure speech recognition:

1. Choose Start > Control Panel > Sounds, Speech, and Audio Devices > Speech > Speech Recognition tab (**Figure 4.67**).

2. In the Language section, choose a speech-recognition engine from the drop-down list or click Settings (if available) to show additional engine properties.

3. In the Recognition Profiles section, click New to create a new recognition profile for your voice.

   Several wizards run to help you set up the profile, calibrate your microphone and speakers, and train your profile.

4. In the Microphone section, set and configure your audio input device.

5. Click OK (or Apply).

To configure text-to-speech translation:

1. Choose Start > Control Panel > Sounds, Speech, and Audio Devices > Speech > Text to Speech tab (**Figure 4.68**).

2. In the Voice Selection section, choose one of the available Text-to-Speech voices or click Settings (if available) to display additional voice properties.

   The selected voice speaks the text in the Preview Voice section.

3. In the Voice Speed section, drag the slider to adjust the voice's rate of speech.

4. Click Audio Output to set the preferred device for voice playback.

5. Click OK (or Apply).

Figure 4.67 You must train a speech recognizer to adapt to the sound of your voice, word pronunciation, accent, and speaking manner.

Figure 4.68 The robotic voice of Windows is named Microsoft Sam.

Figure 4.69 You can open items in folders and on the desktop by single-clicking them, just as you click a link on a web page. To select an item without opening it, move the pointer over it.

Using Alternative Mouse Behavior

The mouse behavior described in "The Mouse" and "Icons" in Chapter 1 is the default. Windows' alternative setting is a weblike interface, letting you open icons by single-clicking—instead of double-clicking, which can be awkward for beginners. (Right-clicking and dragging remain unchanged.)

To open items with a single click:

1. Choose Start > Control Panel > Appearance and Themes > Folder Options > General tab (**Figure 4.69**).

2. In the Click Items As Follows section, select Single-Click to Open an Item (Point to Select).

3. Choose icon title underlining: permanent (like links on a web page) or temporary (only when you point to icons).

4. Click OK (or Apply).

The instructions in this book assume that you use the default behavior, but if you choose the alternative, be aware of the following differences:

◆ The entire concept of double-clicking is eradicated.

◆ To open an icon, click it.

◆ To select an icon, move the pointer over it—don't click.

◆ To select multiple icons, hold down the Ctrl or Shift key while moving the pointer over each desired icon—again, don't click. Ctrl selects individual icons; Shift selects a range of icons.

◆ To rename an icon, point to it; press F2; type the name; then press Enter.

   or

   Right-click it; choose Rename; type the name; then press Enter.

Conserving Power

Environmental and money concerns make power management an issue for desktop as well as laptop users. Control Panel's Power Options utility lets you configure hardware features that reduce power consumption, affect how the power switch works, and extend the life of computer parts by turning them off or switching them to a low-power state. The tabs and controls displayed in the Power Options Properties dialog box depend on the type of computer that you're using (**Figure 4.70**).

Figure 4.70 Power Options detects what's available on your PC and shows you only the options that you can control. A desktop computer has the top set of tabs; a laptop computer has the bottom set.

✔ Tips

■ To use your computer's power-management features, you may have to turn them on in your system BIOS. When you boot your PC you can configure the BIOS by pressing a key combination before Windows starts; read the documentation that came with your computer or motherboard for details, or watch the boot screen carefully for instructions on what key to press. Be quick to press it before Windows starts.

■ If your computer's components don't comply with the industrywide Advanced Configuration and Power Interface (ACPI) specification (also called OnNow), some power-management features may be unavailable or unpredictable. Older, non-ACPI-compliant computers have an APM tab (Advanced Power Management—an older standard) in the Power Options Properties dialog box.

Uninterruptible Power Supply

An Uninterruptible Power Supply (UPS) is a sealed backup battery—connected between the computer and the electrical outlet—that kicks in to keep your computer running if power fails. The UPS's capacity is expressed in minutes available to save your work and shut down normally during a power outage—about 5 minutes for a cheap UPS and up to about 30 minutes for better ones. UPSes also protect against power surges, spikes, and brownouts (low voltage), which damage hardware more than blackouts. Don't forget to plug your monitor into the UPS. You also can plug in a power strip for extra sockets and keep your modem, printer, and electric stapler safe too.

A UPS doesn't really *have* to interact with Windows, but Windows includes built-in support for monitoring that sounds power-failure alerts, displays remaining UPS-battery time, and—if power becomes dangerously low—shuts down the computer automatically. A UPS that plugs into a USB port will install its driver and make the Power Options UPS tab vanish, replacing it with Alarms and Power Meter tabs.

Figure 4.71 The timed power-savings settings depend on the power scheme you choose.

Figure 4.72 The Always Show Icon on the Taskbar option is useful if you're a laptop-computer user who changes between battery and electrical-outlet power occasionally.

To optimize your computer's power use, Windows uses a *power scheme*—a collection of settings that reduces the power consumption of certain system devices or of your entire system. You can use the power schemes provided with Windows or create your own, as you can a desktop theme.

To choose a power scheme:

1. Choose Start > Control Panel > Performance and Maintenance > Power Options > Power Schemes tab (**Figure 4.71**).

2. In the Power Schemes section, choose a scheme from the drop-down list.

3. To customize a power scheme, in the Settings section, change the default time settings.

4. To create a new power scheme, select the time settings that you want; click Save As; type a name; then click OK.

5. To delete a power scheme, select it in the Power Schemes list; then click Delete.

6. Click the Advanced tab (**Figure 4.72**).

7. To put a power-plug (or battery) icon in the notification area, check Always Show Icon on the Taskbar.
   Click this icon to choose a power scheme, or double-click it to open the Power Options utility.

8. To password-protect your computer during standby or hibernation, check Prompt for Password.

9. Click OK (or Apply).

✔ Tips

- On a laptop computer, the Power Schemes tab lets you choose independent settings for battery and plugged-in power.

- Move the mouse or press a key to bring your computer out of standby mode. Press the power button to bring it out of hibernation. Your disks may take a minute to awaken from standby.

- Turning off a monitor makes its screen go dark (and turns the green power light yellow). Turning off a hard disk stops it from spinning.

- Windows puts a computer into Standby more rapidly than it does into Hibernate. This makes sense because you'll want to put the system on standby if you're away briefly and have it hibernate automatically if you're away, say, overnight.

- The details of Stand By and Hibernate modes are listed in Table 1.1 in Chapter 1.

- Older systems may not support standby, hibernation, or software shutdown (powering off without the switch).

Figure 4.73 The Hibernate tab isn't available if your computer doesn't support this feature.

As described in "Logging On and Logging Off" in Chapter 1, you can choose Start > Turn Off Computer to stand by or hibernate manually, but it's faster to use the computer's power or sleep button.

To use the computer's power button to stand by or hibernate:

1. Choose Start > Control Panel > Performance and Maintenance > Power Options > Hibernate tab (**Figure 4.73**).

2. Check Enable Hibernation.

3. Click the Advanced tab (refer to Figure 4.72).

4. In the Power Buttons section, select the action your computer takes when you press the Power or Sleep button.

5. If you're using a laptop computer, choose Stand By from the drop-down list below When I Close the Lid of My Portable Computer.

6. Click OK (or Apply).

For laptop computers, you can set alarms that sound or appear when the battery is almost out of power. Windows gives two distinct warnings: a *low-battery alarm* and the more urgent *critical-battery alarm*. When you hear either you should save your work immediately. The alarm options let you specify which alarms you want (low-battery, critical-battery, or both); how you want to be notified (text, sound, or both); and what the laptop should do in response to the alarm.

To set a warning alarm for a low- or critical-battery condition:

1. Choose Start > Control Panel > Performance and Maintenance > Power Options > Alarms tab (**Figure 4.74**).

2. In the Low Battery Alarm and Critical Battery Alarm sections, check either or both boxes to set the alarms.

3. Drag the slider to change the power-level threshold.

    (Experience with the particular computer helps here.)

4. Click Alarm Action to specify what happens when an alarm goes off (**Figure 4.75**).

5. Click OK (or Apply).

✔ Tip

■ The Power Meter tab offers a graphical "fuel gauge" of remaining battery power, with a separate icon for each battery. Click an icon to get detailed information about that battery.

Figure 4.74 If your battery has a four-hour life, three percentage points is about seven minutes of use, but these settings are approximate.

Figure 4.75 At a critical power level, put your computer in hibernation automatically (thus saving your work if you're away from your PC when the battery dies).

Figure 4.76 The *O* icon indicates an OpenType font; *TT* indicates a TrueType font; and *A* indicates a raster or PostScript font.

Font Utilities

If you work with fonts regularly or your font lists are getting crowded, try a font-management utility such as Suitcase ($100 U.S.; www.extensis.com) or Adobe Type Manager Deluxe ($69; www.adobe.com).

To convert PostScript Type 1 and TrueType fonts between Windows and Mac, try CrossFont ($45; www.asy.com).

To create your own fonts, try Font Creator Program ($50; www.high-logic.com).

For enthusiasts, Metafont, TeX, and LaTeX—the best typography and typesetting software on the planet—is free and available at www.tug.org.

Managing Fonts

Windows includes dozens of fonts used to display text on the screen and in print. Most of these are *TrueType* or *OpenType* fonts that look smooth in all sizes and on all output devices. Windows also supports Adobe's Type 1 fonts for PostScript printers, with no need for Adobe Type Manager. You manage fonts in the Fonts folder.

✔ Tips

- For more font information, visit www.microsoft.com/typography.

- Windows includes a few hideous bitmapped fonts, called *raster* fonts, for compatibility with older programs.

- OpenType fonts also are known as TrueType version 2 fonts.

- To change the fonts used in icons, menus, and other screen elements, see "Choosing a Desktop Theme" earlier in this chapter.

To open the Fonts folder:

- Choose Start > Control Panel > Appearance and Themes; below See Also, click Fonts (**Figure 4.76**).

  or

  In Windows Explorer, open the folder \Windows\Fonts. (\Windows is named \WINNT on some systems.)

✔ Tips

- To match the font names with their file-names, choose View > Details in the Fonts folder.

- To see look-alike fonts, choose View > List Fonts by Similarity.

- To reduce Fonts folder clutter, choose View > Hide Variations (Bold, Italic, Etc.).

To view or print a font:

◆ In the Fonts folder, double-click the font's icon (**Figure 4.77**).

or

In the Fonts folder, select one or more font icons; then press Enter (or choose File > Open).

Windows displays font statistics, the full alphabet, and a type sample at various sizes. Click Print to print a font sample.

✔ Tips

■ Font Viewer displays only a predefined set of characters. To display every character in a font, use Character Map. See "Using the Free Utility Programs" in Chapter 6.

■ Some system fonts (Courier, Symbol, and MS Serif, for example) are hidden because Windows needs them for program windows, dialog boxes, and menus. To view them, in the Fonts folder, choose Tools > Folder Options > View tab > Show Hidden Files and Folders.

■ To view fonts with a program other than Windows Font Viewer, right-click a font icon; choose Properties; then click Change.

To install a new font:

◆ In the Fonts folder, choose File > Install New Font; then navigate to and select the font files to install (**Figure 4.78**).

or

Drag a font file into the Fonts folder.

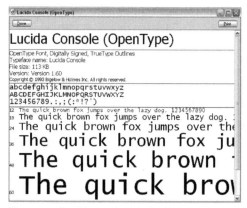

Figure 4.77 Font Viewer shows a font's summary information along with a preview.

Figure 4.78 To install fonts from a network drive without using disk space on your computer, uncheck Copy Fonts to Fonts Folder.

✔ Tips

- After a font is installed, it appears in your programs' Font dialog boxes and lists.

- Windows lets you install only these font types: TrueType (.ttf), OpenType (also .ttf), Adobe Type 1 (.pfm or .pfb), and raster (.fon).

- If a new font appears unexpectedly in your Fonts folder, a recently installed program probably put it there.

To remove a font:

- In the Fonts folder, right-click the font's icon; then choose Delete.

  or

  In the Fonts folder, select one or more font icons; then press Delete (or choose File > Delete).

  or

  Drag one or more font icons out of the Fonts folder (to the Recycle Bin or another folder).

✔ Tips

- If an icon in the Fonts folder has a shortcut arrow, the font is installed but located elsewhere.

- The standard Windows fonts are Courier New (TrueType, including bold, italic, and bold italic), Arial (TrueType, including bold, italic, and bold italic), Times New Roman (TrueType, including bold, italic, and bold italic), Symbol (TrueType), Wingdings (TrueType), MS Serif, and MS Sans Serif.

  If you delete any of the standard fonts, you can restore them by copying icons from the Fonts folder of another Windows computer (pre-XP PCs work fine) or by running Windows Setup.

MANAGING FONTS

Managing Visual Effects and Performance

The Windows interface offers a lot of visual effects such as animation, fading, and shadows. These effects can be entertaining or useful, but they chew up processor time and can degrade performance noticeably (particularly if you're short on RAM or video processor speed). Windows lets you turn off disable individual visual effects, perhaps making your system more responsive. It's worth experimenting.

To turn off visual effects:

1. Choose Start > Control Panel > Performance and Maintenance > System > Advanced tab.

2. In the Performance section, click Settings > Visual Effects tab (**Figure 4.79**).

3. Select Custom; uncheck the boxes for the effects that you want to turn off; then click OK.

4. In the System Properties dialog box, click OK (or Apply).

5. Choose Start > Control Panel > Appearance and Themes > Display > Appearance tab > Effects button.

6. Uncheck the boxes for the effects that you want to turn off; then click OK (**Figure 4.80**).

7. In the Display Properties dialog box, click OK (or Apply).

✔ Tip

■ If you have an elaborate desktop background image, don't turn on Use Drop Shadows for Icon Labels on the Desktop (refer to Figure 4.79, bottom); if you do, you may have trouble reading your desktop icons' text labels.

Figure 4.79 The Performance Options dialog box lets you turn off visual effects.

Figure 4.80 Show Window Contents While Dragging is the most useful effect here, but it can be a drag on responsiveness.

Figure 4.81 A Windows XP desktop with the classic Start menu, Control Panel, and visual style.

Figure 4.82 This setting activates the classic single-column Start menu.

Figure 4.83 Control Panel's task pane lets you remove the extra layer of fluff in category view.

Restoring the Old Windows Look

If you prefer the appearance of Windows 2000, 98, or Me to Windows XP's redesigned interface, you can revert to the classic look (**Figure 4.81**). I've collected the settings here for quick reference. They apply only to the logged-on user.

To switch to the classic Start menu:

◆ Choose Start > Control Panel > Appearance and Themes > Taskbar and Start Menu > Start Menu tab > Classic Start menu option (**Figure 4.82**).

To switch to classic Control Panel view:

1. Choose Start > Control Panel.

2. In the task pane, click Switch to Classic View (**Figure 4.83**).

To hide the task pane in folder windows:

1. Choose Start > Control Panel > Appearance and Themes > Folder Options > General tab.

2. In the Tasks section, select Use Windows Classic Folders (**Figure 4.84**).

To browse folders by using a single window:

1. Choose Start > Control Panel > Appearance and Themes > Folder Options > General tab.

2. In the Browse Folders section, select Open Each Folder in the Same Window (**Figure 4.85**).

To switch to the classic visual style for windows and buttons:

1. Choose Start > Control Panel > Appearance and Themes > Display > Appearance tab.

2. From the Windows and Buttons drop-down list, choose Windows Classic Style (**Figure 4.86**).

Figure 4.84 This option hides the space-consuming task pane in folder windows.

Figure 4.85 This option keeps your desktop from becoming cluttered with folder windows.

Figure 4.86 This setting restores the squared-off, muted look of windows and buttons.

Figure 4.87 The Desktop Items dialog box lets you put system icons back on your desktop.

Figure 4.88 Windows XP still contains a treasure trove of classic-style icons, if you prefer them.

To show My Computer, My Documents, and My Network Places on the desktop:

1. Choose Start > Control Panel > Appearance and Themes > Display > Desktop tab > Customize Desktop button.

2. In the Desktop Icons section, select the icons to show (**Figure 4.87**).

To use earlier versions of desktop icons:

1. Choose Start > Control Panel > Appearance and Themes > Display > Desktop tab > Customize Desktop button (refer to Figure 4.87).

2. Select an icon; click Change Icon; then browse to \Windows\system32\ shell32.dll, which contains most of the old icons (**Figure 4.88**). (\Windows is named \WINNT on some systems.)

✔ Tip

■ When you upgrade to XP, Windows Setup hijacks some file-type associations without telling you. Your default program for .htm and .html (web) files, for example, changes to Internet Explorer. To change your settings back, see "Associating Documents with Programs" in Chapter 6.

RESTORING THE OLD WINDOWS LOOK

Getting General System Information

The General tab in Control Panel's System program is a helpful, information-only window that displays:

◆ The version of Windows installed on your computer (including Service Packs)

◆ The Windows edition (Home, Professional, Media Center, and so on)

◆ Registration information that was entered during Windows Setup

◆ The type and speed of your computer's processor

◆ The total physical memory (RAM) installed on your computer

You'll need some or all of this information when you request tech support over the phone, particularly if you're talking to Microsoft.

To display general system information:

◆ Choose Start > Control Panel > Performance and Maintenance > System > General tab (or press Windows logo key+Break) (**Figure 4.89**).

✔ Tip

■ To get detailed system information, see "Getting System Information" in Chapter 19.

Figure 4.89 The General tab gives information about your Windows version, registration, processor, and RAM.

ORGANIZING FILES AND FOLDERS

Like all modern operating systems, Windows uses files and folders to organize your information so that you aren't overwhelmed by long file lists and can distinguish one set of information from another. A *file* is the basic unit of computer storage; it can be a program, a program's configuration data, a log that the computer itself maintains, or a document that you create or receive. You organize files in containers called *folders* (or *directories*), which can hold additional folders (called *subfolders*) to form a treelike hierarchy. Folders in turn are stored on *disks,* or *volumes*—such as hard drives, floppy disks, CD/DVD drives, USB flash drives, or Zip drives.

Windows creates a few system folders to store its own files and settings but otherwise doesn't care how you structure your tree of folders and files. In this chapter I explain how to use Windows Explorer to navigate and manage your stored information.

Exploring Your Computer

My Computer (**Figure 5.1**), a top-level folder, is the window to your computer's data structure. From it you can open all the files, folders, and disks on your computer (or network), which are categorized as follows:

Files Stored on This Computer lists folders for everyone with a user account on this computer. You see your personal files and folders here. All users can see the community folder named Shared Documents. If you double-click another user's folder that you don't have permissions for, you'll get an error message; see "Sharing Files" in Chapter 17.

Hard Disk Drives lists the hard drives installed on this computer.

Devices with Removable Storage lists floppy, CD, DVD, USB flash, tape, Zip, and other removable media.

Scanners and Cameras shows icons for connected digital cameras and scanners.

Depending on how your PC is configured, more categories (such as Other or Network Drives) may appear.

To see what's on your computer:

1. Choose Start > My Computer.
   or
   Press Windows logo key+E.

2. To see what's on a hard drive, in the Hard Disk Drives section, double-click the drive that you want to see.
   or
   To find a file or folder on a floppy disk, CD, USB flash drive, or other removable media, in the Devices with Removable Storage section, double-click the item you want to see. (You'll get an error message if there's no disk in the drive.)

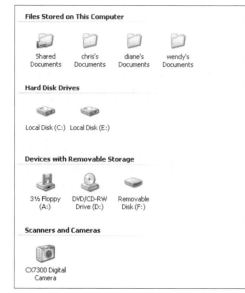

Figure 5.1 The My Computer window shows the top-level folders and disks on your PC, including network drives and other storage devices. Except on factory-fresh computers, no two My Computer folders are ever quite the same.

USB Flash Drives

USB flash drives are small devices that are similar in use to a hard drive; just plug one into a USB port, and its icon appears in My Computer (Removable Disk (F:) in Figure 5.1, for example). USB flash drives are about the size and weight of a car key and have largely supplanted floppy disks and CD-Rs for portable storage. They currently can hold up to 2 GB of data—three times the content of a standard CD (or about 650 three-minute MP3s [33 hours]). Like digital-camera cards, flash drives have no moving parts and can outlast spinning hard disks by years. They cost between $20 and $200 (U.S.), depending on capacity. Some manufacturers give them brand names: the SanDisk Cruzer Mini or Sony Micro Vault, for example. See also "Connecting Devices to Your Computer" in Chapter 8.

or

To find a file or folder, in the Files Stored on This Computer section, double-click a folder.

Keep double-clicking folders to burrow to the file or folder you want. (To return to the previous folder, press Backspace or click the toolbar's Back arrow in the window's top-left corner.)

✔ Tips

■ When you double-click a folder Windows replaces the original window with a new one or opens a separate window atop the current one. Opening new windows makes it easy to move or copy files but clutters the screen quickly. To choose the behavior you prefer, in My Computer, choose Tools > Folder Options > General tab; then select an option in the Browse Folders section.

■ Shift+double-click a My Computer disk or folder icon to jump to Windows Explorer view.

■ To change how My Computer is displayed in the Start menu, see "Customizing the Start Menu" in Chapter 2.

■ To show the My Computer icon on the desktop, see "Restoring the Old Windows Look" in Chapter 4.

■ To show Control Panel in My Computer, see "Using Control Panel" in Chapter 4.

■ You can rename Hard Disk Drives icons.

■ To see how much free space remains on a hard disk, right-click its icon; then choose Properties.

Drive Letters

Like all Windows versions, XP inherits its drive-naming conventions from DOS. Drives are named by a letter followed by a colon:

◆ A: is the first floppy-disk drive.

◆ B: is the second floppy-disk drive (if present).

◆ C: is the first hard-disk drive or the first partition of the first physical hard-disk drive. This drive usually contains Windows itself.

◆ D: through Z: are assigned to other hard-disk drives, CD/DVD drives, mapped network drives, or removable storage devices such as USB flash drives.

Windows assigns drive letters consecutively, but you can use Computer Management to change them; see "Managing Disks" in Chapter 19.

The My Computer folder is the master view of *Windows Explorer,* or simply *Explorer,* the key tool for working with files and folders on your local machine or network.

To open Windows Explorer:

◆ Choose Start > All Programs > Accessories > Windows Explorer (**Figure 5.2**).

or

Right-click the Start button; then choose Explore.

or

Choose Start > Run; type explorer and then press Enter.

During installation Windows Setup creates three top-level system folders:

Documents and Settings contains a subfolder for each user account or for each user who has logged on to a network domain. These subfolders contain the users' personal settings and documents. If you're not an administrator, you can't open other users' subfolders (see Chapter 16). The All Users subfolder stores documents and settings available or common to every user account, administrator or not.

Program Files contains all the programs— Microsoft Word, Internet Explorer, or Adobe Photoshop, for example—that you, Windows Setup, or your PC's manufacturer installed, along with all the support files needed to run those programs. In general you shouldn't need (or want) to touch files in this folder.

Windows (or **WINNT**, if you've upgraded from Windows 2000/NT) contains critical operating-system files. Look but don't touch—with the exception of the Fonts subfolder; see "Managing Fonts" in Chapter 4.

Figure 5.2 The right pane shows the selected folder's contents (or search results). The left pane is an Explorer bar. The Folders bar (shown here) is displayed by default, but you can use the View menu to show other bars.

Printing Directory Listings

Explorer lacks the simple ability to print the contents of a folder (the File menu has no Print command), but you can create a file listing if you're Command Prompt-savvy (see "Using the Free Utility Programs" in Chapter 6). At a prompt, use the cd command to change to the desired directory and then type:

```
dir /a /o:neg /-p > list.txt
```

This command creates the file list.txt in the current directory. Open list.txt in Notepad (or any text editor) for a printable list of the files and folders in the directory. To change the command to suit your preferences, search for *dir* and *command redirection* in Help and Support Center.

Figure 5.3 This setting opens Explorer at the root of the C: drive, but it's more common to specify a personal folder such as "C:\Documents and Settings*<your user name>*\My Documents". If you see the text %SystemRoot% in front of explorer.exe, you can leave it alone or remove it, as desired.

Pathnames

Windows locates and identifies each file or folder by its unique address, called its *pathname* or simply *path*. A pathname is a listing of the folders that lead from the top-level or *root* directory of a disk drive to a particular file or folder. C:\ represents the C drive's root directory, for example. A backslash (\) separates the pathname components. The pathname C:\Documents and Settings\All Users\Documents\ My Pictures\Sample Pictures\Water lilies.jpg traces the route from the file Water lilies.jpg to the C: drive's root directory. For files on a network, the pathname can begin with a double back-slash and a computer or server name instead of a disk drive (\\someserver instead of C:, for example).

The Address toolbar in Windows Explorer displays the pathname of the selected folder. The Target box in a document or program shortcut's Properties dialog box also displays a pathname. You can copy and paste these pathnames if you need them.

✔ Tips

- If "These Files Are Hidden" appears when you click a system folder, click Show the Contents of This Folder to see the folder's contents.

- If you choose Open (instead of Explore) from the Start button's shortcut menu, Explorer opens with the task pane (instead of the Folders bar) displayed.

- If you use Explorer's Favorites menu to view a web page, the menus and toolbars change to those of Internet Explorer (see Chapter 13).

By default Explorer opens with My Documents or Desktop highlighted, but you can modify Explorer's shortcut to highlight a folder of your choice initially.

To open Windows Explorer with a specific folder selected:

1. Right-click a Windows Explorer shortcut (in the Start menu or on the desktop); then choose Properties.

2. In the Target box, type:
   explorer.exe /n, /e, C:*myfolder*
   Replace C:*myfolder* with the pathname of the folder to select initially (**Figure 5.3**). The folder can be on a local, removable, or network drive. If C:*myfolder* contains spaces, surround it with double quotes.

3. Click OK.
   When you double-click the shortcut, Explorer opens with the specified folder highlighted.

✔ Tip

- Another way to open Explorer in a specific folder: Choose Start > Run; type or paste the folder's pathname and then press Enter.

Windows Explorer represents your files, folders, and disks as a hierarchical structure called a *tree* (shown in the Folders bar in the left pane in Figure 5.2). A fully expanded tree is unwieldy, so Explorer shows only the tree's top few levels by default. Use the mouse or keyboard to collapse and expand individual branches selectively.

To navigate folders in Windows Explorer:

◆ To expand or collapse a branch, click the plus sign (+) or minus sign (–) next to a tree icon.

The selected folder's files and nested folders appear in the right pane.

✔ Tips

■ **Table 5.1** lists Explorer's keyboard shortcuts. For more shortcuts, see "Using Keyboard Shortcuts" later in this chapter.

■ If no plus sign appears next to an icon, that branch can't be expanded further because it has no subfolders.

■ If the Folders bar isn't displayed, click Folders on the toolbar (or choose View > Explorer Bar > Folders).

■ If the Folders bar is too narrow to show its contents, drag its right edge of the pane to widen it, or use the horizontal scroll bar at bottom to shift its contents. If you point to a partially hidden folder, a pop-up tip displays its full name.

Table 5.1

Explorer Keyboard Shortcuts	
To	Press
Expand or collapse the selected branch	Right arrow or left arrow
Jump to parent branch without collapsing	Backspace
Jump from top to bottom of expanded branch	Alt+right arrow
Jump from bottom to top of expanded branch	Alt+left arrow
Move up visible branches	Up arrow
Move down visible branches	Down arrow
Expand all branches below selection	* (on numeric pad)
Go to a visible branch	The branch's initial letter
Cycle through visible branches with same initial letter	The initial letter repeatedly
Cycle through the icon pane, folder pane, and address bar	Tab or F6

- Explorer offers information beyond Folders via the View > Explorer Bar submenu. Search displays the Windows search tool; see "Searching for Files and Folders" later in this chapter. Favorites lists your Internet Explorer bookmarks; see "Bookmarking Pages" in Chapter 13. History lists recently visited web pages and recently opened documents, sorted by date; see "Navigating the Web" in Chapter 13.

- If you notice that a folder is missing in Windows Explorer (or that a + appears next to a folder that has no subfolders), press F5 to refresh the display.

- To navigate by using the slightly different method of earlier Windows versions, turn off Simple Folder View. See "Setting Folder Options" later in this chapter.

EXPLORING YOUR COMPUTER

Windows Explorer Alternatives

Windows Explorer is adequate for routine file operations, but power users may prefer an enhanced file-management tool. Third-party alternatives have built-in file search, viewing, compression, synchronization, comparison, download, and other tools. Some good ones are PowerDesk ($50 U.S.; www.v-com.com), Directory Opus ($65; www.gpsoft.com.au), and xplorer² ($28; www.netez.com).

Displaying Links to Common Tasks

The *task pane*, new in XP, occupies the left side of an Explorer window and provides useful commands and links to related locations. Use it to move, copy, or email files; play music; jump to other folders quickly; or get file and folder details, for example (**Figure 5.4**). The task pane is displayed by default; if space is tight you can hide it.

To show or hide the task pane:

1. In Windows Explorer, choose Tools > Folder Options > General tab.

   or

   Choose Start > Control Panel > Appearance and Themes > Folder Options > General tab.

2. Select a Tasks option (**Figure 5.5**).

3. Click OK (or Apply).

✔ Tips

- The task pane is on or off globally; you can't have it appear in some windows but not others.

- Any displayed Explorer bar replaces the task pane. You can't resize the task pane as you can the Folders or Search bar.

- The task pane's Details section (at bottom) acts like a stripped-down Properties dialog box for the selected file or folder. If multiple files are selected, the number of selected files and their total size are displayed.

- You may have to scroll the task pane to see the lower sections.

- To expand or collapse a task-pane section, click the double arrow in the section's top-right corner.

Figure 5.4 The task pane changes dynamically, depending on the selected folder or file. Here, I've selected a music file.

Figure 5.5 Choose Use Windows Classic Folders to hide the task pane in all windows.

182 objects (plus 38 hidden) (Disk free space: 22.1 GB) | 12.5 MB

Figure 5.6 The Windows Explorer status bar shows the number of objects selected, their combined size, and free disk space.

Displaying Summary Information

The *status bar* is the rectangular panel that runs along the bottom of an Explorer window and displays settings and statistics about the selected files, folders, or disks. The status bar is divided into sections that show different information. If you're used to an earlier Windows version, you'll notice that XP hides the status bar by default.

To show or hide the status bar:

◆ In Windows Explorer, choose View > Status Bar to toggle the status bar on or off (**Figure 5.6**).

✔ Tips

■ The status bar displays a short explanation of any menu command that you point to.

■ Double-clicking the status bar's My Computer icon displays the Internet Security Properties dialog box...which makes little sense. Microsoft chose this behavior to make the Windows Explorer status bar act like the Internet Explorer status bar.

■ Status bars appear in many programs—all Microsoft Office and Adobe Creative Suite programs, for example—but their layout and behavior depend on the program. Some sections respond to clicks, double-clicks, or right-clicks; no standard exists. Just try clicking or pointing.

Using Windows Explorer Toolbars

Windows Explorer has three toolbars that you can display in any combination (**Figure 5.7**):

Standard Buttons displays buttons for common Explorer tasks. You can customize these buttons.

Address displays the name or pathname of the selected item. You can type a pathname in the Address text box and press Enter or click Go to go to that item.

Links displays links to Internet Explorer's Favorites > Links folder. You can drag file or web shortcuts onto this toolbar or right-click to delete links.

To show or hide a toolbar:

◆ In Windows Explorer, choose View > Toolbars; then, from the submenu, choose a toolbar to toggle on or off.

or

Right-click any displayed toolbar; then choose a toolbar to toggle on or off.

Drag these handles to move or resize the toolbars.

Links bar   Address bar   Standard Buttons bar

Figure 5.7 The Windows Explorer toolbars.

USING WINDOWS EXPLORER TOOLBARS

✔ Tips

■ To hide the menu bar and all toolbars (except Standard Buttons) and view Explorer full-screen, press F11. Press F11 again to restore toolbars.

■ To remove the redundant Go button from the Address bar, right-click the Go button; then uncheck Go Button. (But don't hurry to do this; the Go button sometimes works better than the Refresh button, even though both controls nominally do the same thing.)

You can rearrange or resize the toolbars and, after you have them looking the way you want, lock them in place.

To move or resize a toolbar:

◆ Drag the vertical dimpled handle on the toolbar's left edge.

✔ Tips

■ To put a toolbar on its own line, drag it up or down.

■ To swap the positions of two toolbars on the same line, drag one of them down; then drag it up to the other side of the second toolbar.

■ You can move the menu bar.

■ If a toolbar is too long to fit in the window, a >> button appears on the toolbar's right edge. Click the button to display the buttons that don't fit.

■ You can't float a toolbar midwindow or dock it against another edge.

■ If you can't move or resize the toolbars, unlock them.

To lock or unlock the toolbars:

◆ Choose View > Toolbars > Lock the Toolbars.

or

Right-click any displayed toolbar; then choose Lock the Toolbars.

✔ Tip

■ The dimpled handle on a toolbar's left edge turns solid when the toolbar is locked.

To customize the Standard Buttons toolbar:

1. Choose View > Toolbars > Customize (**Figure 5.8**).

or

Right-click the Standard Buttons toolbar; then choose Customize.

2. To add a button, select it in the left list; then click Add (or drag it to the right list).

3. To change a button's position, select it in the right list; then click Move Up or Move Down (or drag it to the desired position).

4. To remove a button, select it in the right list; then click Remove (or drag it to the left list).

5. To reposition or hide the buttons' descriptive text, use the Text Options list.

6. To change the size of the toolbar icons, use the Icon Options list.

7. To restore the default set of buttons on the toolbar, click Reset.

8. Click Close.

✔ Tip

■ The left list contains a separator that you can add multiple times to the right list to group buttons logically between vertical bars.

Figure 5.8 If you change the appearance of folders a lot, add a Folder Options button to the Standard Buttons toolbar.

USING WINDOWS EXPLORER TOOLBARS

Figure 5.9 The View menu is available from the menu bar or the toolbar.

Viewing Files and Folders in Different Ways

Explorer lets you view the contents of a folder several ways. You can vary the size of icons, change the details displayed, or view miniature previews of graphics and files, for example. Each view has advantages.

To change the view of a folder's items:

◆ In Windows Explorer, select a folder; then choose a view from the View menu (**Figure 5.9**):

Filmstrip (new in XP) creates a slide show of image files, with the selected file shown as a larger image above the others (**Figure 5.10**).

Thumbnails displays large icons for easy identification (**Figure 5.11**).

Tiles (new in XP) displays large, colorful icons with three lines of text that describe each file (**Figure 5.12**).

continues on next page

Figure 5.10 In Filmstrip view, use the first pair of buttons below the larger image to run forward or backward through the other images in the folder. Use the second pair of buttons to rotate the current picture.

Figure 5.11 Thumbnails view is good for viewing photos, but it's also useful if you want a large icon to click.

Figure 5.12 In Tiles view, the information that appears depends on the file type.

VIEWING FILES AND FOLDERS IN DIFFERENT WAYS

Icons displays items the way icons are shown on the desktop (**Figure 5.13**).

List lists the names of files and folders, preceded by small icons (**Figure 5.14**).

Details displays a columnar list of files, folders, and their properties (**Figure 5.15**).

✔ Tips

■ Right-click an empty area in Explorer's right pane to use the View menu.

■ Filmstrip view is unavailable in Windows Classic Folders. See "Restoring the Old Windows Look" in Chapter 4.

■ In Filmstrip or Thumbnails view, right-click a picture to rotate it or set it as your desktop background via the shortcut menu. Double-click a picture to preview it in Windows Picture and Fax Viewer.

■ You can view pictures as a filmstrip in any My Pictures subfolder or any folder customized as a pictures folder. See "Customizing a Folder" later in this chapter.

■ To make all your folders use the same view, set up one folder the way you want it; then choose Tools > Folder Options > View tab > Apply to All Folders button. You still can apply distinct views to individual folders afterward. (To return all folders to their default views, click Reset All Folders in the same dialog box.)

■ Windows remembers each folder's view when revisited (but forgets the view of seldom-visited folders). To make Windows always forget folder views between visits, choose Tools > Folder Options > View tab > Advanced Settings list > uncheck Remember Each Folder's View Settings. Use Tweak UI's Explorer > Customizations option to set the number of folders to remember. (See the "Tweak UI" sidebar in "Using the Start Menu" in Chapter 2.)

Figure 5.13 Icons view sorts items across rows.

Figure 5.14 List view is the most compact display, showing the most files per window—but it's also the most difficult to select files from.

Figure 5.15 The column headings in Details view list the properties displayed for each file.

Figure 5.16 Explorer offers dozens of properties to display, but a few properties apply only to specific file types.

Figure 5.17 This double-headed arrow appears when you resize the a column by dragging its right-hand vertical divider. To move a column, drag from the column heading's center, not its edge.

Changing the File Details Displayed

Details view contains the most information. By default the columns displayed depend on the type of files in the folder—picture folders show date photographed and image dimensions, for example—but you can choose which columns appear.

To choose details to display:

1. In Windows Explorer, select a folder; then choose View > Details.

2. Choose View > Choose Details; then select the properties that you want to display (**Figure 5.16**).

3. Click OK.

✔ Tips

- Right-click any column heading to choose which columns to display.

- You can reorder columns and set column widths in the Choose Details dialog box, but it's easier to make those changes in the Explorer window itself. To resize a column, drag the column heading's right edge left or right (**Figure 5.17**). To rearrange columns, drag the column headings horizontally.

- Double-click a column's right edge to widen that column just enough to reveal that column's widest item.

Sorting Icons

By default Windows Explorer sorts icons alphabetically by name (listing all folders first, followed by all files), but you can sort them in other ways.

Name	Size	Type	Date Modified
Blue hills.jpg	6 KB	JPEG Image	12/10/2004 11:47 AM
Sunset.jpg	10 KB	JPEG Image	12/10/2004 11:47 AM
Winter.jpg	21 KB	JPEG Image	12/10/2004 11:46 AM
Water lilies.jpg	23 KB	JPEG Image	12/10/2004 11:47 AM

Figure 5.18 Subtle shading indicates the sort column. A small arrow in the column heading points up or down to indicate the sort direction.

To sort icons:

◆ In Windows Explorer, select a folder; choose View > Arrange Icons By; then choose a sorting priority from the submenu:

Name to sort alphabetically by name.

Size to sort by file size, with the smallest first. Folders aren't sorted by size.

Type to sort alphabetically by file type, which keeps files with the same file extension together (.doc for Word files or .exe for programs, for example).

Modified to sort by the date when the file or folder was last modified, with the most recent first.

✔ Tips

■ Right-click an empty area in Explorer's right pane to use the Arrange Icons By menu.

■ In My Computer you can sort by the disks' free space or total size.

■ The Auto Arrange and Align to Grid commands in the Arrange Icons By submenu arrange icons neatly rather than sort them. See "Tidying Your Desktop" in Chapter 2.

Details view offers more sorting options than the other views. You can reverse-sort (from Z to A, for example) and sort by any visible column.

To sort icons in Details view:

◆ Click the heading of the column to sort by.

To reverse the sort order, click the column heading again (**Figure 5.18**).

The sorted column's header shows a small arrowhead pointing up for ascending sort or down for descending sort.

Figure 5.19 These icons are sorted by the dates they were last changed. The Show in Groups feature categorizes them by Today, Yesterday, and so on.

Figure 5.20 When the same icons are sorted by name, they're grouped like a book's index: A, B, C....

Grouping Icons

The Show in Groups feature imposes grouping categories based on how icons are sorted. In a folder sorted by file type, for example, text files appear in one group, Word files appear in another group, and Photoshop files in another. Sorting by size yields, say, Tiny, Small, Medium, and Large groups. Grouping is useful for scanning crowded folders.

To group icons:

◆ In Windows Explorer, select a folder; then choose View > Arrange Icons By > Show in Groups (**Figures 5.19** and **5.20**).

✔ Tips

■ Right-click an empty area in Explorer's right pane to use the Arrange Icons By menu.

■ Grouping isn't available in Filmstrip and List views.

■ Within each time period, the icons in Figure 5.19 are sorted alphabetically by name (listing all folders first, followed by all files).

Customizing a Folder

Windows XP drops the Customize This Folder Wizard of earlier versions in favor of the Customize This Folder command, whose dialog box lets you apply folder templates or custom images. Most of the time, though, you'll be satisfied with the default folder settings.

To customize a folder:

1. In Windows Explorer, select a folder; then choose View > Customize This Folder (**Figure 5.21**).

   or

   Right-click a folder icon; then choose Properties > Customize tab.

2. Select a folder template from the list, and specify whether you want the template applied to all its subfolders as well.

   The Documents template is for generic folders. Other templates are designed for photo, music, or video folders.

3. To place a picture of your choice on a folder in Thumbnails view, click Choose Picture; then navigate to and select an image file.

   If you change your mind, click Restore Default to use default pictures.

4. To change the folder's icon in every view except Thumbnails, click Change Icon; then navigate to and select an icon.

   The icon replaces the standard folder icon.

5. Click OK (or Apply).

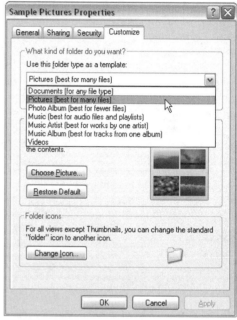

Figure 5.21 The template choice determines the view setting (Tiles, Thumbnails, and so on), task-pane commands, and background image for the folder.

CUSTOMIZING A FOLDER

Figure 5.22 Windows uses up to four images to preview the contents of picture, music, and video folders. For videos, the first frame is displayed. For music downloaded with Windows Media Player, album art is displayed.

✔ Tips

■ Right-click an empty area in Explorer's right pane to choose Customize This Folder.

■ Customize This Folder isn't available for system folders such as Windows (or WINNT), Program Files, Shared Documents, My Documents, and other "Shared" and "My" folders.

■ In Thumbnails view, Windows uses the first four files in a picture, music, or video folder to identify it. The folder's sort order determines which files are displayed (**Figure 5.22**).

Setting Folder Options

Windows offers a trainload of options that control how folders appear and behave. Some options are trivial, but others have default values that can make Windows harder to use.

To set folder options:

1. In Windows Explorer, choose Tools > Folder Options > View tab (**Figure 5.23**).

   or

   Choose Start > Control Panel > Appearance and Themes > Folder Options > View tab.

2. In the Advanced Settings list, select the desired options (**Table 5.2**).

   Changes affect all Explorer windows.

3. To restore the options to their factory settings, click Restore Defaults.

4. Click OK (or Apply).

Figure 5.23 In the Advanced Settings list, you may have to double-click the miniature folder icons to show option groups.

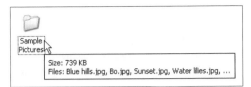

Figure 5.24 A folder tip with size and content information.

Figure 5.25 Turn off Simple Folder View to restore the vertical dotted lines that indicate how deeply a folder is nested.

Figure 5.26 If you click Show the Contents of This Folder in this screen, this warning never reappears, no matter how the option is set.

Table 5.2

Folder Options

Option	Description
Automatically Search for Network Folders and Printers	Turn off this option if you're rarely connected to a network and don't want Windows to scan for network printers, shared folders, and shared disks periodically.
Display File Size Information in Folder Tips	Shows size information in the folder tip that pops up temporarily when your mouse pointer hovers over a folder icon (**Figure 5.24**). If you turn off this option, you still get pop-up contents information; to turn off folder tips, see Show Pop-Up Description for Folder and Desktop Items.
Display Simple Folder View in Explorer's Folders List	When this option is turned on, Windows expands the folder that you click and simultaneously collapses the folder previously expanded. (To stop the previous folder from collapsing, click a plus-sign icon, not a name or folder icon.) I turn off this (misnamed) option to restore the navigation method of earlier Windows versions, which shows vertical lines and never collapses folders automatically (**Figure 5.25**).
Display the Contents of System Folders	By default, Windows displays a "These Files Are Hidden" message when you try to open critical system folders such as Windows or Program Files (**Figure 5.26**). Microsoft added this safety feature to prevent potentially disastrous changes. Turn off this option to suppress the warnings.
Display the Full Path in the Address Bar and Display the Full Path in the Title Bar	When these options are turned on, Explorer shows the selected folder's pathname in the Address bar (if it's showing) and window title bar. The path lets you know where you are in the folder hierarchy; if only *downloads* (rather than C:\Documents and Settings\joe\downloads) appears on a bar, you won't know whose downloads folder you're in. Turn on at least one of these options, preferably the Address bar so you can copy and paste paths. (For information about paths, see "Exploring Your Computer" earlier in this chapter.) If you display the full path on the title bar, Windows also displays the (usually truncated) full path on taskbar buttons too. Hover the pointer over the button to pop up the full path.
Do Not Cache Thumbnails	By default Windows stores the images that appear in Thumbnails view in memory so that it can display them quickly when you revisit the folder. Check this box to free some memory, in exchange for a small delay when opening folders in Thumbnails view.

(table continues on next page)

Figure 5.27 When I save Microsoft's complete home page in Internet Explorer (that is, visit www.microsoft.com, and choose File > Save As), IE creates an HTML file named Microsoft Corporation.htm and a folder named Microsoft Corporation_files that contains the accompanying image (GIF and JPEG) and script files.

Figure 5.28 You can open Control Panel in the Folders bar.

Table 5.2 *continued*

Folder Options

OPTION	DESCRIPTION
Hidden Files and Folders and Hide Protected Operating System Files	By default Windows hides critical files that it doesn't want you to move, delete, or rename. If you show these files, they appear as dimmed icons so you remember to leave them alone. (Technically, a hidden file has its Hidden attribute set, and a system file has its System attribute set.)
Hide Extensions for Known File Types	By default Windows hides the file extension on standard documents and files (.doc for Word files and .exe for programs, for example). Beginners may be tempted to leave this option on to make Windows appear less intimidating, but everyone should turn it off for the reasons discussed in "Associating Documents with Programs" in Chapter 6.
Launch Folder Windows in a Separate Process	By default only one copy of explorer.exe is ever in memory, handling all Explorer windows, the Start menu, the desktop, and much more. Turn this option on to open a new program instance for each Explorer window, so if one crashes, the rest don't. For technical reasons, if the "wrong" one crashes, you may be left without a Start menu and desktop. Favor leaving this option turned off.
Managing Pairs of Web Pages and Folders	When you save a complete web page in Internet Explorer, the page's text is stored in one HTML file, and its images and scripts are stored in a folder named to match (**Figure 5.27**). To make Windows Explorer treat this file-and-folder pair as a single entity, select Show and Manage the Pair As a Single File or Show Both Parts but Manage As a Single File. If you move or delete one item, for example, Windows Explorer takes the same action on the other, maintaining the connection between them. To break the file-and-folder link, select Show Both Parts and Manage Them Individually.
Remember Each Folder's View Settings	Turn on this option to make Explorer remember each folder's view settings independently. If you turn off this option, each folder inherits the view setting from its parent folder.
Restore Previous Folder Windows at Logon	Turn on this option to make Windows Explorer reopen all your previously opened folder windows when you log on. This behavior was automatic in earlier Windows versions but is turned off by default in XP.
Show Control Panel in	Turn on this option to make Control Panel appear in Windows Explorer, below My Computer (**Figure 5.28**).
Show Encrypted or Compressed NTFS Files in Color	Turn on this option to show NTFS-encrypted files and folders in green and NTFS-compressed files and folders in blue. Turn off this option to turn all files black. See "Compressing Files and Folders" and "Encrypting Files and Folders" later in this chapter.
Show Pop-Up Description for Folder and Desktop Items	Turn on this option to see pop-up information about almost any icon you point to. Turn it off if the little yellow pop-up boxes bug you.
PRO Use Simple File Sharing	I turn off this option for security purposes. Never mind that Microsoft recommends it be on. See "Sharing Files" in Chapter 17.

Creating Folders

Here are a few tips for organizing your files and folders:

Use My Documents. Use My Documents as the root folder for all your personal folders and documents, for the reasons given in "Saving Documents" in Chapter 6.

Nest folders deeply. If you create a shallow or "flat" folder structure, you're forced to use long, descriptive filenames rather than succinct ones. A flat structure also makes you fill folders with so many subfolders that it's hard to discern the structure quickly.

Ignore file types. Store all related documents in the same project folder regardless of the programs that created them.

Reduce clutter. Don't store documents on the desktop. Reserve your desktop for only shortcuts to your pending projects. In general, don't put anything—even shortcuts—in the root C:\ folder.

To create a folder:

1. In Windows Explorer, pick a location for a new folder.

2. Choose File > New > Folder.

   or

   Right-click an empty area in the right pane; then choose New > Folder (**Figure 5.29**).

   or

   In the task pane, click Make a New Folder.

3. Type a name for the new folder; then press Enter.

   You can use the Cut, Copy, and Paste keyboard shortcuts (Ctrl+X, Ctrl+C, and Ctrl+V) while editing.

✔ Tips

- To create a new folder on the desktop, right-click an empty area on the desktop; then choose New > Folder.

- The File > New submenu lets you create new empty documents too, depending on which programs are installed. Use Tweak UI's Templates options to set which document types appear. (See the "Tweak UI" sidebar in "Using the Start Menu" in Chapter 2.)

Figure 5.29 You can create a folder inside another folder, on the desktop, at the root of a hard disk, or on a USB flash drive or floppy.

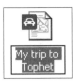

Figure 5.30 To replace the current name, just start typing. To change a few characters in the existing name, use the arrow keys to move to a specific position; then insert, delete, cut, or paste characters.

Naming Files and Folders

You can rename a file or folder to make its name longer, shorter, or more explicit.

To rename a file or folder:

1. In Explorer, select the file or folder that you want to rename.

2. Choose File > Rename (or press F2).

   or

   Right-click the file or folder; then choose Rename.

   or

   In the task pane, click Rename This File (or Rename This Folder).

   or

   Click the file or folder's name (not its icon).

3. Type a new name; then press Enter (or click outside the name area) (**Figure 5.30**).

   You can use the Cut, Copy, and Paste keyboard shortcuts (Ctrl+X, Ctrl+C, and Ctrl+V) while editing.

✔ Tips

- You can rename a file or folder in the General tab of its Properties dialog box.

- Press Esc while editing to revert to the original name.

- You can't rename system folders such as Documents and Settings, Windows (or WINNT), and System32.

- If the folder option Hide Extensions for Known File Types is turned off, you must retype the file extension when renaming the file; otherwise, Windows tracks the file association automatically. See "Setting Folder Options" earlier in this chapter.

Naming Rules and Tricks

A file or folder name can contain up to 255 characters, including the extension (the part after the dot). Spaces and punctuation are permitted but names can't contain these characters: \ / : * ? " < > |. (Note that this paragraph contains 255 characters.)

A folder can't contain two items with the same name. Windows is case-insensitive (it considers MyFile.txt and myfile.txt to be identical), but it preserves the case of each letter.

If you select multiple items and rename one of them to, say, MyFile.txt, Windows renames the others MyFile (1).txt, MyFile (2).txt, and so on. If you bulk-rename a bunch of files accidentally, press Ctrl+Z repeatedly to revert to the original names.

Better File Rename ($30 U.S.; www.publicspace.net/windows/ BetterFileRename) and Lupas Rename (free; www.azheavymetal.com/~lupasrename) are tools for major surgery on filenames. You can find and replace a common phrase in a set of filenames, for example, or add dates and sequence numbers to them. A preview feature lets you see your changes before you commit them.

NAMING FILES AND FOLDERS

Moving and Copying Files and Folders

You can move or copy files and folders to reorganize your folder structure, make back-up copies in a safe location, or move files to the Shared Documents folder to share them with other users. To copy or move items, you must select (highlight) them. For an icon-selection refresher, see "Icons" in Chapter 1.

To move or copy items by choosing a destination:

1. In Windows Explorer, select the item(s) that you want to move or copy.

2. To move the items, choose Edit > Move to Folder (or click Move This File or Move This Folder in the task pane).

   To copy the items, choose Edit > Copy to Folder (or click Copy This File or Copy This Folder in the task pane).

3. Navigate to the destination folder; then click Move (or Copy) (**Figure 5.31**).

Figure 5.31 Windows Explorer gives you several ways to move and copy files, but using a highlighted target is the easiest and most consistent.

Figure 5.32 Here, I'm dragging the file Pyrenees.jpg from Desktop to My Pictures. The destination folder in the left pane darkens automatically as the pointer moves on or close to it. If you hover briefly over a folder that contains subfolders, it will expand.

Figure 5.33 Right-dragging to copy or move items is safer than left-dragging.

To move or copy items by using Cut, Copy, and Paste:

1. In Windows Explorer or on the desktop, select the item(s) that you want to move or copy.

2. To move the items, press Ctrl+X (or right-click a selected item and choose Cut).

   To copy the items, press Ctrl+C (or right-click a selected item and choose Copy).

3. Select the destination folder, disk, or window.

4. Press Ctrl+V (or right-click an empty area and choose Paste).

To move or copy items by dragging:

1. Make sure that the destination folder, disk, or window is visible.

2. In Windows Explorer or on the desktop, select the item(s) that you want to copy or move.

3. Right-drag the items to the destination; then release the right mouse button.

4. Choose Move Here or Copy Here from the shortcut menu (**Figures 5.32** and **5.33**).

You can use the *left* mouse button and drag normally to copy or move items (bypassing the shortcut menu), but the rules that determine whether an item is actually moved or copied are confusing:

◆ If you drag an item to another place on the same disk, it's moved.

◆ If you drag an item from one disk to another, it's copied, not moved.

- To copy an item instead of moving it, hold down Ctrl while dragging.

- To move the item instead of copying it, hold down Shift while dragging.

- If you drag a system icon such as My Computer or Control Panel, it's never moved or copied; instead, a shortcut is created.

Got all that? Me neither. That's why it's easier to *right*-drag to copy or move items.

✔ Tips

- You can move or copy items anywhere on your computer or network, so long as you have privileges to do so.

- If you copy an item to the folder in which it already exists, Windows creates a duplicate named Copy of *<itemname>*.

- You can drag items between Explorer windows, or cut or copy from one window and paste to another.

- Items appear dimmed when they're cut, but they don't actually move until you paste them somewhere. Press Esc to cancel a cut.

- Press Esc during a drag to cancel it.

MOVING AND COPYING FILES AND FOLDERS

Figure 5.34 The Send To menu often is faster than dragging and dropping. Windows adds destinations for removable media automatically. The bottom three menu items are a floppy disk, CD writer, and USB flash drive.

Sending Files and Folders

One of the handiest file-management tools is the Send To menu, which lets you send a copy of a file or folder quickly to:

◆ A floppy disk or USB flash drive

◆ Your desktop (as a shortcut)

◆ Another person via email

◆ Your My Documents folder (or any folder)

◆ A compressed (zipped) folder (see "Compressing Files and Folders" later in this chapter)

◆ Other destinations, depending on the programs installed

To send an item:

1. In Windows Explorer or on the desktop, select the item(s) that you want to send.

2. Right-click one item; choose Send To; then choose a destination from the submenu (**Figure 5.34**).

✔ Tips

■ In Explorer, Send To is available in the File menu.

■ To move an item instead of copying it, hold down Shift when you right-click.

If you perform the same file-management tasks regularly, you can add your own destinations to the Send To menu by adding new shortcuts to your Send To folder (which is hidden by default). Every user on your computer has a separate Send To folder. The destination determines what happens to the item being sent. If the destination is a program, for example, the program is launched with the selected file open. For folder and disk destinations, items are copied.

To add a destination to the Send To menu:

1. Choose Start > My Computer > Local Disk (C:) > Documents and Settings > *<your user name>*.

If Windows is installed on a drive other than C:, choose that drive instead.

2. If the Send To folder is hidden, choose Tools > Folder Options > View tab > Show Hidden Files and Folders.

3. Add the desired shortcuts to the folder (or choose File > New > Shortcut) (**Figure 5.35**).

4. Close the window when you're done adding shortcuts.

✔ Tips

■ If you have a lot of destinations, you can nest folders to create Send To sub-submenus.

■ You can create Send To shortcuts to shared folders on other machines on your network.

■ If you put a shortcut to the Send To folder in the Send To folder itself, you can create Send To destinations quickly by sending them to the Send To folder.

Figure 5.35 Here, I've added a few custom destinations to the standard ones. The Notepad shortcut opens any file in Notepad, regardless of the file's type. The Backups shortcut copies files to a safe place. The printer (HP LaserJet) shortcut prints documents with no need to open their associated applications.

Figure 5.36 The Recycle Bin's icon tells you whether it contains deleted items.

Deleting Files and Folders

When you delete a file or folder, it's not actually erased but compressed and stored in the Recycle Bin on the desktop (**Figure 5.36**). The Recycle Bin is a safeguard from which you can restore (undelete) items if you change your mind or delete them permanently.

To delete items:

1. In Windows Explorer or on the desktop, select the item(s) that you want to delete.

2. Choose File > Delete (or press Delete).

or

Right-click one item; then choose Delete.

3. If an "Are you sure?" message appears, click Yes.

✔ Tips

■ You also can drag items to the Recycle Bin to delete them.

■ To suppress the "Are you sure?" message, right-click the Recycle Bin; then choose Properties > Global tab and check Display Delete Confirmation Dialog.

■ To delete selected items without sending them to the Recycle Bin, press Shift+Delete.

■ You can bypass the Recycle Bin so that all deleted files are erased immediately (good for using a public computer): Right-click the Recycle Bin icon; then choose Properties > Global tab and check Do Not Move Files to the Recycle Bin.

■ Some programs let you delete items within Open and Save As dialog boxes.

■ Items deleted from network drives and removable disks (such as floppies and USB flash drives) bypass the Recycle Bin, as do deletions via the command-line del and erase commands.

DELETING FILES AND FOLDERS

185

To empty the Recycle Bin:

1. Double-click the Recycle Bin icon (**Figure 5.37**).

2. To remove all items, choose File > Empty Recycle Bin (or click Empty the Recycle Bin in the task pane).

   or

   To remove some items, Ctrl+click each item to remove (or click only one item); then press Delete (or choose File > Delete).

3. Click Yes in the "Are you sure?" message.

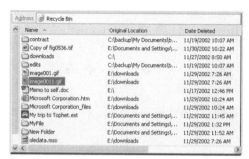

Figure 5.37 Details view tells you when items were deleted and where from.

✔ Tips

- The Delete command also is available in a Recycle Bin item's shortcut menu.

- To empty the Recycle Bin quickly without inspecting its contents, right-click its icon on the desktop; then choose Empty Recycle Bin. (You can't suppress the "Are you sure?" message.)

Undead Files

Deleting files doesn't actually destroy their data—it just makes them harder to find. When you empty the Recycle Bin, Windows doesn't erase files but, rather, *marks* them as deleted, making them invisible to you and to programs but leaving their data intact on disk. Only when Windows later needs disk space will it overwrite deleted files with newly created ones. On a large or sparsely populated drive, deleted files may survive for weeks or months before Windows reclaims the disk space (unless you defragment the disk, which overwrites most deleted files).

To recover deleted files, use an undelete utility soon after you've emptied the Recycle Bin. Some popular ones are FileRestore ($39 U.S.; `www.winternals.com`), Undelete ($30; `www.executive.com`), and PC Inspector File Recovery (free; `www.pcinspector.de/file_recovery/uk/welcome.htm`).

On the other hand, use a *file shredder* to make your files *un*recoverable. File shredders—useful if you're selling your PC or expecting an arrest warrant—overwrite deleted files or entire disks with random data. Shredders let you overwrite a few times (to defeat ordinary undelete software) or many times (to defeat an electron microscope). To shred files, try Eraser (free; `www.heidi.ie/eraser`) or Sure Delete (free; `www.wizard-industries.com`).

Note that Windows' `format` (formerly `fdisk`) command won't shred files. If utterly destroying your data is crucial—you know who you are—smash your hard disk and throw the pieces in a river.

Figure 5.38 Every disk has its own Recycle Bin. If you have more than one drive or have a partitioned drive, you can select Configure Drives Independently and click the separate tabs to set each disk's junk limit.

To restore items from the Recycle Bin:

1. Double-click the Recycle Bin icon (refer to Figure 5.36).

2. Ctrl+click the items that you want to restore (or click only one item).

3. To restore items to their original locations, choose File > Restore (or click Restore the Selected Items or Restore This Item in the task pane).

   or

   To restore items to a specific location, drag them out of the Recycle Bin to the desired folder (in an Explorer window or on the desktop).

✔ Tip

■ The Restore command also is available in a Recycle Bin item's shortcut menu.

The Recycle Bin stores deleted items until it runs out of space, at which point the items are removed automatically, oldest first, to accommodate new items. By default the size of the Recycle Bin folder is 10 percent of the hard drive, but you can change that percentage.

To change the Recycle Bin's capacity:

1. Right-click the Recycle Bin icon; then choose Properties (**Figure 5.38**).

2. On the Global tab, drag the slider to specify how much of each drive can be allocated to the Recycle Bin.

✔ Tips

■ On high-capacity drives 10 percent is a lot of space. On a 100 GB disk, for example, 10 percent is 10 GB of junk. One or two GB should be enough unless you have a lot of music or video files.

■ The Recycle Bin's status bar (choose View > Status Bar) shows how much space the deleted items occupy.

DELETING FILES AND FOLDERS

Compressing Files and Folders

Compressing files and folders reduces the space they occupy on your drives (fixed or removable). Windows offers two compression schemes: Microsoft's proprietary NTFS compression (the same as in Windows 2000) and industry-standard zipped folders (new in XP). You can use either scheme or both; each has its relative advantages. NTFS compression is simple, transparent, and suitable for everyday use, whereas zipped folders are best for:

◆ Emailing large attachments

◆ Archiving files that you no longer need regularly

◆ Transferring files over the internet or via FTP

◆ Gaining the maximum amount of disk space

◆ Compressing encrypted files

NTFS compression

Some important points about NTFS compression are:

◆ It's available only on NTFS-formatted drives, not FAT or FAT32 drives (**Figure 5.39**). See "Getting Ready to Install Windows XP" in the appendix.

◆ You can compress individual files and folders or an entire NTFS drive.

◆ It's easy to use but doesn't save much disk space compared with Zip compression.

Figure 5.39 To determine whether a drive is formatted with NTFS, choose Start > My Computer; right-click a drive; then choose Properties. The file system appears on the General tab.

- NTFS-compressed files and folders act normally in Explorer, programs, and dialog boxes. Windows decompresses and compresses files invisibly and on the fly when you open and close them, at the cost of a small (probably not noticeable) performance hit.

- Don't compress system files in the Windows (or WINNT) folder, because XP uses them frequently.

- If you send an NTFS-compressed file to a non-NTFS disk (via email or dragging, for example), XP expands it to its normal size automatically and invisibly. A file sent to a compressed folder or disk is compressed automatically.

- Windows XP disposes of the awful DriveSpace compression scheme from Windows 9x.

- **PRO** NTFS-compressed files can't be EFS-encrypted (but you *can* encrypt zipped folders). See "Encrypting Files and Folders" later in this chapter.

COMPRESSING FILES AND FOLDERS

To NTFS-compress a file, folder, or drive:

1. Close all files to be compressed.

2. To compress individual files or folders, select their icons in Windows Explorer; right-click one of the selected items; then choose Properties > General tab, click the Advanced button, and check Compress Contents to Save Disk Space (**Figure 5.40**).

   or

   To compress a drive, right-click its icon in My Computer; then choose Properties > General tab and check Compress Drive to Save Disk Space (refer to Figure 5.39).

3. In the Confirm Attribute Changes dialog box, indicate whether you want to compress subfolders too (**Figure 5.41**).

✔ Tips

- Compressing an entire hard disk may take hours. Close all programs before you start; otherwise, Windows halts mid-process to ask you to quit a program.

- To display compressed files and folders in a different color in Windows Explorer, choose Tools > Folder Options > View tab and check Show Encrypted or Compressed NTFS Files in Color. You can use Tweak UI's Explorer > Colors options to change the color. (See the "Tweak UI" sidebar in "Using the Start Menu" in Chapter 2.)

Figure 5.40 If the Advanced button is missing, the selected file or folder isn't on an NTFS drive.

Figure 5.41 Usually, you'll want to compress all subfolders too.

Figure 5.42 An archive looks like a folder, except with a zipper. An archive has a .zip file extension.

Name	Type	Packed	Size	Ratio
Beethoven's 9th.wma	Windows Media Audio file	605,951	618,330	2%
Chapter 4.doc	Microsoft Word Document	44,319	170,496	74%
plutarch.pdf	Adobe Acrobat Document	3,652,431	3,836,764	5%
Water lilies.jpg	JPEG Image	49,493	66,235	25%
web_utilities.html	HTML File	20,610	63,563	68%

Figure 5.43 Details view provides compression information about each file. The Ratio column tells you how much smaller a zipped file is relative to its uncompressed size.

Zipped folders

If you've used the popular WinZip program, you're familiar with the concept of compressing files and folders in Zip format. Some important points about Zip files are:

◆ A zipped folder, called an *archive*, is a collection of files compressed and combined into a single file (**Figure 5.42**).

◆ You can create archives on any drive, not just an NTFS drive. Archives stay compressed when you send them elsewhere. Mac and Unix users can work with them too.

◆ Zipping squashes files much smaller than NTFS compression does. Zipping most image, music, and PDF files won't save much space because they're already compressed, but program, web-page, text, word-processing, spreadsheet, database, bitmap, and WAV audio files shrink a lot.

◆ Though they're actually files, zipped folders still behave like folders in several ways. Double-click an archive to see what's in it (**Figure 5.43**). Double-clicking a document in the archive opens a read-only copy of it; choose File > Save As to save a copy elsewhere. (Or extract it from the archive to work with the original.)

◆ You can password-protect archives to prevent others from extracting files.

To create a new zipped folder:

1. In Explorer, select where you want to create the new archive.

2. Choose File > New > Compressed (Zipped) Folder.

   or

   Right-click an empty area in the right pane; then choose New > Compressed (Zipped) Folder.

3. Type a name for the new archive (keep the .zip extension, if it appears); then press Enter.

✔ Tip

■ To create a zipped folder on the desktop, right-click an empty area; then choose New > Compressed (Zipped) Folder.

To create a new zipped folder from existing files or folders:

1. In Explorer, select the file(s) or folder(s) that you want to archive.

2. Right-click one of the selected items; then choose Send To > Compressed (Zipped) Folder.

To add files or folders to a zipped folder:

1. In Explorer, select the zipped folder that you want to add files or folders to.

2. Right-drag the file(s) into the zipped folder; then choose Copy Here or Move Here.

WinZip

If you zip files only occasionally, Windows' built-in tools work fine; otherwise, get a copy of WinZip ($29 U.S.; www.winzip.com), a superior utility that can:

◆ Zip and email in a single step

◆ Create self-extracting (.exe) archives that unpack themselves automatically when double-clicked

◆ Use wildcard file specifications—like *.doc (Word files) or *.mp3 (MP3s)— to bulk-add files to an archive instead of adding them one by one

◆ Split large archives across disks for easy reassembly later

◆ Encrypt and password-protect archives

◆ Work with many compression standards, not just Zip

WinZip and zipped folders can coexist. When installed, WinZip takes over the .zip file extension and becomes the main way to handle Zip archives (see also "Associating Documents with Programs" in Chapter 6). To reassign .zip back to Windows, in Explorer, choose Tools > Folder Options > File Types tab, select ZIP in the Extensions column, and click the Change button. In the Open With dialog box that appears, choose Compress (Zipped) Folder; then click OK in each open dialog box. Windows is now associated with the .zip extension, but you still can use WinZip by right-clicking a zipped folder.

Sidebar label: COMPRESSING FILES AND FOLDERS

Figure 5.44 Use the Extraction Wizard to specify a destination folder.

To password-protect a zipped folder:

1. Select any item in a zipped folder (not the folder itself).

2. Choose File > Add a Password; then complete the Add Password dialog box. The password applies to every file in the archive.

✔ Tips

- New files added to the zipped folder *aren't* password-protected. To protect them, choose File > Remove Password before adding new files; then reinstate the password. The Has a Password column in Details view indicates a file's password status.

- Password-protection prevents only file *extraction*. Other people can still view a protected archive's filenames and even delete the files, bypassing the Recycle Bin.

To extract files and folders from a zipped folder:

- To extract only some files or folders, double-click the zipped folder to open it; then drag the files or folders to a new location, where they return to their original sizes.

  or

  To extract all files and folders, right-click the zipped folder in Explorer; then choose Extract All (**Figure 5.44**).

✔ Tips

- If a zipped folder window is already open, click Extract All Files in the task pane.

- To compress digital photos for email, see "Emailing Photos" in Chapter 9.

Searching for Files and Folders

Even if you organize your files and folders logically, sooner or later you'll need to find something—newly installed software, a download, or a file whose location you forgot, for example. Often, you'll also want to find all files that meet certain criteria—all or part of a filename, approximate size, modification date, type, and so on.

Search Companion

Windows' built-in Search Companion can find printers, people, and other computers on your network. In this section, I describe how to find files and folders.

To open Search Companion:

◆ On the desktop, choose Start > Search, press F3, or press Windows logo key+F (**Figure 5.45**).

or

In Explorer, press Ctrl+E, press F3, or click the Search toolbar button, or choose View > Explorer Bar > Search.

✔ Tips

■ To widen or narrow the search pane, drag its right edge.

■ To get rid of the animated dog, click the dog itself; then click Turn Off the Animated Character in the menu that appears.

■ Windows veterans prefer the Windows 2000-style interface, which offers the same search options without the hand-holding screens. To invoke it, in Search Companion, choose Change Preferences > Change Files and Folders Search Behavior > Advanced and click OK.

Figure 5.45 The Search Companion occupies the left pane of Windows Explorer, where it replaces the taskbar or Folders bar when visible.

SEARCHING FOR FILES AND FOLDERS

Figure 5.46 The initial Search Companion screen offers specialized searches for digital media (MP3s, JPEGs, WMAs, and so on) or documents (no folders and no program, hidden, help, or system files). Each search entails its own default settings and screens. All Files and Folders is the broadest, most versatile search.

Figure 5.47 Each option that you specify narrows the search.

To search for a file or folder:

1. In Search Companion, click All Files and Folders (**Figure 5.46**).

2. Enter basic search criteria (**Figure 5.47**):

   To search by filename, type the filename or a distinctive part of it in the All or Part of the File Name text box.

   To search by text *inside* files (which can be slow without indexing), type a distinctive word or phrase in the A Word or Phrase in the File text box.

   From the Look In list, choose the drive, folder, or network to search.

continues on next page

3. To narrow this search, click the double down arrows to specify more restrictive criteria (**Figure 5.48**).

4. Click the Search button.

   Search Companion lists the matches progressively in the right pane (**Figure 5.49**). During the search, which can take seconds or minutes, the Search button turns into the Stop button, which you can click at any time.

5. To open a match's parent folder, right-click it and choose File > Open Containing Folder.

   Otherwise, you can treat the results list as you would an ordinary Explorer window. Point to an item for pop-up information, double-click it to open it, drag an item to move or copy it, right-click it for its shortcut menu, click a column heading to sort, and so on.

6. To save the current criteria for repeated searches, choose File > Save Search.

   Search Companion creates a .fnd file (by default, in your My Documents folder). To search again, double-click a .fnd file; then click Search.

Figure 5.48 You can specify a range of dates when the file was modified, search for files of a specified size, or choose among advanced options. Subfolders and system folders (but not hidden folders) are searched by default.

Figure 5.49 The Search Results list contains files and folders that match the criteria. If Search Companion returns the wrong matches (or no matches or too many matches), use the Refine This Search links to try again with more or less restrictive criteria. (Refine This Search does the *entire* search again; it doesn't look in only the current results.)

✔ Tips

- Search Companion searches the Recycle Bin too.

- The results list sometimes contains duplicate entries for files in your My Documents folder.

- You don't have to wait until a search ends before you open or use a file in the results list.

- After a search finishes, if you delete a file or folder or change it so that it no longer meets the search criteria, it disappears from the results list automatically (or appears in it if the change meets the criteria).

- You can use *wildcard characters* to represent one or more filename characters when you don't know what the real character is or don't want to type the entire name. ? substitutes for any single character, and * substitutes for zero or more characters. Type *.do?, for example, to find all files that end in .doc (Word documents) or .dot (Word templates). chapter*.doc finds all Word documents that begin with the word *chapter,* followed by any characters (or no characters).

Indexing

As described in step 2 of "To search for a file or folder," Search Companion lets you search for text *inside* files whose contents you remember but whose names you forget. Fortunately, Windows' indexing service accelerates exhaustive string searches (typically by orders of magnitude). Indexing Service, turned off by default, silently and automatically collects information from the documents on your hard drive and compiles a database, or *catalog*, of file contents. The tradeoff for slashing search time is that Windows must maintain a catalog file that's about 25 percent of the size of the indexed files.

To turn on Indexing Service:

◆ Open Search Companion; then choose Change Preferences > With Indexing Service (for Faster Local Searches) , click Yes, Enable Indexing Service, and then click OK (**Figure 5.50**).

✔ Tips

■ Indexing Service indexes only *your* documents and shared documents. It ignores other users' documents.

■ Indexing Service ignores case. Search Companion can't perform case-sensitive searches with the service running.

■ Indexing Service ignores noise words such as *a, the, to,* and *be,* as well as common pronouns, prepositions, conjunctions, and articles. You can include these words in the search text, but Search Companion treats them as placeholders rather than literal words.

Figure 5.50 Indexing Service updates and maintains its indexes automatically, without your intervention. If the service is busy updating itself, Search Companion performs an ordinary, unindexed search. Updates take lots of time and power but occur only when your PC has been idle for a while. (The initial index may take a few hours.)

- By default Indexing Service catalogs text files, HTML files (their text only), Microsoft Office documents (Office 95 and later), and internet email and news. Third-party filters can index other types of files too. Adobe's free IFilter indexes PDF files; download it from the Acrobat for Windows section of www.adobe.com/support/downloads. To find other filters, search for *indexing service filters* on Google.

- For advanced indexing, go to http://support.microsoft.com/?kbid=317586, "HOW TO: Optimize Indexing Service Performance in Windows 2000."

If you turn off Indexing Service (by disabling it in Figure 5.50), the indexes remain intact. Delete the indexes to save disk space if you don't intend to use indexing again.

To delete indexes:

1. Choose Start > Control Panel > Performance and Maintenance > Administrative Tools > Computer Management > Services and Applications > Indexing Service.

   or

   Choose Start > Run; type ciadv.msc and then press Enter.

   A list of catalogs appears, showing information such as catalog size in megabytes. Each catalog is a different index; most of the time the list contains only one catalog.

2. Right-click the catalog to delete, choose Delete, and then click Yes in the confirmation message.

Other search tools

Search Companion is inadequate for many types of searches; you can't use it to search for all Beethoven MP3s recorded at a particular bit rate, for example. Fortunately, other programs let you search by using sophisticated criteria. The file-management tools described in the "Windows Explorer Alternatives" sidebar in "Exploring Your Computer" earlier in this chapter all have enhanced search features. Some dedicated index-based file finders are blinkx (free; www.blinkx.com), X1 Search ($75 U.S.; www.x1.com), and dtSearch Desktop ($199; www.dtsearch.com).

Google Desktop Search (free; http://desktop.google.com) uses Google's internet search technology to provide a full text search over your email, Office documents, chats, text files, and the web pages that you've viewed. After downloading GDS, you can use Google to search your personal items the way you search the internet (**Figure 5.51**). Microsoft's competing tool, MSN Toolbar Suite (free; http://toolbar.msn.com), places individual search boxes within Outlook, Internet Explorer, Windows Explorer, and the taskbar. Yahoo! offers a free desktop search tool at http://desktop.yahoo.com.

Figure 5.51 Google Desktop Search stores the index that it creates on your own computer.

Google Desktop Search Risks

Google Desktop Search doesn't make your home computer's content accessible to Google or anyone else, but if you use a public, workplace, or other shared computer for email, instant messaging, or web searches, the people who follow you on the PC can see your information (such as online purchases) in the files that GDS indexed. A multicolored swirl ( ) in the taskbar's notification area (system tray) means GDS is running; right-click it to exit the program and prevent it from recording your web, email, and chat sessions.

The GDS help page (http://desktop.google.com/support) answers privacy questions and lists the program files that GDS indexes. You're safe if you use programs that are not on the list, such as (currently) non-AOL chat or a non-Microsoft browser (Mozilla Firefox or Opera).

Searching for Files and Folders

Figure 5.52 When you insert a blank CD, Windows displays this dialog box. Click OK to open a temporary folder that acts as an intermediate staging area for the items to be copied to the CD.

Figure 5.53 The CD Drive window contains the queue of files ready to be copied to the CD. A small down arrow marks items that are ready to be burned.

Copying Files and Folders to CDs

If your PC has a recordable (CD-R) or rewritable (CD-RW) CD drive, Windows lets you copy—or *burn*—files or folders to a recordable CD without the need for third-party software. CDs are excellent for backing up files (they're durable, capacious, and inexpensive) or for exchanging files with Unix and Mac users (CDs are cross-platform).

This section talks about copying *data* files to CDs. To burn *music* CDs, use Windows Media Player. See "Burning Music CDs" in Chapter 10.

To copy files and folders to a CD:

1. Insert a blank CD into the recordable CD drive (**Figure 5.52**).

2. In Windows Explorer, right-click a file or folder (or selection of files and folders) that you want to copy to the CD; then choose Send To > CD Drive.

3. Repeat step 2 for all the items that you want to copy to the CD.

4. Activate the CD Drive window, or if it has disappeared, choose Start > My Computer; then double-click the CD icon (**Figure 5.53**).

continues on next page

5. In the task pane, click Write These Files to CD to start the CD Writing Wizard (**Figure 5.54**).

6. Name the CD, and click Next to start writing files to the CD. (If you're given the option, don't bother creating a HighMAT-compatible CD for a data disc.)

A progress page appears.

7. When the wizard finishes writing the CD, click Finish (**Figure 5.55**).

✔ Tips

■ As an alternative to the Send To command in step 2, you can drag items into the CD Drive folder or use the Copy and Paste commands.

■ To burn a CD, you need temporary free disk space at least twice the size of the items to be copied; otherwise, you'll get a "Cannot complete writing" error from the wizard.

■ The items in the Files Ready to Be Written to the CD list (refer to Figure 5.53) are stored in the hidden folder C:\Documents and Settings\<*your user name*>\Local Settings\Application Data\Microsoft\CD Burning.

■ Calculate the total size of the items before you start copying. In the CD Drive window, press Ctrl+A; then inspect Total File Size in the task pane's Details box. Standard CDs hold around 650 MB. A high-capacity CD holds 800 to 850 MB.

■ After you create a CD, test it immediately to see whether you can use the disc. (CD writers are unreliable.)

Figure 5.54 This page allows you to give the CD a name (up to 16 characters) more meaningful than the current date. You can't change the name of even a CD-RW disc after it has been recorded the first time.

Figure 5.55 In the final page, you can make another copy of the same CD. Click Finish to close the wizard or start copying again, as appropriate.

- If you decide not to create the CD, in the CD Drive window, click Delete Temporary Files in the task pane to clear the storage area.

- Some files contain extra information called *metadata*—the bit rate of an audio track or the dimensions of an image, for example—that can't be copied to a CD. If you get a stream-loss error from the wizard, you can copy the file without the metadata rather than skip it entirely.

- For more recording features, use a program such as Roxio Easy Media Creator ($80 U.S.; www.roxio.com).

Making Network Files and Folders Available Offline

PRO The Offline Files feature isn't available in Windows XP Home edition. Home-edition users can synchronize files with Briefcase, inherited from Windows 98/Me. It's not as easy to use as Offline Files, but it works. Search for *briefcase* in Help and Support Center.

Offline Files is designed for travelers who work with a laptop computer that's often disconnected from the network. When you make a file or folder available offline, Windows makes a temporary copy of it on your laptop; you can work with this copy as you would the original. When you reconnect to the network, Windows *synchronizes* your laptop documents with the network originals so you have up-to-date versions in both places.

✔ Tip

■ You can't use Fast User Switching and Offline Files at the same time. To turn off Fast User Switching, choose Start > Control Panel > User Accounts > Change the Way Users Log On or Off, uncheck Use Fast User Switching, and click Apply Options.

To turn on offline files:

1. In Windows Explorer, choose Tools > Folder Options > Offline Files tab (**Figure 5.56**).

2. Check Enable Offline Files.

3. Check Synchronize All Offline Files Before Logging Off to be sure that you have the latest versions of offline files on your laptop when you log off.

4. Click OK (or Apply).

Figure 5.56 Uncheck the Display a Reminder box, or Offline Files will pester you with warnings when you're disconnected from the network.

To make a file or folder available offline:

1. In My Network Places (on your laptop), right-click the files or folders that you want to be available offline; then choose Make Available Offline.

   The first time you do this, the Offline Files Wizard helps you configure your settings.

2. If you select a folder that contains sub-folders, specify whether to include the subfolders.

✔ Tips

- Instead of using My Network Places, you can double-click a shared network drive icon in My Computer.

- If My Network Places or My Computer contains no network drive icons, choose Tools > Map Network Drive to assign a local drive letter.

- You *must* log off or shut down to effect synchronization. If you simply discon-nect from the network, Windows won't have time to synchronize files.

- You open offline files as though you were working with them online, but Windows displays a special icon (⊞) to remind you that you're working offline.

- Synchronization is at Windows' discre-tion by default. If you've turned off that feature, you can synchronize manually when you're connected to the network: Choose Start > All Programs > Accessories > Synchronize.

- To view a list of available offline files, choose Tools > Folder Options > Offline Files > View Files.

- To make an item *un*available offline, right-click it; then choose Make Available Offline again to uncheck it.

- I've covered only the basics here. For a com-plete description of offline files, search for *offline files* in Help and Support Center.

MAKING NETWORK FILES AVAILABLE OFFLINE

Encrypting Files and Folders

PRO The Encrypting File System isn't available in Windows XP Home edition, but see the sidebar.

Encryption is one of the strongest ways to secure your sensitive documents and personal information. When you encrypt files, Windows' Encrypting File System (EFS) scrambles them so that only you can read them, providing an extra measure of protection over user accounts (Chapter 16). EFS is transparent: Encrypted files and folders change color, but otherwise, you open, edit, and save them in the usual way.

✔ Tips

- EFS works on only NTFS-formatted hard drives (see the appendix). To check a drive, choose Start > My Computer; right-click a drive icon; then choose Properties > General tab. The File System entry should be NTFS.

- NTFS-compressed files can't be EFS-encrypted (but you *can* encrypt Zipped folders). See "Compressing Files and Folders" earlier in this chapter.

- You can't encrypt system files, such as those in the Windows (or WINNT) folder.

To encrypt a file or folder:

1. In Windows Explorer, right-click the file or folder that you want to encrypt; then choose Properties > General tab > Advanced.

    If the Advanced button is missing, the selected file or folder isn't on an NTFS drive

2. Check Encrypt Contents to Secure Data (**Figure 5.57**).

3. Click OK in each open dialog box.

Figure 5.57 If you've selected a folder to encrypt, Windows responds with a Confirm Attribute Change message box asking you whether you want to encrypt just that folder or everything that it contains too.

Stronger Encryption Tools

EFS isn't all that safe, because an administrator can use a Group Policy "back door" to recover your encrypted data. For better protection use a stand-alone encryption tool such as PGP (free; http://web.mit.edu/network/pgp.html). Before you pick a tool, read Matt Curtin's "Snake Oil Warnings: Encryption Software to Avoid" (www.interhack.net/people/cmcurtin/snake-oil-faq.html). And try Bruce Schneier's free monthly Crypto-Gram newsletter (www.counterpane.com/crypto-gram.html). After encrypting files, paranoids should flush RAM and shred the swap file so that enemies can't lift passwords and keys with forensic tools.

A simple alternative to encrypting files is hiding them. (You can't steal what you can't find.) Try Hide Folders XP ($25 U.S.; www.fspro.net), Magic Folders ($30; www.pc-magic.com), or bProtected ($20; www.clasys.com).

ENCRYPTING FILES AND FOLDERS

Figure 5.58 Generally, you should encrypt folders and all their contents so that it's easier to track what's encrypted and what's not.

✔ Tips

■ If you encrypt only a folder, EFS won't encrypt any files in the folder currently, but it will encrypt any new files that you copy, move, or create within the folder.

■ If you encrypt a file in an unencrypted folder, Windows displays an Encryption Warning that lets you choose whether to encrypt only the file or both the file and its parent folder (**Figure 5.58**).

■ EFS encrypts any file or folder that you move into an encrypted folder but won't decrypt one that you drag *out* unless you manually decrypt it by unchecking the Encrypt box in Figure 5.57, drag it to a FAT or FAT32 drive, or transmit it via email or network. (Lesson: Don't keep encrypted material on shared network drives; other users can read it without your account password.)

■ When you decrypt a folder, Windows asks if you want all files and subfolders within the folder to be decrypted as well. If you choose to decrypt the folder only, the encrypted files and folders within the decrypted folder remain encrypted. But EFS won't encrypt new files and folder that you copy, move, or create within the decrypted folder.

■ To display encrypted files and folders in a different color in Windows Explorer, choose Tools > Folder Options > View tab, and check Show Encrypted or Compressed NTFS Files in Color. You can use Tweak UI's Explorer > Colors options to change the color. (See the "Tweak UI" sidebar in "Using the Start Menu" in Chapter 2.) Consider *not* coloring encrypted files so that onlookers won't know that you're using EFS.

ENCRYPTING FILES AND FOLDERS

Using Keyboard Shortcuts

Tables 5.3 and **5.4** list keyboard shortcuts for the desktop, My Computer, Windows Explorer, and other programs. (Table 5.1 in "Exploring Your Computer" earlier in this chapter contains additional Explorer-specific shortcuts.)

Table 5.3

General Keyboard Shortcuts

To	Press
Show the top of the active window or folder list	Home
Show the bottom of the active window or folder list	End
Copy	Ctrl+C (Edit > Copy)
Cut	Ctrl+X (Edit > Cut)
Paste	Ctrl+V (Edit > Paste)
Undo	Ctrl+Z (Edit > Undo)
Delete	Delete
Delete the selected item permanently, bypassing the Recycle Bin (use only if you're sure)	Shift+Delete
Copy the selected item	Ctrl while dragging item
Create a shortcut to the selected item	Ctrl+Shift while dragging item
Rename the selected item	F2
Move the insertion point to the beginning of the next word	Ctrl+right arrow
Move the insertion point to the beginning of the previous word	Ctrl+left arrow
Move the insertion point to the beginning of the next paragraph	Ctrl+down arrow
Move the insertion point to the beginning of the previous paragraph	Ctrl+up arrow
Highlight a block of text	Ctrl+Shift+arrow key
Select more than one item in a window or on the desktop, or select text within a document	Shift+arrow key
Select all contents	Ctrl+A
Search for a file or folder	F3
Show the properties of the selected object	Alt+Enter
Close the active item or quit the active program	Alt+F4
Open the shortcut menu for the active window	Alt+spacebar
Close the active document in programs that allow you to have multiple documents open at the same time	Ctrl+F4
Switch among open windows	Alt+Tab

(table continues on next page)

Table 5.3 *continued*

General Keyboard Shortcuts

To	Press
Cycle through windows in the order in which they were opened	Alt+Esc
Cycle through window panes or desktop elements	F6
Show the Address bar list in My Computer or Windows Explorer	F4
Toggle full-screen mode on and off	F11
Show the shortcut menu for the selected item	Shift+F10
Show the Start menu	Ctrl+Esc
Show a menu	Alt+underlined letter in the menu name
Carry out a menu command	Underlined letter in the command name on an open menu
Activate the menu bar in the active program	F10
Open the next menu to the right or open a submenu	Right arrow
Open the next menu to the left or close a submenu	Left arrow
Refresh the active window	F5
View the folder one level up in My Computer or Windows Explorer	Backspace
Cancel the current task	Esc
Prevent the CD from playing automatically	Shift when you insert a CD into the CD drive

Table 5.4

Windows Logo Key Shortcuts

To	Press
Show or hide the Start menu	Windows logo key
Show the System Properties dialog box	Windows logo key+Break
Show the desktop	Windows logo key+D
Minimize all windows	Windows logo key+M
Restore minimized windows	Windows logo key+Shift+M
Open My Computer	Windows logo key+E
Search for a file or folder	Windows logo key+F
Search for computers	Windows logo key+Ctrl+F
Show Windows Help	Windows logo key+F1
Lock your computer if you're connected to a network domain or switch users if you're not connected	Windows logo key+L
Open the Start > Run dialog box	Windows logo key+R
Open Utility Manager	Windows logo key+U
Cycle through running programs	Windows logo key+Tab

USING KEYBOARD SHORTCUTS

Installing and Running Programs

Windows, like all operating systems, is a launching pad for programs, or *applications*. More programs from more software firms are available for Windows than for any other OS. Fortunately Microsoft and sound design enforce substantial consistency, so you can apply knowledge of a few common operations to many programs. Most programs share user-interface elements—scroll bars, copy-and-paste functions, menus, buttons, and so on—as well as setup and management options.

In this chapter you'll learn how to install, remove, launch, and manage Windows programs. You'll also learn about *documents*, which are self-contained pieces of work (files) that you create with programs.

Installing Programs

If you've upgraded to XP, you'll find some improvements in the installation process. Windows 9x users will find that Microsoft has improved the Add or Remove Programs dialog box. More important, XP won't let poorly designed programs harm your system by installing outdated drivers and system files. Windows 2000 users will find improved compatibility; many programs (especially games) that acted cranky or refused to run in Windows 2000 will run in XP properly. Most installations go smoothly, but be aware of a few things:

Be an Administrator. XP is a multiuser OS that supports Administrator, Limited, and Guest user accounts (see "Setting up User Accounts" in Chapter 16). Only Administrators can install programs without restriction (**Figure 6.1**).

Set a restore point first. Create a System Restore point before you install new software that you don't quite trust. If the new program causes problems, you can undo the installation and return your system to its previous working condition. See "Restoring Your System" in Chapter 19.

Make sure the program is XP-compatible. XP is compatible with fewer programs than Windows 9x but more programs than Windows 2000. Look for an XP compatibility statement or the "Designed for Windows XP" logo on the software's package or web site (and look for patches or updates while you're there). You also can check Microsoft's web site for XP-compatible programs: Choose Start > Help and Support > Find Compatible Hardware and Software for Windows XP; then search for your program.

Figure 6.1 To install software, you need certain permissions. XP-certified programs give these clear instructions, but older Windows 9x programs may display a vague or puzzling message when you try to install them. XP allows a Limited user or Guest to log on as an Administrator to install a program.

INSTALLING PROGRAMS

Close open programs first. Exit all open programs before you install so that support files won't be open—and therefore locked—when Setup tries to replace them. If you have a virus scanner, turn it off; otherwise, it may interpret your new program as being harmful.

✔ Tips

■ Your PC's manufacturer may have added software—Microsoft Office or Works, for example—at the factory. Check the Start > All Programs menu before you install new stuff.

■ If you upgraded an earlier Windows version to XP, Windows Setup configured your existing programs to run; you don't have to reinstall them. If an older program doesn't run in XP, see "Running Older Programs" later in this chapter.

■ If you upgraded from Windows 2000, Power Users group members, in addition to Administrators, can install programs.

INSTALLING PROGRAMS

These days you install most commercial software from a CD. XP's *AutoPlay* feature runs the CD's Setup program automatically when you insert the CD into its drive. But you can use Control Panel to add programs if AutoPlay is turned off, you're installing from a floppy, or AutoPlay can't find the Setup program.

To install a program from CD or floppy disk:

1. Choose Start > Control Panel > Add or Remove Programs.

2. Click Add New Programs.

3. Insert the program's setup disk into the CD or floppy drive.

4. Click CD or Floppy (**Figure 6.2**); then follow the prompts that appear.

   Windows usually can find the Setup program, even if it's not in the top-level folder or named `setup.exe`; it may be an `.ini` or `.inf` file instead.

✔ Tips

- Setup programs usually require you to specify a destination folder, accept a license agreement, choose which components to install, and type a serial number or product key from the CD's envelope or registration card.

- Software publishers create Setup programs with third-party programs such as InstallShield, Wise Installer, or Microsoft's Windows Installer, so you'll see those program names in title bars.

Figure 6.2 Experienced users avoid this installation method; it's quicker to double-click the disk's Setup program (typically, `setup.exe`) in Windows Explorer.

INSTALLING PROGRAMS

Figure 6.3 Support information usually includes the software company's name, the program's version number, and links to relevant web pages.

■ After installation the program's shortcuts are highlighted in orange in the Start > All Programs menu. To turn off high-lighting, right-click the Start button; then choose Properties > Customize > Advanced tab > uncheck Highlight Newly Installed Programs.

■ If you're on a workplace or school net-work, the Add New Programs tab may contain a list of Administrator-approved programs available for installation.

■ Most programs include a Click Here for Support Information link in the Add or Remove Programs dialog box. Click this link to display technical support infor-mation (**Figure 6.3**).

Who Can Use the Program?

A program that you—or any Administrator—install is available to *all* users by default; its shortcuts appear in everybody's All Programs menu. Sometimes shortcuts end up in your *personal* All Programs menu because you (inadvertently) told Setup to do so or because Setup gave you no choice. Recall from "Using the Start Menu" in Chapter 2 that XP inspects two folders to build the All Programs menu: one for All Users and another for the logged-on user. To make a program available to everyone (instead of only you), do the following:

1. Choose Start > All Programs.

2. Right-click the item (icon) that you want everyone to be able to access; then choose Copy.

3. Right-click Start; then choose Open All Users.

4. Right-click the Programs folder; then choose Paste.

Now the program appears in everyone's All Programs menu. If this method doesn't work, or if a program requires per-user settings, log on to each user account and rerun Setup.

The internet is the preferred (sometimes only) distribution method for many software vendors. You can use Internet Explorer (Chapter 13) to download any of the thousands of commercial, shareware, demo, and free programs (and updates) available at vendors' web sites and at independent sites such as www.download.com and www.tucows.com.

To download and install software:

1. In Internet Explorer, click a link that initiates a download.

2. In the File Download – Security Warning dialog box, click Save (**Figure 6.4**).

3. In the Save As dialog box, select a destination folder for the download (**Figure 6.5**).

   The download almost always will be an executable (.exe) file or a compressed (.zip) file.

4. After the download completes, double-click the file in Windows Explorer.

   If the download is an executable file, Setup starts automatically. If it's a Zip archive, extract its files (see "Compressing Files and Folders" in Chapter 5); then look for a read-me file (readme.txt or readme.html) or double-click the installer program (usually named setup.exe) among the extracted pieces.

✔ Tips

■ You can delete the download file (or its unzipped pieces) after installation.

■ If you download with a browser other than Internet Explorer, the steps are the same, but the dialog boxes differ slightly.

■ To install Windows updates from the Microsoft web site, see "Updating Windows XP" in Chapter 19.

Figure 6.4 This dialog box appears when you click a link to download a file. Blame virus writers worldwide for the paranoid tone of the message.

Figure 6.5 Choose or create a destination folder where you won't lose the downloaded file. Desktop isn't a bad choice, but it's better to create a dedicated folder for all your downloads.

■ Some software download sites let you install a program directly online rather than locally from a downloaded file. Installing locally gives you more control and leaves you a copy of the program if you have to reinstall.

Removing Programs

When you install a program, it scatters its components all over your folder structure, not just in the Program Files subfolder it creates. Only an unwanted program's uninstall utility can remove it completely. Don't just delete the program's folder; if you do, you'll leave behind shortcuts, support files, hidden folders, registry entries, and other litter on your hard drive.

✔ Tip

■ Always exit the program that you're going to remove. If you're using Fast User Switching (see "Logging On and Logging Off" in Chapter 1), make sure that no other logged-on users are using the program.

To remove a program:

1. Choose Start > Control Panel > Add or Remove Programs > Change or Remove Programs.

2. In the Currently Installed Programs list, click the program that you want to remove (**Figure 6.6**).

continues on next page

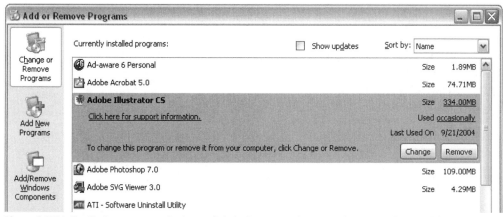

Figure 6.6 This list displays a program's size on disk, its frequency of use over the past 30 days, and the date you last used it. If you have a lot of programs, use the Sort By list (top-right corner) to select a sorting option.

3. Click the Change/Remove button (or Remove button), and confirm the removal if a message box appears.

Windows runs the program's uninstall utility (which varies by program). Follow any onscreen directions.

✔ Tips

■ Some uninstallers let you remove program components selectively; others eradicate the entire program.

■ The folder that contained the program may persist after uninstallation, usually because it contains documents created with the program. Games, for example. often leave keyboard-binding and saved-game files. If you don't need those documents, you can delete the folder and its files safely.

■ Most uninstallers display a progress bar, explain what they're removing or not removing, and tell you whether you must restart your computer to complete the removal.

■ You may get a midprocess message asking whether Windows should remove a shared file that other programs may need. Beginners should keep such files; other users can delete them unless they know a reason not to.

■ If a program doesn't appear in the Currently Installed Programs list, look for removal instructions in the program's read-me file (if any) or at the vendor's web site. Or search the web for *uninstall* and the program's name. As a last resort, drag the program's folder into the Recycle Bin.

Figure 6.7 Some list items, such as Internet Explorer, are single programs; others, such as Accessories and Utilities, are groups. If you choose a group, click the Details button to install or remove that group's programs individually.

Adding and Removing Windows Components

By default Windows Setup omits some accessory programs that Microsoft deemed inessential (mostly network and administration tools). If you feel otherwise, you can install them from the Windows CD. You also can remove optional Windows components if disk space is tight or you don't want them cluttering your All Programs menu.

To add or remove Windows components:

1. Choose Start > Control Panel > Add or Remove Programs > Add/Remove Windows Components.

2. In the Components list, check a box to install a component; uncheck a box to remove it (**Figure 6.7**).

3. Click Next.

4. If you're prompted for the Windows CD, insert it and continue.

✔ Tips

- To learn about a component, click its name (not its check box). A description appears below the list.

- To the right of each component name is the space it occupies on your hard disk.

- For some components, Windows might ask you to restart your PC.

- To uninstall Windows updates downloaded from the Microsoft web site, see "Updating Windows XP" in Chapter 19.

Launching Programs

Windows gives you many ways to launch (open) a program. Even Windows veterans may not know all of them.

To start a program:

◆ Choose Start > All Programs; then click the program's icon.

or

On the left side of the Start menu, click the program's icon (if it appears).

or

On the Quick Launch bar, click the program's icon (if it appears).

or

Choose Start > My Computer > Local Disk (C:) > Program Files. In the program's subfolder, double-click the program's icon (or select the icon and press Enter) (**Figure 6.8**).

or

Right-click the program's icon; then choose Open.

or

Press the keyboard shortcut that you assigned to the program's icon.

or

Choose Start > Run (or press Windows logo key+R); type the program's name and then press Enter (**Figure 6.9**).

You may have to include the path. See "Exploring Your Computer" in Chapter 5.

or

Type the program's name in the Address bar (in Windows Explorer, Internet Explorer, or on the taskbar); then press Enter.

Again, you may have to include the path.

Figure 6.8 Here, I've highlighted the program files for Microsoft Office applications. Finding programs by name may take a little hunting because executable (.exe) filenames sometimes are short and cryptic. Application files are easier to find in Explorer if you switch to Details view (View > Details) and sort by type (View > Arrange Icons By > Type).

Figure 6.9 The Run dialog box (or the Address toolbar) may seem old-fashioned, but for many experienced users and rapid typists it's the fastest way to open a program or document.

LAUNCHING PROGRAMS

✔ Tips

- You can use any of these methods to open a document with its associated program. If you created the document stuff.doc in Microsoft Word, for example, double-click the document's icon to start Word and open that file automatically.

- Most Setup programs put an icon in the All Programs menu or on the desktop. To move these icons, see "Using the Start Menu" in Chapter 2.

- To customize the Quick Launch bar, see "Adding Toolbars to the Taskbar" in Chapter 2.

- To assign a keyboard shortcut to a shortcut icon, see "Managing Shortcuts" in Chapter 2. Or try Hotkeycontrol XP (free; www.digital-miner.com/hkcontrol.html).

- You can open a programs or document at a command prompt just as you can from the Run dialog box or Address bar. See "Using the Free Utility Programs" later in this chapter.

Launching Programs Automatically

The Start > All Programs > Startup folder contains programs that open automatically every time you start Windows. To save yourself a few clicks or keystrokes every time you log on, you can place your own shortcuts to programs or documents in this folder.

To open an item each time you start Windows:

1. Choose Start > All Programs; right-click Startup; then choose Open.

   Choose Open All Users (instead of Open) to change the Startup folder that applies to all users, not only yourself.

2. In Windows Explorer or My Computer, navigate to the disk, folder, program, or document that you want to open automatically.

3. Right-drag the item to the Startup window; then choose Create Shortcuts Here (**Figure 6.10**).

4. Close the windows you've opened.

   From now on, the item opens each time you (re)start your PC or log on.

✔ Tips

- For an uncluttered desktop, open Startup programs as taskbar buttons rather than as windows. Right-click a Startup shortcut; choose Properties > Shortcut tab; then choose Minimized in the Run list.

- To identify startup programs, choose Start > Run; type `msconfig.exe` and then press Enter. You can use the Startup tab's check boxes to isolate startup problems. Try also Startup Control Panel (free; `www.mlin.net/StartupCPL.shtml`).

Figure 6.10 Items in the Startup folder open automatically when Windows starts. It's not uncommon to put a My Documents shortcut in Startup.

Unwelcome Startup Programs

Too many programs add their own shortcuts silently to the All Users Startup folder (or the registry). Many of these programs are unnecessary, slow the boot process, and run invisibly in the background, chewing up processor time. If you know that you can delete a Startup shortcut without affecting your system or a program adversely, do so. (You'll want to keep some programs, such as virus scanners.) If you have trouble identifying a Startup item, visit `www.pacs-portal. co.uk/startup_index.htm` for help.

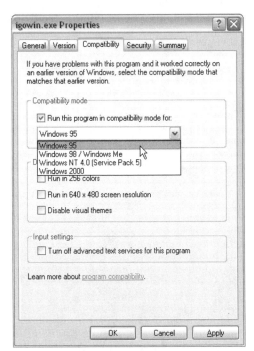

Figure 6.11 Choose the previous version of Windows that the old program was made for.

Running 16-Bit Programs

Windows 3.1 and DOS programs are called *16-bit programs*. Programs written for Windows 95, NT, and later are called *32-bit programs*. The 16-bit programs run slowly because XP runs them in a leakproof, emulated space called a *virtual machine* that draws on a common memory pool. If one 16-bit program crashes, they all crash. To run DOS programs, choose Start > All Programs > Accessories > Command Prompt. See also "Killing Unresponsive Programs" and "Using the Free Utility Programs" later in this chapter.

If XP displays an incompatibility message when you try to install or run a 16-bit program, don't ignore it. Either find a patch (update) or scrap the program.

Running Older Programs

If you upgraded from XP's forebear, Windows 2000, you know that its designers sacrificed some compatibility for stability; many Windows 9*x* programs (games in particular) won't run on 2000. With XP, Microsoft made a largely successful effort to run older programs written for Windows 9*x* and even Windows 3.1/DOS. But if XP has trouble running a program that ran fine in Windows 9*x*, NT, or 2000, you can try tricking the program into thinking that it's running on the older OS.

To run a troublesome older program:

1. Right-click a program's executable (.exe) file or shortcut icon; then choose Properties > Compatibility tab (**Figure 6.11**).

2. Change the compatibility settings for the program; then click OK.

   The next time that you open the program, XP tries to fool it into running.

✔ Tips

- Never try to coerce obsolete hardware-dependent system utilities to run on XP. Upgrade to the latest version of your virus scanner, backup program, hard-disk partitioning tool, CD burner, or whatever.

- The Compatibility tab is available only for programs installed on your hard drive. If the program is on a CD, floppy, or network drive, use Program Compatibility Wizard instead: Choose Start > All Programs > Accessories > Program Compatibility Wizard.

- To run old LucasArts and SCUMM-based adventure games (Monkey Island, Day of the Tentacle, and Sam and Max), try ScummVM (free; www.scummvm.org).

Switching Programs

You'll probably have multiple programs running simultaneously so that you can juggle, say, a word processor, email program, and web browser. You have several techniques for switching programs.

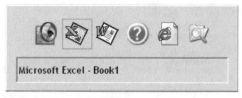

Figure 6.12 Alt+tabbing pops up a small list of icons representing running programs. Hold down Alt and press Tab repeatedly to highlight a program. If you press and release Alt+Tab quickly, you swap between only two programs instead of cycling through them all.

To switch among running programs:

◆ If the program's window is visible in the background, click it. (But click an empty area, not a button or menu, lest you activate it accidentally.)

or

Click the program's taskbar button. (The darkest button indicates the active program.)

or

Hold down Alt, press Tab repeatedly until the desired program is highlighted in the pop-up window, and then release both keys (**Figure 6.12**).

or

Hold down Alt, press Esc repeatedly until the desired program appears, and then release both keys.

✔ Tips

■ Alt+Esc, unlike Alt+Tab, has no pop-up window; doesn't cycle through *minimized* programs; and doesn't swap between two programs. (It simply sends the active program to the bottom of the pile.)

■ Windows logo key+Tab is equivalent to Alt+Tab.

■ Shift+Alt+Tab and Shift+Alt+Esc cycle *backward* through running programs.

■ If a program's taskbar button shows a small arrow and a number, button grouping is active. Clicking the button doesn't activate the program but displays a menu of documents.

Other Switchers

Alt+tabbing is by far the most common way to switch programs, and a few souped-up versions are freely available.

You can use Tweak UI's General > Alt+Tab options to set the number of rows and columns that appear in the pop-up icon list. (See the "Tweak UI" sidebar in "Using the Start Menu" in Chapter 2.)

The Task Switcher PowerToy enhances the Alt+Tab shortcut by showing a thumbnail preview of each window in the pop-up icon list. See "Using the Free Utility Programs" later in this chapter.

For true multitaskers, TaskSwitchXP (free; http://taskswitchxp.sourceforge.net) offers a large pop-up icon list, per-user configuration, thumbnail previews, and mouse and keyboard navigation.

Figure 6.13 Pressing Alt+F4 is quicker than choosing File > Exit.

Exiting Programs

When you finish using a program, you should exit (or quit or close) it to get it out of your way and to let Windows reclaim its memory for other use.

To exit a program:

◆ Choose File > Exit (**Figure 6.13**).

or

Press Alt+F4.

or

Click the program's Close button (⊠).

or

Double-click its control-menu icon (at the left end of the title bar).

or

Right-click its taskbar button; then click Close.

or

Activate the program's window; press Alt+spacebar; then press C.

✔ Tip

■ Before exiting, the program prompts you to save any unsaved work.

Killing Unresponsive Programs

Programs that crash/freeze/lock up/hang are said to be "not responding" in Microsoft vernacular; you can move the pointer within the program's window, but the program itself won't respond to clicks or keystrokes. If you're coming from Windows 9*x*, you'll be glad to hear that an unresponsive program rarely forces you to restart your computer. Instead, use Task Manager (inherited from Windows 2000) to send the frozen program to its grave.

✔ Tip

- Before you kill a program, make sure that it's really not responding. Wait a minute or two; Windows may be struggling to allocate extra memory. If you're running a Visual Basic macro in Word or Excel, the program may appear frozen while VB has control. Global reformatting or a find-and-replace operation can keep a word processor hypnotized for minutes. An open dialog box may prevent you from doing anything else in the program; look for one hiding behind another window.

Desperate Measures

If killing an unresponsive program as described doesn't work, you still have these options, in order of preference:

- ◆ Click the Processes tab in Task Manager, click the program's image name, and then click End Process.

- ◆ Exit all other programs and log off.

- ◆ If you can't log off but other users are logged on (via Fast User Switching), right-click another user in Task Manager's Users tab; choose Connect to switch to that user; then use Task Manager to log off (Disconnect) *yourself*.

- ◆ If none of these measures works, press your PC's Reset button or do an emergency shutdown (see "Logging On and Logging Off" in Chapter 1).

Figure 6.14 After Windows terminates the program, you can launch it again immediately without repercussions.

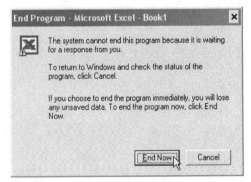

Figure 6.15 If you're lucky, Windows will ask whether you want to save your unsaved work before it kills the program. Sometimes, alas, even if Windows gives you the chance, the program itself won't.

To kill an unresponsive program:

1. Press Ctrl+Alt+Delete or Ctrl+Shift+Esc to open Task Manager.

   or

   Right-click an empty area of the taskbar; then choose Task Manager.

2. On the Applications tab, select the name of the unresponsive task (**Figure 6.14**).

3. Click End Task.

4. In the End Program dialog box, click End Now (**Figure 6.15**).

✔ Tip

■ As an alternative to killing programs via Task Manager, you can use the command-line programs `tskill` and `taskkill`, which allow more control than Task Manager. `tskill` is available for both XP Home and Pro editions, but `taskkill`, which offers more options, is available only for Pro. For usage and syntax, search for *tskill* or *taskkill* in Help and Support Center. To use the command prompt, see "Using the Free Utility Programs" later in this chapter.

KILLING UNRESPONSIVE PROGRAMS

Reporting Errors to Microsoft

When a program or Windows itself terminates abnormally, a new XP feature lets you report the error to Microsoft over the internet (**Figure 6.16**). If enough people report the same error, then (one assumes) Microsoft will fix the bug or at least post a Knowledge Base article. Microsoft swears that only technical information is sent for purely technical purposes—not for marketing or license compliance. You can fine-tune error reporting or turn it off.

To configure error reporting:

1. Choose Start > Control Panel > Performance and Maintenance > System > Advanced tab > Error Reporting (**Figure 6.17**).

   or

   Press Windows logo key+Break; then choose Advanced tab > Error Reporting.

2. To turn off error reporting, select the Disable Error Reporting option.

   or

   To report errors, select the Enable Error Reporting option; then select the types of errors that you want to report.

3. Click OK in each open dialog box.

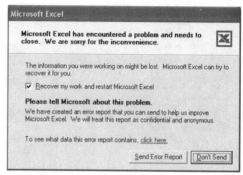

Figure 6.16 A "Please tell Microsoft" dialog box appears after a program crashes or after you reboot following a Windows "blue screen of death" system error. Click Send Error Report to transmit the error details to Microsoft; otherwise, click Don't Send. Sometimes, as shown here, you can have Windows try to recover your unsaved work.

Figure 6.17 You can choose to report only Windows system errors, only program errors, or both (or neither). Click Choose Programs if you want to report errors for some programs but not others.

Figure 6.18 Launch utility programs from the Start > All Programs > Accessories menu or one of its submenus.

Figure 6.19 Choose File > Import > Other Address Book to import names from other popular address-book programs and formats.

Using the Free Utility Programs

The All Programs menu teems with free programs that are part of the standard Windows installation. Some of these programs (such as Internet Explorer and Outlook Express) are heavy hitters that rate their own chapters. But Microsoft also includes useful utility programs, described here.

✔ Tips

■ These programs are available in the Start > All Programs > Accessories menu (or its submenus) (**Figure 6.18**) or Start > All Programs > Games, if appropriate.

■ To get program-specific help for a utility program, use its Help menu (or press F1).

Address Book

Address Book offers a centralized directory where you can store names, postal and email addresses, phone numbers, and other contact information (**Figure 6.19**). You can retrieve this information from programs such as Outlook Express, Outlook, and Start > Search > Computers or People.

Calculator

In Standard mode, Calculator offers add, subtract, square root, invert, and other basic functions. Scientific mode (**Figure 6.20**) adds trigonometric, statistical, logarithmic, and base functions. To operate Calculator, click its buttons with your mouse or press the corresponding keyboard keys. Help > Help Topics gives keyboard shortcuts for Scientific mode.

✔ Tip

- Some better calculators are the Power Calculator PowerToy (see "PowerToys" later in this section), which lets you graph and evaluate functions and convert units; and Calc98 (free; www.calculator.org), an engineering, scientific, statistical, and financial calculator. You also can type equations in the Google search box and press Enter (see www.google.com/help/features.html#calculator).

Character Map

Character Map (**Figure 6.21**) displays all characters and symbols for a particular font. Use it to copy and paste diacritical marks, currency symbols, copyright signs, and all the other characters that don't appear on your keyboard.

✔ Tip

- If you're using Word, the Insert > Symbol command is faster than Character Map.

Figure 6.20 Choose View > Scientific to reveal Calculator's geeky secret identity.

Figure 6.21 Here are the characters for the Arial font. Double-click characters to put them in the Characters to Copy text box; then click Copy. Now you can Edit > Paste them into any document. The pop-up tip is for typography experts and programmers: it shows the character's hexadecimal code.

Figure 6.22 To quit Command Prompt, type exit and then press Enter.

Command Prompt

Command Prompt (formerly called DOS Prompt) lets you type commands rather than point and click (**Figure 6.22**). Rapid typists, Unix junkies, and people impatient with Windows safeguards love the command line, but new users find it cryptic and intimidating (experience teaches them to appreciate its efficiency). Command Prompt is handy for many routine tasks, but it shines when it's impractical to use a graphical interface. (Network administrators don't add 1,000 user accounts by pointing and clicking, for example.) You also can use Command Prompt to (try to) run your old 16-bit DOS programs and games. Hundreds of commands are available; search for *command shell overview* and *command-line reference* in Help and Support Center. The basic commands are cd (or chdir), cls, copy, del, dir, exit, md (or mkdir), more, move, path, rename, rmdir, set, tree, type, and xcopy.

✔ Tips

- Command Prompt remembers the commands you've typed. Press the up- and down-arrow keys to review your command history.

- To customize Command Prompt, right-click its title bar and choose Properties. A few recommendations: On the Options tab, turn on QuickEdit Mode, which lets you drag over text and press Enter to copy it to the clipboard; on the Font tab, switch the font to Lucida Console, bold, 14-point; on the Layout tab, set the Window Size to 80 width and 40 height; on the Colors tab, choose black text on a white background. Click OK, and choose to modify the shortcut that started the window.

continues on next page

USING THE FREE UTILITY PROGRAMS

■ You can use Tweak UI's Command Prompt options to set filename completion keys. (See the "Tweak UI" sidebar in "Using the Start Menu" in Chapter 2.).

■ Command-line utilities include the Open Command Window Here Power Toy (see "PowerToys" later in this section), which gives you a right-click command that opens a command window pointing at the selected folder in Explorer; Command Prompt Explorer Bar (free; www.codeproject.com/csharp/commandbar.asp), which opens a command-prompt pane within Explorer; and MCL (free; www.mlin.net/MCL.shtml), which places a versatile command line right on your desktop.

Games

The Games menu offers world-class productivity killers Solitaire, FreeCell, Pinball, and Minesweeper. You also can play a few games with strangers over the internet; the games match you with other players on www.zone.com.

HyperTerminal

HyperTerminal (in the Communications submenu) lets you connect to remote computers via modem. In days of yore, people used HyperTerminal to dial into bulletin-board services; now they use it to access remote systems that offer text-only Telnet service. Two nearby computers with identical HyperTerminal settings can swap files over an Ethernet connection or null-modem cable. HyperTerminal is robust, but it's not easy to use.

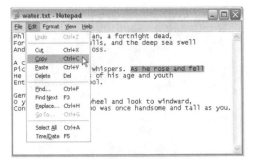

Figure 6.23 If you find Notepad too limiting, you can find many excellent shareware editors.

Notepad

Notepad, a bare-bones text editor, is one of the most useful tools in Windows (**Figure 6.23**). Use it to open, create, or edit *text files*, which contain only printable characters—no fonts, formatting, invisible codes, colors, graphics, or any of the clutter usually associated with a word processor. Notepad is the default program for .txt and .log files, but you can use it to view or edit .html files (saved web pages), .ini files (program initialization settings), or any other text-based file types.

✔ Tips

■ Notepad does offer a few handy features: Press F5 to insert a timestamp (useful for keeping logs); choose Format > Font to set the display font; or choose File > Page Setup to set headers and footers for printouts.

■ Notepad alternatives abound. A few of the better ones are TextPad ($31 U.S.; www.textpad.com), EditPlus ($30; www.editplus.com), and NoteTab ($10; www.notetab.com).

■ If you use Notepad to take notes and jot down reminders, look at ATnotes (free; http://atnotes.fr.st), a sticky-notes and alarm-clock program that lives in your notification area (system tray). If you need an outliner to organize your thoughts, try KeyNote (free; www.tranglos.com/free/index.html).

Paint

Paint is a no-frills image editor with a few drawing, color, and manipulation tools (**Figure 6.24**). Use it to create your own works of art or to view or touch up graphic files that were created in other programs (such as Adobe Photoshop) or that you scanned or downloaded. Paint supports bitmap (.bmp), JPEG, GIF, TIFF, and PNG file formats.

✔ Tip

- Paint alternatives include Paint Shop Pro ($119 U.S.; www.jasc.com); Adobe Photoshop Elements ($100; www.adobe.com), Oriens Enhancer ($15; www.oriens-solution.com), and The Gimp (free; www.gimp.org).

WordPad

WordPad (**Figure 6.25**) is a simple, stripped-down word processor associated with .doc files (unless you've installed Microsoft Word), .rtf files (Rich Text Format), and .wri files (Microsoft Write). You also can use it to edit plain-text files, but Notepad is more appropriate for that task.

✔ Tip

- WordPad's native file format is an old Microsoft Word version called 6.0/95. Word can open all WordPad files, but not vice versa.

Figure 6.24 The Image menu lets you flip, rotate, and stretch images.

Figure 6.25 Like any word processor, WordPad lets you apply formatting (italic, justification, colors, fonts, and so on) to text. The Insert > Object command lets you embed images, sounds, movies, charts, spreadsheets, and other objects in your document.

Figure 6.26 The most useful PowerToy is Tweak UI, which lets you change many aspects of the standard user interface without the risk of messing with the Windows registry directly.

PowerToys

PowerToys is a popular suite of utility programs that Microsoft felt experienced users would appreciate. They're free and available for download at www.microsoft.com/windowsxp/downloads/powertoys/xppowertoys.mspx. (They're not on the Windows XP CD.) PowerToys includes tools for changing the user interface, supercharging existing features, viewing images, and more (**Figure 6.26**). I've mentioned a few PowerToys at relevant places in this book; see the web site for a complete list.

GNUWin

GNUWin is a free software compilation for Windows. It's a huge suite that includes alternatives to expensive commercial products. The suite offers OpenOffice for Microsoft Office, The Gimp for Photoshop, gzip for WinZip, Abi Word for Word, and dozens more. It's possible that GNUWin will let you set up your PC completely while spending no money on programs or utilities.

You can order GNUWin on CD or download it from http://gnuwin.epfl.ch/en/index.html. All GNUWin software is Open Source (www.opensource.org), which means that it's free, not privately owned, spyware-free, and dependable. (You can even have the source code.)

Saving Documents

Most programs let you save your work as documents, which you can return to later, print, send to other people, back up, and so on. Documents generally are thought of as being word-processed materials, but they can be images, spreadsheets, presentations, databases, email, web pages, digital photos, text files, or any other user-created work. Nearly all programs use Windows' standard Save dialog box. The first time that you save a document, Windows asks you to name it and pick a folder to store it in. (Two files in the same folder can't have the same name.)

Figure 6.27 The Save dialog box appears the first time you save a file or when you choose File > Save As.

To save a document:

1. Choose File > Save (**Figure 6.27**).

    or

    To save a copy of a file under a different name or in a different folder, choose File > Save As.

Save Your Work in My Documents

Windows 98 introduced the My Documents folder (whose name you can change, by the way; right-click it and choose Rename). If you're a stalwart still storing your documents elsewhere, consider moving them to the My Documents folder, because it:

♦ Is easy to open from the Start menu and Windows Explorer task pane.

♦ Is where most programs expect you to save and open files.

♦ Segregates documents and programs (which are stored in \Windows\Program Files), obviating accidental document deletion when you remove or upgrade programs.

♦ Makes it easier to back up your work by archiving only My Documents (and its subfolders) rather than folders scattered about your hard disk.

♦ Keeps your personal files private. To share files, move them to the Shared Documents folder. (Shared Documents isn't available if you're on an XP Pro network domain.)

♦ Has specialized personal subfolders (My Music, My Videos, and My Pictures).

If your user name is, say, John, your My Documents folder appears as John's Documents to other logged-on users (who can't access it without permission).

Figure 6.28 From left to right, these buttons go to the last folder visited, go up one level in the folder hierarchy, create a new folder, and change the view of the listed files and folders in the dialog box. Extra buttons in Microsoft Office and other programs let you search the web, delete files, map network drives, and more.

2. Navigate to the folder where you want to store the document.

You have several ways to navigate. Double-click folder icons in the folder box to drill down the folder hierarchy. Use the left-side buttons (the Places bar) to go to a common destination quickly. Use the top-side Save In list to pick a different drive. The toolbar also helps you navigate (**Figure 6.28**).

3. In the File Name box, type the name of the file.

You can use the Cut, Copy, and Paste keyboard shortcuts (Ctrl+X, Ctrl+C, and Ctrl+V) while editing. For file-naming rules, see "Naming Files and Folders" in Chapter 5.

4. To save a file in a format other than the program's default (native) format, choose a target format from the Save As Type list.

This feature lets you, say, save a Word document as text (.txt), Rich Text Format (.rtf), or HTML (.html) so that users without Word can open it in a text editor, WordPad, or a web browser.

5. Click Save.

SAVING DOCUMENTS

✔ Tips

- To bypass step 2, type the filename's full path in step 3. See "Exploring Your Computer" in Chapter 5.

- The folder box lists documents as well as folders. Click a document to make its name appear in the File Name box; then click Save to overwrite the existing document or edit the name to save a new document. The latter technique saves typing when you're saving similarly named documents.

- The folder box acts like an Explorer window. You can right-click any item to, say, rename or delete it. You even can drag items into and out of this box or use the standard navigation keys.

- You must close the Save dialog box before you can use another part of the program.

- Some older programs use the old-style Save dialog box, which lacks some of the navigation features of the new dialog box.

- You can't save your work in some utility and game programs such as Calculator and Solitaire.

- Some programs can auto-save your work at a regular time interval that you set.

- You can use Tweak UI's Common Dialogs > Places Bar options to customize the Places bar. (See the "Tweak UI" sidebar in "Using the Start Menu" in Chapter 2.).

Figure 6.29 The Open dialog box works like the Save dialog box described in the preceding section.

Opening Documents

You have several ways to reopen a document that you've already named and saved.

To open a document:

◆ In the program that created the document, choose File > Open; navigate to the document; then click Open (**Figure 6.29**).

or

In Windows Explorer or on the desktop, double-click the document's icon (or select it and then press Enter).

or

If the document was opened recently, choose it from the Start > My Recent Documents menu.

My Recent Documents is turned off by default. To turn it on, see Table 2.1 in "Customizing the Start Menu" in Chapter 2.

or

Choose Start > Run (or press Windows logo key+R); type the document's name and path and then press Enter.

✔ Tips

- You also can open a document by using any of the techniques described in "Launching Programs" earlier in this chapter.

- Like the Save dialog box, the Open dialog box must be closed before you can use another part of the program.

- To open a file that's not associated with a particular program, right-click the file; choose Open With; then select the name of a program. See "Associating Documents with Programs" later in this chapter.

- If you open a document that somebody else already has open, the program usually will warn you or open a *read-only* copy of the document, unless it's a multiuser document such as a database.

- Explorer's Favorites menu lets you add documents—not only web pages—to your Favorites list, which you can access quickly in the Open and Save dialog boxes.

Table 6.1

EXTENSION	DESCRIPTION OR PROGRAM
.ai	Adobe Illustrator
.avi	Windows Media Player
.bmp	Bitmap image
.dll	System file (not a document)
.doc	Microsoft Word (or WordPad)
.exe	Program (not a document)
.gif	GIF image
.htm/.html	Web page (Internet Explorer)
.indd	Adobe InDesign
.jpg/.jpeg	JPEG image (for photos)
.mdb	Microsoft Access
.pdf	Portable Document Format (Adobe Reader)
.png	PNG image
.ppt	Microsoft PowerPoint
.psd	Adobe Photoshop
.qxd	QuarkXPress
.tmp	Temporary file
.txt	Text file (Notepad)
.wpd	WordPerfect
.xls	Microsoft Excel
.zip	Compressed Zip file

Common Filename Extensions

Viruses and Extensions

Viruses disguised as innocuous attachments often arrive via email. A virus file with the extension .exe is a program that runs when you double-click it, infecting you. (Some other extensions are dangerous too.) Virus writers will try to trick you into thinking a file is safe by naming it, say, `iloveyou.txt.exe`. If extensions are hidden, you see only `iloveyou.txt`, which appears to be a harmless text file.

Even with extensions showing, the file `FreeMP3s.txt                .exe` will appear to be harmless if the embedded spaces hide the .exe extension in a narrow column.

Associating Documents with Programs

When you double-click a Word document, Windows launches Word with that document open. Windows knows to launch Word—rather than, say, Paint or Outlook Express—because a document's file type is embedded in its filename, as the (usually three) characters appearing after the name's last dot. These characters, called an *extension* or *filename extension,* associate a document with a particular program. **Table 6.1** gives a short list of common extensions; go to www.filext.com for a comprehensive list.

Microsoft hides extensions by default to make Windows appear friendlier. But even beginners should show extensions for these reasons:

◆ An icon alone can be insufficient to distinguish a file's type (particularly the tiny icons in Details and List views).

◆ Extensions impart the types of like-named files quickly (`resume.doc` vs. `resume.txt` vs. `resume.html`, for example) without making you read the Type column in Explorer.

◆ Extensions make it plainer to, say, choose among Photoshop, Paint, Internet Explorer, and Windows Picture and Fax Viewer to open .jpg (JPEG) files.

◆ If a newly installed program hijacks an extension's association without asking your permission (both rude and common), you can reassociate the extension with your preferred program.

◆ If you don't learn about extensions, you'll remain mired in beginner status and pester people with trivial problems.

To show extensions:

◆ In Windows Explorer, choose Tools >
Folder Options > View tab > Advanced
Settings list > uncheck Hide Extensions
for Known File Types (**Figures 6.30**
and **6.31**).

To change the program associated with an extension:

1. In Windows Explorer, choose Tools >
Folder Options > File Types tab
(**Figure 6.32**).

2. In the Registered File Types list, select
the extension that you want to change.

3. Click Change.

4. In the Open With dialog box, select
another program to associate the extension with (**Figure 6.33**).

5. Click OK in each open dialog box.

Figure 6.30 Uncheck this box to show filename extensions in Explorer, on the desktop, and in dialog boxes.

Figure 6.31 Explorer windows that hide (top) and show (bottom) extensions.

Figure 6.32 Each program must register its file type(s) with Windows to appear in this list.

✔ Tips

- The Details section in Explorer's task pane contains file-type information for the selected file.

- Some file types have multiple extensions (.htm/.html and .jpg/.jpeg, for example). Repeat the association for each form of the extension.

- If you double-click a file with an unknown extension, Windows lets you choose a program or try to look up the extension on Microsoft's web site (**Figure 6.34**).

continues on next page

Figure 6.33 At the top of the list are programs that Windows thinks appropriate for the selected file type, but you can choose or browse for a different program.

Figure 6.34 This dialog box appears when you double-click a file with an extension that Windows doesn't recognize. A file with an unknown extension (or no extension) often is a text file; try opening it in Notepad before asking Windows to hunt for a program.

- If you want to open a file with a program other than the associated one (without actually changing the association by reassigning the file type), right-click the file's icon; then choose a program from the Open With submenu (**Figure 6.35**).

- To change the icon for a file type, follow steps 1 and 2; then click Advanced > Change Icon (**Figure 6.36**). You also can find icons by using Search to look for *.ico files. Unfortunately, most icon collections are hidden in .dll files. `shell32.dll` has a bunch, but finding others will take some work.

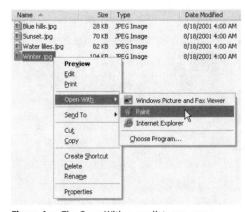

Figure 6.35 The Open With menu lists programs capable of opening the selected file. Click Choose Program to pick a program that's not in the menu.

Figure 6.36 You can't change the icon for an individual file, but you can change it for a file *type* (JPEG files, here). If you don't like any of the replacement icons that Windows offers, you can browse.

PRINTING AND FAXING

7

Paperless-office propaganda notwithstanding, computer users have felled forests to feed printers and preserve paper trails. In Windows the operating system, rather than individual programs, handles printing. When you print something in any program, you activate Windows' intermediary printing system, which accepts print jobs from programs and feeds them to the printer. This process, called *background printing,* lets you keep working in your program while your documents print.

Printer installation and configuration is easy. After hardware connection and setup you can print individual documents with the default settings or override them for special purposes. In this chapter you'll learn basic printer properties, printing tasks, and a few topics beyond the routine. I'll also describe how to save paper by using your computer to send and receive faxes without a fax machine.

Installing a Printer

A *local printer* connects directly to your computer through a USB, parallel, serial, or infrared port. Your printer's manual describes how to attach it to the back of your computer; it's simple. Newer printers attach through a USB (Universal Serial Bus) port; older ones attach through a parallel or (rarely) serial port. You can use a cableless infrared connection if both your printer and computer (typically a laptop) have infrared lenses. Printers also accept wireless Bluetooth USB adapters. For information about ports, see "Connecting Devices to Your Computer" in Chapter 8.

When you connect a printer to your computer, Windows often recognizes the device and searches its extensive collection of built-in drivers to run printers. A *printer driver* is software that lets programs send commands to a particular printer. If your printer doesn't appear on Windows' built-in list, you can use the driver on the CD or floppy that came with the printer. If you upgraded from an earlier Windows version, XP inherited the existing printer driver and settings, and your printer may work fine. In any case, check the printer manufacturer's web site for a more recent driver.

✔ Tips

- You must be an Administrator to install a printer. See "Setting up User Accounts" in Chapter 16.

- Turn off your PC before connecting or disconnecting a parallel or serial cable. (Your PC can remain on for USB, Bluetooth, and infrared connections.)

- Skim the manual before installation. Some manufacturers supply software to be used instead of Windows' Add Printer Wizard.

INSTALLING A PRINTER

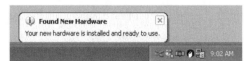

Figure 7.1 You'll see this notification-area message for Plug and Play printers. It means that Windows completed the installation automatically. Go ahead and start printing.

Figure 7.2 When Windows says "printer," it means "printer driver."

Figure 7.3 The Add Printer Wizard tells you not to use the wizard if your printer connects to a USB, IEEE 1394 (FireWire), infrared, or Bluetooth port.

Figure 7.4 Uncheck the Automatically Detect box to spare Windows a fruitless search for your non–Plug and Play printer.

- Installation is trivial for printers that support Plug and Play, which lets Windows detect and configure a connected device automatically. Printers that use USB, Bluetooth, or infrared connections always support Plug and Play. Parallel connections might support it; serial connections never do. For more information about Plug and Play, see "Installing Plug and Play Devices" in Chapter 8.

To install a local printer:

1. Connect your printer to the appropriate port, and turn on the printer.

   On the Windows desktop, one of these three things happens:

   ▲ A Found New Hardware alert appears (**Figure 7.1**), meaning that Windows knows about your printer and has installed the appropriate driver. You're ready to print; skip the rest of these steps.

   ▲ The Add Printer Wizard appears, meaning that Windows detected the printer but lacks a driver for this model. Skip to step 7.

   ▲ Windows didn't detect the printer and does nothing. Continue to step 2.

2. Choose Start > Control Panel > Printers and Other Hardware > Printers and Faxes.

3. In the task pane, click Add a Printer (**Figure 7.2**).

   The Add Printer Wizard opens.

4. On the Welcome page, click Next (**Figure 7.3**).

5. On the Local or Network Printer page, select Local Printer Attached to This Computer; uncheck Automatically Detect and Install My Plug and Play Printer; then click Next (**Figure 7.4**).

continues on next page

6. On the Select a Printer Port page, select a port from the list (**Figure 7.5**); then click Next.

In almost all cases, LPT1 (the default) is the correct port.

7. On the Install Printer Software page, select the manufacturer and model of your printer; then click Next (**Figure 7.6**).

or

If your printer model isn't listed, insert the printer's installation CD or floppy; click Have Disk; then follow the onscreen instructions to install your printer.

(If Windows refuses your installation disk, download the current printer driver from the printer manufacturer's web site.)

8. On the Name Your Printer page, type a name for your printer or accept the default name; indicate whether this printer is the one that you'll usually or always print with (the default); then click Next (**Figure 7.7**).

9. On the Printer Sharing page, select Do Not Share This Printer; then click Next (**Figure 7.8**).

Figure 7.5 For most printer setups you can accept the default settings. Windows refers to a parallel port as an *LPT port* and a serial port as a *COM port*.

Figure 7.6 Clicking an entry in the Manufacturer list (left) displays XP's standard drivers for that manufacturer in the Printers (right) list. The Windows Update button connects you to Microsoft's web site for drivers that were updated since XP came out.

Figure 7.7 Use a short printer name that will fit easily in messages and dialog boxes. If you're going to print from an old DOS-based program, use a name with eight or fewer letters (no spaces or punctuation).

Figure 7.8 To share a printer on a network, see the next section in this chapter.

INSTALLING A PRINTER

Figure 7.9 Print a test page to confirm that your printer is working properly.

Completing the Add Printer Wizard

You have successfully completed the Add Printer Wizard.
You specified the following printer settings:

Name: HP LaserJet 2100
Share name: <Not Shared>
Port: LPT1:
Model: HP LaserJet 2100
Default: Yes
Test page: Yes

Figure 7.10 This page echoes the settings you've chosen in the Add Printer Wizard.

10. On the Print Test Page page, choose Yes to print a test page; then click Next (**Figure 7.9**).

11. On the completion page, click Finish (**Figure 7.10**).

continues on next page

Same Printer. Different Purposes.

You can install multiple drivers with different settings for the same physical printer and then switch among these "virtual" printers easily to suit what you're printing. If your printer has two paper trays, create "Letterhead" and "Plain" printers; to switch between printing high-resolution graphics and low-res text documents, create "1200 dpi" (dots per inch) and "300 dpi" printers. Separate "Landscape" and "Portrait" printers are popular too. To create another printer:

1. Install the printer a second time, but under a different name that indicates its purpose (see step 8).

2. After installation, right-click the printer's icon in the Printers and Faxes window (refer to Figure 7.12), choose Printing Preferences; then select the settings appropriate to its role.

3. In the Printers and Faxes window, right-click the icon for the printer that you use most of the time; then choose Set As Default Printer. (This command appears only when you right-click a printer that isn't already the default.)

A check mark appears on the default printer's icon.

From now on you can choose the appropriate printer in any program's Print dialog box. See "Printing Documents" later in this chapter.

12. In the pop-up confirmation dialog box, click OK if the test page printed or Troubleshoot if it didn't (**Figure 7.11**).

After successful installation, the printer's icon appears in the Printers and Faxes window (**Figure 7.12**).

✔ Tips

- If the manufacturer provides no XP driver for your printer, try the Windows 2000 driver. If no 2000 driver exists, try the Windows NT driver. No luck? Try a NT/2000/XP driver for a different printer from the same manufacturer—but keep it in the family; inkjet printers can't use laser-printer drivers, for example. *Still* no luck? Try *printer emulation.* Check the manual to see whether your printer can mimic a different printer, and use *that* printer's driver. Many non–Hewlett-Packard laser printers can work with HP LaserJet drivers, for example.

- To remove a printer that you no longer use, right-click its icon in the Printers and Faxes window; then choose Delete.

- For information about installing fonts, see "Managing Fonts" in Chapter 4.

- To put a Printers and Faxes shortcut in the Start menu, see "Using the Start Menu" in Chapter 2.

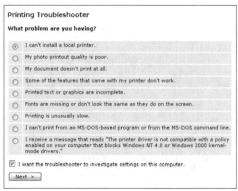

Figure 7.11 If the test page looks garbled (or doesn't print at all), click Troubleshoot to have Windows help you try to solve the problem.

Figure 7.12 Right-click a printer icon to show common printer tasks (many of which are duplicated in the task pane at left). Tiles view (shown here) and Details view display printer status information. Note the link to the printer manufacturer's web site in the task pane's See Also section.

Figure 7.13 Type a short name, without spaces or punctuation, that everyone on the network will recognize.

Figure 7.14 You can install additional printer drivers on your system so that users running other Windows versions can connect to your printer without being prompted to install missing drivers.

Sharing a Network Printer

Computers on a network (see Chapter 17) can share the same printer. Step 9 in the preceding section showed you how to use the Add Printer Wizard to set up a shared network printer, but that option isn't available if you let Windows detect your Plug and Play printer automatically. Here's how to set up a network printer manually.

To share a printer on a network:

1. At the computer attached to the printer to be shared, choose Start > Control Panel > Printers and Other Hardware > Printers and Faxes.

2. Right-click a printer; then choose Sharing.

3. Select Share This Printer; then type a share name for the printer (**Figure 7.13**). You can make up this name, but it has to be unique on the network.

4. To share the printer with users using different Windows versions or computer hardware, click Additional Drivers; choose the environment and operating system for the other computers (**Figure 7.14**).

5. Click OK in each open dialog box.

After you've set up a shared printer, other users on the network can add it to their own Printers and Faxes window and print with it.

To use a shared printer:

1. Choose Start > Control Panel > Printers and Other Hardware > Printers and Faxes.

2. In the task pane, click Add a Printer (refer to Figure 7.2); then click Next.

3. On the Local or Network Printer page (refer to Figure 7.4), select A Network Printer, or a Printer Attached to Another Computer; then click Next.

4. On the Specify a Printer page, if you know the printer's address, type it; then click Next.

   or

   Select the second option to type a network path (such as \\server_name\printer_name); then click Next.

   or

   Select the third option to type an internet address (URL); then click Next.

   or

   If you don't know the printer's address, select Browse for a Printer (**Figure 7.15**); then click Next.

5. If you selected Browse for a Printer in the preceding step, select the printer to use (**Figure 7.16**); then click Next.

Figure 7.15 You can browse for a shared printer or type its network address or URL.

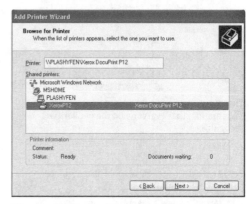

Figure 7.16 When you browse for a printer, the Shared Printers list appears—empty. Wait a few seconds for Windows to populate it with the names of available network printers.

Table 7.1

Printer Icons	
ICON	DESCRIPTION
	A local printer has a normal printer icon.
	A shared local printer has a hand below it.
	A remote printer on the network has a cable below it.
	The default printer has a check mark on it.

6. Enter your user account name and password if you're asked.

7. If you have more than one printer installed, specify the one to be your default (primary) printer.

8. Click Finish.

   The shared printer appears in the Printers and Faxes window.

✔ Tips

■ **Table 7.1** shows how a printer's icon reflects its status.

■ If you share a printer with DOS or Windows 3.*x* computers, use eight or fewer letters for the printer's share name (no spaces or punctuation); a network share is named with the same rules as a file.

■ The terms *shared printer* and *network printer* are synonymous.

■ When you share a printer connected to your PC, everybody's print jobs go through *your* copy of Windows, draining your system resources. Busy networks use a *print server* to arbitrate print requests. Stand-alone Ethernet or wireless print servers (which require no dedicated PC) cost about $50 to $120 (U.S.).

SHARING A NETWORK PRINTER

Setting Printer Properties

You can change a printer's default settings through its Properties dialog box. This dialog box varies by printer model because the manufacturer supplies the drivers whose features appear there. Options common to all printers include those in the General and Advanced tabs.

Figure 7.17 If you're sharing a printer, add its location and a few helpful comments for other network users to see.

To change a printer's default settings:

1. Choose Start > Control Panel > Printers and Other Hardware > Printers and Faxes.

2. Right-click a printer icon; then choose Properties.

3. On the following tabs, set the printer's default properties:

   General. Change the printer's name, location, or comments. To test the printer, click Print Test Page (**Figure 7.17**).

   Sharing. See "Sharing a Network Printer" earlier in this chapter.

   Ports. Review the printer's port assignment and configuration. You'll rarely want to change these settings.

   Advanced. Change settings such as printer access hours and spooling (queuing) behavior. (*Don't* select Print Directly to the Printer; it turns off background printing.) Click Printing Defaults to view or change the default document properties for all users. Click Separator Page to add or change a separator page that prints between documents (**Figure 7.18**).

   Device Settings. These options differ by printer model depending on its features (**Figure 7.19**).

4. Click OK (or Apply).

✔ Tip

- To set print server properties that affect *all* networked printers, right-click an empty area of the Printers and Faxes window; then choose Server Properties.

Figure 7.18 With shared printers, separator pages make it easy to find your documents among others at the printer. You can create custom separator pages.

Figure 7.19 Printer-dependent settings affect such things as color, tray selection, fonts, printer memory, and duplex printing.

Figure 7.20 Print dialog boxes vary by program and printer model, but you'll find some common settings. Here are Print dialog boxes for Notepad (top), Microsoft Word (middle), and Microsoft Streets & Trips (bottom).

Printing Documents

After your printer is up and running, printing a document is simple.

To print a document:

1. Open the document that you want to print.

2. Choose File > Print (or press Ctrl+P).

3. In the Print dialog box (**Figure 7.20**), select the printer and print options.

   This dialog box varies by printer model and program, but the basic settings are:

   Select Printer. Choose a local or network printer from the list or scrolling panel. If you've created several icons for different modes of the same printer, choose among them here.

   Preferences/Properties. Click this to open the Preferences or Properties dialog box (**Figure 7.21**).

   continues on next page

Figure 7.21 This dialog box, which varies by printer, lets you specify paper size (for multitray printers), orientation (landscape or portrait), print quality (dots per inch), and so on. These settings apply to the current printout, not to the printer in general.

Page Range. Specify which pages of the document to print. The Selection option is dimmed if you didn't highlight any text before you opened the Print dialog box.

Copies. Specify the number of copies to print. You'll usually want to turn on collation for multiple copies.

Program-specific settings. Any program can add extra features to the Print dialog box. Right-click an option; then click What's This? for pop-up help.

4. Click Print or OK (or press Enter).

✔ Tips

■ During printing, a status icon appears in the notification area (**Figure 7.22**).

■ To bypass the Print dialog box and use the default printer and settings to print, click the Print button on a toolbar (**Figure 7.23**).

■ Internet Explorer's Print dialog box lets you print a web page's frames and links (**Figure 7.24**).

■ You can print a document right from Windows Explorer or the desktop without opening it; right-click the document's icon and choose Print. Or drag a document's icon to a printer icon in the Printers and Faxes window, to a print spooler window, or to a desktop printer shortcut.

■ Most programs have additional print commands in the File menu or a toolbar. Page Setup sets margins, orientation, and other layout options. Print Preview shows how a document will look when you print it.

■ If you have a color printer, see the discussion of color management in "Configuring the Monitor" in Chapter 4.

■ **PRO** If you're a domain member, the Print dialog box has a Find Printer button that you can click to search the network for a particular printer.

Figure 7.22 Point to this icon (without clicking) to see how many print jobs are pending.

Figure 7.23 The standard Print toolbar button (shown here in Microsoft Office) looks like this. The pop-up tip displays the destination printer.

Figure 7.24 Click the Options tab in IE's Print dialog box. If a web page is divided into independent rectangular sections (*frames*), you can print them selectively. You also can print all the linked pages and a table at the end of the printout that lists all the page's links.

Controlling Printouts

When you print a document, it's intercepted by an intermediary program, called the *print spooler,* on its way to the printer. The print spooler holds your documents (on disk or in memory) until your printer can accept them. The delay is short for text files but can be substantial for large graphics files. The spooler puts each document in a *print queue* (or just *queue*) where it waits its turn to be printed. You can change the order of queued documents, pause or resume printing, or cancel specific print jobs. Spooling occurs in the background, so you can keep working in your program—or even quit the program—and documents still print.

Printer Troubleshooting

When you're having printer troubles, you want to determine whether the problem lies with the printer, Windows, or a particular program. Here are some things to check:

◆ Make sure that the printer is plugged in and turned on. Check for snug cable connections on the printer and computer ports.

◆ Remove the paper tray, pop the printer's lid, and check for a jammed paper path.

◆ Streaks of white space in printouts mean you're low on toner (ink).

◆ Turn the printer off and on to clear its memory.

◆ Create a file in Notepad, and print it from the command prompt. Choose Start > All Programs > Accessories > Command Prompt, type `print filename.txt` and then press Enter. (Replace *filename.txt* with the name of your homemade text file.) If it prints, you have a software problem; otherwise, you have a hardware problem.

◆ Consult the printer's manual and print a test page. (If the page prints, delete and reinstall the printer driver.)

◆ Use XP's built-in troubleshooter: Choose Start > Help and Support > Printing and Faxing topic > Fixing a Printing Problem (in the left pane) > Printing Troubleshooter (in the right pane). (Refer to Figure 7.11.)

If you still can't determine the problem's source, you may have a malfunctioning port (somewhat complex) or motherboard (get out your wallet).

To manage the print queue:

1. Choose Start > Control Panel > Printers and Other Hardware > Printers and Faxes; then double-click a printer icon.

   or

   Double-click the notification-area printer icon (refer to Figure 7.22).

2. In the print spooler window, do any of the following (**Figure 7.25**):

   To cancel printing a document, right-click that document; then choose Cancel.

   To cancel printing all documents, choose Printer > Cancel All Documents.

   To pause (or resume) printing a document, right-click that document; then choose Pause (or Resume).

   To pause (or resume) printing all documents, choose Printer > Pause Printing. (Choose it again to resume printing.)

   To add another document to the queue, drag the document's icon from Explorer or the desktop into the print spooler window.

   To rearrange the printing order, right-click a document; choose Properties; then drag the Priority slider. Higher-priority documents print before lower-priority documents. (You can't reorder the documents by dragging them.)

✔ Tip

- FinePrint ($50 U.S.; www.fineprint.com) is a printing utility that saves ink, paper, and time by controlling print jobs. Some of its options: Print multiple pages on one sheet of paper; scale web pages to fit on standard paper sizes; and convert colored text to black and skip graphics (saving ink).

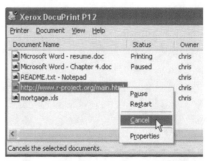

Figure 7.25 The print-spooler window lists the documents waiting to print. The first document is printing, the second one is paused, and I'm about to cancel the fourth one. If you're on a network, by default you can pause, resume, restart, or cancel your own documents but not those of other users.

Your Printer Is Lying

Printer manufacturers make money on replacement ink (toner) cartridges like razor manufacturers make money on blades. Cartridges are priced about 10 times higher than the cost of producing them, so be skeptical of your printer's "low ink" warnings, especially inkjet printers—some multicolor cartridges shut down if even only one color runs out. For laser printers, remove the cartridge and shake it for some extra life.

You have a few money-saving options. Try the free version of InkSaver (www.inksaver.com) to see if it saves ink for your printer. You can buy low-priced inkjet cartridges at Amazon Imaging (www.amazonimaging.com), PrintPal (www.printpal.com), or other stores. To find discount ink stores, visit www.buyinkcartridges.com. Don't throw out or return empty laser cartridges; look for a local computer-supplies store that will refill them (or ask an online store). Be wary of printer-makers that use lock-out codes to prevent cartridge refills.

Faxing

Windows' Fax program lets you send and receive faxes through your PC, without an actual fax machine. You'll need a phone line and almost any modem. Even an old 33.6 Kbps modem can send a multipage fax in a minute or two.

✔ Tips

- Install the modem (a conventional modem, not a DSL or cable modem) *before* you start the Fax setup process. Make sure that the modem is connected to a phone line and the phone line is connected to a working jack.

- You can't use your DSL or cable connection for faxing...yet...but *VoIP* (Voice Over Internet Protocol) technology will change this.

- To fax documents that aren't computer files, you'll need a scanner (see Chapter 9). Faxes are sent in black and white at a default resolution of 150×150 dpi, which any scanner can manage.

- If you don't want to buy a modem or tie up your phone line, consider one of the internet-based fax services listed at http://directory.google.com/Top/Computers/Internet/Internet_Fax/Services.

PC-Based Faxing Advantages

Faxing through Windows offers these advantages over a traditional fax machine:

- Conserves paper.

- Saves money on paper and fax-machine cartridges.

- Faxes documents without printing them.

- Faxes from your computer via the File > Print command.

- Lets you read incoming faxes onscreen or print them automatically.

- Lets you manage incoming faxes as you would any documents: Read, save, or delete them, or attach them to email.

- Generates cleaner, more legible faxes than ones sent via fax machine.

Windows Setup ignores Fax, so you must install it manually. Exception: If you upgraded to XP from a Windows version that had a Fax component, Setup installed the XP Fax component automatically during the upgrade. You can import your existing faxes into Fax. Choose Start > All Programs > Accessories > Communications > Fax > Fax Console. In Fax Console, choose Help > Help Topics; then read the topic Fax After Upgrading to Windows XP.

To install Fax:

1. Choose Start > Control Panel > Printers and Other Hardware > Printers and Faxes > Set up Faxing (in the task pane) (**Figure 7.26**). (If the task pane is hidden, choose File > Set up Faxing.)

2. Insert your Windows XP CD when prompted, close the blue Welcome to Windows window when it appears, and continue.

3. When the installation is complete, a Fax icon appears in the Printers and Faxes window (**Figure 7.27**), and new programs appear in Start > All Programs > Accessories > Communications > Fax.

Figure 7.26 Use Control Panel's Add or Remove Programs extension to install Fax. See "Adding and Removing Windows Components" in Chapter 6.

Figure 7.27 When you install XP's Fax Services component, a fax icon appears in your Printers and Faxes window.

Figure 7.28 You can set up Fax to only send faxes, only receive them, or both.

Figure 7.29 The TSID is mandatory in some areas. This identification information usually appears in the header area of a received fax and serves to identify the sending fax machine. Some fax-routing software depends on TSIDs to determine where to direct incoming faxes.

Before you can send or receive faxes you must use the Fax Configuration Wizard to configure Fax.

To configure Fax:

1. Choose Start > All Programs > Accessories > Communications > Fax > Fax Console.

   The Fax Configuration Wizard opens.

2. Click Next to skip the Welcome page.

3. On the Sender Information page, type your name or business name and your fax number; then click Next.

   The fields all are optional, but information from here appears on the fax cover sheet, so include enough for the recipient to contact you if a fax doesn't go through completely.

4. On the Select Device for Sending or Receiving Faxes page, make sure that your modem is selected; set send and receive options; specify whether you'll answer incoming faxes manually or automatically (**Figure 7.28**); and click Next.

5. On the Transmitting Subscriber Identification (TSID) page (which appears only if you checked Enable Send in step 4), enter your business name and fax number (**Figure 7.29**); then click Next.

continues on next page

FAXING

6. On the Called Subscriber Identification (CSID) page (which appears only if you checked Enable Receive in step 4), enter your name (or business name) and fax number again; then click Next.

The CSID is displayed on the sending fax machine. This helps confirm that the fax is being sent to the correct recipient.

7. On the Routing Options page (which appears only if you checked Enable Receive in step 4), specify how incoming faxes will be handled; then click Next.

All faxes are stored in Fax Console automatically, but you can print a copy or store it in a local or shared folder (**Figure 7.30**).

8. Confirm the settings; then click Finish (**Figure 7.31**).

To send a fax:

1. Open the document that you want to print.

2. Choose File > Print (or press Ctrl+P).

3. In the Print dialog box, click the Fax icon or choose Fax from the list; then click Print or OK, or press Enter (**Figure 7.32**). The Send Fax Wizard opens.

4. Click Next to skip the Welcome page.

Figure 7.30 Check Print It On if you want each received fax to be printed automatically (on the selected printer). Check Store a Copy in a Folder to create a backup copy of each fax (in addition to the copies saved by Fax Console).

Figure 7.31 The Fax Configuration Wizard closes, and the Fax Console window opens. Now the computer is configured to send or receive faxes.

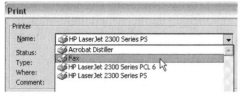

Figure 7.32 After configuration, a Fax icon appears in the Printer list of each program's Print dialog box.

FAXING

Figure 7.33 If Use Dialing Rules is turned off, type the recipient's fax number as it should be dialed. (Parentheses, commas, and hyphens are ignored.) If Use Dialing Rules is turned on, click Dialing Rules, and choose one of the dialing setups, or click Add to create one.

Figure 7.34 Click the More button to see the detailed status of each outgoing fax. Click Hide if you prefer Windows to do its faxing invisibly in the background. A pop-up message appears in the notification area (system tray) when a fax is sent successfully (or fails).

5. On the Recipient Information page, type the recipient's name and fax number (**Figure 7.33**); click Add to send a fax to multiple recipients; then click Next.

or

Click Address Book; select one or more recipients; then click Next.

6. On the Cover Page page, select a cover page if you want one; add a subject line and a note to appear on the cover page; then click Next.

7. On the Schedule page, specify when you want to send the fax and its priority; then click Next.

Priority determines the sending order if you're stacking a bunch of faxes to send at a particular time.

8. On the completion page, confirm the settings; then click Finish. (Click Preview Fax if you want to inspect the fax.)

If you're sending the fax now, the Fax Monitor window appears after a few seconds (**Figure 7.34**).

✔ Tips

■ To fax from a Microsoft Office program (such as Word or Outlook), choose File > Send To > Fax Recipient. The Office Fax Wizard asks for information and then hands off to the Send Fax Wizard.

■ To fax someone a quick one-page note, choose Start > All Programs > Accessories > Communications > Fax > Send a Fax.

■ Cover pages help when you fax to big institutions where the fax might be misrouted. The built-in cover pages work fine, but you can design your own: In Fax Console, choose Tools > Personal Cover Pages > New.

FAXING

To receive a fax, you must have checked Enable Receive in the Fax Configuration Wizard in step 4 of "To configure Fax." To change that setting (and others) without stepping through the wizard again, in the Printers and Faxes window (refer to Figure 7.27), right-click the Fax icon; then choose Properties > Devices tab > Properties button > Receive tab (**Figure 7.35**).

Faxes received in Automatic answer mode (best for dedicated fax lines) appear in the Fax Console's Inbox, discussed next. You'll prefer Manual answer mode if your computer and telephone share a line.

To receive a fax manually:

1. When the phone rings, click the animated fax icon or the pop-up message (**Figure 7.36**) that appears in the notification area (system tray).

2. To view the received fax, look in the Fax Console's Inbox, discussed next.

To manage and view faxes:

1. Choose Start > All Programs > Accessories > Communications > Fax > Fax Console (**Figure 7.37**).

2. In the left pane, click the plus (+) icon to expand the Fax folder, if necessary.

    Fax contains the following subfolders:

    Incoming contains faxes that you're receiving now.

    Inbox contains faxes that you've received.

    Outbox contains faxes that Fax will send later.

    Sent Items contains faxes that you've sent successfully.

3. In the left pane, click the folder that you want.

4. In the right pane, right-click a fax; then choose a command.

Figure 7.35 Select Manual answer mode if you receive a fax occasionally on a telephone line that you use mostly for talking.

Figure 7.36 If you're expecting a fax, click this message; Fax Monitor (refer to Figure 7.34) appears and downloads the fax. If you're expecting a person to call, just pick up the phone, and this message disappears.

Figure 7.37 Click Properties to see the status of the fax.

Figure 7.38 When a fax doesn't go through the first time, Fax tries again later automatically.

To control fax-transmission behavior:

1. In the Printers and Faxes window (refer to Figure 7.27), right-click the Fax icon; then choose Properties.

2. On the Tracking tab, set options for notifications and when the Fax Monitor should open.

3. On the Archives tab, specify whether incoming and outgoing faxes should be saved and, if so, where.

4. On the Devices tab, click the Properties button.

5. On the Send tab, specify the number of times to retry sending a fax (in case of a busy signal) and how long to wait between tries (**Figure 7.38**).

6. Click OK in each open dialog box.

SETTING UP HARDWARE

8

In the broadest sense, *hardware* is your computer and whatever connects to it; everything else is software. Windows generally uses the term to refer to a *peripheral*—nowadays usually called a *device*—which is any part of a computer other than the processor (CPU), motherboard, and memory (RAM and ROM). Your monitor, mouse, keyboard, hard disks, and printer are devices, as are digital cameras, MP3 players, backup drives, video recorders, external speakers, USB flash drives, and PDA synchronization cradles.

Windows treats any gadget connected to your PC as a device and requires you to install the software that controls it, called its *device driver* or simply *driver.* A driver translates a device's outgoing commands to Windows and the incoming commands from Windows programs that are using the device. Modern Plug and Play devices install easily, and Windows offers wizards to help you install older non–Plug and Play devices.

Installing Plug and Play Devices

Almost all hardware made since 1995 is *Plug and Play* (PnP), which means you can install a PnP device (plug it in) and use it (play with it) immediately—no configuration needed. To work properly, Plug and Play requires:

◆ A Plug and Play-compliant operating system, which XP is.

◆ A device that identifies itself to Windows and lets Windows configure it and install its drivers. Look for the "Designed for Windows" logo when you buy.

◆ The PC's system startup chip on the motherboard (called the *BIOS*) must be Plug and Play-compatible. Any computer with enough horsepower to run XP has a PnP BIOS.

The port or slot (discussed next) that a device plugs into may indicate its compatibility:

◆ All USB, IEEE 1394 (FireWire), Bluetooth, and PCMCIA (PC Card) devices support Plug and Play fully.

◆ Most PCI and parallel devices are Plug and Play-compliant.

◆ No ISA or serial devices are Plug and Play-compliant. Most such devices are old. If their manufacturers still exist, check their web sites for a Windows XP/2000/NT4 driver. If there's no such driver, you may need to replace the gizmo.

✔ Tip

■ Remember that the *serial* in *serial port* and the *serial* in *Universal Serial Bus* (USB) aren't the same thing. A serial port has a D connector with nine pins. A USB port is a small rectangular hole that accepts a pinless metal plug.

Hardware Compatibility List

Windows XP's hardware compatibility is better than that of its parent, Windows 2000, but if you've upgraded from Windows 98/Me you may find that hardware that worked fine before abruptly ceases to.

First, check the manufacturer's web site for updated drivers. Then visit www.microsoft.com/whdc/hcl to inspect Microsoft's Hardware Compatibility List (HCL), a huge list of equipment that's certified to work with XP by Microsoft's Windows Hardware Quality Labs (WHQL). Also look for the "Designed for Windows XP" logo on the product's package or web site.

Your device might still work fine with XP even if isn't on the HCL. The manufacturer may have declined to pay WHQL the fee for XP-specific certification. Many devices that were WHQL-certified for Windows 2000/98/Me work fine with XP (and an XP driver, if available).

Connecting Devices to Your Computer

When you install a new device for your computer, you'll either connect it to a port on the front or back of the computer, or insert it into a slot inside the computer case. The port or slot provides the channel that the computer and device use to exchange data.

Ordinarily there's more to installing a device than just connecting it, but I'll cover connecting here and the larger process of installing in the next section.

New-computer manuals usually contain diagrams labeling the PC's internal slots and back-panel connectors. Look in the manual for the *motherboard* (also called the *mainboard* or *desktop board*). Here's an example back-panel diagram from an Intel reference:

External devices

External devices—ones that you can connect without opening your PC's case—plug into *ports* on the computer's front or back panel. **Table 8.1** lists the common PC ports and connections. If your PC doesn't have a particular port, you must install an expansion card to get it.

Table 8.1

Ports and Connections	
PORT	DESCRIPTION
Parallel (DB-25)	A long, narrow, female port with 25 holes along 2 rows. If your printer doesn't plug into a USB port, it plugs into this port (usually called a printer port). Older backup, tape, CD, and other external drives use this port too. Windows calls it an LPT port. In modern equipment, USB connections have replaced parallel connections.
Serial	A short, slightly D-shaped male port with 9 pins along 2 rows, used for any type of serial device—an older mouse, external modem, or serial printer, for example. Windows calls it a COM port. USB connections are much faster than serial connections and have replaced them on new hardware.
PS/2	A small, round, female port with six holes. If your mouse and keyboard don't plug into USB ports, they plug into two PS/2 ports. Look for small pictures of a mouse and a keyboard, each next to its proper port. USB has mostly replaced PS/2.
USB (Universal Serial Bus)	A small, thin, rectangular port that accepts almost all Plug and Play devices: mice, USB flash drives, external drives, scanners, digital cameras, MP3 players, keyboards, printers, and so on. Most PCs have at least two USB ports, but you can buy an internal or external USB hub if you need extra ports. USB ports are hot-pluggable, allowing you to connect and disconnect devices without shutting down your PC; Windows automatically loads or unloads the drivers as needed. USB ports can provide power as well as data to the devices they connect. USB 2.0 equipment is much faster than USB 1.1 equipment. USB 2.0 requires Service Pack 1 (SP1) or later.
IEEE 1394 (FireWire)	A small, rectangular, very fast port with a tapered (>-shaped) plug. These ports are ideal for video, external disk, multiplayer gaming, and network devices. Like USB, FireWire is Plug and Play-compliant and hot-pluggable, and can provide power to peripherals. You can buy an internal or external hub to add IEEE 1394 ports to your computer.
Video (VGA)	A rectangular, female port with 15 holes along 3 rows. Your monitor plugs in here. Laptop computers use this port to connect external monitors.
Ethernet (RJ-45)	A jack (which looks like a wide telephone jack) for Ethernet and network connections. If your computer doesn't have an RJ-45 jack, buy a network interface card (NIC) to add one.
Modem (RJ-11)	A ordinary telephone jack that lets you run a telephone line from the wall to your computer for faxing or dial-up internet connections. Laptops, but not desktops, usually have built-in RJ-11 jacks. If you need one, buy a 56K modem card.
Sound	A row of small circular holes for connecting external speakers, headphones, microphones, and audio sources. Most PCs also have built-in sound ports, but adding a good sound card gives you high-quality surround sound.
S-Video	A small, circular, female port for connecting projectors, TVs, and VCRs.
Infrared (IrDA)	A small red lens on laptops that uses line-of-sight infrared light to transfer data from the computer to a similarly equipped device (such as an infrared PDA or printer) without cables.

If you set up your own computer, you're familiar with ports because the monitor, keyboard, mouse, and printer all have cables or adapters that connect to ports. Different shapes for different port types make it hard to plug a cable into the wrong port, but examine the plug and port, and don't force a connection; you'll bend the pins.

To connect an external device:

◆ If the device is hot-pluggable (USB or IEEE 1394), simply plug the device's cable or adapter into the appropriate port.

   or

   If the device isn't hot-pluggable, turn off the computer and the device; plug the device's cable into the appropriate port; then turn on the computer and device.

✔ Tips

■ Some PC also have built-in slots for reading digital-camera memory cards.

■ If you want to add both USB and IEEE 1394 ports to your PC, save some money and buy an (internal or external) hub that has them both.

Safely Removing Hardware

A small icon (🥄) appears in the notification area (system tray) when a USB, IEEE 1394, or other hot-pluggable removable storage device is plugged into your PC. If no data is being transferred between the device and the computer, you can unplug the device safely. Usually a light on the device or an onscreen warning signals whether data transfer is active. USB flash drives have a green activity light that blinks during read-write operations, for example.

If you want to be extra safe when you remove a device (make sure that an external drive's disks have stopped spinning, for example), you can stop the device before unplugging it:

1. Right-click the notification-area icon; then choose Safely Remove Hardware.

2. In the dialog box that appears, select the device in the Hardware Devices list; then click Stop.

3. Click OK in the confirmation dialog box.

   The notification-area icon disappears, and it's safe to unplug the device.

Internal devices

Internal devices are connected inside your PC's case. Storage devices such as CD, DVD, floppy, tape, backup, and hard drives are mounted on stacked shelves, called *bays,* at the front of the case. Printed circuit boards with edge connectors—such as sound cards, video adapters, graphics accelerators, internal modems, Ethernet (network) adapters, and USB hubs—are called *expansion boards* or *cards.* These cards plug into *expansion slots* (or simply *slots*) on the main circuit board (*motherboard*). **Table 8.2** lists the common PC slots. You must open your computer's case to see which slots are empty.

Each type of slot has a different shape and color, so you're unlikely to insert a card into the wrong slot. Inserting a card into a slot takes a little courage and practice. You must seat the card firmly and accurately by using neither too much force nor too little.

Table 8.2

Slots	
SLOT	DESCRIPTION
PCI	A white-cased socket about 3.25 inches (8.25 cm) long, with a white crossbar about three-quarters of the way down the slot. PCI (Peripheral Component Interconnect) slots, developed by Intel but supported by all manufacturers, are the most common type.
ISA	A black-cased socket about 5.25 inches (13.3 cm) long, with a black crossbar about two-thirds of the way down the slot. Some computers include both ISA (Industry Standard Architecture) slots for older, slower devices and PCI slots for modern ones.
AGP	A brown-cased slot about 3 inches (7.6 cm) long, with a brown crossbar about one-third of the way down the slot. AGP (Accelerated Graphics Port) is based on PCI but gives 3D graphics cards faster access to main memory than PCI. A PC has only one AGP port, occupied by a video card or accelerated graphics card.
PCMCIA (PC Card)	A slot on the side or back of a laptop computer that accepts a metal PC Card about the size of a credit card. A PC Card adds a particular feature to a laptop: a modem, Ethernet port, wireless antenna, or extra memory, for example. PC Cards are Plug and Play-compliant and hot-pluggable, and can provide power to peripherals.

✔ Tips

- Before touching the motherboard or handling a card outside its protective packaging, touch a grounded metal surface (such as the computer case or a pipe) to discharge static electricity.

- Plugging a card into an expansion slot connects it to the *bus*—the shared collection of hardware conductors that allows computer components to exchange data.

- PC Cards are hot-pluggable, so you don't have to power down your laptop to insert them.

To connect an expansion card:

1. Shut down Windows, turn off the computer, and unplug the power cord.

2. Remove the computer's cover.

3. Remove the cover plate of an empty slot (to let the card's ports protrude from the computer case).

4. Seat the card in the slot firmly, according to the manufacturer's instructions.

5. Replace the screw that held on the cover plate, tightening it through the hole in the bracket on the back of the card.

6. Replace the cover, reconnect the power cord, and turn on the computer.

   Windows will detect the new card after it starts.

Bluetooth

Bluetooth is a wireless technology that provides short-range (about 30 feet) radio links among desktops, laptops, PDAs, cellphones, printers, digital cameras, mice, keyboards, and other Bluetooth-equipped devices. It aims to eliminate cable clutter while simplifying communications, sharing, and data synchronization between computers and devices. Bluetooth doesn't need a line-of-sight connection (as infrared does), so you can, say, listen to MP3 music from the laptop in your briefcase on a hands-free headset.

Bluetooth adapters plug into any USB port on your computer—the product's user's guide will have instructions.

Bluetooth requires Service Pack 1, but Service Pack 2 further improves support. To learn more, search for *bluetooth* in Help and Support Center. If you're having problems, go to http://support.microsoft.com/?kbid=883258, "How to Troubleshoot Bluetooth Detection and Connectivity Problems in Windows XP Service Pack 2."

Bluetooth is an open standard (that is, it's not owned by Microsoft or anyone else); see also www.bluetooth.com.

Installing a New Device

Installing a new device requires both new hardware and new software. The steps you take depend on the device's Plug and Play status and whether Windows has an appropriate driver on hand.

✔ Tips

■ Windows stores thousands of drivers on your hard drive (in the file `\Windows\Driver Cache\i386\driver.cab`) and many more on the Windows CD. Running Windows Update adds new drivers as Microsoft certifies them. See "Updating Windows XP" in Chapter 19.

■ After hardware installation, Windows—or the device maker's instructions—may ask you to restart your computer.

■ You must be an Administrator to install hardware. See "Setting up User Accounts" in Chapter 16.

To install a new device:

1. Run the device's setup program (if any).

   Many new devices come with a Setup CD or floppy that includes driver files. Run this program *before* you connect the device so that Windows can copy the drivers to your hard drive and have them handy for the next steps.

2. Connect the device to your PC, as described in the preceding section.

   On the Windows desktop, one of the following three things will happen:

   ▲ A Found New Hardware pop-up message appears (**Figure 8.1**), meaning that Windows has installed the appropriate driver for your Plug and Play hardware. You're done.

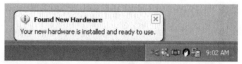

Figure 8.1 When you install a Plug and Play device, Windows pops up messages in the notification area (system tray). You might see several such messages, ending with the one shown here. If you do, you're in luck; the new hardware is ready to use.

Driver Information (.inf) Files

When Windows searches for a driver, it's actually looking for an information (.inf) file, which lists the driver files to use and registry entries to make. Windows veterans may recognize that .inf files and Windows 9x initialization (.ini) files are quite similar. But .inf settings are subtler than .ini settings. Never edit an .inf file to try to solve your driver problems.

Hardware setup software can include an .inf file; a .sys file (the actual driver); and subordinate library (.dll), help (.hlp), Control Panel (.cpl), and web-page (.htm) files. Some device drivers are *only* .inf files. A monitor, for example, may be set up by a single .inf file listing the valid resolutions, refresh rates, and other display settings.

Figure 8.2 You'll see the Found New Hardware Wizard if your device isn't Plug and Play—or if it is but Windows can't find an appropriate driver. This wizard helps you install the driver manually.

Figure 8.3 You have two choices here: Click Finish to give up the installation (at least for now), or click Back to enter the driver's specific location. Check Don't Prompt Me Again if you don't want to be nagged to install this particular piece of hardware each time you restart Windows.

▲ The Found New Hardware Wizard appears (**Figure 8.2**), meaning that Windows detected the device but can't find an appropriate driver. Follow one of the "To install a device driver" procedures later in this section.

▲ Windows does nothing, meaning that it didn't detect the device. See the next section, "Installing Non–Plug and Play Hardware."

✔ Tip

■ The driver packed with the hardware may turn on specific features that the Windows driver doesn't. If you want to use the manufacturer's unsigned driver instead of a signed driver included with Windows, follow "To install a device driver from a specific location" later in this section. (See also the later tips about unsigned drivers.)

To install a device driver from an installation CD or floppy:

1. Insert the device's setup disk into a drive.

2. On the Welcome page (refer to Figure 8.2), select the first option, Install the Software Automatically (Recommended); then click Next.

   The wizard searches the CD, floppy disk, and all removable drives.

   If the wizard finds one compatible driver, it installs the driver automatically. If it finds several compatible drivers, it lets you choose one from a list. If it can't find any compatible drivers, the wizard displays **Figure 8.3**.

To install a device driver downloaded from the internet:

1. On the Welcome page (refer to Figure 8.2), select the second option, Install from a List or Specific Location (Advanced); then click Next.

2. On the Search page (**Figure 8.4**), select the first option, Search for the Best Driver in These Locations.

3. Check Include This Location in the Search.

4. Type or browse to the location (full pathname) of the folder that contains the downloaded driver and information (.inf) files.

5. Click Next.

   The wizard searches the specified location for the driver.

6. Follow the onscreen instructions.

✔ Tip

■ A downloaded driver usually comes as a self-extracting executable (.exe) file or a compressed (.zip) file that you must decompress before installation. Look for setup instructions on the web page or, after unzipping, in a `readme.txt` file.

Figure 8.4 If you've downloaded a driver to a local or network drive, use this page to specify its location.

INSTALLING A NEW DEVICE

Figure 8.5 If you're installing drivers from a CD or floppy, it isn't important to pick the correct hardware type; the driver information (.inf) file will specify that.

Figure 8.6 Clicking an entry in the Manufacturer list makes the Model list display the drivers that XP has on tap for that manufacturer. If you don't see your model (or something compatible), click Have Disk to install a driver from a CD or floppy.

Figure 8.7 This warning appears if Windows thinks that you've chosen a driver that won't work with your new device. Click Yes if you're sure that you want to install the driver; click No otherwise.

To install a device driver from a specific location:

1. On the Welcome page (refer to Figure 8.2), select the second option, Install from a List or Specific Location (Advanced); then click Next.

2. On the Search page (refer to Figure 8.4), select the second option, Don't Search, I Will Choose the Driver to Install; then click Next.

3. On the Hardware Type page, select the type of hardware that you're installing (**Figure 8.5**); then click Next.

   If the device doesn't fit any entry in the list, select Show All Devices.

4. On the Select Device Driver page, choose a manufacturer and model (**Figure 8.6**); then click Next.

   You're probably in this page, however, to install a driver that Windows *doesn't* have. In that case, click Have Disk; type or browse to the location (full pathname) of the manufacturer's installation disk; then click Next.

5. Follow the onscreen instructions.

   You may be asked to choose among several drivers, select settings or a port, or insert the Windows CD. When you click Finish, you may be prompted to restart your PC.

✔ Tips

- If Windows thinks that you've picked an incorrect driver, it displays an Update Driver Warning message (**Figure 8.7**).

continues on next page

INSTALLING A NEW DEVICE

- When you try to install an *unsigned driver,* Windows displays **Figure 8.8**. A *signed driver* is one that Microsoft has digitally stamped to certify that it works properly with Windows XP and that it hasn't been tampered with since its creation. Microsoft's driver-signing program combats the sloppily written, system-destabilizing, third-party drivers that plagued earlier Windows versions.

- Windows uses the icon ( ) to identify a signed driver.

- Unsigned drivers are adventures. They may work perfectly (particularly those that worked fine in Windows 2000), or they may cause system lockups and blue screens. To synchronize your driver security policy with your own degree of paranoia, choose Start > Control Panel > Performance and Maintenance > System > Hardware tab > Driver Signing (**Figure 8.9**).

- Windows maintains its own list of drivers known to cause serious stability problems. XP's driver-protection feature refuses to install these drivers, regardless of your security policy. Windows warns you when such a driver is blocked (**Figure 8.10**).

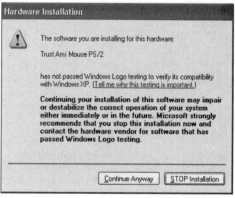

Figure 8.8 The most stable systems run only signed drivers; installing an unsigned driver is a gamble. If you see this message, check the device maker's web site for an updated driver. If you decide to click Continue Anyway, create a System Restore checkpoint first (see "Restoring Your System" in Chapter 19).

Figure 8.9 Ignore lets you install an unsigned driver without having to click through a warning message. Warn (the default) lets you install after you override the warning message. Block prohibits installation of any unsigned driver.

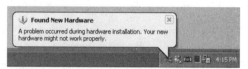

Figure 8.10 Windows displays several warnings when it blocks a driver, culminating with this one. You also may see an Incompatible Hardware or Software message box that provides details about the bad driver.

Figure 8.11 You can't skip this search for non–Plug and Play hardware, even though it's unsuccessful in most cases.

Installing Non–Plug and Play Hardware

Use the Add Hardware Wizard to set up older, non–Plug and Play devices. This wizard is a lot like the Found New Hardware Wizard, described in the preceding section, but it doesn't appear automatically.

✔ Tip

■ You must be an Administrator to install hardware. See "Setting up User Accounts" in Chapter 16.

To install a non–Plug and Play device:

1. If the device includes a setup program on CD or floppy, or if you've downloaded one from the manufacturer's web site, run it now.

2. Connect the device to your PC, as described in "Connecting Devices to Your Computer" earlier in this chapter.

3. Choose Start > Control Panel > Printers and Other Hardware > Add Hardware (under See Also in the task pane).

4. Click Next to skip the Welcome page.
   The wizard searches for the new device (**Figure 8.11**).
   If the wizard finds it, you can install the correct driver, follow the onscreen instructions to finish the wizard, and skip the rest of these steps. Most of the time, the wizard won't find the device and instead prompts *you* to find it; continue to the next step.

5. On the Is the Hardware Connected page, select the first option, Yes, I Have Already Connected the Hardware; then click Next.

continues on next page

6. On the next page, select the device that you're trying to install (**Figure 8.12**).

7. On the next page, specify how you want to install the device:

▲ To search your computer's ports and slots for non–Plug and Play devices, select the first option, Search for and Install the Hardware Automatically (Recommended) (**Figure 8.13**).

▲ To skip the automated detection process, select the second option, Install the Hardware That I Manually Select from a List (Advanced).

8. On the next page, select a hardware type in the list, or select Show All Devices (refer to Figure 8.5); then click Next.

9. On the next page, select the device manufacturer and correct model (**Figure 8.14**); then click Next.

10. Follow the onscreen instructions.

You may be asked to choose among several drivers, select settings or a port, or insert the Windows CD. When you click Finish, you may be prompted to restart your PC.

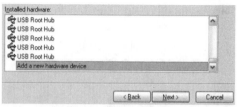

Figure 8.12 If your device doesn't appear in the list of installed devices, scroll to the bottom of the list and choose Add a New Hardware Device.

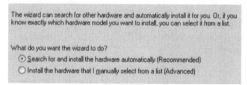

Figure 8.13 If you select this option and Windows finds the new device, it installs the driver automatically, and you're done. If Windows doesn't find the device, proceed to the next step.

Figure 8.14 Click Have Disk if the driver resides on a local or network drive, a CD, or a floppy.

Figure 8.15 Click a + symbol to expand a category branch and list all installed devices that fit into that category. Right-click a particular device for a shortcut menu, or double-click it to show its Properties dialog box.

Managing Device Drivers

Device Manager is a powerful tool that lets you inspect, manage, and troubleshoot drivers for the hardware already installed on your computer. It lists every device in or attached to your system in an Explorer-like tree (**Figure 8.15**).

✔ Tip

- You must be an Administrator to perform many Device Manager tasks. See "Setting up User Accounts" in Chapter 16.

To open Device Manager:

◆ Choose Start > Control Panel > Performance and Maintenance > System > Hardware tab > Device Manager.

or

Right-click My Computer (in the Start menu); then choose Properties > Hardware tab > Device Manager.

or

Choose Start > Run; type `devmgmt.msc` and then press Enter.

✔ Tips

- Choose View > Show Hidden Devices to display *legacy* (non–Plug and Play) devices.

- To expand all branches of the Device Manager tree, select the top-level (root) entry; then press * (on the numeric keypad).

Like any file, a device driver has properties that determine its behavior.

To show a device's properties:

◆ In Device Manager, right-click the device; then choose Properties (refer to Figure 8.15).

or

Double-click the device's name.

The tabs of the Properties dialog box vary by device. The standard ones are:

General shows the name, type, physical location, and status of the device (**Figure 8.16**).

Advanced (if it appears) contains device-specific properties. A network adapter, for example, may have a connection-type property.

Driver shows information about the currently installed driver and has buttons that let you manage it (**Figure 8.17**).

Resources lists the system hardware resources (such as interrupts and memory range) that the device uses.

✔ Tip

■ Some devices install their own Control Panel extensions, which let you view or change additional properties.

Figure 8.16 The General tab tells you whether a device is working properly. If you're having problems, click Troubleshoot to display Help and Support Center's troubleshooting wizard.

Figure 8.17 The Driver tab tells you the driver's provider (which, unhelpfully, is its distributor, not its manufacturer), its date and version, and whether it has a signature.

Welcome to the Hardware Update Wizard

Windows will search for current and updated software by looking on your computer, on the hardware installation CD, or on the Windows Update Web site (with your permission).

Read our privacy policy

Can Windows connect to Windows Update to search for software?

- Yes, this time only
- Yes, now and every time I connect a device
- No, not this time

Click Next to continue.

This wizard helps you install software for:

Intel(R) PRO/100 VE Network Connection

 If your hardware came with an installation CD or floppy disk, insert it now.

What do you want the wizard to do?

- Install the software automatically (Recommended)
- Install from a list or specific location (Advanced)

Figure 8.18 If SP2 is installed on your PC, the top page appears when you launch the wizard. Without SP2, the wizard skips right to the bottom page.

You can use Device Manager to install a driver that's newer than the current one. But newer doesn't always mean better or more stable. If a driver isn't broken, don't update it unless updating improves things.

To update a device driver:

1. In Device Manager, right-click the device whose driver you want to update; then choose Update Driver (refer to Figure 8.15).

2. Use the Hardware Update Wizard to install the new driver.

   If Service Pack 2 is installed, **Figure 8.18, top** appears as the first page. Select one of the Yes options to have Windows scour the Microsoft web site for an updated driver. Or select No if you already have a driver to install; then click Next to advance to **Figure 8.18, bottom.** (Without SP2, this page appears first.) Select the second option, Install from a List or Specific location (Advanced), and point the wizard to the new driver's location.

   The remaining steps are the same as those in the Found New Hardware and Add Hardware wizards, described earlier in this chapter.

✔ Tip

- Some devices have proprietary update programs that don't support the Hardware Update Wizard.

MANAGING DEVICE DRIVERS

283

If a fresh driver causes more problems than it solves (not uncommon for unsigned drivers and prerelease drivers), the driver rollback feature lets you uninstall and replace it with the previous one.

To roll back a device driver:

◆ In Device Manager, right-click the device whose driver you want to roll back; then choose Properties > Driver tab > Roll Back Driver (refer to Figure 8.17).

✔ Tips

■ The rollback feature is available only if the driver has been updated since Windows was installed.

■ When you install a prerelease (*beta*) driver, you're helping the software developer. Don't install a beta driver unless it fixes a flaw that's bugging you.

Troubleshooting Hardware

If you install and uninstall enough hardware on your system, you're going to have to deal with error messages and system conflicts. When trouble comes, the first step is to use Windows' built-in troubleshooters: Choose Start > Help and Support > Hardware > Fixing a Hardware Problem > Hardware Troubleshooter (under Fix a Problem). Use the wizardlike screens to try to resolve the problem.

No luck? Use Device Manager: Double-click a device (refer to Figure 8.15) to show its Properties dialog box and then click the General tab. If the device isn't working, the Device Status box shows an error message and code (refer to Figure 8.16). For an explanation of the problem and advice on how to fix it, go to http://support.microsoft.com/?kbid=125174, "Explanation of Error Codes Generated by Device Manager." Or click the Troubleshoot button for a device-specific troubleshooter.

Before you become aggressive, back up your drivers with DriverGuide Toolkit ($20 U.S.; www.driverguidetoolkit.com) or WinRet (free; http://winret.sourceforge.net).

You can remove a driver permanently and erase all the configuration settings for its device. Generally you uninstall a driver to reclaim system resources after you've removed hardware from your PC. But you can remove a troublesome driver completely, to scrap it or to reinstall it from scratch.

To uninstall a device:

◆ In Device Manager, right-click the device whose driver you want to uninstall; then choose Uninstall (refer to Figure 8.15).

✔ Tips

■ You can uninstall a Plug and Play device's driver only if the device is plugged in, because otherwise, the driver isn't in memory. To reinstall the driver without unplugging, in Device Manager, choose Action > Scan for Hardware Changes.

■ If Device Manager displays icons for duplicate devices (such as two mice), uninstall *both* of them; then restart your PC. If you uninstall only one, Windows detects it again when you restart. Click No if Windows asks you to restart after you uninstall the first duplicate; restart manually after removing the second.

If you want to turn off a device without the hassle of removing it, you can disable it. Windows ignores a disabled device's existence and releases the system resources that it uses.

Generally you disable and enable devices to create hardware profiles (see the next section), but you also can use this technique to resolve device conflicts. If two devices are competing for the same resource, disable one of them; restart; and then see whether the other one starts working.

To disable a device:

◆ In Device Manager, right-click the device that you want to disable; then choose Disable (refer to Figure 8.15).

A red X appears on the disabled device's icon (**Figure 8.19**).

✔ Tips

■ To enable a disabled device, repeat the procedure. (The Disable command becomes the Enable command.)

■ A black-on-yellow exclamation mark (!) on the icon of a malfunctioning device (**Figure 8.20**) indicates a driver problem.

■ In Windows 9*x*, conflicts were frequent because too many devices fought over scarce IRQs. An *IRQ,* or *interrupt request,* is a hardware line that a device uses to communicate with the CPU. Windows XP copes with this problem by letting devices share IRQs when possible (**Figure 8.21**).

Figure 8.19 A red X means that a device isn't working, either because you've disabled it or because it's incompatible with Windows or your PC. Check the Resources and General tabs of the Properties dialog box for an explanation of the problem.

Figure 8.20 A yellow ! means that you (or Windows) installed the wrong driver; that the device is trying to use the same resources as another device; or that the driver can't find its device, perhaps because it's been removed or disconnected.

Figure 8.21 Choose View > Resources by Connection to see different devices sharing the same IRQ—16 and 17, in this case.

Figure 8.22 Windows names the default hardware profile Profile 1. If you have a laptop with a Plug and Play docking station, you'll see Docked and Undocked profiles too. Give new profiles meaningful names, such as In the Office or On the Road.

Figure 8.23 The General tab of a device's Properties dialog box lets you enable or disable that device in the prevailing hardware profile.

Using Hardware Profiles

A *hardware profile* tells Windows which devices to start when you boot your computer. Profiles are especially useful if you're a traveling laptop user. When you're in the office, you want your laptop to recognize your network card, external mouse, keyboard, and monitor. When you're in transit, you don't want your laptop to waste time and battery power by looking for these devices. You can create a profile for each situation.

To create a hardware profile:

1. Choose Start > Control Panel > Performance and Maintenance > System > Hardware tab > Hardware Profiles (**Figure 8.22**).

2. Select a profile in the list; then click Copy. The copied profile serves as a starting point for the new one.

3. In the Copy Profile dialog box, type a name for the new profile; then click OK.

4. In the Hardware Profiles Selection section, specify how Windows should load a profile during startup; then click OK.

5. Restart your computer.

6. On the startup screen (a black, DOS-like text screen), choose the profile that you want to modify.

7. Open Device Manager (see the preceding section), and adjust the settings for each device that you want to enable or disable (**Figure 8.23**).

8. Close Device Manager.

9. To modify other profiles, repeat steps 6–8 for each profile.

CAMERAS AND SCANNERS

9

Windows XP comes with programs and features that let you download, view, and manage digital images on your computer.

The **Scanner and Camera Wizard** transfers digital photos from your camera to your computer. Other wizards help you print pictures or publish them on the web.

Windows Explorer enhancements help you organize image files. The Filmstrip and Thumbnails views, for example, let you browse miniature versions of your photos.

Windows Picture and Fax Viewer lets you view, rotate, magnify, and annotate images—and put up a slide show—without opening an image-editing program.

Windows also can make your scanner behave (somewhat) like a digital camera, and manipulate scanned documents and images just like digital photos.

Transferring Photos to Your Computer

After connecting your camera to your PC, you can use the Scanner and Camera Wizard to download and save pictures in your My Pictures folder or any folder that you choose.

Most cameras come with a cable that plugs into your PC's USB port. Windows includes and installs drivers for many camera models, sparing you the chore of manual setup. If your camera is too old (pre-2000) to understand XP's automated download features, your best bet is to buy an external *memory card reader* that plugs into a USB port. Insert a memory card into the reader, and Windows treats it like a floppy disk (**Figure 9.1**). Multislot readers can handle Secure Digital (SD), SmartMedia, CompactFlash, MultiMedia, Memory Stick, xD, and other formats.

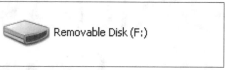

Figure 9.1 If you connect a digital camera to your PC, the top icon appears in the My Computer window. If you connect a memory card reader, the bottom icon appears.

✔ Tips

- For information about USB and connecting hardware to your computer, see Chapter 8.

- Installed cameras also are accessible in Control Panel's Scanners and Cameras extension. Choose Start > Control Panel > Printers and Other Hardware > Scanners and Cameras.

Figure 9.2 Your choices may differ depending on the photo-management software—which may have come with your camera—installed on your computer. Check Always Use This Program for This Action (or Always Do the Selected Action) if you don't want to be nagged by this dialog box every time you download photos.

To transfer photos to your computer:

1. Connect your digital camera to your computer with the USB cable, or connect your card reader to your computer and insert a memory card.

   If a dialog box or the Scanner and Camera Wizard doesn't appear, see the sidebar later in this section.

2. If Windows asks you what you want to do, choose Microsoft Scanner and Camera Wizard; then click OK (**Figure 9.2**).

3. Click Next to skip the Welcome page (**Figure 9.3**).

4. On the Choose Pictures to Copy page, choose the photos that you want to work with on your computer (**Figure 9.4**); then click Next.

   It's usually easier to copy *all* photos from camera to hard disk and then delete the ones that you don't want in Windows Explorer, which displays larger preview images.

continues on next page

Figure 9.3 Instead of walking through the wizard (by clicking Next), you can click the link Advanced Users Only (which isn't that advanced) to work with individual photo files in Windows Explorer.

Figure 9.4 The Clear All and Select All buttons in the bottom-right corner are handy if you want to include or exclude only a few pictures. The bottom-left buttons let you rotate pictures and see their properties.

TRANSFERRING PHOTOS TO YOUR COMPUTER

5. On the Picture Name and Destination page, name the group of pictures and specify a folder to copy them to (**Figure 9.5**); then click Next.

If you name the group, say, My Bar Mitzvah, Windows creates the folder My Documents\My Pictures\My Bar Mitzvah and puts the photos in it unless you click Browse or type a different pathname.

The wizard displays a progress page (**Figure 9.6**).

6. On the Other Options page, select the third option, Nothing, I'm Finished Working with These Pictures (**Figure 9.7**); then click Next.

7. You're done; click Finish (**Figure 9.8**).

The wizard tacks serial numbers onto the group name to create each photo's file name (`Picture 001.jpg`, `Picture 002.jpg`, and so on). You can rename the photos as you would any other files.

Figure 9.5 Check Delete Pictures from My Device After Copying Them if you want to erase your camera or memory card after the transfer.

Figure 9.6 Twiddle your thumbs while Windows copies the photos to your hard drive. You can click Cancel to stop copying.

Figure 9.7 The first two options cost money.

Completing the Scanner and Camera Wizard

6 picture(s) were copied.

To see your pictures on your computer or network, click the location below:
My Pictures\Rainy San Francisco Trip

Figure 9.8 Before clicking Finish, you can click the link to open the folder that contains your downloaded photos.

Figure 9.9 With these options selected, Windows automatically creates a subfolder in the specified folder (by using the current date), copies all the photos from the camera to that folder, and then erases the photos from the camera's memory or card.

If you find the Scanner and Camera Wizard to be cumbersome, you may prefer an option that downloads all your photos automatically to a specified folder whenever you plug in your digital camera.

To transfer photos to your computer automatically:

1. With the camera connected and powered on, choose Start > My Computer.

2. Right-click the camera icon; then choose Properties > Events tab.

3. Adjust the settings shown in **Figure 9.9.**

4. Click OK (or Apply).

✔ Tip

■ This option doesn't apply to memory card readers (removable disks).

Installing a Camera Driver Manually

The Scanner and Camera Wizard won't appear when you connect your camera to your PC if

◆ It's an older (pre-2000) camera that doesn't comply with the WIA (Windows Image Acquisition) standard, or

◆ The camera's driver didn't come preinstalled in XP.

In either case, you can install the necessary software manually by using the CD that came with the camera:

1. Choose Start > Control Panel > Printers and Other Hardware > Scanners and Cameras.

2. Below Imaging Tasks (in the task pane), click Add an Imaging Device.

3. In the Scanner and Camera Installation Wizard, click Next.

4. Click Have Disk.

5. Insert the disk containing the camera software; then follow the onscreen instructions.

You also can install a camera driver by using Control Panel's Add Hardware Wizard. See Chapter 8.

Viewing and Managing Photos

Windows XP's official storage locations for photos are the My Pictures folder and any subfolders that you create for it. You can store your pictures elsewhere, but My Pictures is easy to open from the Start menu and Explorer's task pane. It's also where most programs and wizards assume that you'll save and open image files.

My Pictures offers many options for viewing and managing digital pictures. From within this folder, you can view photos at different sizes, view a slide show, rotate photos, print them, email them, or publish them on the web. Don't miss the list of special tasks in the task pane on the left side of the window (**Figure 9.10**).

To view photos as a filmstrip:

1. Choose Start > My Pictures.

2. Double-click subfolder (if any) containing your photos.

3. Choose View > Filmstrip (**Figure 9.11**).

Figure 9.10 The Picture Tasks links give you quick access to common image tasks. You also can right-click an image icon (or group of icons) to see specialized photo tasks, as well as the usual file tasks (Copy, Rename, Properties, Delete, and so on).

Figure 9.11 The enlarged image shows the selected photo. To select another one, click the left or right arrow below the large image; click one of the smaller images in the bottom row; or press the left- or right-arrow key.

Figure 9.12 You can drag and drop photos to rearrange their order in Thumbnails view. If you're viewing 50 photos, for example, you can drag your favorites—one by one or in groups—to the top of the folder. When you reopen that folder, you still see all 50 photos, but the first few are your favorites.

✔ Tips

■ If My Pictures doesn't appear in your Start menu, right-click the Start button; choose Properties > Customize > Advanced tab; then choose Display As Link (below My Pictures) in the Start Menu Items list.

■ In step 3, choose View > Thumbnails to see the images presented as miniatures arranged in rows and columns (**Figure 9.12**).

■ To free screen space for displaying photos, press F11. Press F11 again to return to normal screen layout.

■ To use a photo as your desktop background, select a photo; then click Set As Desktop Background in the task pane (refer to Figure 9.10).

■ To use your photos as a screen saver, see "Setting a Screen Saver" in Chapter 4.

■ Edit photos in Paint or an alternative image-editing program; see "Using the Free Utility Programs" in Chapter 6.

■ For more information about viewing images in Explorer, see "Viewing Files and Folders in Different Ways" and "Customizing a Folder" in Chapter 5.

VIEWING AND MANAGING PHOTOS

To start a slide show:

1. In the task pane on the left, in the Picture Tasks section, click View As a Slide Show (refer to Figure 9.10).

Your screen fills with a self-advancing slide show of every picture in the folder.

2. View the slide show, using the appropriate controls.

As the slide show begins, an onscreen toolbar offers controls to start, pause, advance, reverse, or stop the show. You also can use the left- and right-arrow keys to move backward and forward, or click the photo itself to advance. To stop the show, click Exit on the toolbar or press Esc.

To rotate a photo:

◆ In Filmstrip or Thumbnails view, right-click the photo that you want to rotate; then choose Rotate Clockwise or Rotate Counterclockwise.

or

Double-click the photo to open it in Windows Picture and Fax Viewer; then click the Rotate Clockwise or Rotate Counterclockwise button at the bottom of the window (**Figure 9.13**).

✔ Tip

■ Sometimes Windows warns that rotating a photo may reduce its image quality. The change usually is imperceptible, but if you're worried, make a copy of the image before rotation.

Figure 9.13 If your photo is sideways (because you held the camera sideways when you took it), you can rotate it in 90-degree increments.

To zoom in or zoom out on a photo:

◆ In My Pictures, double-click the photo to open it in Windows Picture and Fax Viewer; then click the Zoom In or Zoom Out button at the bottom of the window as many times as you need to.

✔ Tips

■ When you click Zoom In, the pointer becomes a magnifying glass. Wherever you place the pointer before you click becomes the new center of the displayed image when you click. This method is handy for examining details before you edit an image.

■ Microsoft's Photo Story is a free program that lets you create "video" stories by adding music, narration, pans, zooms, and other effects to your photos. Download it at www.microsoft.com/windowsxp/using/digitalphotography/photostory/.

Windows Picture and Fax Viewer

Windows Picture and Fax Viewer (refer to Figure 9.13) isn't a freestanding application—you won't find it in the Start menu—but a miniature program that appears only when you double-click an image file. The Viewer is associated by default with .emf, .gif, .jpg, .bmp, .png, .tif, and .wmf files unless you've assigned them otherwise (see "Associating Documents with Programs" in Chapter 6).

At the bottom of the Viewer window are buttons for advancing, reversing, rotating, zooming, printing, and deleting images, among other things. To learn what a button does, hover the pointer over it for a pop-up tip. When you view a TIFF file, the toolbar sprouts extra buttons for navigation, drawing, and annotation.

Windows Picture and Fax Viewer is quick and convenient but too lightweight for serious use. If you manage a lot of photos, look into Picasa (free; www.picasa.com), IrfanView (free; www.irfanview.com), ACDSee ($50 U.S.; www.acdsee.com), ThumbsPlus ($50; www.cerious.com), or FlipAlbum ($20; www.flipalbum.com).

VIEWING AND MANAGING PHOTOS

Printing Photos

The Photo Printing Wizard walks you through the printing process and lets you print multiple photos per page, saving you money on expensive photo-quality paper.

To print photos:

1. Choose Start > My Pictures; then choose the subfolder (if any) containing your photos.

2. To print all the photos in the folder, click Print Pictures in the task pane (refer to Figure 9.10).

   or

   To print some photos, select them and then click Print This Picture (or Print the Selected Pictures) in the task pane.

   The Photo Printing Wizard appears.

3. Click Next to skip the Welcome page.

4. On the Picture Selection page, check the box above each thumbnail you want to print; uncheck the others (**Figure 9.14**); then click Next.

5. On the Printing Options page, choose a printer; then click Next.

   If you're using photo-quality paper, also click Printing Preferences to set paper tray, color, and resolution options.

6. On the Layout Selection page, specify how you want the photos arranged on the page (**Figure 9.15**); then click Next.

   The wizard sends your photos to the printer.

Figure 9.14 This page shows you the selected photos or, if you made no selection, all the current folder's photos.

Figure 9.15 The wizard rotates, sizes, and crops images to fit. To prevent unpleasant surprises, the layout preview shows you which parts of the images you'll lose on paper.

Figure 9.16 This page varies by print processor. Heed the warning icons (such as the yellow ! shown here) next to print sizes; they mean that the image's resolution is too low to produce good print quality at that size. The same file may make a good 4"x 6" print but a grainy 5"x 7" print, for example.

Ordering Prints Online

The Online Print Ordering Wizard walks you through getting digital photos printed via the internet. You select the photos to be uploaded to an online photo processor (such as Fujifilm, Shutterfly, or Kodak) and enter credit-card and shipping information. Your prints arrive by mail in about a week.

To order prints via the internet:

1. Choose Start > My Pictures and then the subfolder (if any) containing your photos.

2. Select the photos that you want to order.

3. In the task pane at the left, click Order Prints Online (refer to Figure 9.10). The Online Print Ordering Wizard appears.

4. Click Next to skip the Welcome page.

5. On the Change Your Picture Selection page, check or uncheck the box above the thumbnails to choose the prints to order; then click Next.

6. On the Select a Printing Company page, select a company to print your photos; then click Next.

7. Select the pictures, print sizes, and quantities that you want (**Figure 9.16**); then click Next.

8. Follow the onscreen instructions to complete the wizard. You'll be prompted for shipping and payment information.

...ng Photos

...photos to be printed can be too ...rge for emailing. You may have trouble sending photos if your (or your recipient's) ISP or mail service bounces attachments larger than 1 or 2 MB. Even if the transfer is successful, you may overload your recipients' inboxes and annoy them. Windows solves this problem with image-shrinking tools.

To email photos:

1. Choose Start > My Pictures and then the subfolder (if any) containing your photos.

2. Select the photos to send.

3. In the task pane at the left, in the File and Folder Tasks section, click E-Mail This File or E-Mail the Selected Items, if you selected more than one.

4. In the Send Pictures via E-Mail dialog box, click Show More Options to expand the dialog box (**Figure 9.17**).

5. Make a selection, and click OK (**Figure 9.18**).

✔ Tips

- Windows compresses bitmap (.bmp) and TIFF (.tif) files before resizing them. GIF (.gif) and JPEG (.jpg) files already are compressed, so Windows resizes them without more compression.

- If you want to compress photos *without* emailing them, select the icons in the Attach header of the email message (refer to Figure 9.18) and drag them to the desktop or to any folder other than My Pictures. Then close the email without saving.

Figure 9.17 The default settings compress and resize images to 640 x 480 pixels, which is fine for onscreen viewing. A larger size shows more detail and prints better, at the cost of bigger files and slower emailing.

Figure 9.18 Windows opens your email program, creates a new message, and attaches the compressed files. You type the recipient's address, add your own note, and send the message.

EMAILING PHOTOS

Figure 9.19 Suggested sites are configured specifically to hook into the Web Publishing Wizard. MSN is free, but its storage limit is 3 MB (about a dozen photos), and it requires a .NET Passport (see "Getting a .NET Passport" in Chapter 15). You can't use the wizard to use sites hosted by other ISPs.

Figure 9.20 Large images on the web increase page-loading times and waste server space. Choose Small to reduce your photos to web-friendly sizes.

Publishing Photos on the Web

The Web Publishing Wizard lets you compress photos and post them on selected web sites for the world to see. MSN and some of the other sites are free.

To post photos on the web:

1. Choose Start > My Pictures and then the subfolder (if any) containing your photos.

2. Select one or more photos, or a whole folder, to post.

3. In the task pane at the left, in the File and Folder Tasks section, click the Publish to the Web link.
   The Web Publishing Wizard appears.

4. Click Next to skip the Welcome page.

5. Check or uncheck the boxes above the thumbnails to choose the photos to post; then click Next.

6. Select an internet service provider to host your web site (**Figure 9.19**); then click Next.

7. Follow the onscreen instructions for your chosen service provider. When you arrive at **Figure 9.20**, you'll generally want to choose Small image sizes.
   After Windows uploads your photos to the website, the wizard's final page opens your browser to the new web page. Windows creates a shortcut to that site in Internet Explorer's Favorites menu.

✔ Tips

- You can use the Web Publishing Wizard to post other types of files, such as Microsoft Word documents.

- Skip the wizard and use one of the better photo-sharing sites, such as www.ofoto.com, www.shutterfly.com, www.dotphoto.com, or www.photoworks.com.

Using Scanners

When you connect a Plug and Play scanner to your PC, the Scanner and Camera Wizard appears, just as it does for a camera. The wizard's pages are similar to those described in "Transferring Photos to Your Computer" earlier in this chapter, with these differences:

◆ On the Choose Scanning Preferences page, specify black-and-white, color, or grayscale scanning and the part of the page you want scanned.

◆ On the Picture Name and Destination page, select an image format listed in **Table 9.1**.

✔ Tip

■ If you save an image in the wrong format, you can open it in Paint and save it in another format by choosing File > Save As. To open Paint, choose Start > All Programs > Accessories > Paint.

Table 9.1

Image-File Formats	
FORMAT	DESCRIPTION
Bitmap	Windows bitmap (.bmp) images tend to be large, because this format can't be compressed. BMP is almost always the wrong choice for scanned documents and photos.
JPEG	Joint Photographic Experts Group (.jpg/.jpeg) files are highly compressed and an excellent choice for scanning photos, particularly if you're going to post them on the web. But the JPEG process sacrifices image detail permanently during compression. In most cases, the loss is invisible for onscreen viewing.
PNG	Portable Network Graphics (.png) files, which all modern browsers support, is patent- and license-free, and retains all detail during compression.
TIFF	Tagged Image File Format (.tif) files are compatible with most image-editing programs, even ancient ones. TIFF is a good choice for scanning text documents and grayscale images. TIFF's compression, like PNG's, preserves detail but results in larger files than JPEG. You can scan multiple pages into a single TIFF file; the Windows Fax program does this to store faxes.

WINDOWS MEDIA PLAYER

Windows Media Player is Microsoft's free program that plays most of your digital media, including music, videos, CDs, and DVDs. It also acts like a digital jukebox that helps you find and organize digital media files. XP's Media Player is more versatile than the anemic attempts in early Windows versions; it lets you listen to internet radio stations, rip tracks from audio CDs to your hard drive, burn music CDs, download songs to your portable music player, shop at online stores, and more.

✔ Tips

- Many Windows XP installations include Media Player 8 or 9. This chapter covers Media Player 10, which Microsoft released in September 2004. You can download the latest version free via Windows Update or at www.microsoft.com/windowsmedia. (Media Player 10 isn't part of Service Pack 2.)

- To use Media Player in all its capacities, you should have a 1.5 GHz processor or faster and at least 512 MB RAM.

Getting Started with Media Player

Media Player's gee-whizzery makes for a crowded interface, as you see in **Figure 10.1**. You can hover your mouse pointer over any control for a pop-up tip, but there are wheels within wheels. The interior section changes depending on the Media Player feature that you're using; Figure 10.1 shows Now Playing.

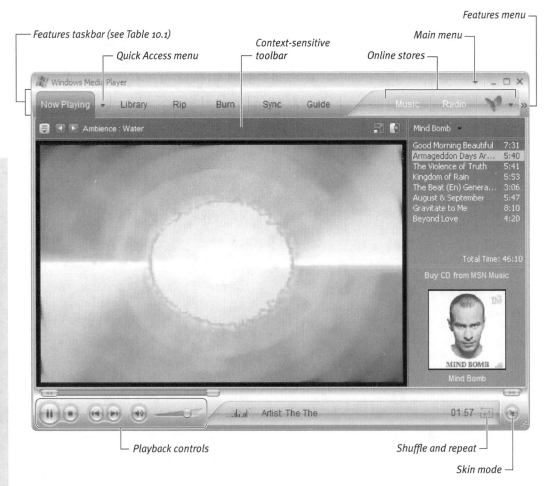

Features menu

Features taskbar (see Table 10.1)   *Context-sensitive toolbar*   *Main menu*

Quick Access menu   *Online stores*

Playback controls   *Shuffle and repeat*

Skin mode

Figure 10.1 Windows Media Player controls

Figure 10.2 Double-clicking a file with any of these file types opens Media Player. Click a file-type name (not its check box) to make a description appear below the list. A dimmed box means that the file type was associated with a different player; you can double-click the box to give Media Player full ownership of that type.

Table 10.1

Features Taskbar Buttons	
CLICK	TO
Now Playing	View a video, visualization, song list, or information about whatever is playing.
Library	Organize digital music and video files by using a Windows Explorer-like interface or compile your media files into sets of favorite songs and videos (playlists).
Rip	Copy (rip) tracks from a music CD to your hard drive.
Burn	Create (burn) your own music CDs from the tracks stored on your hard drive.
Sync	Transfer music and videos to a portable music or video player.
Guide	Go online to pitiless hype machine WindowsMedia.com to read about (or buy) the latest movies, music, and videos.
Online Stores	The buttons in the Online Stores area vary by the store that you've picked. You'll find music, radio, video, and other content.

To start Media Player:

◆ Choose Start > All Programs > Windows Media Player.

or

Click the Media Player icon ( ) on the Quick Launch toolbar, located on the taskbar.

or

Double-click any associated media file.

or

Choose Start > Run; type wmplayer and then press Enter.

✔ Tips

■ Naturally you need speakers or headphones to hear anything. If you have an older computer without built-in sound support (look on the back panel for a row of small circular ports), you can buy a sound card; the cards are cheap and easy to install. A pricier sound card plays multichannel audio (surround sound) and High Definition Compatible Digital (HDCD) content. If you're buying speakers, get ones that come with a subwoofer.

■ The Features taskbar has buttons for quick access to Media Player's main features. See **Table 10.1** for a summary and later sections for details.

■ To see the file types that Media Player will open by default, choose Tools > Options > File Types tab (**Figure 10.2**). Check the box next to a file type to make Media Player its default player or uncheck it to use another player. For information about file-type associations, see "Associating Documents with Programs" in Chapter 6.

■ The old version of Media Player, without all the clutter, is still around but hidden. To open it, choose Start > Run; type mplay32 and then press Enter.

GETTING STARTED WITH MEDIA PLAYER

The Media Player menu bar keeps itself out of the way until you summon it in its horizontal or vertical form.

To summon the Media Player menu bar:

◆ Move the mouse pointer to where the menu bar *should* be (**Figure 10.3**).

or

Press and release the Alt key.

or

Click the down-pointing triangle at the right end of the title bar.

or

Right-click anywhere on the title bar, the Features taskbar, or the area to the right of the playback controls.

✔ Tips

■ Use the View > Menu Bar Options submenu to set menu-bar preferences. Press Ctrl+M to freeze the menu bar in its proper place. Ctrl+Shift+M auto-hides it again. This submenu also lets you show or hide the Features taskbar.

■ The controls shown in Figure 10.1 also are available in the View and Play menus. The View > Go To submenu is equivalent to the Features taskbar, for example.

■ Media Player is complex enough to get its own troubleshooting web site. Choose Help > Troubleshooting to open the site in your browser. If the player displays an error with an error ID (800704CF, for example), press F1 to open Media Player Help; click the Search tab; then search for *error center help*.

Figure 10.3 The menu bar springs into existence when you move your pointer above the window's top edge.

QuickTime and Real

Media Player doesn't play a few of the most popular media formats: QuickTime, RealAudio, and RealVideo. To play these files, you can download the free QuickTime Player (www.apple.com/quicktime) and RealPlayer (www.real.com). I don't like either player, because QuickTime keeps bugging me to upgrade to the $30 Pro version and RealPlayer is notorious for installing spyware and hijacking filename extensions. Instead, search on Google for *"QuickTime Alternative"* and *"Real Alternative"* (include the quotes) for players that are both free and nuisance-free.

Figure 10.4 Normally, you'll want to play the music CD. You also can rip tracks to your hard drive (covered later), open a standard folder window with an icon for each song, or have the CD sit in the drive silently.

Figure 10.5 Media Player features the standard playback controls used on VCRs and other consumer toys. You can drag the Seek slider to move to a different place within the item that's playing.

Figure 10.6 When you've turned on mini-Player mode and minimized Media Player, the playback controls appear in the Windows taskbar.

Playing Music CDs

Playing a music CD on your PC isn't too different from playing it on a conventional CD player. You can play music while you're working with other programs.

You can set your CD (or DVD) drive's *AutoPlay* options to make Windows detect various discs when you insert them.

To play a music CD:

1. Insert a music CD into your computer's CD drive.

2. If Media Player is open already, the CD starts playing automatically.

   or

   If **Figure 10.4** appears, select Play Audio CD; then click OK.

3. Click the Now Playing button on the Features taskbar to show artist, title, and track information, if you like (see the next section).

✔ Tips

■ The buttons and slider in **Figure 10.5** control playback.

■ If Media Player is minimized, you can use the mini-Player toolbar to perform basic playback functions. To turn on mini-mode, right-click an empty area on the Windows taskbar; then choose Toolbars > Windows Media Player (**Figure 10.6**).

continues on next page

- Media Player plays through the playlist (**Figure 10.7**) in order, once, unless you turn on Shuffle (Play > Shuffle or Ctrl+H) to randomize the tracks or Repeat (Play > Repeat or Ctrl+T) to play them forever. If the playlist is hidden, choose View > Now Playing Options > Show Playlist.

- If Media Player doesn't play your CD automatically—or if it plays something else—choose your CD from the Quick Access menu (to the right of the Now Playing button on the taskbar).

- To eject a CD, choose Play > Eject or press Ctrl+E. You also can use this command to open and close the CD tray.

- If the music skips too much (assuming that your CD is clean and unscratched), try switching to analog playback: Choose Tools > Options > Devices tab; select your CD drive; click Properties; then choose Analog (below Playback). If that doesn't work, go back to Digital playback but check Use Error Correction this time.

To change the AutoPlay behavior of a CD or DVD drive:

1. On the Windows desktop, choose Start > My Computer.

2. Right-click the icon for the CD or DVD drive; then choose Properties > AutoPlay tab.

3. From the drop-down list, choose a disc type (**Figure 10.8**).

4. In the Actions section, choose Select an Action to Perform; then choose the action that you want Windows to take every time you insert that disc type.

5. Click OK.

Figure 10.7
The playlist lists the CD's track names and durations. Point to a track for pop-up information, or right-click a track for properties and related commands (such as skipping tracks). The drop-down menu at top (labeled with the album name) lets you change the playlist. Click the album art for detailed album information.

Figure 10.8 You can specify the action that Windows takes when you insert a specific type of disc, thus suppressing dialog boxes like Figure 10.4. Select the Prompt Me Each Time option if you don't want Windows to do the same thing each time. (Here, the drop-down list is hiding some actions.)

Customizing the Now Playing Area

The Now Playing area has several panes that you can use to view videos, visualizations, media information, audio and video controls, and the current playlist. **Figure 10.9** shows these panes, which you can show or hide to suit your needs. **Table 10.2** (on the following page) describes each pane.

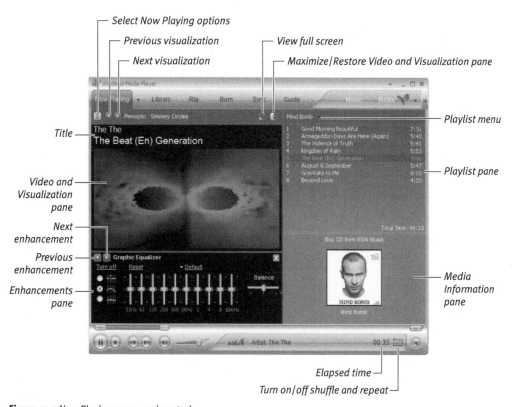

Figure 10.9 Now Playing panes and controls

To show the Now Playing area:

◆ Click Now Playing on the Features taskbar.
or
Choose View > Go To > Now Playing.

To show or hide Now Playing panes:

◆ To show the **Video and Visualization pane,** choose View > Visualizations; then choose a visualization from the submenu (see the next section).

or

To show the **Info Center View pane,** choose View > Info Center View.

or

To show or hide the **Enhancements pane,** choose View > Enhancements > Show Enhancements.

or

To show or hide the **Media Information pane,** choose View > Now Playing Options > Show Media Information.

or

To show or hide the **Playlist pane,** choose View > Now Playing Options > Show Playlist.

or

To show or hide the **Title,** choose View > Now Playing Options > Show Title.

✔ Tips

■ Right-click any pane to show its shortcut menu. In the Playlist pane, right-click a specific song in the playlist.

■ To resize panes, drag the horizontal or vertical lines that separate them. The cursor becomes a double-headed arrow when you place it over a separator line.

■ If you're connected to the internet, Media Player retrieves CD information and album art from the All Music Group (AMG) web site (www.allmusic.com) and displays it in the Info Center View and Media Information panes. (If AMG's information is inadequate, try www.gracenote.com.)

Figure 10.10 The Info Center View pane. The MSN Music link at the top of the pane reveals more album details and lets you buy individual tracks.

Table 10.2

Now Playing Panes	
PANE	**DESCRIPTION**
Video and Visualization	Displays the current video or visualization that you're playing. If you're playing a video or DVD, rather than music, this pane appears automatically.
Info Center View	Displays detailed information—if available—about what's playing. You can't display the Video and Visualization pane and the Info Center View pane at the same time. **Figure 10.10** shows Info Center View.
Enhancements	Contains several controls that you can use to adjust graphic-equalizer levels, video settings, audio effects, play speed, and the color of Media Player. You also can use this pane to share a streaming media clip with a friend. Figure 10.9 shows the graphic equalizer.
Media Information	Displays summary information—if available—about what's playing. For music copied from a CD, for example, this pane displays the album art and album title.
Playlist	Displays the current playlist. For a CD, this pane displays the track names and durations. For a DVD, it displays the title and chapter names.
Title	The artist and title of what's playing.

Figure 10.11 Media Player comes with scores of preinstalled visualizations, but you can download more from the internet: Choose Tools > Download > Visualizations.

Viewing Visualizations

Media Player lets you not only hear music but also see it with *visualizations*—splashes of color and shape that follow the music's beat. The Video and Visualization pane displays the current visualization.

To view a visualization:

1. Play a song.

2. Click Now Playing on the Features taskbar.

3. Choose View > Visualizations; then choose a visualization from the submenu (**Figure 10.11**).

   or

   If you're already viewing one, click the Previous/Next Visualization buttons (refer to Figure 10.9) to cycle through available visualizations. (Or right-click a playing visualization and choose another one from the shortcut menu.)

✔ Tips

- You can click the Select Now Playing Options button (refer to Figure 10.9) to choose a visualization.

- To fill your screen with a visualization, choose View > Full Screen (or press Alt+Enter). To return to normal, click the mouse or press Esc (or Alt+Enter again).

- To show or hide the CD's title in the Video and Visualization pane, choose View > Now Playing Options > Show Title.

- Choose Album Art from the Visualizations submenu to show the CD's album cover instead of an abstract visualization.

VIEWING VISUALIZATIONS

Changing Player Appearance with Skins

You can change Media Player's appearance by applying design schemes called *skins*. Each skin offers the essential controls—Play/Pause, Stop, Previous Track, Next Track, and Volume, and the usual Minimize, Maximize, and Close buttons—but skin appearance and features vary. Some skins link to visualizations or include playlists and audio controls; play around to see which skin has what.

To apply a skin:

1. Choose View > Skin Chooser.

2. Select a skin from the list (**Figure 10.12**).

3. Click Apply Skin on the toolbar (or press Alt+A).

When you apply a skin, the player's user interface is in *skin mode* (**Figure 10.13**, for example). You can return easily to *full mode*—the default state in which all features are displayed.

To switch modes:

◆ To switch to full mode: Press Ctrl+1 or click the Full Mode button.
   or
   To switch to skin mode: Press Ctrl+2 or click the Skin Mode button (in the bottom-right corner of the Media Player window; refer to Figure 10.1).

✔ Tips

■ In Skin Chooser, click More Skins on the toolbar (or press Alt+S) to download skins from Microsoft's web site.

■ To delete a skin from the skins list, select it; then press Delete or click the red *X* in the toolbar.

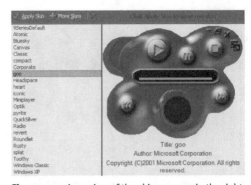

Figure 10.12 A preview of the skin appears in the right pane. Some skins are a triumph of form over function; it may take some hunting to find the Play button and other controls.

Figure 10.13 Media Player in skin mode. You can change skins as often as you like, but you must be in full mode to do so.

■ To make the player float over all other windows, choose Tools > Options > Player tab; then check Keep the Player on Top of Other Windows.

■ Right-click a skin to display its shortcut menu.

CHANGING PLAYER APPEARANCE WITH SKINS

Figure 10.14 The guide is mostly pandering celebrity-driven gossip, but click the Site Index link on the toolbar to find news, business, sports, and other subjects. The search box searches only the WindowsMedia.com site, not the entire web.

Shopping Online

If you're connected to the internet, you can use Media Player's Guide and online stores to find digital media on the web.

The guide is a live, frequently updated internet "magazine" hosted by WindowsMedia.com, containing links to the latest movie trailers, music, and video. The content will play in Media Player or open a web page in your browser.

The online stores are web sites that offer digital media content for purchase or by subscription.

To use the guide:

1. Click Guide on the Features taskbar.

2. To view or listen to an item, click a link (**Figure 10.14**).

   or

   To find an item, use the search feature on the web page.

✔ Tips

- If the player displays a Getting Started page instead of WindowsMedia.com, click the Guide link on that page.

- If moving around the guide in Media Player feels cramped, visit www.windowsmedia.com in a web browser instead.

- Some videos let you choose your modem speed with the links 56k | 100k | 300k. Click 100k or 300k if you have a DSL, cable, or T1 connection; click 56k if you have a dial-up modem. 56K videos play haltingly but usually sound fine. You can right-click a video to decrease its size, which may improve playback.

Online stores are displayed at the right end of the Features taskbar (refer to Figure 10.1). Music, video, and radio online stores from MSN Entertainment are the default online stores unless you specify that a different online store be the default. You can use Media Player to look for and register with online stores any time you're online.

To browse an online store:

1. Choose View > Online Stores, and choose a store from the submenu.

   or

   Click the Online Stores button on the Features taskbar, and choose a store (**Figure 10.15**).

2. If necessary, click one of the Music, Radio, Video, or other content buttons in the Online Store area on the Features taskbar.

   The content buttons change depending on which online store you've picked. **Table 10.3** lists the content available at the various stores.

3. Use the store's search function or help links to navigate the store.

✔ Tips

■ Content from a store may be available only as long as you're registered with that store, and you won't be able to copy downloaded media files that have DRM (Digital Rights Management) safeguards. Learn about your digital rights at the Electronic Frontier Foundation (EFF) web site, www.eff.org.

■ If you buy copy-protected content, back up your licenses to a floppy disk or USB flash drive in case they become lost or corrupted. Choose Tools > Manage Licenses to back up and restore licenses.

■ Downloaded digital media content is displayed in your library in the All Music and All Video categories.

Figure 10.15 Choose Browse All Online Stores in the Online Stores menu to see a Media Player page with links to all the online stores.

Table 10.3

Online Stores Content	
CONTENT	STORES
Music	MSN Music, Napster, MusicNow, Musicmatch, Wal-Mart, fye, Puretracks, PassAlong
Radio	MSN Music, Napster, MusicNow, Musicmatch, Wal-Mart, XM Radio Online, fye, Puretracks, Live365
Video	Court TV, fye, MSN Music, MLB
Audio	Audible, MLB
Movies	MSN Music, CinemaNow

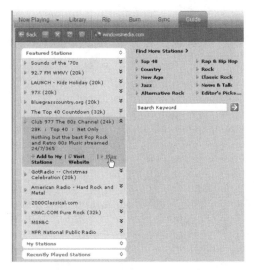

Figure 10.16 Radio Tuner's left side is divided into three expandable sections: Featured Stations (starter stations chosen by Microsoft), My Stations, and Recently Played Stations. The right side contains genre links and a search feature.

Figure 10.17 You can browse radio stations around the world by genre. Hidden by the expanded drop-down list are two search boxes that let you find stations by keyword (enter a talk-show host's name, for example) or zip code (U.S. only). Advanced search criteria such as country, language, and call sign also are available.

Listening to Radio Stations

Radio stations around the world stream their signals over the internet. Media Player, an internet connection, and speakers will bring in these stations without a radio, extra software, or extra hardware. You can add your favorite stations to a preset list to access them quickly.

To listen to an internet radio station:

1. Click Guide on the Features taskbar.

2. Click the Radio Tuner link (not the Radio link) in the Guide pane.

   You might need to click the Home button to display the page that includes the Radio Tuner link.

3. To listen to a featured, preset, or recently played radio station, click the green arrow next to the station's name on the left side; then click Play (**Figure 10.16**).

   or

   To find a radio station, click Find More Stations on the right side (**Figure 10.17**).

To add a radio station to a preset list:

1. Click the desired radio station's name or the double down arrows to the name's right.

   The station name expands to show details and links (refer to Figure 10.16).

2. Click Add to My Stations.

   The station is added to the My Stations section of the Radio Tuner home page.

✔ Tips

- You may have to wait a few seconds for a station to tune in.

- The Speed column lists the stations' streaming speeds. Faster means better sound. Don't listen to a 56K station with a 28K modem.

- Playing a station may open that station's web site in your browser.

- Some of the online stores let you listen to radio; see the preceding section.

- To save streaming music to your hard drive, try Super MP3 Recorder ($20 U.S.; www.supermp3recorder.com).

Figure 10.18 Media Player 10 lets you rip MP3 files directly, so you don't have to buy a separate MP3 add-in as you did with earlier versions. The link at the bottom of this dialog box launches a web page that compares MP3 and WMA (from Microsoft's point of view).

Figure 10.19 This dialog box lets you embed useful information such as the track number, song title, and bit rate in the track's filename.

Ripping CDs to Your Hard Drive

Media Player lets you copy (*rip*) an entire album or selected tracks from a music CD to your hard drive. Each track winds up as a double-clickable file in your My Music folder. Disk-based music means no more CD hunts; you can use your CD drive for other things while you play music files. You can organize your tracks into custom playlists, burn them on custom music CDs, or copy them to your portable music player.

Before you copy your first CD, you'll want to set a few default options.

To set options for ripping CDs:

1. Choose Tools > Options > Rip Music tab (**Figure 10.18**).

2. Click Change if you want to store the ripped tracks somewhere other than your My Music folder.

3. Click File Name to specify which details to include in the filenames (**Figure 10.19**).

4. Choose a music format from the drop-down Format list.

   Usually you'll want to create MP3 (.mp3) files rather than Windows Media Audio (.wma) files, Microsoft's proprietary, more compact, and vastly less popular format. If you choose the WMA format, uncheck Copy Protect Music so you can transfer tracks to other computers and portable music players.

continues on next page

5. Drag the Audio Quality slider to set the bit rate.

Set the slider in the middle of the range for a good sound-quality/file-size trade-off or experiment with different settings to see what suits your ears.

6. Click OK.

✔ Tip

■ A little hunting around on the internet should find you a way to rip CDs that give you copying troubles.

To rip tracks from a music CD:

1. Insert a music CD into your computer's CD drive.

Media Player probably starts playing the CD on insertion. The player can play and copy tracks at the same time, but click Stop if you prefer silence while you copy tracks.

2. Choose File > CDs and Devices > Rip Audio CD. (If you have more than one CD drive, click the drive that contains the music CD.)

The Rip feature appears with all tracks checked or, if you ripped them previously, unchecked (**Figure 10.20**).

If you're connected to the internet, the player gleans the album's title and track names from AMG (www.allmusic.com) and lists them in the Rip pane. If AMG doesn't recognize your CD, see the side-bar in this section.

3. Uncheck the boxes for the tracks that you don't want to rip.

The topmost check box selects or clears all the tracks.

4. Click the Rip Music button in the taskbar (or press Alt+C).

Figure 10.20 To rename a song title, right-click it; then choose Edit. (You also can change the artist, composer, and genre this way.) To rearrange the tracks, right-click the titles and choose Move Up or Move Down. This figure shows the player in the middle of ripping an album, so the Rip Music button has changed to Stop Rip.

Figure 10.21 The Rip Options dialog box includes a sales pitch for Microsoft's WMA music format.

5. If **Figure 10.21** appears, select Keep My Current Format Settings and click OK.

Select the Change My Current Format Settings option only if you want to change the default settings (refer to Figure 10.18).

6. Media Player begins copying tracks to your hard drive. The Rip Status column shows its progress.

The Rip Music button changes to Stop Rip, which you can click (or press Alt+S) to stop the current rip operation.

✔ Tips

■ The selected tracks are copied by default to your My Music folder. In My Music is a subfolder labeled with the artist's name (or labeled Various Artists). In that folder is a subfolder labeled with the album name.

■ The copied tracks are listed in the library. See "Organizing Your Library" later in this chapter.

If AMG Doesn't Recognize Your CD

If you lack an internet connection or if AMG doesn't recognize your CD, the album title *Unknown Album* appears in Figure 10.20, along with the tracks Track 1, Track 2, and so on, all by Unknown Artist. At this point, you can accept the default names and copy the tracks anyway; they'll sound fine, but you'll have a hard time finding them in Windows Explorer or the library. Instead, take the time to type the names yourself before you copy the tracks.

To do so, click Find Album Info on the toolbar. A wizard appears to help you search for the CD in AMG's online database. If you still can't find it, click the wizard's Edit button; enter the album and track information in the text boxes; then click Next to accept the names.

Organizing Your Library

Over time, your hard drive will become crowded with music and video files that you've copied or downloaded. Media Player's library is a master list that helps you play and keep track of all your media files.

To show the library:

◆ Choose View > Go To > Library.

or

Click Library on the Features taskbar (**Figure 10.22**).

Details pane

Contents pane

List pane

Figure 10.22 The library uses an Explorer-like display of categories and subcategories. The Contents pane lets you access your music by artist, album, genre, or other category. The Details pane shows information about the selection in the Contents pane. The List pane shows a Now Playing, Burn, or Sync list, depending on the menu choice above the pane.

Figure 10.23 The folder structure of My Music matches the Media Player library.

✔ Tips

■ The Details pane works like Windows Explorer in Details view. To choose which columns appear, right-click a column heading; then click a column in the pop-up list. To sort by a column, click that column's heading. To rearrange columns, drag the column headings left or right.

■ To show or hide the List pane, click the Library Options button above the Details pane; then click Show List.

■ Behind the scenes, Media Player populates the library by inspecting your My Music folder (among other locations). Choose Start > My Music to see the folder (**Figure 10.23**).

■ The library also lists your music subscriptions, TV, video, and other digital media.

Before you can create playlists, burn CDs, or copy files to portable music players, you must add (to the library) links to digital media files. CDs copied to your hard drive become part of the library automatically. You can add links to other media files in several ways.

To add items to your library:

◆ Choose Tools > Search for Media Files (or press F3) (**Figure 10.24**).

or

Choose File > Add to Library (or click Add to Library below the Contents pane); then choose a submenu command to search your computer; add an individual file, playlist, or folder; or add media files automatically from folders that you want Media Player to monitor.

or

Drag items from the desktop, My Computer, or an Explorer window to the Details pane.

✔ Tips

■ By default, the Search function ignores small audio and video files to filter system files used by XP (such as the logon melody). To change the search settings, choose Tools > Options > Library tab.

■ To add files to the library automatically when played (either on your computer or from the internet), choose Tools > Options > Player tab; then check Add Music Files to Library When Played.

■ You can't add other users' media files to your library if you lack permission to read the folders containing those files. See "Sharing Files" in Chapter 17.

■ The Now Playing pane lists the item that's playing currently even if that item hasn't been added to the library.

Figure 10.24 Media Player can populate the library list by searching your drives for media files.

Privacy and Security

Media Player relies on the internet to get information about the music and DVDs that you play. You also can use the player to buy content from online stores and share your library with other users. All these third-party interactions can expose information about yourself that you'd rather keep private. The relevant options are on the Privacy tab and the Security tab in the Tools > Options dialog box. You should inspect them, changing them if necessary to suit your preferences. the player's help pages describe each setting and its effects: In the Option dialog box, click the Privacy tab; then click Help. Do the same for the Security tab.

Also read Richard Smith's "Serious Privacy Problems in Windows Media Player for Windows XP" (and Microsoft's response) at www.computerbytesman.com/privacy/ wmp8dvd.htm. To read Microsoft's privacy statement, choose Help > View Privacy Statement.

You can search for library items and then play the ones that meet your search criteria or add them to a playlist.

To search for items in your library:

1. In the library, type the text that you want to search by in the box next to the Search button.

2. Click Search 🔍 (or press Alt+S).
   The search results are displayed in the Details pane.

3. To play the items that were found, in the Contents pane, right-click Search Results and choose Play.

   You also can use the shortcut menu to add the search results to the Now Playing, Burn, or Sync list or to a new playlist.

In your library, you can delete links to files and playlists on your computer. When you delete a link, the file or playlist that it's linked to isn't deleted unless you choose to do so.

To delete items from your library:

1. In the library, right-click the item to delete; then choose Delete.

2. If prompted, choose whether to delete only the link or delete the file on your hard drive as well (to land in the Recycle Bin).

✔ Tips

- Duplicate items will appear in your library if you delete a file on your hard drive without removing the corresponding link in your library and then add the item to your library again. To remove duplicates, choose File > Add to Library > By Searching Computer; in the Search On list, choose the folder or drive where the previously deleted item was stored; then click Search.

- You can delete several items at the same time. To select adjacent items, click the first item; then Shift+click the last item. To select nonadjacent items, Ctrl+click each item. Right-click the selected items; then click Delete.

ORGANIZING YOUR LIBRARY

Working with Playlists

A *playlist* is a list of media files that you want to watch or listen to. Media Player generates a temporary playlist automatically when you play a CD (refer to Figure 10.7), but you also can create your own playlists that group any mix of songs and videos in the order in which you want them to be played. You can create a playlist that includes several tracks from various CDs, a radio-station link, and a video clip, for example. Classical-music fans use playlists to compare the same piece performed by different artists. You also can use playlists to burn your own CDs or copy files to portable music players.

Figure 10.25 The playlists that you create appear in the My Playlists category in the Contents pane.

To create a playlist:

1. Choose File > New Now Playing List.

2. In the List pane, choose Now Playing List > New List > Playlist (**Figure 10.25**).

3. Drag items from the Contents or Details pane in your library to the List pane to add them to the new playlist.

4. In the List pane, choose New Playlist > Save Playlist As.

5. In the Save As dialog box, type the playlist name in the File Name text box (**Figure 10.26**).

6. Click Save.

    The new playlist is added to the My Playlists category in the Contents pane.

Figure 10.26 By default, playlists are saved as .wpl files in the My Playlists folder (usually located in your My Music folder). You also can save playlists with the .m3u, .asx, .wax, or .wvx extension.

Figure 10.27 You can specify multiple filters for items to be included in (or excluded from) an auto playlist. Media Player updates the list automatically each time you open it.

Figure 10.28 You can explore the auto playlists that come with the library to get ideas for your own auto playlists.

An *auto playlist* is a playlist that Media Player compiles automatically, based on criteria that you specify. Auto playlists are updated each time you open them.

To create an auto playlist:

1. Choose File > New Now Playing List.

2. In the List pane, choose Now Playing List > New List > Auto Playlist (refer to Figure 10.25).

3. In the New Auto Playlist dialog box, type the name of the new auto playlist.

4. Specify criteria for the items in the auto playlist (**Figure 10.27**).

5. Click OK.

   The new auto playlist is added to the Auto Playlists category in the Contents pane (**Figure 10.28**).

To add items to a playlist:

1. Choose File > New Now Playing List.

2. In the List pane, choose Now Playing List > Edit Playlist; then click a playlist name (if one is displayed). The items in the playlist are displayed in the List pane.

   or

   If some of your playlists are hidden in the Edit Playlist submenu (because there's not enough room to show them), click Additional Playlists to open the Add to Playlist dialog box; then click the playlist that you want to add the item to.

3. Add the items to the playlist by dragging them to the List pane or by right-clicking the selected items, and then choosing a playlist name in the Add To submenu.

WORKING WITH PLAYLISTS

To play a playlist:

◆ Choose a playlist from the Quick Access menu's My Playlists or Auto Playlists submenu (**Figure 10.29**).

or

In the Contents pane, expand My Playlists or Auto Playlists; then double-click a playlist (or select a playlist and click the Play button).

The double-click technique works only if you click the Library Options button above the Details pane and then choose Play All Items on Double-Click.

To edit a playlist:

1. Choose File > New Now Playing List.

2. In the Contents pane, expand My Playlists; select the playlist that you want to change; then drag it to the List pane.

3. Choose Now Playing List > Edit Using Playlist Editor.

4. In the Edit Playlist dialog box, add, delete, or rearrange playlist items (**Figure 10.30**).

5. Click OK.

Figure 10.29 Your playlists and auto playlists are available to play even if you're not in the library.

Figure 10.30 You can use the *X* and arrow buttons below the right list to delete and rearrange playlist items.

✔ Tips

■ You can select several items at once and then drag them to the List pane. To select adjacent items, click the first item; then Shift+click the last item. To select non-adjacent items, Ctrl+click each item. (You also can drag items from the desktop, My Computer, or an Explorer window.)

■ Instead of dragging items to the List pane, you can add the items by double-clicking them. To turn on this option, click the Library Options button above the Details pane; then choose Add to List on Double-Click.

■ Right-click a playlist or auto playlist to rename, delete, or edit it (refer to Figure 10.28).

■ Media Player plays through a playlist in order, once, unless you turn on Shuffle (Play > Shuffle or Ctrl+H) to randomize the tracks or Repeat (Play > Repeat or Ctrl+T) to play them forever.

■ To save an auto playlist as a regular playlist, right-click the auto playlist; then choose Save As New Playlist (refer to Figure 10.28). The playlist no longer auto-updates after conversion.

WORKING WITH PLAYLISTS

Burning Music CDs

If you're a fan of heavy-metal bands, you're aware that they insist on putting at least one cringe-inducing ballad on every album. If you have a CD burner, you can take your revenge by creating personal CDs of music that *you* like, without appalling filler tunes.

To burn a music CD:

1. As described in the preceding section, create a playlist of tracks to be burned, in the desired playback order.

2. Click Burn on the Features taskbar.

3. In the Items to Burn pane on the left, select the playlist or category of tracks that you want to burn.

4. Uncheck the check boxes for tracks that you don't want to burn.

5. Insert a blank CD-R or CD-RW into your CD drive.

6. If necessary, when using a CD-RW disc, click the Erase Disk button to erase the CD.

7. If you want to change recording or data CD settings, such as the CD write speed or quality level, click the Display Properties and Settings button (![button]) on the toolbar.

8. In the Items on Device pane on the right, select the type of CD that you want to create (**Figure 10.31**).

   Typically you'll choose Audio CD. HighMAT Audio doesn't work in every CD player, and Data CD isn't appropriate for music CDs.

9. Click Start Burn (or press Alt+B).

   The process takes a bit of time and disk space.

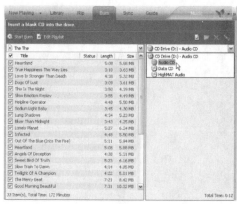

Figure 10.31 If "Will not fit" appears in the Status column (left pane) for some tracks, you must uncheck some check boxes until all the selected tracks fit. "Will not fit" appears even if the length of the selected tracks exactly matches the CD length, because Media Player inserts two-second intervals between tracks.

Copying Music to a Portable Player

The process for copying music to a portable player—such as a Rio, Nomad, or iRiver—is the same as the process for burning a music CD. Just connect the player to your PC, and choose its name from the drop-down list at the top of the right pane (in step 8). Some players play MP3 but not WMA files; see "Ripping CDs to Your Hard Drive" earlier in this chapter. If you own an Apple iPod, go to www.apple.com/itunes and download the Windows version of iTunes to use instead of Media Player.

✔ Tips

- To add items from other playlists or categories to the burn playlist, or to remove items from the burn playlist, click the Edit Playlist button (or press Alt+A).

- You can rearrange the items in the Items to Burn pane by dragging them to new positions in the burning order.

- If you're using a CD-R, you can't burn additional tracks to the CD after burning completes. If you're using a CD-RW, you can erase the entire CD before burning tracks again.

- To burn a data CD (not an audio CD), see "Copying Files and Folders to CDs" in Chapter 5.

Burning Problems

CD burners are so cranky and skittish that you should close all other programs, leave your PC alone, and not stomp around until Media Player ejects the completed CD. If you still get music files that skip and pop, try slowing the burning speed: Choose Tools > Options > Devices tab; select your CD drive; click Properties > Recording tab; then select a slower speed than Fastest in the Select a Write Speed list.

You also can try switching to analog ripping: In the same dialog box, click the Audio tab and select Analog (below Rip). If that doesn't work, check Use Error Correction and try again.

To make an exact duplicate of a CD, try Nero Burning ROM ($70 U.S.; www.nero.com) or Exact Audio Copy (free; www.exactaudiocopy.de). If you're recording from vinyl LPs, try WAVclean ($30; www.excla.com/WAVclean/English) or WaveCorrector ($45; www.wavecor.co.uk). The TweakMP PowerToy (free; www.wmplugins.com) provides automatic volume leveling for CD burns.

BURNING MUSIC CDS

Playing DVDs

If you have a DVD drive, you can use Media Player to watch DVD movies. The Play menu lets you display closed captions and subtitles, choose a language track, and use other movie-specific features.

✔ Tips

- To play a DVD's special features, choose View > DVD Features > Root Menu.

- The Play menu contains commands for using a DVD's language and subtitle features.

- To capture a DVD image as a bitmap or JPEG file, choose View > DVD Features > Capture Image (or press Ctrl+I). To turn on the image-capture feature, choose Tools > Options > Performance tab > Advanced; then, in the DVD Video area, check Use Video Mixing Renderer.

- Media Player also can play VCDs (video CDs).

To play a DVD:

1. Insert a DVD into your computer's DVD drive.

2. Depending on the AutoPlay settings that you made (refer to Figure 10.8), Media Player opens automatically or offers to do so.

   If not, open Media Player; then choose Play > DVD, VCD or CD Audio > [your DVD drive].

3. In the Playlist pane on the right, click a DVD title or chapter name, if appropriate.

   If the playlist is hidden, choose View > Now Playing Options > Show Playlist.

DVD Decoders

DVD playback requires a software *decoder*. If you bought your system with Windows and a DVD drive installed, you probably can play any DVD on your PC as is. If you have an older system, you may have to download and install a decoder from the internet. If Media Player is unable to play a DVD, it displays an error message that links you to Microsoft's web site, where you can purchase (for about $15 U.S.) and download a DVD Decoder Pack. But first check your computer or DVD-drive manufacturer's web site for free, updated XP DVD decoders.

Table 10.4

DVD Keyboard Shortcuts	
To	PRESS
Play/pause	Ctrl+P
Stop	Ctrl+S
Rewind	Ctrl+Shift+B
Fast-forward	Ctrl+Shift+F
Previous/next chapter	Ctrl+B/Ctrl+F
Play louder/quieter	F9/F10
Mute	F8
Eject	Ctrl+E
Play fast	Ctrl+Shift+G
Play slow	Ctrl+Shift+S
Turn on or off captions and subtitles	Ctrl+Shift+C

4. To enlarge the picture to fill the screen, press Alt+Enter (or choose View > Full Screen).

To return to normal, press Esc or Alt+Enter again (**Figure 10.32**).

You can control playback with the onscreen controls or the keyboard shortcuts listed in **Table 10.4**.

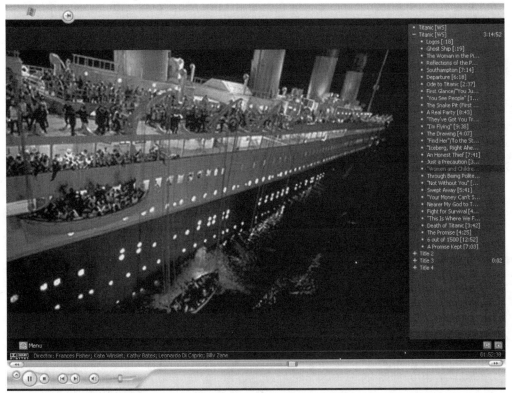

Figure 10.32 In full-screen mode, the playback controls appear automatically when you move the mouse and disappear after the mouse is idle for a few seconds. To control playback, you can right-click the movie or use the keyboard shortcuts listed in Table 10.4. The playlist (on the right) divides the movie into discrete "chapters"; double-click a chapter to jump to a particular scene. An exclamation mark (!) next to the chapter name means that the player can't skip to that chapter.

Using Keyboard Shortcuts

Table 10.5 lists Media Player's keyboard shortcuts. Table 10.4 in the preceding section also contains some keyboard shortcuts.

Table 10.5

Media Player Keyboard Shortcuts	
To	Press
Open a file	Ctrl+O
Specify a URL or path to a file	Ctrl+U
Close or stop playing a file	Ctrl+W
Create a new playlist	Ctrl+N
Edit the current playlist	Ctrl+D
Shuffle the playlist	Ctrl+H
Repeat the playlist	Ctrl+T
Search specified locations for digital media files	F3
Quit Media Player	Alt+F4
Switch to full mode	Ctrl+1
Switch to skin mode	Ctrl+2
Display the menu bar in full mode	Ctrl+M
Auto-hide the menu bar in full mode	Ctrl+Shift+M
Display video in full screen	Alt+Enter
Zoom to 50%	Alt+1
Zoom to 100%	Alt+2
Zoom to 200%	Alt+3
Get help	F1

WINDOWS MOVIE MAKER

Windows Movie Maker lets you transfer audio and video to your computer from a video camera, VCR, web camera, or other video source and use that as raw material for your own movies. You can combine footage, still photos, music tracks, videos, voice-over narratives, and other media files. Then you can edit; add titles, video transitions, and special effects; and save the result as a stand-alone file in Windows Media Audio/Video (.wmv) format. Your movie is ready to play or to share with friends and enemies via email, web, or disk.

✔ Tips

- Video editing is a computer-intensive activity that requires at least a 2 GHz processor, 1 GB of RAM, and a fast hard disk (7200 rpm or better) with a lot of free space.

- Many Windows XP installations include Movie Maker 1 or 2. Microsoft released Movie Maker 2.1 as part of Service Pack 2, but you can download it independently via Windows Update or at www.microsoft.com/windowsxp/moviemaker.

Getting Started with Movie Maker

Like all video-editing software, Movie Maker is a complex program; using it effectively isn't a simple matter of opening, editing, saving, and closing a document. Before you work with Movie Maker, you'll need to explore the interface and grasp a few concepts. **Figure 11.1** shows Movie Maker's main sections, which are described in **Table 11.1**. You can point (without clicking) to any Movie Maker control for a pop-up tip.

Figure 11.1 Movie Maker is divided into three main horizontal sections: the menu bar and toolbar, the panes, and the storyboard/timeline.

Version 2.1 Changes

Judging by my email, most readers skip this chapter. I suspect that most people open Movie Maker; kick the tires; and then go out and buy a real video editor from Adobe, Avid, or Pinnacle. Microsoft, perhaps realizing this, has offered only a few changes in the upgrade from version 2 to 2.1:

◆ Increased compatibility with other video programs (Tools > Options > Compatibility tab).

◆ Digital video (DV) pass-through (`www.microsoft.com/windowsxp/using /moviemaker/21/dvpassthrough.mspx`).

◆ A new default capture setting. In the Video Capture Wizard, the new default capture setting is a constant bit rate (CBR) profile rather than a variable bit rate (VBR) profile.

To determine which version you have, choose Help > About Windows Movie Maker.

To start Movie Maker:

◆ Choose Start > All Programs > Windows Movie Maker.

or

Choose Start > All Programs > Accessories > Entertainment > Windows Movie Maker.

or

Choose Start > Run; type `moviemk` and then press Enter.

✔ Tips

■ You can't display the Movie Tasks pane and the Collections pane, or storyboard view and timeline view, at the same time. Use the View menu or toolbar buttons to show, hide, or toggle panes and views.

■ Right-click any section (or specific item in a section) to show its shortcut menu.

■ To resize sections, drag the horizontal or vertical lines that separate them. The cursor becomes a double-headed arrow when you place it over a separator line.

■ Choose Tools > Options to change Movie Maker's default settings.

Table 11.1

Movie Maker Sections

FEATURE	DESCRIPTION
Movie Tasks pane	Lists common moviemaking tasks, such as capturing or importing video, editing a movie, adding effects, and saving or sending a movie.
Collections pane	(Not shown) Displays your collections in an Explorer-like tree. A collection is a container of video clips, audio clips, and pictures that you've captured or imported. Each clip is a smaller continuous segment of audio and video. (Not everything in a collection must appear in a final movie.) See "Organizing Your Clips" later in this chapter.
Contents pane	Displays the clips that are contained in the selected collection, including all the video, audio, pictures, video transitions, and video effects that you can add to the storyboard/timeline to include in your movie.
Storyboard view	Displays the sequence of the clips in your project and lets you rearrange them easily. This view also lets you see any video transitions or video effects that you've added.
Timeline view	(Not shown) Lets you review or modify the timing of clips in your project. You can zoom in or out on project details, record narration, add background music, adjust audio levels, and trim unwanted portions of a clip (among other things). See "Editing a Project" later in this chapter.
Monitor	Plays individual clips or an entire project. Use this feature to preview your project before saving it as a movie.

Capturing and Importing Content

You edit and create movies with Movie Maker by using footage transferred from camera to computer. *Capturing* is the process of recording audio and video as digital data in a file.

✔ Tip

■ Captured and imported content appears in the My Videos folder inside your My Documents folder. My Videos also contains sample video files that you can practice on. To view My Videos, choose View > My Videos Folder.

To capture video:

1. Connect your camera to your computer (see the sidebar in this section).

2. Choose File > Capture Video (or press Ctrl+R).

   or

   In the Movie Tasks pane, below Capture Video, click Capture from Video Device.

3. Follow the onscreen instructions in the Video Capture Wizard.

   The wizard lets you choose a capture device, specify video settings, and select a capture method (**Figures 11.2** and **11.3**). You can capture:

   ▲ The entire video from a tape in a DV camera

   ▲ Parts of video from a tape in a DV camera

   ▲ Video from tape in an analog camera or VCR

   ▲ Live video

   Movie Maker imports the captured content into a new collection with the same name as the specified video file.

Figure 11.2 The Video Capture Wizard helps you download audio and video from your analog or digital camera to your computer.

Figure 11.3 The quality level that you choose determines how big the video file will be.

✔ Tips

■ For help choosing video settings, choose Help > Help Topics > Index tab; type the keyword *video;* then double-click the Capturing subtopic.

■ Copy-protected tapes may show up as onscreen garbage.

Your movie can combine footage that you've captured from your video camera with audio clips, still photos, and other video files that you've downloaded from the internet, copied from CDs, transferred from a digital camera, or scanned into your computer.

To import existing pictures, sounds, and video:

1. Choose File > Import into Collections (or press Ctrl+I).

   or

   In the Movie Tasks pane, below Capture Video, click one of the Import links.

2. In the Import File dialog box, locate the file that you want to import. You can import these types of files:

   Audio and music files: .aif, .aifc, .aiff, .asf, .au, .mp2, .mp3, .mpa, .snd, .wav, .wma

   Picture files: .bmp, .dib, .emf, .gif, .jfif, .jpe, .jpeg, .jpg, .png, .tif, .tiff, .wmf

   Video files: .asf, .avi, .m1v, .mp2, .mp2v, .mpe, .mpeg, .mpg, .mpv2, .wm, .wmv

   For a description of each file type, go to http://support.microsoft.com/?kbid=316992, "Windows Media Player Multimedia File Formats."

3. If you're importing a video file, check Create Clips for Video Files to have Movie Maker separate the video automatically into smaller, more manageable clips. Or uncheck the box to import the video as one whole clip.

4. Click Import.

✔ Tips

- When you capture or import a file, a new clip appears in the Contents pane (**Figure 11.4**).

- If you create clips in step 3, Movie Maker uses *clip detection* to begin a new clip each time it encounters a substantial change from one frame of the video to the next. (The minimum duration of a clip is 1 second.) To create clips *after* you've imported or captured a video, select the clip in the Contents pane; then choose Tools > Create Clips.

- Imported files actually remain in their original locations. Movie Maker doesn't create copies; instead, a clip in the Contents pane is a shortcut that points to the source file. If you move, rename, or delete a source file after you import it, you'll break the link. Movie Maker tries to find moved or renamed files automatically, but sometimes, you'll have to import them again.

- Movie Maker 2 and later versions import and upgrade your Movie Maker 1 clip collections automatically, so you don't have to reimport files. To import a Movie Maker 1 collection manually, choose Windows Movie Maker 1.x Collection Files from the Files of Type list in the Import File dialog box (step 2).

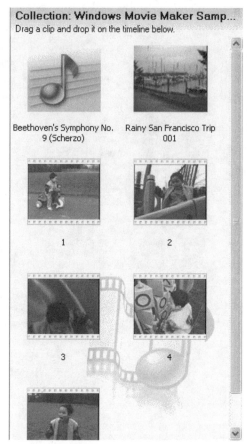

Figure 11.4 Imported and captured clips appear as thumbnails in the Contents pane. Icons indicate the clip type: The top-left clip is an audio file, the top-right clip is a still photo, and the bottom five clips are videos. The five video clips actually come from a single file; I let Movie Maker divide the video into smaller segments during import, so they're ready to edit.

Connecting a Video Camera to Your Computer

A variety of hardware *capture devices* can transfer content to your computer from your analog video camera, VCR, DV camera, or webcam. These are only guidelines about connecting; specific configuration will depend on your hardware. See Chapter 8 for tips on installing hardware.

Analog cameras and VCRs. Connect a VCR or analog camcorder (which uses VHS, 8mm, or Hi-8 tapes) to a *video capture card* installed in your PC, which provides extra video and probably audio ports. For video capture, you can connect your camera's video line-out to the card's video line-in port. For audio capture, you could then connect the left and right audio lines (usually, through RCA-style single-channel connectors to a 3.5mm stereo plug Y-adapter) to the line-in port on a sound card or a video capture card with audio ports. If both your camera and video capture card have *S-video* connectors, you can attach those connectors to record video while the attached audio connectors capture sound.

Digital cameras. Connect a digital camera (which uses miniDV, microMV, or Digital8 tapes) to your PC's IEEE 1394 port (also known as a FireWire or i.Link port). If your PC didn't come with IEEE 1394 ports, you'll have to buy and install a card that provides them. These connections transfer high-quality content very quickly because they're designed to transmit digital data like your camera's audio and video information. Use the cable that came with your camera to connect the camera's DV-out port to the IEEE 1394 port. The cable transfers both audio and video. Many digital cameras also have analog outputs, which you can connect to a video capture card to transfer video and audio to your computer, but converting the signal from digital to analog and back again will degrade picture and sound quality.

Web cameras. A webcam connects to a USB port, to an IEEE 1394 port, or (if it's a video composite camera) to a video capture card. Some webcams have a built-in microphone for capturing audio too.

Audio only. To capture audio only, you can use a stand-alone microphone connected to a sound card's line-in port or to a USB port.

TV. You can capture video from TV if you have a TV tuner card installed in your computer.

Organizing Your Clips

After capturing or importing clips, you can organize them in *collections*—Explorer-like folder hierarchies (**Figure 11.5**). A collection doesn't apply to any specific movie project; you can use it many times over in different movies.

To create a collection:

1. If the Collections pane is hidden, choose View > Collections.

2. In the Collections pane, right-click the collection folder where you want to add your new collection; then choose New Collection (refer to Figure 11.5).

3. Type a name for the collection; then press Enter.

✔ Tips

- Right-click a collection to rename or delete it. Deleting a collection or clip deletes only pointers; source files remain in their original locations on your hard drive.

- Collections are stored as .dat files in the hidden folder \Documents and Settings\<*your user name*>\Local Settings\ Application Data\Microsoft\Movie Maker. Again, backing up a collection file doesn't back up the source files.

Figure 11.5 Here's a reasonable way to organize clips in a collection hierarchy. Alternatively, you can organize your clips by event rather than by clip type. If you have only a few clips, you can stick them all in one collection folder.

Figure 11.6 You also can arrange clips via the shortcut menu; just right-click an empty area of the Contents pane. (You can't drag and drop clips in this pane to reorder them.)

To store a clip in a particular collection folder, just drag the clip's icon from the Contents pane to the folder. You can sort the clips in the Contents pane.

To arrange clips:

1. In the Collections pane, click the collection folder that contains the clips you want to arrange.

   The clips appear in the Contents pane.

2. To change how much detail is displayed, choose View > Details or View > Thumbnails.

3. Choose View > Arrange Icons By; then choose a property to display (**Figure 11.6**).

Creating a Project

Your works in progress in Movie Maker are stored in *projects*. A project (.mswmm) file isn't an end-result movie but a framework containing the arrangement and timing information of audio and video clips, video transitions, video effects, and titles that you've added to the storyboard/timeline. Project files also have properties that you can define and use to organize your projects.

You open and save existing projects with the usual Open, Save, and Save As commands in the toolbar or File menu.

To create a new project:

◆ Choose File > New Project.

✔ Tips

■ You can have only one project open at a time.

■ Project files are saved by default in the My Videos folder inside your My Documents folder (choose View > My Videos Folder).

■ Like most Microsoft applications, Movie Maker opens by default with a blank, untitled project. If you'd rather start editing where you left off, choose Tools > Options > General tab; then check Open Last Project on Startup.

To view a project's properties:

◆ Choose File > Properties (**Figure 11.7**).

✔ Tips

■ The properties that you enter become part of the project file *and* of your final, saved movie. Don't enter any information in the Project Properties dialog box that you don't want others to see.

■ To view an individual clip's properties (such as duration and source file), right-click the clip; then choose Properties.

Figure 11.7 You can specify values for different properties (except Duration, which is preset) and use Windows Explorer to search for specific projects or organize them according to title, author, and so on.

Figure 11.8 Use the storyboard to look at the sequence of clips in your project and rearrange them, if necessary. You can preview all the clips and see any video effects or video transitions that you've added. Audio clips aren't displayed on the storyboard, but they are in the timeline.

Figure 11.9 Use the timeline to review or modify the timing of clips; use its buttons to change the view, zoom in or out, record narration, or adjust audio levels. Click the small + icon next to the Video track to expand it and display Transition and Audio tracks.

Editing a Project

Now comes the fun. To begin editing your project, you add captured or imported video, audio, or pictures to the storyboard/timeline. The storyboard/timeline clips become the contents of your project and future movie.

The storyboard and timeline both display your work in progress, but from different perspectives. The storyboard displays the *sequence* of clips (**Figure 11.8**); the timeline displays the *timing* of clips (**Figure 11.9**).

You can preview your entire project or a particular clip in the Monitor.

To switch between storyboard and timeline view:

◆ Press Ctrl+T (or choose View > Storyboard or View > Timeline).

   or

   Click the Show Storyboard/Timeline button on the toolbar.

✔ Tips

■ Timeline time is displayed as hours: minutes:seconds.hundredths of a second (h:mm:ss.ss).

■ Some editing tasks can be performed in both storyboard and timeline views; others, in only one view.

EDITING A PROJECT

To add a clip to a project:

1. In the Collections pane, click the collection that contains the clip that you want to add to your project.

2. In the Contents pane, click the clip that you want to add (or Ctrl+click to select multiple clips).

3. Drag the clip (or multiple clips) onto the storyboard/timeline in whatever order you like (or choose Clip > Add to Storyboard/Timeline).

✔ Tips

- To rearrange your clips, just drag them to a different location on the storyboard/timeline. You also can move or duplicate clips with the usual Cut, Copy, and Paste commands in the Edit menu.

- To move a clip only slightly, select it; then choose Clip > Nudge Left/Right (timeline view only).

- To remove a clip from the storyboard/timeline, right-click it; then choose Delete (or select it and press Delete). To remove all clips, press Ctrl+Delete or choose Edit > Clear toryboard/Timeline.

- If the timeline's clips become too cramped or too spread out, you can zoom to change the level of detail displayed. From the View menu, choose Zoom In, Zoom Out, or Zoom to Fit (or press Page Down, Page Up, or F9, respectively).

Timeline Tracks

Each timeline track (refer to Figure 11.9) shows specific items that you've added to a project:

Video. Shows video clips, pictures, and titles. If you add video effects to a clip, a small star icon appears on that clip.

Transition. Shows video transitions between clips.

Audio. Shows the audio that's included in any video clips.

Audio/Music. Shows audio clips that aren't part of the video track, such as narration and background music.

Title Overlay. Shows any titles or credits.

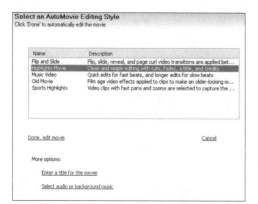

Figure 11.10 AutoMovie analyzes the selected video, audio, and picture clips, and combines them to make one movie based on the automatic editing style that you choose.

To preview a project or clip:

◆ To preview a project, choose Play > Play Storyboard/Timeline.

or

To preview a clip, select the clip; then choose Play > Play Clip.

✔ Tips

■ The Play menu and the Monitor's playback controls let you play the current selection continuously or frame by frame.

■ Press Alt+Enter to preview in full-screen mode. Press Esc (or Alt+Enter again) to go back to normal.

Movie Maker's AutoMovie feature creates a movie quickly and automatically based on the selected clips or collection.

To create a movie automatically:

1. Select a collection in the Collections pane or select multiple clips in the Contents pane.

    The selected clips must contain video and/or pictures that have a combined duration of at least 30 seconds. (An audio clip must be at least 30 seconds long.)

2. Choose Tools > AutoMovie.

3. Select an AutoMovie editing style.

4. If desired, click the More Options links to enter a movie title and select audio or background music (**Figure 11.10**).

5. Click Done, Edit Movie.

✔ Tip

■ After you create an AutoMovie, you can save it with the Save Movie Wizard or make further edits, just as you would when creating a project and movie manually.

Editing Clips

You have several ways to edit the clips that you've arranged on the storyboard/timeline.

You can *split* an audio or video clip into smaller, more manageable clips. By splitting a clip, you can, say, insert a video transition or title into the middle.

To split a clip:

1. In the Contents pane or on the storyboard/timeline, select the clip that you want to split.

2. Press the spacebar to play the clip; then press the spacebar again to pause at the point at which you want to split the clip.

   or

   On the Monitor, move the seek bar to the point at which you want to split the clip.

3. Choose Clip > Split (or press Ctrl+L).

Conversely, you *combine* an audio or video clip that's divided into small clips. You can combine only contiguous clips. (The second clip's start time immediately follows the first clip's end time.)

To combine a split clip:

1. In the Contents pane or on the storyboard/timeline, hold down the Ctrl key; then select two or more contiguous clips that you want to combine.

2. Choose Clip > Combine (or press Ctrl+M).

You can *trim* a clip to hide its unwanted parts. By trimming an audio or video clip, you edit its starting and ending points, therefore editing its length. Trimmed content isn't removed but merely hidden from the movie's audience.

To trim a clip:

1. Choose View > Timeline.

2. Select the clip that you want to trim.

3. Drag the trim handles to set the start and end trim points (**Figure 11.11**).

✔ Tips

- For precise trimming, use the Monitor's playback controls to pause at a trim point; then use the Clip menu's Set Trim Point commands.

- To clear trim points, select the trimmed clip on the timeline; then choose Clip > Clear Trim Points.

Figure 11.11 Drag the trim handles to set start and end trim points. The start trim point determines when the clip will begin to play; the end trim point determines when the clip will stop playing.

Adding Visual Content

You can embroider your movies with video transitions, video effects, and titles and credits.

A *video transition* controls how your movie plays from one video clip or picture to the next.

To add a video transition:

1. Choose Tools > Video Transitions (**Figure 11.12**).

2. In storyboard view, drag a video transition to the video-transition marker between two video clips or pictures (**Figure 11.13**).

   or

   In Timeline view, drag a video transition between two clips on the Video track.

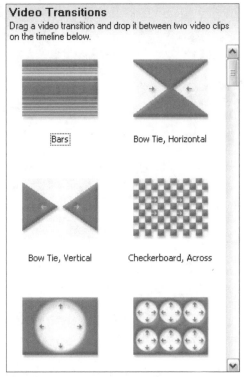

Figure 11.12 Several video transitions appear in the Contents pane. Double-click a transition to test it in the Monitor.

Figure 11.13 The box between these clips shows a checkerboard transition, which plays before the first clip ends and while the other clip starts to play. In Timeline view, you can drag the transition's left edge to change its duration. The starred boxes in each clip's bottom-left corner indicate video effects. You can right-click a transition or effect to delete it.

Video Effects

Drag a video effect and drop it on a video clip on the storyboard below.

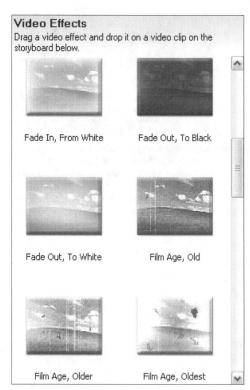

Fade In, From White Fade Out, To Black

Fade Out, To White Film Age, Old

Film Age, Older Film Age, Oldest

Figure 11.14 These effects are maintained when you split, cut, copy, or move a video clip or picture. You can add multiple video effects to each clip.

A *video effect* is a special effect that determines how a video clip, picture, or title appears in a movie. The effect lasts for the clip's entire duration.

To add a video effect:

1. Choose Tools > Video Effects (**Figure 11.14**).

2. In storyboard view, drag a video effect to a clip's video-effects box (refer to Figure 11.13).

   or

   In Timeline view, drag a video effect to the Video track.

Titles and credits add text-based information, such as a movie title or your name, to a movie. You can add multiple titles to a track at different points in a movie. The titles overlay the video.

To add a title or credit:

1. Choose Tools > Title and Credits.

2. On the pane that appears, select where you want to add text.

3. Type the text.

   Use the More Options link to tailor the text's appearance.

4. Click Done, Add Title to Movie.

ADDING VISUAL CONTENT

Adding Audio Tracks

If you've imported music or audio files, you can add them to your movie as background music or sounds.

If you have a microphone connected to your PC, you can add audio narration to video clips. Your narration is synchronized with the video automatically, so the narration describes the action in your movie as it plays.

To add audio:

1. Choose View > Timeline.

2. In the Collections pane, click the collection that contains the audio clip that you want to add to your project.

3. Drag the clip from the Contents pane to the timeline's Audio/Music track (**Figure 11.15**).

Figure 11.15 You can drag an audio clip left or right to adjust its position in the movie or drag the clip's left or right edge to trim its length. (The Audio track—above the Audio/Music track—holds the *video's* audio track.) You can add video clips to the Audio/Music track if you want the audio, but not the video, to play in your movie.

Figure 11.16 Click Show More Options to set additional recording options. If the Limit Narration box is unchecked, you can keep talking past the end of the movie.

Figure 11.17 Sound Recorder is a free—and underrated—Windows program. You can record, mix, play, and edit sounds with it; choose Help Topics from its Help menu for instructions.

To narrate the timeline:

1. Choose View > Timeline.

2. Move the timeline's playback indicator (the square with a vertical line; refer to Figure 11.15) to an empty point on the Audio/Music track where you want to begin your audio narration.

3. Choose Tools > Narrate Timeline (**Figure 11.16**).

4. Click Start Narration; then speak into the microphone to narrate the movie as it progresses.

5. Click Stop Narration.

6. Save the file.

✔ Tips

■ You can record audio clips in Sound Recorder and import them into your project. To start Sound Recorder, choose Start > All Programs > Accessories > Entertainment > Sound Recorder (**Figure 11.17**).

■ Right-click an audio clip to adjust its volume levels or to delete it.

Saving a Movie

Now you're ready to use the Save Movie Wizard to save your final project as an actual movie. The wizard lets you choose among several destinations: You can store the movie on your computer, burn it on a CD-R or CD-RW, send it as an email attachment, post it on the web with a video hosting provider, or record it to a tape in your DV camera. The wizard's pages vary by the destination. In this section, I'll describe how to save a movie on your hard drive.

To save a movie to your computer:

1. Choose File > Save Movie File (or press Ctrl+P).

2. Select My Computer (**Figure 11.18**); then click Next.

3. Type a file name and choose a location for the saved movie (**Figure 11.19**); then click Next.

4. Select the settings for your new movie (**Figure 11.20**); then click Next.

5. After your movie is saved, click Finish.

   By default, your movie plays in Windows Media Player.

✔ Tips

- Movies are saved in Windows Media Audio/Video (.wmv) format. You can watch them in Windows Media Player version 7 or later, Internet Explorer, or any media player that can play .wmv files.

- You also can start the Save Movie Wizard from the Finish Movie section of the Movie Tasks pane.

Figure 11.18 The Save Movie Wizard simplifies and automates the process of assembling your clips and compressing digital video to create movies.

Figure 11.19 Your My Videos folder is the movie's default location, but you can store it anywhere on your hard drive.

Figure 11.20 Movie Maker suggests a setting for intended use, bit rate and display size, but you can choose any setting you like. The setting details and the potential movie file size appear in the bottom half of this screen.

CONNECTING TO THE INTERNET 12

After you finish using your computer to write memos, create spreadsheets, and cook books, you can connect to the internet to browse the web, pirate music, flirt with strangers, send email, and chat online. Windows' New Connection Wizard simplifies internet connections, but realistically, hooking up to the internet can induce stress in even war-weary network administrators.

As an individual, you can't connect to the internet directly. You must pay a go-between *internet service provider (ISP)* and rely on it to provide setup information, turn on your service, equip and maintain dependable connections, and help you when things go wrong.

In this chapter, you'll learn how to choose a connection type and set it up, as well as how to armor your computer against outside attacks. Subsequent chapters show you how to browse, send email, and chat after you're hooked up.

Understanding Connection Types

First, you can skip this chapter if:

You upgraded from a previous Windows version that had internet access. Windows Setup preserved the configuration; your XP connection should work fine.

You want to transfer internet connection settings from another PC. Use the Files and Settings Transfer Wizard; see "Transferring Existing Files and Settings" in the appendix.

Your PC is on a local area network (LAN) at work or school. You have internet access through the network. Ask your network administrator about connection details.

You want to share an internet connection provided by another computer. Use Internet Connection Sharing (or a router); see "Sharing an Internet Connection" in Chapter 17.

If you're not in any of these situations, you can set up your own internet connection by using:

◆ A *dial-up connection* through an analog modem over ordinary phone lines, or

◆ A high-speed *broadband connection* such as DSL or cable

Picking a Connection Type

If you want to get online but don't know the best way to do it, here's some help.

Dial-up connections are the most popular type. Each time you connect to the internet, your analog modem dials your ISP over a standard phone line. (If you have only one line, callers can't reach you while you're online.) Dial-up connections are slow compared with broadband, but they're a good choice for frequent travelers, because big ISPs provide local access numbers over large geographic areas. In some areas, dial-up is your *only* choice. Dial-up service costs about $20 (U.S.) a month for unlimited access (plus your cost for the calls).

DSL and cable (broadband) connections are growing in popularity because they're:

◆ *Fast.* Broadband modems are 10 to 50 times faster than dial-up modems.

◆ *Persistent.* Broadband connections are always on. No dialing is involved.

◆ *Easy to set up.* In many cases, a technician comes to your home to install and configure everything. Otherwise, the ISP will mail you a kit with equipment and setup instructions.

continues on next page

UNDERSTANDING CONNECTION TYPES

For either connection type, you'll need an account with an ISP. If you have one already, see "Setting up an Existing Internet Account" later in this chapter. If not, ask a friend or colleague to recommend one; find an online PC and visit www.dslreports.com; or look in your local Yellow Pages under, say, *Computers—Online Services*. After you've signed up, see "Setting up an Existing Internet Account" later in this chapter.

If you'd rather skip the ISP hunt and sign up online with a Microsoft-recommended ISP, see "Creating a New Internet Account" later in this chapter.

✔ Tip

■ Internet junkies use traditional ISPs, which provide direct, unsanitized internet access. Beginners like online services, such as America Online (AOL) and Microsoft's MSN, because they're easier to use and set up, and they have their own little nonhostile online communities. Online services give you an all-in-one application to browse, send email, create web sites, and so on. With traditional ISPs, you choose your programs: Internet Explorer or Mozilla Firefox for browsing, Outlook Express or Eudora for email, Windows Messenger or AIM for chatting, and so on. Windows includes a complete suite of internet software.

Picking a Connection Type
(continued)

◆ *Cheaper (maybe)*. Broadband service costs about $25 to $50 a month for unlimited access (plus one-time setup and equipment costs, ranging from zero to a few hundred dollars). Dial-up's $20 monthly fee is cheaper, but with broadband, you don't need to pay for a second phone line for internet access or for the extra connect time needed for big downloads.

DSL (Digital Subscriber Line) uses a DSL modem to operate over a standard phone line without interfering with normal voice calls. DSL is available if you're no more than 3 miles from a phone-company central office. (The closer you are, the faster the connection speed.)

Cable uses a cable modem to operate over a cable TV line (coaxial cable). If you're wired for cable TV, you can get a connection through your cable company. Cable speed can drop precipitously when too many people in your area use the system.

Other connection types include satellite or ISDN (an older, slower sort-of-DSL). If your connection doesn't fit neatly into a particular category, your setup still may be similar to those described in the following sections. In any case, your ISP will provide equipment, instructions, and possibly an on-site technician.

UNDERSTANDING CONNECTION TYPES

Creating a New Internet Account

Read this section if you don't have an internet account and want to use Microsoft's referral service to sign up with an ISP online. This service lists only ISPs that cut a special deal with Microsoft; with a little legwork, you probably can find a better deal with a local ISP (in which case, skip to the next section).

✔ Tip

- You need a modem for this procedure. See "Dial-up connections" later in this chapter.

To create a new internet account:

1. Choose Start > All Programs > Accessories > Communications > New Connection Wizard.

   The New Connection Wizard appears (**Figure 12.1**).

2. Click Next to skip the Welcome page.

3. On the Network Connection Type page, select Connect to the Internet; then click Next.

4. On the Getting Ready page, select Choose from a List of Internet Service Providers (ISPs); then click Next.

5. On the Completing page, click Finish.

   The wizard closes, and the Online Services window opens.

6. In the Online Services window, double-click the icon Refer Me to More Internet Service Providers.

   The Internet Connection Wizard starts.

Figure 12.1 This wizard also lets you set up a network or connect to a small network. Here, you'll use it to establish an internet account.

7. On the first page of the Internet Connection Wizard, click Next.

   The wizard dials out (toll-free) on your modem, downloads information about ISPs, and then displays **Figure 12.2.**

8. Follow the onscreen instructions.

   When you're done, a new connection icon appears in the Network Connections window.

9. Choose Start > All Programs > Accessories > Communications > Network Connections.

10. Double-click the connection icon to go online or right-click it to see its properties.

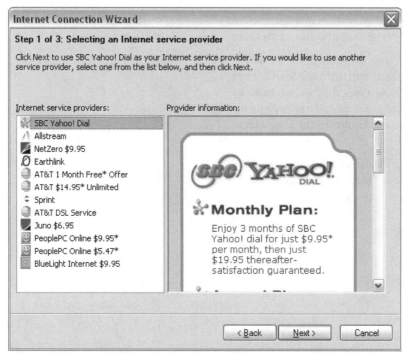

Internet Connection Wizard

Step 1 of 3: Selecting an Internet service provider

Click Next to use SBC Yahoo! Dial as your Internet service provider. If you would like to use another service provider, select one from the list below, and then click Next.

Internet service providers:
- SBC Yahoo! Dial
- Allstream
- NetZero $9.95
- Earthlink
- AT&T 1 Month Free* Offer
- AT&T $14.95* Unlimited
- Sprint
- AT&T DSL Service
- Juno $6.95
- PeoplePC Online $9.95*
- PeoplePC Online $5.47*
- BlueLight Internet $9.95

Provider information:

(SBC) YAHOO! DIAL

Monthly Plan:

Enjoy 3 months of SBC Yahoo! dial for just $9.95* per month, then just $19.95 thereafter- satisfaction guaranteed.

< Back   Next >   Cancel

Figure 12.2 The listed ISPs basically are identical; use price and the availability of local dial-up numbers as your selection criteria. During the sign-up process, Windows dials a toll-free number to send your name, address, credit-card number, chosen email address, and other information to your new ISP. If Windows can't find an ISP in your area, you'll have to find one yourself and set it up manually (see the next section).

Setting up an Existing Internet Account

Read this section if you have an existing dial-up or broadband internet account that you want to set up manually or if your PC connects to the internet through your school or workplace network. The setup procedure depends on whether you have a dial-up connection or a DSL, cable, network, or other high-speed connection.

✔ Tips

- Before you start, look in the Network Connections window for existing connections; choose Start > Control Panel > Network and Internet Connections > Network Connections (**Figure 12.3**).

- Always favor your ISP's own instructions over the generic instructions given here.

- To add Network Connections to the Start menu, right-click the Start button; then choose Properties > Customize > Advanced tab > select Link to Network Connections Folder (in the Start Menu Items list).

- Set up a firewall as soon as you're connected; see "Securing Your Computer" later in this chapter.

Figure 12.3 The Network Connections window lists your current internet and network connections. Type descriptive connection names when you're prompted; the names appear as icon labels in this window.

Figure 12.4 The different types of connections are described in the sidebar in "Understanding Connection Types" earlier in this chapter.

Silencing Your Modem

I listen to the squawks, static, and pings that my telephone modem makes when it dials so I can track the progress and success of a connection. If you prefer silence, do the following:

1. Choose Start > Control Panel > Printers and Other Hardware > Phone and Modem Options.

2. In the Phone and Modem Options dialog box that appears, choose Modems tab > Properties > Modem tab.

3. Drag the Speaker Volume slider to Off. (You have two choices: On or Off. You can't drag the slider midway between them.)

4. Click OK in each open dialog box.

By the way, silencing the modem is a bad idea if you think that you may get a dialer virus; see "Securing Your Computer" later in this chapter.

Dial-up connections

You need an analog modem for a dial-up connection. Plug the telephone cable from your wall jack into the modem's *Line* (not *Phone*) jack. If you have to run your modem and a phone off the same line at the same jack, run a second cable from the modem's *Phone* jack to the telephone's *Line* jack. If your PC didn't come with a built-in modem, buy a 56 Kbps model and install it (see Chapter 8).

To set up a dial-up connection:

1. Choose Start > All Programs > Accessories > Communications > New Connection Wizard.
   The New Connection Wizard appears.

2. Click Next to skip the Welcome page.

3. On the Network Connection Type page, select Connect to the Internet; then click Next.

4. On the Getting Ready page, select Set up My Connection Manually (refer to the first three pages of Figure 12.1); then click Next.
   Detour: If you have an AOL or other installation CD, select Use the CD I Got from an ISP; click Next; click Finish; insert the CD; then follow the onscreen instructions and skip the rest of these steps.

5. On the Internet Connection page, select Connect Using a Dial-Up Modem (**Figure 12.4**); then click Next.

6. On the Connection Name page, type a connection name; then click Next.
   If you're a traveler with multiple dial-up connections on your laptop, use names like *AOL (New York)* or *SBC (San Francisco)*.

7. On the Phone Number to Dial page, type the phone number that connects your PC to your ISP (including a prefix and area code, if necessary); then click Next.

continues on next page

8. On the Internet Account Information page, type your user name and password; check or uncheck the connection options (**Figure 12.5**); then click Next.

Check Use This Account Name and Password When Anyone Connects to the Internet from This Computer to let *all* logged-on users use this connection; uncheck it if you don't want to share the connection.

Check Make This the Default Internet Connection if this connection is the one that you use most often to dial up the internet.

9. On the Completing page, review your settings; then click Finish.

A new connection icon appears in the Network Connections window (refer to Figure 12.3).

10. Double-click the connection icon to go online or right-click it to see its properties.

✔ Tips

■ To suppress the Connect dialog box (**Figure 12.6**), right-click the connection icon; then choose Properties > Options tab > uncheck Prompt for Name and Password, Certificate, Etc.

■ To have Windows connect automatically when needed, right-click the connection icon and choose Set as Default Connection. Next, choose Start > Control Panel > Network and Internet Connections > Internet Options > Connections tab > select Always Dial My Default Connection.

■ To add alternative dial-up numbers to a connection, right-click its icon; then choose Properties > General tab > Alternates.

■ To create another connection quickly, right-click an existing connection icon; choose Create Copy; then right-click the new icon and edit its properties.

Figure 12.5 Contact your ISP if you don't know your user name and password.

Figure 12.6 This dialog box appears when you start a connection.

High-speed connections

As noted earlier, sometimes a technician sets up your broadband or network connection, but you can set up (or troubleshoot) it yourself. Before setup, make sure that there's a cable running from your PC's Ethernet (network) port to a DSL modem, a cable modem, or a network jack. The correct lights on the modem must be lit. (Typically you want to see four steady green lights, but refer to the documentation.)

Next, ask your ISP or network administrator if you have a static or dynamic IP address. An *IP address* identifies your computer uniquely on the internet. A *static* (or *fixed*) IP address stays the same every time you connect; a *dynamic* IP address changes each time. Unlike a static IP connection, a dynamic IP connection (also called a *PPPoE, DHCP,* or—rarely—*DDNS* connection) requires a user name and password, and must be initiated *(leased)* each time that you reconnect to the internet. For some ISPs, your connection hardware can handle reconnection; for others, you have to initiate it yourself, like a dial-up connection.

Windows often refers to *connection* as *enabling* and to *disconnection* as *disabling*.

Hanging Up

An icon (🖳) in the notification area (system tray) reminds you that you're online; if you don't see it, check Show Icon in the connection's Properties dialog box (see Figure 12.8 later in this chapter). You can point to or click the icon for connection status.

When you close your browser or other internet program, your dial-up connection doesn't hang up automatically; it ties up your phone line until you disconnect it manually. To hang up, right-click the notification-area icon; then choose Disconnect. (You don't have to disconnect broadband connections. They don't cost extra or tie up the telephone line when connected.)

To make a connection hang up automatically after an inactivity period, right-click the connection icon in the Network Connections window; choose Properties > Options tab; then select a time limit from the Idle Time Before Hanging Up list.

To set up a dynamic IP connection:

1. Choose Start > All Programs > Accessories > Communications > New Connection Wizard.

   The New Connection Wizard appears.

2. Click Next to skip the Welcome page.

3. On the Network Connection Type page, select Connect to the Internet; then click Next.

4. On the Getting Ready page, select Set up My Connection Manually (refer to the first three pages of Figure 12.1); then click Next.

5. On the Internet Connection page, select Connect Using a Broadband Connection That Requires a User Name and Password (refer to Figure 12.4); then click Next.

6. On the Connection Name page, type your ISP's name; then click Next.

7. On the Internet Account Information page, type your user name and password; check or uncheck the connection options; then click Next (refer to Figure 12.5).

8. On the Completing page, review your settings; then click Finish.

   A new connection icon appears in the Network Connections window (refer to Figure 12.3).

9. Double-click the connection icon to go online or right-click it to see its properties.

✔ Tip

- To suppress the Connect dialog box (refer to Figure 12.6) or to have Windows connect automatically when needed, see the Tips in "To set up a dial-up connection" earlier in this chapter.

Why Dynamic IP Addresses?

Dynamic IP addresses are more complicated than static ones, but they're needed because of the IP-address shortage. About 4.3 billion addresses exist (ranging from 0.0.0.0 to 255.255.255.255), but along with the growing number of networked computers, "IP-aware" cellphones and consumer toys, car navigation systems, shipping containers, and other devices are swallowing them up.

The problem with static addresses is that once an IP address is allocated to a particular computer or device, it's off the market—even when that machine is offline. With dynamic addresses, an online machine asks the server, "Got an IP address I can use temporarily?", and the server replies, "Take this one while you're here." It's a technically more difficult but more efficient use of a scarce resource.

Figure 12.7 Your Ethernet (network) port appears in the LAN or High-Speed Internet section of the Network Connections window.

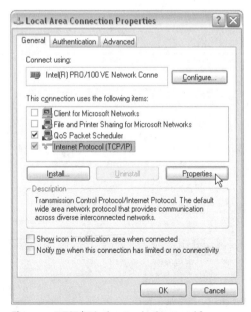

Figure 12.8 TCP/IP is the standard protocol for computer communications over the internet.

To set up a static IP connection:

1. Choose Start > Control Panel > Network and Internet Connections > Network Connections.

2. Right-click the Local Area Connection icon; then choose Properties (**Figure 12.7**).

3. On the General tab of the Local Area Connection Properties dialog box, double-click Internet Protocol (TCP/IP) in the connections list (**Figure 12.8**).

continues on next page

4. On the General tab of the Internet Protocol (TCP/IP) Properties dialog box, select Use the Following IP Address; select Use the Following DNS Server Addresses; then type your IP addresses (**Figure 12.9**).

5. Click OK in each open dialog box.

✔ Tip

■ If Windows ever prompts you to connect to the internet, choose Start > Control Panel > Network and Internet Connections > Internet Options > Connections tab; then select Never Dial a Connection.

Figure 12.9 Your ISP may have sent you your IP addresses, but you can type these settings while you've got your DSL provider, cable company, or network administrator on the phone.

Troubleshooting Tools

Windows includes a few tools that let you inspect and troubleshoot your internet and network connections.

To use Windows' built-in diagnostics tool, choose Start > Help and Support > Networking and the Web > Fixing Networking or Web Problems > Diagnose Network Configuration and Run Automated Networking Tests > Scan Your System.

These command-line commands are faster and more useful than almost anything else in the graphical interface: ipconfig, netsh, netstat, pathping, ping, and tracert. Also try 3D Traceroute (free; www.hlembke.de/prod/3dtraceroute).

To determine your actual internet connection speed (as opposed to what your ISP tells you), go to www.bandwidthplace.com/speedtest or http://speedtest.dslreports.com.

Securing Your Computer

Computer security is no longer an afterthought, and a four-pronged defense will protect you from most attacks:

Firewall. A *firewall* is a secure boundary between your computer (or network) and the internet, protecting you against external threats such as crackers and malicious programs.

Software updates. Automatic Updates, a Control Panel program, monitors the Microsoft web site for new security patches, updates, bug fixes, and hardware drivers, which it downloads and installs promptly.

Antivirus software. An antivirus program searches hard drives and monitors downloaded files and email attachments for viruses, and then removes any viruses it finds. Most antivirus programs include an auto-update feature to counter emerging threats.

Antispyware software. An antispyware program, like an antivirus program, scours your hard drive for spyware and removes it.

Service Pack 2 adds a new Control Panel program named Security Center, which monitors the status of your firewall, software updates, and antivirus software. You'll have to handle the antispyware software on your own.

✔ Tips

■ If you're a savvy user who already has a firewall and anti-whatever software, you still should install SP2 because it has many buried, geeky changes such as boot-time, buffer-overflow, and anonymous-RPC protections. To install SP2, see "Updating Windows XP" in Chapter 19.

■ The Microsoft Windows Malicious Software Removal Tool detects and removes infections by specific malicious software, including prevalent viruses and worms. Microsoft releases an updated version of this tool on the second Tuesday of each month. New versions are available through Windows Update or www.microsoft.com/security/ malwareremove/default.mspx.

■ Baseline Security Advisor is a little-known but excellent Microsoft tool that scans your PC for security holes and suggests how to fix them. Download it for free at www.microsoft.com/technet/ security/tools/mbsahome.mspx. Its diagnoses contain some technical language but make clear where the problems lie.

■ A good general site on web privacy and security is www.junkbusters.com.

Viruses and Spyware

Malicious software *(malware)* comes in two broad categories: viruses and spyware. They can resemble each other— they're both installed without your knowledge or consent and make your system unstable—but have some important differences.

A *virus* (or *worm*) is a self-replicating program that infects your computer. The type of attack depends on the skill and intent of the virus writer. A virus can erase or corrupt files, steal your financial data, spread other viruses, email copies of itself to people in your address list, chew up memory to slow or halt your system, install a backdoor that lets remote attackers log on to your computer...or may only display a practical-joke screen. A virus often arrives as an innocent-looking email attachment with an executable filename extension such as .exe, .scr, .bat, or .pif (see "Associating Documents with Programs" in Chapter 6).

A *Trojan horse* is a destructive program disguised as legitimate or enticing software, or even as a logon screen. (A file named `sexy.exe` or `FreeMP3s.bat` probably is dangerous.) Trojans don't replicate themselves like viruses, but they can be just as destructive. A exceptionally vicious program, called a *dialer,* uses your modem to make calls to premium-rate telephone numbers (at, say, $20 per minute).

Spyware (or *adware*) relies on people's credulity or ignorance—children are a favorite target— to download and install it. Trickery or bait often are part of the repertoire. If a pop-up window that looks like a legitimate Windows dialog box appears onscreen when you're browsing, don't click Agree, OK, or Close (which might trigger spyware installation); always click the red Close button (☒) or press Alt+F4 in this situation. Other programs, such as the popular Kazaa file-swapping program, promise free music or software but also install spyware surreptitiously. Some spyware exploits security flaws in Internet Explorer to install itself when you simply *visit* a web site (usually an X-rated or Free Stuff! site); it's not unusual for these *drive-by downloads* to install dozens of spyware programs on your PC in a single visit.

Like those of viruses, spyware's effects depend on the creator's intent. Spyware can report your browsing habits to third parties, highjack your browser's home page, redirect your web searches, inundate you with ads (even when you're offline), steal online-store affiliate commissions, or plant a new barnaclelike toolbar in your browser. You also may notice system slowdowns and instability, but these are only side effects; spyware's aim is profit, not destruction.

Security Center

If you've just bought a new computer, upgraded to XP, or installed SP2, you'll probably be greeted with a Security Center warning message in the notification area (system tray) the first time you log on (**Figure 12.10**). This message and icon, or sometimes only the icon, appear if Security Center thinks that your computer has insufficient protection (or if it doesn't recognize the firewall and antivirus software that you're using).

Figure 12.10 This message means that your computer's security settings need attention.

To open Security Center:

◆ Click the Security Center icon ( ) or pop-up message, if it appears.

or

Choose Start > Control Panel > Security Center (**Figure 12.11**).

or

Choose Start > Run; type `wscui.cpl` and then press Enter.

Show security information on the internet and in Help and Support Center

Change Security Center alert options

Security status reports

Open Control Panel programs

Figure 12.11 Security Center displays security-related settings and links in a single window.

Figure 12.12 Unchecking these boxes turns off Security Center alerts but leaves on monitoring.

Security Center has a dashboard of indicator "lights" for your PC's Firewall, Automatic Updates, and Virus Protection components. For each item, a blue bar and green light labeled ON mean that everything is okay. Otherwise you'll see an orange or red bar and light labeled OFF, CHECK SETTINGS, NOT FOUND, NOT MONITORED, or OUT OF DATE. Click one of the headings to expand that section and to learn what the problem is and what to do about it. Security Center offers a status report and provides links to the relevant help screens, online resources, and Control Panel programs that you'll need to fix things.

If you don't want to be bothered with alerts, you can turn them off selectively. You might want to turn off alerts if Security Center doesn't recognize your firewall or antivirus program, either because it's an obscure brand or it came out before SP2 was released.

To turn on or off Security Center alerts:

1. In Security Center, click Change the Way Security Center Alerts Me.

   The Alert Settings dialog box appears (**Figure 12.12**).

2. Check or uncheck the boxes to turn each alert on or off.

3. Click OK.

✔ Tip

- **PRO** If you're an XP Pro user on a network domain, Security Center doesn't display your security status or send alerts. (Your security settings typically are managed by your network administrator.)

Firewalls

A *firewall* is a piece of software or hardware that helps screen out crackers and viruses that try to reach your computer over the internet. It's the most important security component on your PC or network; attackers can compromise your computer easily if you don't have one. Always turn on a firewall *before* you connect to the internet, no matter how you connect. It's no exaggeration to say that unprotected computers often are compromised minutes after going online. XP provides Windows Firewall for free, but you have other choices, in order of preference:

Router (hardware). A router is a small box that distributes the signal from your modem (DSL, cable, or dial-up) to the computers on your network (**Figure 12.13**). Most routers have a built-in firewall and appear to the outside world to be a computer without programs and hard drives to attack or infect; it's the safest type of firewall, because it protects your entire network and is always on. Even if you're not on a network, you can put a router between your PC and your modem. (Chapter 17 covers routers in more detail.)

If you're on a network, a router won't protect you from *other* computers on the network if one of them becomes infected because someone downloaded a virus. For that kind of protection, you'll need a software firewall on your individual PC. Also, laptop users will want a software firewall so that they don't have to lug around a router. If all you need is a router, turn off the Windows (software) firewall, ignoring the dire warning that appears.

Figure 12.13 This Linksys firewall router is popular for home and small-office networks. Other brand-name router makers include 3Com, D-Link, Netgear, Belkin, SMC, and Microsoft.

Figure 12.14 ZoneAlarm asks you if you want to allow or forbid a program to access the internet from your computer (it might surprise you how many programs try this). Check Remember This Setting to always allow or always deny a program access, suppressing this dialog box for that program.

Third-party firewall (software). You can use a non-Microsoft firewall instead of Windows' built-in one. The popular brand-name software firewalls include BlackICE, McAfee, Norton, and Tiny Personal Firewall, but most people opt for ZoneAlarm (free; www.zonealarm.com). Windows Firewall blocks only inbound traffic, but ZoneAlarm provides two-way protection by blocking *outbound* traffic too—a major advantage that can stop spyware and viruses on an already-infected PC from sending your personal information out. Every time that a program (*any* program) tries to access the internet, ZoneAlarm intercepts it and asks for your approval (**Figure 12.14**).

Security Center recognizes popular third-party firewalls and turns off its own firewall automatically. (Don't run two software firewalls at the same time; you might not be able to get online.) If Security Center doesn't know your firewall, turn off Windows Firewall manually—and look for a post-SP2 update of your firewall.

Windows Firewall (software). Prior to Service Pack 2, XP had Internet Connection Firewall, which was weak, hard to find, and turned off by default. SP2 replaces ICF with Windows Firewall, which is stronger, available in Control Panel, and turned on by default.

SECURING YOUR COMPUTER

To turn on or off Windows Firewall:

1. Choose Start > Control Panel > Network and Internet Connections > Windows Firewall (**Figure 12.15**).

   or

   In Security Center, click the Windows Firewall link (refer to Figure 12.11).

   or

   In the Network Connections window (refer to Figure 12.7), right-click a network connection; then choose Properties > Advanced tab > Settings (below Windows Firewall).

   or

   Choose Start > Run; type `firewall.cpl` and then press Enter.

2. On the General tab, click On or Off; then click OK.

✔ Tips

- In the Network Connections window, a small padlock appears in the icon of each connection that Windows Firewall is protecting (**Figure 12.16**).

- You can check Don't Allow Exceptions to block *all* unsolicited incoming traffic, even traffic that normally would be permitted by an exception (described next). Use this extra-secure mode when you connect to a public wireless (Wi-Fi) hotspot in a café, hotel, or airport, or when a virus is spreading over your network.

- An easier way to protect yourself from wireless hotspot hazards is HotSpotVPN ($8.88 per month U.S.; www.hotspotvpn.com).

Figure 12.15 In general, the only reason to switch off Windows Firewall is if you've installed a third-party firewall. (Windows Firewall turns itself off automatically if you install a popular one.)

Figure 12.16 The Windows Firewall padlock should appear for all your broadband, dial-up, and network (LAN) connections. (The padlock won't appear if you're using a third-party firewall.)

Figure 12.17 Online gamers see this dialog box a lot. You'll never see it on a public or network PC where the administrator has blocked *all* exceptions.

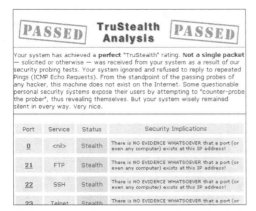

Figure 12.18 A sterling security report for a firewalled computer.

Traffic flows in and out of your computer through *ports*—small, authorized doors in the firewall. (These ports aren't the same as the hardware ports that you connect devices to.) A port number identifies each port uniquely, and certain ports handle only a specific type of traffic. Port 80 is used for HTTP (web) traffic, for example. Other ports allow instant messages, printer sharing, and so on. (You can find others by searching for *"well-known ports"* in Google.)

Windows Firewall leaves some ports open by default (File and Printer Sharing, Windows Messenger, FireWire connectors, and your local network connections, for example) but blocks most of them to incoming traffic, so when a new program wants to get online, the firewall displays a dialog box asking you if it's okay (**Figure 12.17**). Click:

Unblock if you recognize the program name. The firewall opens the relevant listening port temporarily for incoming connections.

Keep Blocking if you don't know which program the firewall is asking about. The program might not work properly if it can't accept incoming traffic (desirable in some cases).

Ask Me Later to deny permission this time but want to be asked again the next time you run the program.

✔ Tip

- To test your computer for online vulnerabilities, go to www.grc.com and navigate to the ShieldsUP! page; then run the tests (**Figure 12.18**). (The tests take some reading and clicking to find.) This web site also contains a lot of useful internet security information, as well as free and for-pay software.

Common sense applies to opening ports: Open one only when you really need it, never unblock a program that you don't recognize, and close a port when you no longer need it. But sometimes you'll change your mind about a program or will be tricked into unblocking a hostile program named to fool you. Windows Firewall lets you create *exceptions* for these programs and manage them manually.

To configure programs and ports:

1. Open Windows Firewall.

2. Click the Exceptions tab (**Figure 12.19**).

3. Do any of the following:

To open or close ports for specific programs, check or uncheck the boxes.

To add a program, click Add Program; then select it in the list or browse to it.

To delete a program, select it in the list; then click Delete. (You can't delete the preconfigured programs.)

To open an individual port by number, click Add Port; then type the port name (any name) and number. (Windows assumes that you're geeky enough to know the port number yourself or that you read it in the program's documentation.)

4. Click OK in each open dialog box.

✔ Tips

■ Adding a program is preferable to opening a specific port because it's easier to do, you don't need to know which port number to use, and the firewall is open only while the program is waiting to receive the connection.

■ Advanced users can open ports for, and configure the scope of, individual connections to minimize opportunities for intruders to connect to your computer or network. In Windows Firewall, click the Advanced tab; then use the settings under Network Connection Settings.

Figure 12.19 The Exceptions tab lists every program that's been granted an open port in the firewall.

SECURING YOUR COMPUTER

Figure 12.20 To open Automatic Updates, click the link in Security Center or choose Start > Control Panel > Automatic Updates.

Is Antivirus Software Necessary?

No. Plenty of people—including me—use no virus protection and don't get infected. I don't like antivirus programs because they display chronic Chicken Little warnings that interfere with my workflow, program installations, and routine internet transactions. If you think that you have a virus, run an antivirus program to eradicate it. The 24/7 protection that continuously running antivirus programs promise is cold comfort. The best way to avoid viruses is to behave safely: Use a firewall, delete executable or risky attachments (even from friends), browse with Mozilla Firefox instead of Internet Explorer, don't download "free" music and movie file-sharing programs, and use an aggressive spam filter. Also, ignore virus myths, publicity stunts, hoaxes, chain letters, and hysteria; see Crypt Newsletter (http://sun.soci.niu.edu/~crypt) or Vmyths (www.vmyths.com).

Automatic Updates

Security Center alerts you with a CHECK SETTINGS or OFF message if Automatic Updates is set to anything other than Automatic (**Figure 12.20**), which checks Microsoft's Windows Update web site regularly for important fixes and, if they're available, downloads and installs them automatically. For more information, see "Updating Windows XP" in Chapter 19.

Virus protection

Security Center warns you if you have no antivirus software installed and running. Unlike the firewall feature, Microsoft doesn't provide an antivirus program, but if you click the Recommendations button (visible in Figure 12.11) and then click the How? link in the dialog box that appears, you're taken to a web page that offer free time-limited trials of various third-party products. Save yourself some money and get AVG Anti-Virus (free; www.grisoft.com).

After you've installed antivirus software, Security Center responds with a green ON light in the Virus Protection section. If Security Center doesn't recognize your brand, you can turn off the antivirus alert manually, as described earlier in this section.

✔ Tips

- McAfee's free online scanner checks your computer for viruses: Go to www.mcafee.com; click the Home & Home Office link; then click the FreeScan button. Symantec has a similar scanner at http://security.symantec.com. These tools detect—but don't remove—viruses.

- Antivirus programs designed specifically to kill Trojan horses include TDS-3 ($49 U.S.; www.diamondcs.com.au), Trojan Hunter ($49; www.misec.net), and Ewido ($35; www.ewido.net/en).

SECURING YOUR COMPUTER

Spyware protection

You can download Microsoft AntiSpyware at www.microsoft.com/spyware (**Figure 12.21**). No spyware cleaner can detect every spyware program, so use a second cleaner in tandem. Try Ad-Aware (free; www.lavasoftusa.com), Spybot Search & Destroy (free; www.safer-networking.org), or Spy Sweeper ($40; www.webroot.com). Don't bother with the antispyware components that come bundled with antivirus programs from Symantec, McAfee, and others.

Spyware is very difficult to remove without a spyware cleaner (and sometimes with one), so do a little research before you download a suspicious program. Use Google to search for the program name and "spyware". A *kazaa spyware* search, for example, yields more than 1 million hits. Or read the product's editorial or user reviews at www.download.com or www.nonags.com. Here are some sites that list clean freeware:

◆ www.pricelessware.org

◆ www.onlythebestfreeware.com

◆ www.majorgeeks.com

Figure 12.21 A clean spyware report from Microsoft AntiSpyware.

Spyware Lineup

You're most likely to pick up spyware when you download free file-sharing (*peer-to-peer*), shopping, animated-buddy, weather, or toolbar utilities. Here are a few culprits:

- BearShare
- BingoFun
- BonziBUDDY
- ClipGenie
- CoolWebSearch
- Dashbar
- eAcceleration Software Station and Threat Scanner
- Freeze.com's Living Rainforest screen saver
- Grokster
- Hotbar
- iMesh
- Kazaa
- LimeWire
- Morpheus
- Messenger Plus!
- Panicware Pop-Up Stopper
- PuritySCAN
- Smiley Central
- WeatherBug
- XXXtoolbar

PC Pitstop publishes a regularly updated "Top 25 Spyware and Adware" list at www.pcpitstop.com/spycheck/top25.asp.

✔ Tips

- Run your antispyware programs at least once a month.

- The home sites of some utilities—Kazaa and LimeWire, for example—swear that they're spyware-free, but they define "spyware" very narrowly.

- Some spyware-laden programs fraudulently promise to *remove* spyware. Spyware Warrior (www.spywarewarrior.com) publishes a list of such products (click the Rogue/Suspect Anti-Spyware link). The same site has a review of antispyware programs (click the Anti-Spyware Testing link). Other worthwhile sites are www.benedelman.org and www.spywareinfo.com.

Browsing the Web with Internet Explorer 13

After your internet connection is working (Chapter 12), use Internet Explorer (IE) to browse the web. If you've used IE before, turn the page; otherwise, you need to improve your vocabulary:

◆ The *internet* is a global network that connects millions of computers. Unlike online services like AOL, the internet is decentralized—by design. You can use to it exchange data, news, opinions, ideas, and things (you can buy or sell almost anything on it).

◆ The *World Wide Web,* or simply *web,* is a way of viewing and sharing information over the internet via specially formatted documents—*web pages*—that support text, graphics, sounds, video, and links to other web pages. A *web site* is a group of related web pages.

◆ A *web browser* is an application that locates and displays web pages, and downloads files to your hard drive.

✔ Tip

■ The web is a *portion* of the internet. (The terms are not synonyms.) The internet contains not only the web, but also channels for email and news-groups (Chapter 14), as well as instant messages (Chapter 15).

Getting Started with Internet Explorer

Figure 13.1 shows Internet Explorer's main controls. You can point (without clicking) to any control for a pop-up tip. The important part of IE is not the program itself but the web pages and resources that it gives you access to. You'll spend most of your browsing time working within the web itself—reading, searching, scrolling, clicking links, filling out forms, downloading files—rather than using IE's controls and menus.

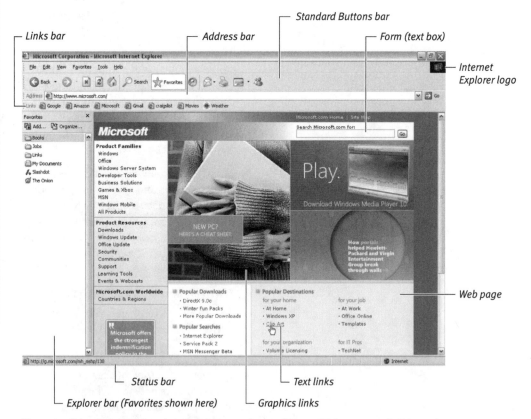

Figure 13.1 Internet Explorer's main panel shows a web page (Microsoft's home page, in this case).

To start Internet Explorer:

◆ Choose Start > Internet Explorer (or Start > All Programs > Internet Explorer).

or

Click the Internet Explorer icon (🔵) on the Quick Launch toolbar on the taskbar.

or

Double-click an internet shortcut.

or

Choose Start > Run; type `iexplore` and then press Enter.

Mozilla Firefox

IE is popular because it's included with Windows, but Mozilla Firefox (free; `www.mozilla.org/products/firefox`) is a far better browser. It features built-in pop-up blocking and tabbed browsing, which lets you flip quickly among pages all within one window. (IE makes you Alt+Tab among a clutter of browser windows.) Firefox is smaller, faster, simpler, more secure, and updated more frequently. You can customize it with easily installed extensions (free add-ins) that include a Google toolbar; Flash-animation suppressor; banner-ad killer; weather-forecast display; and hundreds more for blogging, creating bookmarks, downloading, navigation, searching, tabbing, privacy, security, and miscellany. Firefox can import and export IE settings and bookmarks. And it has an extension that opens a web page in IE in case it doesn't display properly in Firefox (which happens occasionally).

Opera (free; `www.opera.com`) is another strong IE alternative.

IE vs. Windows Explorer

Web pages are HTML (.htm or .html) files that sit on a dedicated computer called a *web server*. Requesting a page makes the server upload it to IE for display. So why use IE to access files on a web server's hard drive and Windows Explorer (Chapter 5) to access files on a local drive or network drive? Microsoft knows that it's silly to treat files differently depending on where they're located, so it blurred the distinction between local and remote files by making IE and Windows Explorer two faces of the same program. You can access *any* file from either program. Choosing a web site in Windows Explorer's Favorites menu, for example, makes Windows Explorer transform into IE and display the site. Similarly, using IE's Search or Favorites bar to locate or manage files on your PC's hard drive makes IE morph into Windows Explorer.

Navigating the Web

You have three ways to move among web pages:

◆ Type a web address (URL) (**Figure 13.2**).

◆ Click a navigation button (**Figure 13.3**).

◆ Click a *link,* or *hyperlink* (**Figure 13.4**).

✔ Tips

■ Text links typically are underlined blue phrases. Pictures and buttons also can be links. Some links sprout a menu when you point to them. If links are hard to spot at first, watch your pointer; wherever it turns from an arrow into a finger-pointing hand, you've discovered a link.

■ To show or hide toolbars, use the View > Toolbars submenu. To move, resize, lock, or customize toolbars, see "Using Windows Explorer Toolbars" in Chapter 5.

■ To visit a page on a particular site, go to the site's home page; then use *the site's* search and navigation tools to find your target. **Table 13.1** lists a few sites to get you started.

■ If an error message ("Cannot find server" or "The page cannot be displayed") appears instead of a web page, you may have mistyped the URL, or the web page may have been moved or removed.

■ The status bar shows IE's progress ("Opening page..." or "Done") and displays the target URL of any link that you point to. If the status bar is hidden, choose View > Status Bar.

■ While the IE logo (top right) is waving or spinning, your PC is downloading a web page.

Figure 13.2 The Address bar displays the address (URL) of the current web page. Type a new address to go to a different page.

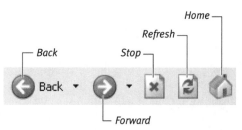

Figure 13.3 The Standard Buttons toolbar's navigation buttons.

Figure 13.4 Links take you to a new web page (or another place on the same page).

Table 13.1

Web-Site Sampler	
TOPIC	SITE
Auctions	www.ebay.com
City guides	www.citysearch.com
Classifieds	www.craigslist.org
Dating	www.match.com
Encyclopedia	www.wikipedia.org
Geek news	www.slashdot.org
Great books	www.bartleby.com
Internet security	www.cert.org
Jobs	www.monster.com
Legal	www.nolo.com
Movie reviews	www.rottentomatoes.com
Search	www.google.com
Shareware	www.download.com
Shopping	www.amazon.com
Tech terms	www.webopedia.com
Travel	www.orbitz.com
U.S. government	www.firstgov.gov
Weather	www.weather.gov
Web design	www.useit.com

URLs

A *URL* (Uniform Resource Locator) is a case-insensitive address that identifies a web page uniquely. The URL for Microsoft's home page, for example, is http://www.microsoft.com. The transmission standard for all web pages is http://, so you don't type it (IE fills it in for you). The rest of the address specifies the web server and the web page's location on it. Some URLs don't need the www., and others require additional dot-separated elements.

The server name's last part (called the *top-level domain,* or *TLD*) tells you about the web site's owner or country. .com is a business, .gov is a government, .edu is a school, and .org is a not-for-profit organization, for example. .uk is a United Kingdom site; .ca is a Canadian site, and so on. For a list of TLDs, see www.iana.org/domain-names.htm.

Like your own documents, web-page files are organized in folder trees on the server, so a long URL (www.microsoft.com/windowsxp/support, for example) works like a pathname. Complicated URLs that contain ?, =, and & symbols often are pages created on-the-fly in response to a query. Note that URLs use forward slashes, not backslashes as in Windows pathnames.

By the way, articulate each letter: *U–R–L.* Don't say *earl.*

To visit a web page by typing a URL:

1. Click the Address bar (or press Alt+D).

2. Type or paste the URL; then press Enter (or click Go).

✔ Tips

■ The Address bar auto-completes—that is, proposes a list of matching sites that you've visited recently. Keep typing, or use the down-arrow key to select a match; then press Enter. To show or hide the Address list manually, press F4.

■ Typing shortcut: To visit a commercial site, type only the business name; then press Ctrl+Enter. IE adds the http://www. and .com bits automatically. (Even without this shortcut, IE adds http:// if you don't.)

■ When you're editing a URL, Ctrl+left arrow or Ctrl+right arrow jump back or forward to the URL's next logical break (dot or slash).

NAVIGATING THE WEB

To visit a web page via navigation buttons or links:

◆ Click a link on a web page.

or

Click a link in an email message or document.

or

To revisit the page that you were just on, click Back on the toolbar (or press Backspace or Alt+left arrow) (**Figure 13.5**).

or

After you've clicked Back, click Forward on the toolbar (or press Alt+right arrow) to return to the page you were on when you clicked Back.

or

To return to a page you've visited in the past few weeks, click History on the toolbar (or press Ctrl+H); then click a link on the History bar (**Figure 13.6**).

or

To go to a bookmarked page, choose it from the Favorites menu (see "Bookmarking Pages" later in this chapter).

✔ Tips

■ To stop downloading a page, click Stop on the toolbar (or press Esc).

■ To reload a stale or incomplete page, click Refresh on the toolbar (or press F5). But Refresh decides for itself what and what not to fetch from the web server; Ctrl+Refresh forces a reload of everything and may bring you newer content.

■ To change the number of days that pages are saved in the History list, choose Tools > Internet Options > General tab > History section (**Figure 13.7**).

Figure 13.5 Click the Back button's small triangle to reveal a menu that lets you jump back several pages. The Forward button has a similar menu.

Figure 13.6 The History bar is an organized list of pages that you've visited recently. Click a time-period icon to list the web sites visited during that period; then click a web-site icon to view each page visited within that site. To sort the sites, click the View button (at top) and choose By Date, By Site, By Most Visited, or By Order Visited Today.

Figure 13.7 If you don't want people peeking at the sites you've visited, click Clear History; then set Days to Keep Pages in History to zero, thus covering your tracks and disabling the History feature.

You can move around a web page by using scroll bars, but it's faster to use keyboard shortcuts or the mouse wheel. Almost all web scrolling is up/down; some poorly designed pages or large images will make you scroll left/right.

To move around a web page:

◆ To scroll down or up incrementally (or line by line), press the down- or up-arrow key or spin the mouse wheel.

or

To scroll up or down by a window, press Page Up or Page Down.

or

To scroll to the beginning or end, press Home or End.

or

To move the cursor forward or back through web-page items, the Address bar, and the Explorer bar, press Tab or Shift+Tab.

If a link is highlighted, press Enter to activate it.

✔ Tips

■ If the insertion point isn't blinking in a text box or the Address bar, press the spacebar or Shift+spacebar to scroll up or down.

■ To close a page (and IE), press Ctrl+W. To launch a new IE session, press Ctrl+N.

Searching the Web

Search engines index billions of web pages and put them at your fingertips. Google is best for all-around searching, but you may prefer other engines for specialized searches or if Google doesn't do what you want. (No one engine knows about every web page.) Some engines, such as Teoma (www.teoma.com) and Open Directory (www.dmoz.org), have their own spin on analyzing and organizing relevant links. You can find search-engine recommendations, news, tips—and about everything else you'd want to know about the subject—at www.searchenginewatch.com.

To search by using Google:

1. In your browser, go to www.google.com (**Figure 13.8**).

2. Type a search phrase in the box; then click Google Search.

   Google responds with a list of links, ordered by relevancy (**Figure 13.9**).

3. Click any result link to visit the page.

✔ Tips

- To bypass the results list and go straight to the most relevant page, click I'm Feeling Lucky (instead of Google Search) in step 2.

- To increase the accuracy of your searches by adding operators that fine-tune your keywords, click the Advanced Search link (visible in Figure 13.8).

- The Google toolbar adds a search bar to IE that lets you search from any web page (it also blocks pop-up ads). The Google Deskbar adds a search box to the taskbar. Get them—and other free search tools—at www.google.com/downloads.

Figure 13.8 Click the Preferences link to set your language(s) and the number of search results to display per page.

Figure 13.9 Search engines are fast. Here, Google's results bar shows more than 3 million matches for *human genome project* in about a fifth of a second. Search engines rank pages by using proprietary (and competing) "relevance" formulas; Google's is called PageRank.

- Google's simple interface hides a lot of features and sophisticated technology. Click the About Google link (visible in Figure 13.8) and browse the Our Search section for help, search features, services, and tools.

What are you looking for?

Type your question below. For best results, use complete sentences.

human genome project

Sample question:

➜ Buy a book online

You may also want to...

Search this computer for files

Change preferences

Search

Figure 13.10 The search results appear in the pane to the right of the Search Companion.

You also can use IE's Search Companion to search the web.

To search by using Search Companion:

1. ☌ Search Click Search on the toolbar (or press Ctrl+E).

2. Type a search phrase in the text box; then click Search (**Figure 13.10**).

✔ Tips

■ Search Companion uses MSN Search by default. To use a different search engine, click Change Preferences (in Figure 13.10); click Change Internet Search Behavior; select With Classic Internet Search; select an engine; then click OK.

■ To search directly from the Address bar, press Alt+D; type go, find, or ?, followed by a space and a search phrase; then press Enter.

■ After you go to a web page, choose Edit > Find (on This Page) or press Ctrl+F to search for specific text on that page.

■ Beware of advertisements posing as "sponsored links" interlaced with results. Reputable search engines like Google color-code paid links or set them apart from legitimate results.

■ A *metasearch engine* or *metaengine* queries other search engines and compiles the results that it receives. Try www.dogpile.com or www.vivisimo.com.

■ A good alternative search bar is Dave's Quick Search Bar (free; www.dqsd.net).

SEARCHING THE WEB

.comBAT

When you search for information about health, science, weather, scholarly disciplines, government services, high culture, charitable causes, not-for-profits, news, and religion (not shopping, sports, or celebrities), favor `.org`, `.gov`, `.edu`, and other noncommercial domains over `.com` sites. A comparison should convince you: Visit `www.weather.gov` (the U.S. government's National Weather Service site) and `www.weather.com` (The Weather Channel's commercial site), and behold:

- The NWS site loads quickly, has no ads, shows only weather information, uses graphics sparingly and effectively, plants no cookies, has an obvious search function, and shows a clear map of nationwide weather and warnings.

- The Weather Channel site greets you with pop-up ads; has banner ads that occupy substantial screen real estate; plays Flash animations; is inundated with sales pitches, self-promotion, and slow-loading images; plants a cookie; and has one tiny weather map.

Google's `site` operator can help you. To search for, say, philosophy pages at only educational sites, use the query `philosophy site:edu`. To search at only United Kingdom academic sites, use `philosophy site:ac.uk`.

Figure 13.11 Press Ctrl+D to make the current page appear instantly at the bottom of your Favorites list (bypassing the dialog box in step 3).

Figure 13.12 Drag shortcuts up or down to organize the list. Click a list item and use the buttons at left to rename it, delete it, or stick it in a folder.

Bookmarking Pages

You can keep track of web pages that you like and open them quickly in the future.

You can add a page to your Favorites list. Any time that you want to open that page, click Favorites on the toolbar (or press Ctrl+I); then click the shortcut in the Favorites list. (Or use the Favorites menu.)

To add a page to your Favorites list:

1. Go to the page that you want to add.

2. Choose Favorites > Add to Favorites (**Figure 13.11**).

3. Type a new name for the favorite, if you like.

4. *Optional.* Click Create In to choose the folder (or create a new folder) to store the favorite in.

5. Click OK.

✔ Tip

■ As your Favorites menu grows, you can organize your bookmarks into folders: Choose Favorites > Organize Favorites (or press Ctrl+B) (**Figure 13.12**). It's easier, however, to work in the Favorites folder directly than to use the Organize Favorites dialog box. In Windows Explorer, navigate to C:\Documents and Settings\<*your user name*>\Favorites, and use it as you would any other folder.

You can add a few pages that you visit often to the Links bar for one-click access.

To add a page to your Links bar:

1. Go to the page that you want to add.

2. Drag the page icon from the Address bar to the Links bar (**Figure 13.13**).

Your *home page* appears each time you start Internet Explorer. When you first open IE, you may see www.msn.com or your PC manufacturer's page, but you can change that.

To change your home page:

1. Go to your desired home page.

2. Choose Tools > Internet Options > General tab > Home Page section (refer to Figure 13.7).

3. Click Use Current to set the web page that you have open as your home page.

   or

   Click Use Default to use the home page that was set when Internet Explorer was first installed.

   or

   Click Use Blank to use a blank HTML page as your home page.

✔ Tip

■ To return to your home page, click the Home button on the toolbar (or press Alt+Home).

Figure 13.13 You can drag a link to the Links folder in your Favorites list. If the Links bar is hidden, choose View > Toolbars > Links. Right-click a link to rename it, delete it, or see its properties. Drag links around the Links bar to rearrange them.

Bookmark Tools

The Import/Export Wizard lets you import and export your bookmarks (and cookies) to other browsers or files. In IE, choose File > Import and Export; then follow the onscreen instructions.

AM-DeadLink (free; http://aignes.com/deadlink.htm) scans your bookmarks for dead links and duplicate links, and lets you delete them.

BookmarkBridge (free; http://bookmarkbridge.sourceforge.net) lets you synchronize and share your bookmarks among all your browsers.

Figure 13.14 The Information bar (new in SP2) appears near the top of the browser window to alert you when IE blocks a pop-up window or a download file that might not be safe.

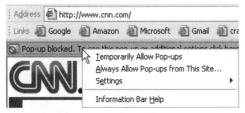

Figure 13.15 Click the Information bar to reveal a menu of pop-up customization options.

Blocking Pop-Up Windows

Pop-up and *pop-under ads* are separate windows that appear uninvited above or beneath your browser window. When you visit a web page and the taskbar starts sprouting new buttons, you have pop-unders. Kill this pestilence with IE's Pop-Up Blocker, added in Service Pack 2 (finally). Pop-Up Blocker is on by default. You should need to turn it on only if someone has turned it off. You also can customize its settings to let certain pop-ups through. Pop-ups are useful in some circumstances, such as showing small help windows, seating diagrams for concert halls or airplanes, and larger versions of thumbnail images.

To block pop-up windows:

◆ Choose Tools > Pop-Up Blocker > Turn on Pop-Up Blocker.

From now on, when IE blocks a pop-up, the *Information bar* appears with a "Pop-up blocked" message (**Figure 13.14**).

To see a blocked pop-up:

1. Click the Information Bar when it notifies you that a pop-up has been blocked (**Figure 13.15**).

2. Click Temporarily Allow Pop-Ups.

To see pop-ups from a specific web site:

1. Choose Tools > Pop-Up Blocker > Pop-Up Blocker Settings (**Figure 13.16**).

2. In the Address of Web Site to Allow box, type the address (URL) of the web site that you want to see pop-ups from; then click Add.

   Use the Remove and Remove All buttons to delete previously added sites.

✔ Tips

- If you've installed the Google Toolbar (or other third-party utility) to block pop-ups, you can turn off the IE blocker: Choose Tools > Pop-Up Blocker > Turn off Pop-Up Blocker.

- Pop-Up Blocker doesn't block pop-ups that appear when you click a link...unless you've chosen the High filter level (refer to the bottom of Figure 13.16). To see pop-ups when you have this setting turned on, hold down the Ctrl key while the web page loads.

Figure 13.16 This dialog box lets you manage your list of approved sites. You also can turn off the "blocked pop-up" sound, suppress the Information bar, and adjust the aggressiveness of the pop-up filter.

Unblockable Pop-Ups

Some reasons why you still may see pop-ups when Pop-Up Blocker is turned on:

- ◆ The site is on your approved list (refer to Figure 13.16).

- ◆ The ad designer found a way to circumvent Microsoft's blocking method (nothing you can do about this).

- ◆ You have spyware. Remove it (see "Securing Your Computer" in Chapter 12).

- ◆ It's a window with animated content that Pop-Up Blocker doesn't block.

- ◆ It's a web site in the Local Intranet or Trusted Sites web content zone. Choose Tools > Internet Options > Security tab; click the zone that you want to block pop-ups from; click Sites; in the Web Sites box, click the web site for which you want to block pop-ups; then click Remove.

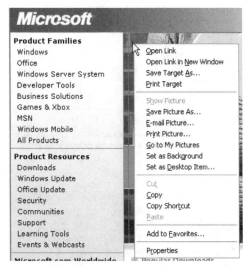

Figure 13.17 This shortcut menu appears when you right-click an image link. Note that you can save a copy of a web image on your own disk.

Figure 13.18 Each frame is really a separate web page. The three sets of scroll bars show that this page has three frames. On some pages, frame boundaries are invisible.

Browsing Tips

This section contains tips for browsing the web and using Internet Explorer's features.

Shortcut menus. Right-click toolbars, Explorer bars, shortcuts, links, or images to select commands quickly (**Figure 13.17**).

Keyboard shortcuts. For a complete list of IE's keyboard shortcuts, choose Help > Contents and Index > Index tab; type the keyword *keyboard;* then double-click the subtopic *shortcuts*.

Frames. Some web pages are divided into independent rectangular sections called *frames* (**Figure 13.18**). To move forward between frames, press Ctrl+Tab (or F6); to move backward, press Shift+Ctrl+Tab (or Shift+F6).

Text size, font, and color. To change the size of text displayed in web pages, choose a relative size from the View > Text Size submenu. Press F5 to refresh the page, if necessary. If you have a mouse wheel, hold down Ctrl and spin the wheel to resize text.

To change the text's typeface or link colors, click the Fonts or Colors button (refer to Figure 13.7). Some rude web pages won't let you change text properties. To override this restriction, click Accessibility (same figure).

Full-screen browsing. Press F11 to toggle between full-screen and normal view. In full-screen view, you can right-click the Standard Buttons toolbar at the screen's top edge and choose Auto-Hide. The toolbar will vanish, and you'll have real full-screen browsing; when you move the pointer close to the screen's top edge, the toolbar reappears.

Printing web pages. To preview a web page before printing, choose File > Print Preview; then use the toolbar to view each page to be printed. To set margins, headers, footers, and other printing options, choose File > Page Setup. To print a web page, choose File > Print (or press Ctrl+P) (**Figure 13.19**); or click Print on the toolbar to bypass the Print dialog box.

Saving pages. To save a web page on your hard drive, choose File > Save As. From the Save As Type drop-down list, choose Web Archive, Single File (*.mht) to save the page as a single file. If you want to edit the page rather than simply view it, use one of the other options to save the page as a group of files or save only parts of the page. To open the saved web page, double-click it or, in IE, choose File > Open. To specify how Windows treats saved web pages, see the folder option Managing Pairs of Web Pages and Folders in "Setting Folder Options" in Chapter 5.

Viewing pages offline. IE takes saved web pages one step further with *offline viewing,* which lets you update saved pages automatically to synchronize their contents with what's on the web site. To make a page available offline, right-click it in the Favorites menu or Links bar (see "Bookmarking Pages" earlier in this chapter); choose Make Available Offline; then use the Offline Favorite Wizard to set up a synchronization schedule (**Figure 13.20**). To get the latest version of your pages before you go offline, choose Tools > Synchronize. When you're ready to work offline, choose File > Work Offline.

✔ Tip

■ HTTrack (free; www.httrack.com) lets you download entire web sites so that you can browse them offline.

Figure 13.19 The Print dialog box's Options tab lets you print a web page's frames and links. Be sure to click the desired frame before you print.

Figure 13.20 If you make, say, weather and news pages available offline, you can update them periodically to get the latest forecasts and headlines. (Web pages saved with File > Save As, by comparison, are static.)

Figure 13.21 The Image toolbar appears when you point to a picture. Click the Resize button (bottom-right corner) to toggle a picture between its normal and shrink-to-fit sizes.

Figure 13.22 The same page with (top) and without (bottom) banner ads.

Graphics features. Right-click a picture to save it, email it, print it, or use it as a static or updating desktop image (refer to Figure 13.17). Or use the pop-up toolbar that appears when you point to an image (**Figure 13.21**). IE resizes large images automatically to fit in your browser window; click the pop-up Resize button to restore the image to its original size. To turn off the image toolbar and image resizing, choose Tools > Internet Options > Advanced tab; then uncheck the Enable Image Toolbar (Requires Restart) and Enable Automatic Image Resizing boxes. For faster browsing with *no* graphics, uncheck Show Pictures. (To see a particular picture, right-click it; then choose Show Picture.)

Removing banner advertisements. In Service Pack 2, Microsoft added a pop-up blocker to stop pop-up ads and disabled the Messenger service to stop messenger spam (pop-up message boxes that contain advertisements). That still leaves *banner ads*—rectangular "billboards" at the edges of a page. You can remove them with a third-party filter such as Privoxy (free; www.privoxy.org), Muffin (free; http://muffin.doit.org), WebWasher (free; www.webwasher.com/client/download/index.html), or AdSubtract ($30; www.adsubtract.com) (**Figure 13.22**).

✔ Tips

- For fast and sophisticated ad-blocking, you can modify your HOSTS file; see www.everythingisnt.com/hosts.html.

- A list of advertising techniques is at www.useit.com/alertbox/20041206.html.

continues on next page

Detect web bugs. *Web bugs* are transparent one-pixel graphics on web pages and in HTML email messages that determine when you view a message or a page, when you did so, how many times, how long you kept the message open, and so on. You can squash them with Bugnosis (free; www.bugnosis.org). The ad-blocking programs in the preceding tip also catch web bugs.

Security settings. IE's Tools > Internet Options > Security tab features help prevent intruders from seeing your personal information, such as credit-card numbers that you enter when shopping online. Security features also can protect your PC from unsafe software (**Figure 13.23**).

Temporary files. When you visit a page, IE stores, or *caches* (say "cashes"), temporary internet files on your hard disk. These files speed the display of pages that you visit frequently or already have seen, because IE can open them from your hard disk instead of from the web server. To view or manage these files, choose Tools > Internet Options > General tab > Settings button (**Figure 13.24**). To delete existing files, click Delete Files (refer to Figure 13.7). Drag the slider to decrease or increase the cache size (a browsing-speed/disk-space trade-off).

Figure 13.23 Click the Custom Level button to specify individual security settings for add-ons, downloads, scripting, and more. Or choose a preset group of settings. The High option provides the safest way to browse but may inactivate some web sites.

Figure 13.24 Drag the slider to the right to increase the size of the cache folder so that revisited pages load faster. If IE displays stale pages from the cache instead of fresh ones from the web, select an option that makes IE check for newer versions more frequently than Automatically.

Figure 13.25 The more paranoid you are, the higher you should move this slider (click Default to show it). Tip: Always block third-party cookies, which come from spying advertisers. Click Sites to specify web sites that are always or never allowed to use cookies, regardless of your privacy-policy setting. Click Advanced to override automatic cookie handling.

Cookies and privacy. *Cookies* are messages given to IE by web sites and stored in text files on your hard disk. A cookie's main purpose is to identify you and possibly prepare customized web pages for you. When you enter shopping preferences and personal information at, say, Amazon.com, they're stored in a cookie, which Amazon can read when you return. (Other sites can't read the Amazon cookie.) Most cookies are innocuous and spare you from having to fill out forms repeatedly, but some sites and advertisers use *tracking cookies* to record your browsing history. To control how IE handles cookies, choose Tools > Internet Options > Privacy tab (**Figure 13.25**). To delete existing cookies, click Delete Cookies (refer to Figure 13.7).

✔ Tips

- You can manage cookie files manually in Windows Explorer. They're stored in C:\Documents and Settings\<*your user name*>\Cookies.

- Cookie Pal ($15 U.S.; www.kburra.com/cpal.html) is a graphical cookie-management system.

- AT&T Privacy Bird (free; http://privacybird.com) is a green icon in the notification area (system tray) that turns red when you visit a site set up to sell your data.

continues on next page

BROWSING TIPS

Content Advisor. IE's Content Advisor
(Tools > Internet Options > Content tab >
Content Advisor section > Enable) purport-
edly filters material (sex, violence, nudity,
language) that you may find offensive or may
not want your kids to see. Don't bother—
Content Advisor and all programs that make
similar claims are 21st-century snake oil. They
invariably filter legitimate topics (such as
breast cancer) and let offensive stuff through.

AutoComplete. You met AutoComplete
earlier in this chapter when you typed
an address in the Address bar (refer to
Figure 13.2). IE also can auto-complete
forms (text boxes), user names, and passwords. To turn AutoComplete on or off,
choose Tools > Internet Options > Content
tab > AutoComplete (**Figure 13.26**).

Internet connections. To display and manage your internet connections (Chapter 12),
choose Tools > Internet Options >
Connections tab (**Figure 13.27**).

Figure 13.26 AutoComplete shows a list of
suggested matches based on the previous
entries you've typed. For security, uncheck
User Names and Passwords on Forms.

Figure 13.27 Configure your existing internet
connections or create a new one on this page.

BROWSING TIPS

Figure 13.28 To bypass this dialog box, right-click a download link; then choose Save Target As.

Figure 13.29 When the download completes, click Open Folder to open a window containing the downloaded file.

Set the default browser. A newly installed browser usually assumes default-browser status. To reinstate IE, choose Tools > Internet Options > Programs tab; then check Internet Explorer Should Check to See Whether It Is the Default Browser. You also can use the this tab to specify the default programs for other internet programs, such as email. Alternatively, you can pick your default browser via the Start menu: Right-click the Start button; choose Properties > Customize; then select a browser in the Show on Start Menu list.

Downloading files. When you click a link to a file that you can download to your PC, IE displays **Figure 13.28**. Click Save; specify a download location on your hard drive; then click Save to start the download. After the download completes (**Figure 13.29**), you can move, double-click, or rename the new file.

View HTML. Web pages are created with *HTML* (Hypertext Markup Language). To view a page's source HTML, choose View > Source.

Add-ons. For web pages with video, sounds, and animation, you need free plug-in programs called *add-ons*. The most popular add-ons are QuickTime (video), Flash and Shockwave (animations), Adobe Reader (documents), and RealPlayer (music and audio). When a web site tries to install a plug-in, ActiveX control, or toolbar, IE will warn you with the pop-up Information bar (refer to Figure 13.14). Click the bar and install the software only if you trust the source (**Figure 13.30**). Service Pack 2 makes it easier for you to track and manage add-ons: Choose Tools > Manage Add-Ons. The Manage Add-Ons dialog box (**Figure 13.31**) lets you see where add-ons came from (usually), turn them on and off individually, and update them.

Java applets. The *Java virtual machine* (or Java run-time environment) is a useful add-on that may be missing from IE, depending on your version of XP and IE. The JVM (or JRE) runs many stock tickers, games, and other complex web programs, called *applets*. IE should prompt you to download the JVM the first time that it encounters an applet, but you can get it at http://java.sun.com. If you're having trouble, visit www.microsoft.com/java/xp.htm.

Cut/Copy/Paste. You can copy (but not cut, of course) selected text and images from web pages and paste them into other programs by using the usual Edit-menu commands or keyboard shortcuts.

Figure 13.30 Here, IE asks for my permission to let the Apple Computer site install the QuickTime ActiveX control. (An ActiveX control is a small program that runs within the browser window.)

Figure 13.31 If you think that an add-on has been causing trouble or crashes, turn it off. In the Show drop-down list, select Add-Ons That Have Been Used by Internet Explorer; click an entry in the Name column; then click Disable. Keep an eye on the Publisher column for mysterious, and possibly untrustworthy, companies.

BROWSING TIPS

Figure 13.32 Dozens of settings are available to make browsing faster, stop animations, strengthen security, and so on.

Other options. IE has a slew of other options that you can change to suit your preferences; choose Tools > Internet Options > Advanced tab (**Figure 13.32**).

MSN Explorer. If MSN is your ISP, your default browser may be *MSN Explorer,* a "friendlier" all-in-one program that integrates browsing, email, chat, and so on. Most experienced users forgo MSN Explorer for IE, Outlook or Outlook Express, Windows Messenger, and so on.

Anonymous surfing. Surfing the web exposes certain information about you, including (possibly) your IP address, rough geographic location, browsing history, clipboard contents, cache contents, and machine name. You can see what you're exposing by taking the tests at www.anonymizer.com/snoop. To surf anonymously, use a service such as Anonymizer (free; www.anonymizer.com), the-Cloak (free; www.the-cloak.com), or JAP (free; http://anon.inf.tu-dresden.de/index_en.html).

✔ Tip

- These services are called *anonymous proxy servers*. Your browser doesn't visit a site directly. Instead, it tells the proxy server which site to visit and deliver back with no direct contact from you. The price of anonymity is slower surfing as you're relayed through a chain of servers and, for some sites, oddly displayed text and graphics.

BROWSING TIPS

401

Bypass site registration. Some sites, such as www.nytimes.com, require you to register before you can read their content. Registration usually means handing over your location and email address so that the site can compile marketing and demographic databases. You simply can, like most people, enter fake details, but it's still a waste of time. Instead, use BugMeNot (free; www.bugmenot.com) to bypass logging on to web sites that require compulsory registration (**Figure 13.33**).

Tweak UI settings. You can use Tweak UI's Internet Explorer options to change the toolbar, logo, and other aspects of IE. (See the "Tweak UI" sidebar in "Using the Start Menu" in Chapter 2.)

Figure 13.33 To get logons for registration-required web sites, use the BugMeNot home page (shown here) or install the BugMeNot add-on for Internet Explorer (or Mozilla Firefox). You can link to BugMeNot with, for example, http://bugmenot.com/view.php?url=www.nytimes.com.

OUTLOOK EXPRESS— EMAIL AND NEWS

Other Email Programs

A few other (better) email programs are available. Trying an alternative doesn't lock you into it; email programs can import one another's messages and account settings.

Eudora (www.eudora.com) existed before Outlook and Outlook Express, is still going strong, and is still the choice of serious emailers. It has all sorts of features that you won't find elsewhere. You have a choice: a free version with ads, an ad-free version for $50 U.S., or a free light version with no ads but some features turned off.

Thunderbird (free; www.mozilla.com/products/thunderbird) is from the same folks who brought you the Mozilla Firefox browser. It has enough features to compete with Outlook as well as Outlook Express, and it's updated more frequently. (Microsoft doesn't improve Outlook Express much anymore.)

Email is a fast, convenient, and cheap way to exchange written messages and files over the internet. Windows includes Outlook Express to let you send and receive email, as well as read newsgroups (internet discussion forums). You can communicate with anyone who has an email account. Your recipient doesn't have to have Outlook Express to read and reply to your messages; any email program can talk to any other one.

You can't use Outlook Express to manage your email with any of the free, web-based mail services—Gmail, Yahoo!, and Excite, for example—except for Hotmail and MSN, both of which belong to Microsoft.

✔ Tip

■ Don't confuse Outlook Express with Outlook, its bigger brother in the Microsoft Office suite. Outlook is a complex program that manages your email, schedule, meetings, contacts, and more.

Getting Started with Outlook Express

Figure 14.1 shows Outlook Express's main panes and controls. If your copy of Outlook Express doesn't look like the pictured one, it's configured differently; choose View > Layout to show, hide, customize, or rearrange the panes. To resize panes, drag the gray horizontal or vertical lines that separate them.

To start Outlook Express:

◆ Choose Start > Outlook Express (or Start > All Programs > Outlook Express).

 or

 Choose Start > Run; type `msimn` and then press Enter.

Figure 14.1 The parts of Outlook Express. Click a message name in the Message list to make the message itself appear in the Preview pane. (Most of my email is spam.)

Figure 14.2 This name appears in the From header of email that you send. Don't type something cute or clever; people or spam filters may mistake your messages for junk mail.

Figure 14.3 A email address has two parts. To the left of the @ is the *alias*, which you choose. To the right is the *domain*, which depends on your ISP.

Setting up an Email Account

Before you set up an email account, you must connect to the internet (Chapter 12). If you used the New Connection Wizard, your email settings may be in place already, and you can skip this section. Otherwise, the Internet Connection Wizard appears the first time that you start Outlook Express. The wizard helps you enter the addresses (provided by your ISP) that let Outlook Express find your electronic mailbox.

To set up an email account:

1. On the Your Name page, type your display name (**Figure 14.2**); then click Next.

2. On the Internet E-Mail Address page, type the email address that you chose when you signed up with your ISP (**Figure 14.3**); then click Next.

3. On the E-Mail Server Names page, type the information that your ISP provided about its mail servers (see the sidebar) (**Figure 14.4**); then click Next.

continues on next page

Figure 14.4 Your ISP provides server names, which usually look like this. For Hotmail accounts, choose HTTP from the mail-server drop-down list.

4. On the Internet Mail Logon page, type your logon name and password; check Remember Password to avoid being prompted for it each time you check your mail (**Figure 14.5**); then click Next.

5. Click Finish to create the account.

Now you should be able to send and receive email.

✔ Tips

■ If you have multiple email accounts, choose Tools > Accounts > Add > Mail. The Internet Connection Wizard reappears, ready to accept another account.

■ For computers with separate user accounts (Chapter 16), each user must create his own email account when logged on.

Figure 14.5 Check Log on Using Secure Password Authentication (SPA) only if your ISP tells you to.

Email Protocols

Mail servers are networked computers that manage your mailbox. ISP server administrators limit the number and size of messages that you can send or receive, as well as how much space is available in your mailbox. A server handles *incoming* messages by using one of three standards, or *protocols.* (Your ISP can tell you which protocol it uses.)

A *POP3* server (the most common type) transfers your messages to your hard drive before you read them and then deletes its server copies. You save, manage, delete, and back up messages yourself.

An *IMAP* server lets you read, delete, and search your messages while they're still on the server. Then you can choose which messages to download to your hard drive. If your server mailbox reaches its capacity, incoming messages bounce back to their senders.

An *HTTP* server, such as Gmail, Yahoo!, or Hotmail, lets you send, receive, and manage your email with any web browser. (Messages remain on the server.) If your server mailbox reaches its capacity, incoming messages are thrown away, often with a warning and a sales pitch for a higher-capacity premium account.

SMTP servers handle *outgoing* messages.

Figure 14.6 The two sections of a message are the *headers* (top), which contains information about the message, and the *body* (bottom), which contains the message itself. Each message window contains its own menu bar and toolbar.

Sending Email

After you've set up your email account, you can compose a message and send it.

To compose and send a message:

1. Choose Message > New Message (or press Ctrl+N).

   or

    Click Create Mail on the toolbar.

   A new message window appears (**Figure 14.6**).

2. Type the recipient's email address in the To box.

   To send the message to more than one person, separate the addresses with semicolons (;).

   As you type, Outlook Express auto-completes each address (or ordinary name) with an entry from your address book. If auto-complete guesses wrong, keep typing; if it guesses right, press Tab to jump to the Cc box, or press the semicolon to stay in the To box and type another address.

3. To send a copy of the message to other recipients, type additional email addresses in the Cc box, pressing Tab when you're finished.

   Each address auto-completes as before.

   Cc (carbon-copy) recipients receive the same message as To recipients, but Cc lets them know that you sent them the message as a courtesy and that you're not expecting them to reply.

4. Type the message's topic in the Subject box; then press Tab.

   Recipients appreciate a descriptive subject rather than, say, "Hi," which makes your mail look like junk.

continues on next page

5. Type the text of your message.

You can use Cut, Copy, Paste, and all the standard editing techniques.

6. Click Send on the toolbar (or press Alt+S).

Your PC sends the message over the internet, first connecting to it if necessary.

Figure 14.7 Attached files appear in the Attach header. To remove a file from the outgoing message, right-click its icon; then choose Remove.

✔ Tips

- ■ To attach a file to a message, click Attach on the toolbar; locate the file; then click Attach. Alternatively, drag files from Windows Explorer to the message window (**Figure 14.7**). ISPs usually limit attached-file sizes to a few megabytes, and many email programs block executable attachments, so zip your files before attaching them (see "Compressing Files and Folders" in Chapter 5). See also "Receiving Attachments" later in this chapter.

- ■ To embed (rather than attach) an image in a message, while in the message body, choose Format > Rich Text (HTML); choose Insert > Picture; browse to the image to insert; then click OK. Your recipient won't have to open a viewing program to see the picture.

- ■ Names that you add to your address book (press Ctrl+Shift+B or click Addresses on the toolbar) appear in your Contacts list (**Figure 14.8**) and let Outlook Express auto-complete email addresses. To add the sender of a message to your address book quickly, right-click the message in the Message list; then choose Add Sender to Address Book.

- ■ If Microsoft Word is installed on your PC, click Spelling on the toolbar (or press F7) to spell-check your message.

Figure 14.8 To scroll quickly to a contact name, type its first few letters. Right-click a name to send email, edit it, or delete it. Double-clicking a name opens a new, blank message window addressed to the contact.

Plain Text or HTML?

You can format your message body as plain text or HTML. Plain-text messages contain only unadorned text without italics, boldface, colors, custom font sizes, and so on. HTML—the language used to format web pages—permits fancy formatting. In general, use plain text because:

◆ Some older email programs (especially on Unix) can't read HTML formatting.

◆ Amateurish HTML formatting irritates recipients.

◆ Most junk email (spam) uses HTML formatting. *Your* HTML messages may be caught by filtering software and routed—unread—to the recipient's trash.

◆ HTML formatting is inconsistent across programs. What looks good on your screen might look bad on your recipient's.

◆ Extra formatting increases download and display times.

To change the *default* format for all new messages, choose Tools > Options > Send tab > Mail Sending Format section; select HTML or Plain Text; then click OK (see Figure 14.21 later in this chapter).

No matter what the default format, you can switch it for individual messages: In the New Message window, choose Format > Plain Text or Format > Rich Text (HTML). Choosing HTML activates the HTML toolbar, with buttons for styles, formatting, hyperlinks, and so on. Choosing Plain Text brings up a warning that certain embellishments, such as images, won't be possible.

■ A *signature* is a distinctive bit of text— usually, your choice of contact information, a Bartlett's quotation, or something flippant—added at the bottom of outgoing messages. To create signatures, choose Tools > Options > Signatures tab > New; then type a signature in the Edit Signature box. Click New again if you want to create multiple signatures. You can add a signature to *all* messages by checking Add Signatures to All Outgoing Messages in this dialog box or to individual messages by choosing Insert > Signature in the New Message window.

■ The Bcc (blind carbon copy) header is hidden by default. To show it, choose View > All Headers in the message window. Bcc recipients receive the same message as To and Cc recipients, but *secretly*, without the other recipients' knowing. If you send, say, a joke or announcement to many recipients, it's polite to put them *all* in the Bcc list; then no one has to scroll through the long list of To or Cc names that appears at the top of the message, and individual email addresses aren't revealed to the entire list.

■ To save an incomplete message in the Drafts folder, choose File > Save, and finish composing it later.

■ To keep a copy of all outgoing messages, choose Tools > Options > Send tab > check Save Copy of Sent Messages in the "Sent Items" Folder.

■ If you've defined multiple email accounts and want to send from an account other than the current one, click the From box; then click the account that you want to use.

SENDING EMAIL

Reading Email

When you open Outlook Express, it retrieves (downloads) your messages automatically from your ISP's mail server. If you keep Outlook Express running, it checks for new mail every 30 minutes, but you can change the interval or check on demand.

To check immediately for new messages:

◆   Click Send/Recv on the toolbar (or press Ctrl+M).

✔ Tips

■ The preceding method receives messages *and* sends any messages in your Outbox. To *receive* only, choose Tools > Send and Receive > Receive All, or click the small arrow on the Send/Recv button and choose Receive All (**Figure 14.9**).

■ If you've defined several email accounts, you don't have to check them *all*. To turn off an account, choose Tools > Accounts > Mail tab; double-click the account's name; then uncheck Include This Account When Receiving Mail or Synchronizing. To check a disabled account occasionally, choose its name at the bottom of the Send/Recv menu (refer to Figure 14.9).

■ To change the mail-retrieval interval, choose Tools > Options > General tab; then change the time period for Check for New Messages Every __ Minutes.

Figure 14.9 Click the Send/Recv button's small arrow to reveal a drop-down list, where you can choose to send messages, receive them, or both. To check an individual email account (rather than all of them), click its name at the bottom of the list.

Organizing Your Messages

Use the Folders list (refer to Figure 14.1) to organize your messages. It contains the following folders initially (but you can create new ones):

Inbox holds mail that you've received.

Outbox holds mail that you've written but haven't sent.

Sent Items holds copies of messages that you've sent.

Deleted Items holds received mail that you've deleted.

Drafts holds mail that you're working on but aren't ready to send.

The Folders list acts like a normal Windows Explorer tree. Click a folder to see what's in it. Choose File > New > Folder (Ctrl+ Shift+E) to create a new folder. Right-click a folder that you've created to rename or delete it. To file a message, drag it from the Message list to a folder icon, or right-click it and choose Move to Folder or Copy to Folder. To save a message in a Windows Explorer folder, choose File > Save As.

Figure 14.10 The names of new (unread) messages appear in bold in the Message list (on the right). Folders (on the left) containing new messages appear in bold, too, along with the number of unread messages.

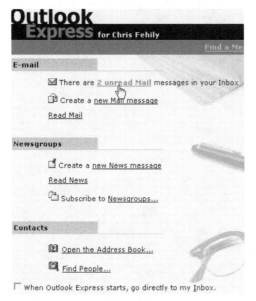

Figure 14.11 Outlook Express' opening screen shows your Inbox status and provides links to common tasks.

Newly arrived messages land in your Inbox (**Figure 14.10**) unless they're redirected by rules (see "Applying Message Rules" later in this chapter). Arrivals display an icon in the notification area (system tray) near the taskbar clock and play a sound.

When you open Outlook Express, you may see **Figure 14.11** instead of the Message list and Preview pane. Click the Unread Mail link to display the Inbox. To display the Inbox at startup, check When Outlook Express Starts, Go Directly to My Inbox at the bottom of Figure 14.11, or check the similar box in Tools > Options > General tab.

To read messages:

1. Click Inbox (or another folder) in the Folders list.

2. To view a message in the Preview pane, click the message in the Message list.

   or

   To view a message in a separate window, double-click the message in the Message list.

3. To move back or forward through messages, press Ctrl+<, Ctrl+>, or (in preview mode) the up- or down-arrow key.

   or

   To view the next *unread* message, press Ctrl+U.

✔ Tips

- To view all of a message's information, right-click it; then choose Properties.

- To switch a message's read/unread status manually, right-click the message; then choose Mark As Unread or Mark As Read.

- To read, send, and manage messages from any browser, anywhere, visit a POP3-access web site such as www.mail2web.com. Your ISP also may provide a web page that lets you manage your mail in a browser.

- To hide read messages, choose View > Current View > Hide Read Messages.

- The Message list behaves like Windows Explorer in Details view. Choose View > Columns to choose which columns to display. To resize a column, drag its heading's right edge left or right (or double-click the right edge to auto-size the column). To rearrange columns, drag the headings horizontally. To sort by a column, click its heading; click again to reverse sort order.

- Outlook Express comes with a "very special" message, *Welcome to Outlook Express 6,* from Microsoft. This message didn't arrive via the internet; read and delete it.

After you've read a message, you can print it, delete it, reply to it, forward it (that is, pass it on to a third person), or file it in a folder (see the "Organizing Your Messages" sidebar). You can process a message that's displayed in the Preview pane or one that's open in a separate window.

To print, delete, forward, or file multiple messages simultaneously, Ctrl+click each message to select it. (Ctrl+clicking again deselects it.) To select a group of contiguous messages, click the first message; then Shift+click the last.

To print a message:

◆ [Print] Select a message; then click Print on the toolbar (or press Ctrl+P).

To delete a message:

1. [Delete] Select a message; then click Delete on the toolbar (or press Delete).

   Deleted messages aren't erased but are placed in the Deleted Items folder.

2. To remove *all* deleted messages permanently, choose Edit > Empty Deleted Items Folder.

   or

   To remove a specific deleted message permanently, select it in the Deleted Items folder; then press Delete.

   or

   To delete messages automatically when you quit Outlook Express, choose Tools > Options > Maintenance tab > check Empty Messages from Deleted Items Folder on Exit.

3. To rescue a deleted message, drag it from Deleted Items to another folder.

Stopping Spam

You can't, really. *Spam*—unsolicited commercial email—will clog your Inbox eventually. Practicing safe email (posting disguised addresses in newsgroups, for example) only delays it. Spammers scour the web for email addresses, and nothing stops ISPs (yours or your recipients') from selling your address. Eventually, you'll end up on a spammer's list—and soon thereafter, on hundreds of them.

Short of getting a new email address, the only effective way avoid spam is to use filters to redirect it to the trash. Applying individual message rules (described next) isn't effective, because the rules are hard to maintain, miss too much spam, and discard too much legitimate email identified as spam. Your ISP probably has a server-based spam filter that you can turn on. Otherwise, you can get your own spam killer. Try MailWasher (free; www.mailwasher.net) or xTerminator (free; www.artplus.hr/adapps/eng/xterminator.htm). Experienced users should try POPFile (free; http://popfile.sourceforge.net/old_index.html) or SpamBayes (free; http://spambayes.sourceforge.net).

To learn more about spam, visit http://spam.abuse.net or the web sites listed at http://directory.google.com/top/computers/internet/abuse/spam.

To reply to a message:

1. To reply to only the sender, select a message; then click Reply on the toolbar (or press Ctrl+R) (**Figure 14.12**).

or

To reply to everyone in the To and Cc lines (for group discussions), select a message; then click Reply All on the toolbar (or press Ctrl+Shift+R).

2. Type a response to the message.

3. Click Send on the toolbar (or press Alt+S).

To forward a message:

1. Select a message; then click Forward on the toolbar (or press Ctrl+F).

A new message opens, containing the original message's text.

2. Type the email addresses of the recipients (see "Sending Email" earlier in this chapter).

3. Edit the subject line or original message, or add your own comments, if you want.

4. Click Send on the toolbar (or press Alt+S).

✔ Tips

■ When you receive an important message, you can *flag* it for later reference. Select a message and choose Message > Flag Message, or click the flag column next to the message. A small red flag appears (refer to Figure 14.10). You can click a flag icon to remove it or click the flag-column header to sort flagged messages together.

Figure 14.12 A preaddressed reply opens with *Re:* (regarding) added to the subject line and the original message's text (which you can edit, cut, or commingle with your own comments) in the body. To turn off the original-text feature, choose Tools > Options > Send tab > uncheck Include Message in Reply.

- Message headers contain detailed information about who sent a message and the path it took. Outlook Express hides headers, which is fine for everyday use, but you can reveal them if you're curious or want to troubleshoot messages that bounce back to you. In the message window, choose File > Properties > Details tab.

- If your mailbox fills up, and your friends complain that their messages to you are bouncing back, choose Tools > Accounts; click the proper account; then choose Properties > Advanced tab. If Leave a Copy of Messages on Server is checked, check Remove from Server After __ Days, and change 5 (the default) to 1 or 2.

- The Preview pane (refer to Figure 14.1) has two major problems. First, after a few seconds it marks messages as "Read" whether or not you've actually read them. Second, it responds to web bugs (see "Detect web bugs" in "Browsing Tips" in Chapter 13). To turn off the Preview pane, choose View > Layout > uncheck Show Preview Pane. If you want to keep the Preview pane but not mark messages as read, choose Tools > Options > Read tab > uncheck Mark Message Read After Displaying for __ Seconds.

- For instructions to back up your email and address book, go to `http://support.microsoft.com/?kbid=270670`, "OLEXP: How to Back up and Recover Outlook Express Data."

READING EMAIL

Receiving Attachments

If someone has sent a you a file, a paper-clip icon appears next to the message name in the Message list (refer to Figure 14.10). Outlook Express stores an attachment with its message in a single, specially encoded mail file. You can open an attachment from the mail file or save it separately as a normal file on your hard drive. (To send attachments, see the Tips in "Sending Email" earlier in this chapter.)

To open an attachment:

◆ In the Preview pane, click the paper-clip icon in the header; then choose the file name (**Figure 14.13**).

   or

   At the top of the message window, double-click the file icon in the Attach header (refer to Figure 14.7).

To save an attachment:

1. In the Preview pane, click the paper-clip icon in the header, then choose Save Attachments (refer to Figure 14.13).

   or

   Select the message; then choose File > Save Attachments.

2. Select a folder for the file; then click Save (**Figure 14.14**).

Figure 14.13 If the selected message has files attached, a paper-clip icon appears on the right side of the Preview pane header. Click the icon for a shortcut menu; then choose the name of the attached file to open (in Microsoft Word, Microsoft Excel, or whatever), or choose Save Attachments to save it to your hard drive.

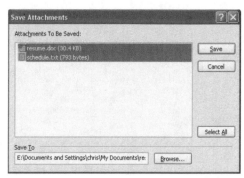

Figure 14.14 After you've saved an attachment on your hard drive, you can delete the message it came with.

RECEIVING ATTACHMENTS

Figure 14.15 Uncheck the Always Ask box if you don't want to be bothered by future security warnings.

Service Pack 2 installs Attachment Manager, a background security program that handles email attachments and internet downloads. Attachment Manager is part of Windows, but Outlook Express, Windows Messenger, and Internet Explorer—and possibly other programs in the future—use it.

To combat email-borne viruses, Outlook Express blocks attachments with high-risk extensions because you could infect your computer if you open them. The extensions include common ones such as .exe and .bat (the sidebar has a complete list). In the message window or Preview pane header, you'll see a warning strip letting you know that the file has been blocked. You can unblock the file if you're sure that it isn't dangerous.

To unblock and open a blocked attachment:

1. Choose Tools > Options > Security tab > uncheck Do Not Allow Attachments to Be Saved or Opened That Could Potentially Be a Virus > click OK.

2. Save the attachment to your hard drive (as described in "To save an attachment" earlier in this section).

3. In Windows Explorer or on the desktop, double-click the file.

4. If an Open File - Security Warning dialog box appears, click Run (**Figure 14.15**). The file opens normally.

Risky File Types

.ade, .adp, .app, .asp, .bas, .bat, .cer, .chm, .cmd, .com, .cpl, .crt, .csh, .exe, .fxp, .hlp, .hta, .inf, .ins, .isp, .its, .js, .jse, .ksh, .lnk, .mad, .maf, .mag, .mam, .maq, .mar, .mas, .mat, .mau, .mav, .maw, .mda, .mdb, .mde, .mdt, .mdw, .mdz, .msc, .msi, .msp, .mst, .ops, .pcd, .pif, .prf, .prg, .pst, .reg, .scf, .scr, .sct, .shb, .shs, .tmp, .url, .vb, .vbe, .vbs, .vsmacros, .vss, .vst, .vsw, .ws, .wsc, .wsf, .wsh

RECEIVING ATTACHMENTS

✔ Tips

- Instead of steps 3 and 4, you can right-click the file and choose Properties. The Properties dialog box that appears contains an Unblock button. Clicking it is the same as unchecking the Always Ask box in Figure 14.15. (And it removes the Unblock button from future Properties dialog boxes.)

- Even attachments from friends are risky because a self-forwarding virus may have picked your name out of your friend's address book.

- To remove viruses, see "Securing Your Computer" in Chapter 12. Virus scanners can check your incoming and outgoing messages automatically.

- For Attachment Manager details, go to http://support.microsoft.com/ ?kbid=883260, "Description of How the Attachment Manager Works in Windows XP Service Pack 2."

Blocked Pictures

Outlook also blocks graphics in HTML-format email—not attached graphic files, but *references* to graphics that sit on a web server somewhere. When you open such a message, Outlook Express won't fetch the image from the server because most of these images come from spammers trying to confirm (and sell) your email address. To download images and see them in the message, click the Some Pictures Have Been Blocked warning strip that appears in the message header. To turn off this feature, choose Tools > Options > Security tab > uncheck Block Images and Other External Content in HTML E-Mail. You might want to disable this feature if you get a lot of email containing photos from online dating sites.

Figure 14.16 This rule, named Resumes, moves a message to my Hiring folder if the message is addressed to *fehily* directly, contains *editorial assistant* in the Subject line or message body, and has an attachment (presumably, a résumé).

Applying Message Rules

Outlook Express lets you define *message rules* that answer, redirect, or delete incoming messages automatically, based on subject, sender, message text, size, or other criteria.

To set up message rules:

1. Choose Tools > Messages Rules > Mail (**Figure 14.16**).

2. In the top box, specify selection criteria for messages.

   To look for messages from a certain person, for example, check Where the From Line Contains People.

3. In the second box, specify what happens to messages that meet the selection criteria.

   You can define complex rule systems that move, copy, delete, reply to, forward, flag, ignore, or highlight messages automatically.

continues on next page

APPLYING MESSAGE RULES

4. In the third box, click underlined phrases to specify which people, words, or values the message rules apply to (**Figure 14.17**).

5. In the bottom text box, type the rule's name; then click OK.

The Message Rules dialog box appears (**Figure 14.18**).

✔ Tips

■ Don't expect to get all your rules right the first time. Outlook Express applies the rules in the Message Rules dialog box from top to bottom. You may find that an earlier rule contradicts a later one or that legitimate messages are deleted inadvertently. After creating a new rule, watch how it's applied as new mail arrives.

■ To create a rule based on a selected message, choose Message > Create Rule from Message.

■ Message rules apply to all defined accounts.

Figure 14.17 Enter the values to watch for in the dialog box that appears when you click an underlined phrase.

Figure 14.18 All the rules that you've created appear in this dialog box. Select a rule to see what it does, or double-click it to edit it. Use the Move Up and Move Down buttons to change the order in which rules run.

APPLYING MESSAGE RULES

Figure 14.19 For dial-up connections, use the drop-down list to tell Outlook Express how, or whether, to connect to check for new mail.

Figure 14.20 Uncheck the first box to stop Outlook Express from marking your messages as read automatically.

Configuring Outlook Express

Rather than explain each of Outlook Express' scores of options, I'll describe the 10 tabs in the Tools > Options dialog box. (Most tabs have buttons that open *more* dialog boxes.) Many options are self-explanatory, but you can right-click an option for a "What's This?" pop-up tip.

General options control what happens when Outlook Express starts and when messages are sent and received (**Figure 14.19**).

Read options control how Inbox messages are treated, and let you change their font and font size (**Figure 14.20**).

Receipts adds a *return receipt* to your outgoing messages, letting you know when your message has been read (*if* the recipient agrees to return it). Return receipts generally annoy recipients, and not all email programs support them.

Send options control how outgoing messages are treated and let you change the default sending format (**Figure 14.21**).

Compose lets you specify the font for outgoing messages, add fancy *stationery* to HTML messages (don't bother), and include electronic business cards with outgoing messages so that your recipients can add you to their address books.

Signatures is described in the Tips in "Sending Email" earlier in this chapter.

Spelling configures the spell-check feature, which works only if Microsoft Word is installed on your computer.

Security has options for virus protection and sending secure email, as well as using encryption and digital IDs.

Connection controls dial-up options and your internet connection (Chapter 12), which Outlook Express shares with Internet Explorer.

Maintenance has housekeeping features for cleaning up old messages and downloads.

Figure 14.21 For dial-up connections, uncheck Send Messages Immediately to stop Outlook Express from dialing every time you click the Send button. When you're ready to send a batch of messages (from your Outbox), press Ctrl+M.

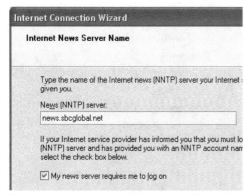

Figure 14.22 Get your user name, password, and NNTP news-server address from your ISP. If your ISP doesn't provide access to newsgroups, try www.newsguy.com, www.easynews.com, or www.mailgate.org.

Figure 14.23 A newsgroup name is a series of dot-separated words that indicates the newsgroup's topic in increasingly narrow categories, such as microsoft.public.windowsxp.help_and_support.

Using Newsgroups

The internet's uncensored anarchy is evident in the tens of thousands of online forums, called *newsgroups* (or *Usenet*), that cover almost every conceivable interest. A newsgroup consists of messages and follow-up posts, which are (supposed to be) related to the original message's subject line. A message and its follow-ups are called a *thread*. To view and post newsgroup messages, use Outlook Express as a *newsreader*. Setting up a news account is similar to setting up an email account, described earlier in this chapter.

To set up and use a news account:

1. Choose Tools > Accounts > Add > News.

2. Follow the onscreen instructions; then click Finish when you're done (**Figure 14.22**).

3. Click Yes when you're prompted to download newsgroups.

   You may have to wait a few seconds or minutes.

4. In the Newsgroup Subscriptions dialog box that appears, type a term of interest in the text box. As you type, newsgroups that *don't* match that text are hidden (**Figure 14.23**).

   To summon Newsgroup Subscriptions at any time, choose Tools > Newsgroups (Ctrl+W).

5. When you find an interesting newsgroup, select it; then click Subscribe.

   An icon appears near the newsgroup name.

   continues on next page

6. When you finish subscribing to news-groups, click OK.

The new newsgroups appear in the Folders list, below the news-server name.

7. In the Folders list, click a newsgroup name to download its recent threads (**Figure 14.24**).

8. Click (or double-click) a header in the Message list to read the message.

Reply to or post newsgroup messages as you would normal email. Note the Reply (to individuals) and Reply Group (for public posts) toolbar buttons.

✔ Tips

- Usenet, home of newsgroups, is one of the oldest parts of the internet and is encrusted with etiquette and rules, some of which may seem silly. They're not. Before you post extensively to a news-group, observe it silently *(lurk)* for a few days to test the waters.

- Learn the ropes by joining and reading news.answers and news.announce. newusers. Find out what *crossposting* is and how not to do it.

- Usenet, like chat, will gobble your life if you dive into it headlong. Don't plan on joining more than three or four news-groups, but if you do, make yourself cut back to what really interests you.

- If you join a newsgroup, find and read its *FAQ* (frequently asked questions) file, which may answer your questions before you ask the group.

Figure 14.24 Lurk on a newsgroup before participating. Asking recently answered (or dumb) questions irritates people and marks you as a fool. You also can use Google's Groups service to search newsgroups.

CHATTING ONLINE WITH WINDOWS MESSENGER

Windows Messenger (formerly MSN Messenger) is instant gratification for those of you impatient with email delays. Messenger lets you *chat* privately with other people on the internet—one or several at a time—by typing live comments in a small window. This communications channel, called *instant messaging*, also is the idea behind AOL Instant Messenger (AIM), Yahoo! Messenger, and ICQ. Unfortunately, whoever you want to chat with must use the same messaging system that you do, so if you chat with a lot of friends, it's not unusual to have two or three of these programs on your computer. In fact, the shareware program Trillian (free; www.ceruleanstudios.com) helps you run several of these at the same time.

Besides chatting or even while you're chatting, you can monitor your email, exchange files, have a teleconference, make free voice calls, or work collaboratively with a whiteboard program.

Connection Requirements

To use Windows Messenger, you need an internet connection (Chapter 12). High-speed DSL or cable connections are ideal, but chatting on 28 Kbps or 56 Kbps dial-up connection is adequate.

If your connection goes directly to a cable or jack without passing through a router, you can set a Windows Firewall exception to let Messenger traffic through (see "Securing Your Computer" in Chapter 12). To connect from behind a proxy server, use the settings in Tools > Options > Connections tab.

Getting a .NET Passport

Along with your internet connection, you need a Microsoft *.NET Passport* to run Messenger, even to chat within your local area network. Your Passport is Microsoft's way of identifying you uniquely on the internet. It's free and requires only a (real) email address.

If you already have a Passport, and it's linked to your user account, you can skip this section. Windows sometimes nags you to set up a Passport (**Figure 15.1**), or if you open Messenger, the .NET Passport Wizard appears when you try to sign in. You also can launch the wizard yourself.

To get a .NET Passport:

1. Choose > Start > Control Panel > User Accounts; click your user-account icon; then click Set Up My Account to Use a .NET Passport.

   The .NET Passport Wizard appears (**Figure 15.2**).

2. Click Next to skip the Welcome page.

3. On the Do You Have an E-Mail Address? page, specify whether to use your existing email address or sign up for a new, free one with MSN.com (**Figure 15.3**); then click Next.

4. Follow the onscreen instructions, and click Finish when you're done.

   Along the way, you're asked for your name, location, and other personal information. (Your Passport password doesn't have to be the same as your Windows password.)

   When the wizard finishes, Windows starts Messenger and signs you in automatically.

✔ Tips

- Go to www.passport.net and click Member Services to edit your Passport profile, change your password, or recover a forgotten password.

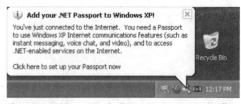

Figure 15.1 This pop-up balloon appears periodically in the notification area (system tray).

Figure 15.2 Microsoft implies otherwise, but a .NET Passport is required for Messenger only, not for other Windows programs or features.

Figure 15.3 Any (nonbogus) email address works; earlier Passport versions required a Hotmail or MSN address.

- After you sign up, Microsoft sends a message to your Passport email address. Reply to this message to make your Passport official. Until then, other Messenger users see you as "E-Mail Address Not Verified."

Figure 15.4 The Messenger icon appears whether or not you're online and signed in. The left icon indicates that you're offline; the right one means you're online and signed in.

Figure 15.5 Your sign-in screen will be more elaborate than this one if you've signed in before.

Signing in to Messenger

If Messenger doesn't sign you in automatically when you go online, you must do so manually. When you're finished using Messenger, sign out.

To open Messenger and sign in:

1. Choose Start > All Programs > Windows Messenger.

   or

   Double-click Messenger's notification-area (system-tray) icon on the taskbar (**Figure 15.4**).

   or

   Choose Start > Run; type msmsgs and then press Enter.

2. Click the link titled Click Here to Sign In (**Figure 15.5**).

3. Type your Passport email address and password.

   continues on next page

4. If you don't want to type your password every time you sign in, check Sign Me In Automatically (**Figure 15.6**).

Don't check this box on public PCs or a PC where your user account is shared.

5. Click OK to go online (**Figure 15.7**).

To sign out:

◆ Choose File > Sign Out.

Signing out doesn't break your internet connection or close Messenger. When you sign out, you'll appear offline to others, but you'll still be online.

✔ Tips

■ To stop Messenger from starting auto-matically, choose Tools > Options > Preferences tab > uncheck Run This Program When Windows Starts. You can start Messenger manually from the Start menu.

■ After you sign in the first time, Messenger's sign-in screen will show your email address. To sign in with a different Passport, click To Sign in with a Different Account, Click Here.

Figure 15.6 Passwords are case-sensitive.

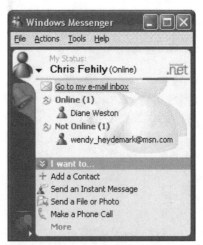

Figure 15.7 Messenger's main window appears after you sign in.

Figure 15.8 The wizard checks whether this person has a Passport and, if so, adds the name to your contact list.

Figure 15.9 When someone adds *you* to her contact list, you can choose whether to allow the contact or block it. Check the box to add that person to *your* contact list. To see everyone who's added you, choose Tools > Options > Privacy tab > View button.

- To add a contact from within Outlook Express, right-click the person's name in the Contacts list (refer to Figure 14.8 in Chapter 14); then choose New Online Contact.

Creating a Contact List

To send instant messages, you need a list of contacts who have Passport accounts and Windows Messenger (or MSN Messenger) installed. The best way to add a contact is to specify an email address, as described here. You can search a directory for contacts, but these usually don't work. Messenger scans only your Outlook Express address book and Microsoft's Hotmail Member Directory, which people often decline to be listed in.

To add a contact:

1. Choose File > Add a Contact.

2. Select By E-Mail Address or Sign-In Name; then click Next.

3. Enter the person's email address (**Figure 15.8**); then click Next.

4. Click Next to add another contact or Finish to quit the wizard.
   Contact names appear in the main window.

✔ Tips

- As a privacy precaution, Messenger displays the dialog box shown in **Figure 15.9** on a new contact's screen.

- To allow others to add you without seeking your approval, choose Tools > Options > Privacy tab > uncheck Alert Me When Other Users Add Me to Their Contact Lists.

- If the person whose email address you specified doesn't have a Passport, the wizard offers to send that person an email message (from you) with instructions on how to get one.

- To remove a contact, choose Tools > Manage Contacts > Delete a Contact; then double-click the contact to delete.

Chatting Online

After you've created a contact list, you're ready to chat with anyone who's running Messenger in the background. All parties to the conversation must be connected to the internet.

✔ Tip

■ Before starting your first chat, you may want to change your Messenger display name. Choose Tools > Options > Personal tab; in the text box, type your name as you want other users to see it (**Figure 15.10**). (Unlike AIM, Windows Messenger doesn't demand that your screen name be unique.)

To send an instant message:

1. In your contact list, double-click the name of someone who's online (refer to Figure 15.7).

   The conversation window opens.

2. Type your message in the box at the bottom of the window; then click Send (or press Enter) (**Figure 15.11**).

   Your message appears in the top section of the window.

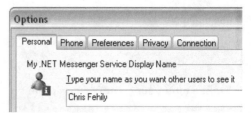

Figure 15.10 Use your real name or a nickname (to protect your anonymity). Don't use your email address; spammers will get it.

Figure 15.11 To start a new line while typing, press Shift+Enter. Each instant message can contain up to 400 characters.

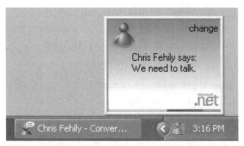

Figure 15.12 The other person hears a chime and sees this pop-up invitation, which she can click to open a conversation window. The Messenger taskbar button, shown here, changes color and blinks to get her attention.

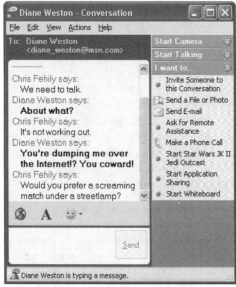

Figure 15.13 You can see when the other person is typing by looking at the bottom of the window. The date and time of the last message that you received appear here as well.

3. The other person receives an onscreen invitation to chat (**Figure 15.12**) and (presumably) replies.

4. Type your reply in the bottom box; then click Send (or press Enter).

Now you're chatting. You can use Cut, Copy, Paste, and all the standard editing techniques. The conversation's transcript rolls down the top box, identifying each message's speaker (**Figure 15.13**).

5. Close the conversation window when you're done chatting or leave it open to continue the conversation later.

You remain signed in to Messenger when you close a conversation window.

Chatting Tips

This section contains tips about chatting on the web and using Windows Messenger's features.

Choose commands quickly. A conversation window's toolbar and right sidebar contain links to common tasks (refer to Figure 15.13). To show or hide the toolbar or sidebar, choose View > Show Toolbar or View > Show Sidebar.

Change fonts. Change the font or color of your messages to distinguish them from the other person's messages. In the main window, choose Tools > Options > Personal tab > Change Font; or, in a conversation window, choose Edit > Change Font. Both of you will see the change (assuming that you have similar fonts installed). You can't change the other person's font in your window, but you can change text size with the View > Text Size submenu.

Add other chatters. To add more people to a chat, in a conversation window, choose Actions > Invite Someone to This Conversation; then double-click the name of an online contact.

Cold-shoulder someone. To block somebody from chatting with you:

◆ In a conversation window with the person you want to block, choose Actions > Block, or click Block on the toolbar.

   or

   In the main window, right-click a contact's name; then choose Block.

   or

   In the main window, choose Tools > Options > Privacy tab; click the victim's name; then click Block.

If a dialog box explaining your action's consequences appears, click OK. To unblock someone, repeat the Block command. (Block toggles to Unblock.)

Ignore people. If you step away from your computer or don't want to be bothered, broadcast your status by using the File > My Status submenu in the main window. (Choose Busy, Be Right Back, On the Phone, and so on.)

Express your feelings. On the toolbar near the bottom of a conversation window is a drop-down list of smiley-face icons. You can insert these *emoticons* into your messages to indicate how the message should be interpreted (that is, your mood—embarrassment, anger, surprise, delight, whatever). Emoticons may be annoying, but they help prevent misunderstandings if your correspondent has no sense of irony. Messenger converts common text emoticons to graphic ones automatically; type :) to make a smiley face, for example. To turn off autoconversion, choose Tools > Options > Personal tab > uncheck Show Graphics (Emoticons) in Instant Messages.

Save conversations. To save a transcript of your chat as plain text on your hard drive, in a conversation window, choose File > Save As. If you'd rather preserve the transcript's colors and fonts, click in the transcript pane; choose Edit > Select All (or press Ctrl+A) to highlight all the text; then copy and paste the text into WordPad or Microsoft Word.

Keep Messenger in sight. To make Messenger remain in front of all other windows unless minimized, in the main window, choose Tools > Always On Top; or, in a conversation window, choose View > Always On Top.

Configure Messenger. The Tools > Options dialog box contains tabs for setting personal preferences, Messenger settings, and privacy options. "What's This?" pop-up help doesn't work here; click Help instead.

Get help from a friend. To start a Remote Assistance session from Messenger, see "Allowing Others to Connect to Your Computer Remotely" in Chapter 3.

Exchange files. To send a file to your chat partner, drag a file icon from Explorer or your desktop to the chat window. Or click Send a File or Photo in the right sidebar; then, in the Send a File dialog box that appears, locate and double-click the file. Use this feature to circumvent ISP-imposed file-size limits on email attachments.

Messenger asks the other person to Accept (Alt+T) or Decline (Alt+D) the file. Or *you* can Cancel (Alt+Q) the file transfer. If the recipient accepts the file, Messenger displays a dire virus warning, followed by a download-progress readout. If you have Service Pack 2 installed, Messenger uses the Attachment Manager service to block risky files (see "Receiving Attachments" in Chapter 14).

Add voice to a conversation. Free long distance! If you and your chat partner have USB headsets or microphones and speakers attached to your PCs, you can have a live, not-quite-phone-quality conversation. To do so, in the main window, right-click an online contact and choose Start a Voice Conversation; or, in a conversation window, click Start Talking in the right sidebar. If you haven't set up your audio equipment, Messenger runs Audio and Video Tuning Wizard; otherwise, speaker and microphone controls appear in the right pane. Start talking when your chat partner accepts the call. To hang up, click Stop Talking.

Add video to a conversation. If you (or your chat partner) have a digital video camera or webcam hooked up to your PC, you can add grainy, jerky video to your voice conversation. To do so, in a conversation window, click Start Camera in the right sidebar. When your contact accepts, a video picture appears in the right pane. Below the picture is an Options menu that lets you see a tiny version of your picture embedded in your contact's picture or stop sending your image to the contact. To end the conversation, click Stop Talking or Stop Camera. If your contact doesn't have a camera and you do, she'll see you, but you won't see her.

Send a pager message. To send a text message to a cell phone or pager, in the main window, right-click a contact name; then choose Send a Message to a Mobile Device. To receive a message, a person must have mobile information set up (Tools > Options > Phone tab).

Share applications. Application Sharing lets your chat partner use any program on your PC—Word, Microsoft Excel, and so on—even if it's not installed on her PC. Only open programs can be shared; you can open them before or after you send the invitation. (Don't block the view of the shared program with other windows.) To share a program, in the main window, right-click an online contact, and choose Start Application Sharing; or, in a conversation window, click Start Application Sharing in the right sidebar. After the invitation is accepted, select the program in the Sharing dialog box; click Share; then click Allow Control. To take control of the program, the chat partner clicks Request Control. In response, you click Accept. To retake control, press Esc.

CHATTING TIPS

Use a whiteboard. Whiteboard is a graphics window that allows you to work with someone else simultaneously. Anything that you draw, type, or paste in this window appears on your chat partner's screen (and vice versa). To start Whiteboard, in the main window, right-click an online contact and choose Start Whiteboard; or, in a conversation window, click Start Whiteboard in the right sidebar.

Check your email. In the main window, right-click a contact; then choose Send E-Mail to open your email program with a preaddressed message to the contact. To check your email, choose File > My E-Mail Inbox.

Play alert sounds. Messenger can alert you with a sound when contacts sign in or send a message. Choose Tools > Options > Preferences tab > Alerts section. Check the Play Sound box to hear sounds or uncheck it for silence. To change the sounds, click the Sounds button in the same dialog box; click the Sounds tab; then scroll the Program Events list to Windows Messenger. For more information, see "Configuring Sound and Audio Devices" in Chapter 4.

Chat without Messenger. Microsoft Chat is an older no-Passport-required program for chatting with someone connected to your network (LAN). To open Chat, choose Start > Run; type winchat and then press Enter. To have a videoconference without Messenger, use Microsoft NetMeeting: Choose Start > Run; type conf and then press Enter.

✔ Tips

- Among veteran chatters, blocking is a mild to significant insult, depending on circumstances. If you're trying to remain open to some people while avoiding others, Messenger doesn't give you many options; the best probably is to set yourself as Away or Busy and continue your chats of choice while letting others think you're not at the keyboard.

- For the same purpose, you can use the Appear Offline setting, but that's of less use than it might be. You can see who's online and they can't see you, but you also can't send a message without changing your visibility setting first.

- Messenger's size limit for a single message is 400 characters, and if you exceed it, your typing stops as though you'd hit a wall. If you must continue one thought over two messages, it's polite to back up a bit and end the first message with [more] or >>.

- If you want to save the transcript, you must do so explicitly (in Word or Notepad) before you close your session. Otherwise, the traffic is discarded when you exit Messenger.

- Unlike some other chat clients, and unlike email, Messenger doesn't stamp its saved messages with the date and time. The only such record you have is the creation date and time of the saved file.

- Microsoft will send you periodic pop-up notifications that a new version of Messenger is available.

MANAGING USER ACCOUNTS

16

Windows XP is a true multiple-user OS that lets several people use one PC without intruding on—or even viewing—one another's files, settings, and tastes. To start a Windows session, you log on to your *user account,* which gives you personalized access to the system. You, like each user, have your own desktop, Start menu, My Documents folder, Control Panel settings, email account, internet details (Favorites, History, cookies, and cached web pages), program settings, permissions, network connections, and other odds and ends. Your private files, folders, and preferences are stored in C:\Documents and Settings*<your user name>,* which lets Windows personalize your desktop each time that you log on.

In this chapter, you'll learn to create, edit, and delete user accounts as an administrator. If you're an ordinary user who's not called on to administer, you still need to know (and will learn) how to maintain your own account.

Workgroup vs. Domain

The type of network (Chapter 17) that you're on determines how you administer accounts.

A *workgroup* is a simple home or small-business network whose computers each maintain separate user accounts and security settings. These informal networks exist primarily to help users share printers, folders, files, and other resources. User accounts don't float around the network; you need a separate account on each networked PC to access its files.

PRO A *domain* is a large, business-oriented, centrally administered network. Files can reside on local hard disks or on a network *server* that distributes files across the network. Centralized user accounts let you log on to any domain computer. XP Home supports only workgroups; Pro supports both workgroups and domains.

Setting up User Accounts

Use Control Panel's User Accounts program to set up user accounts on a workgroup PC or a stand-alone (non-networked) PC. If you're an XP Pro user on a domain, skip to the Tips later in this section.

Your computer will have at least one account: yours. It might have other accounts if you upgraded from an earlier Windows version. If your PC is new, its manufacturer may have created a predefined account named, say, *Owner*. See "Logging On and Logging Off" in Chapter 1.

To see existing accounts:

◆ Choose Start > Control Panel > User Accounts (**Figure 16.1**).

   or

   Choose Start > Run; type `nusrmgr.cpl` and then press Enter.

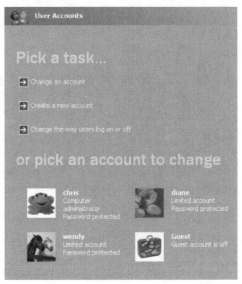

Figure 16.1 This window lists everyone who has a user account.

Account Types

An *account type* defines a user's *privileges*—rights to perform specific tasks. The account type appears below each user's name.

A *computer administrator* has sweeping systemwide rights to create, change, and delete user accounts and passwords; access *all* files (including other users' files); and install programs and hardware. Many of the settings described in this book require administrative privileges, which you should grant to few users besides yourself. XP must have at least one *Administrator* account, and if you installed Windows or maintain it, this is *your* account type.

If you're not an Administrator, you're an everyday *Limited* user who can change your own password, picture, .NET Passport, desktop theme, and Start menu; change some Control Panel settings (you can't change the system time, for example); and access files in your My Documents folder (everyone else's files are off limits) and the Shared Documents folder (which Windows Setup creates automatically as a shared location for all users).

Windows also comes with a no-password *Guest* account that has the same privileges as a limited account. This account, intended for visitors, is turned off by default and should stay that way.

User Accounts offers straightforward controls to create, change, and delete accounts.

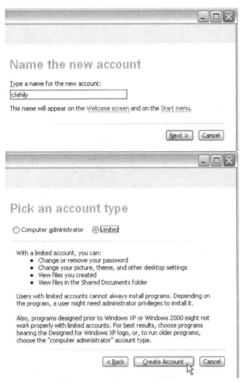

Figure 16.2 Best practice: Don't use spaces in a user name because they may cause problems with some programs and command-line tools. Capitalization doesn't matter, but favor only lowercase letters. Most punctuation is forbidden. Use a short name that will fit easily in messages and dialog boxes.

What do you want to change about diane's account?

- ➔ Change the name
- ➔ Change the password
- ➔ Remove the password
- ➔ Change the picture
- ➔ Change the account type
- ➔ Delete the account

diane
Limited account
Password protected

Figure 16.3 Administrators have full access to all accounts. Some options are available for only your account; other options, for only others' accounts. Limited users see fewer options; they can't change their name or account type, nor can they modify other users' accounts.

To create an account:

1. In User Accounts, click Create a New Account.

2. Type a user name for the account; then click Next.

   You'll also use this name to log on to domains and to computers without the Welcome screen.

3. Select an account type (see the "Account Types" sidebar) (**Figure 16.2**); then click Create Account.

   The new account will appear in the User Accounts window.

After creating a user account, you edit it to set up its other information. You can change a user account's details, such as its password and picture, at any time after creating it.

To edit an account:

1. In User Accounts, click the name or icon of the account that you want to change.

   Don't bother with the extra click of the Change an Account link.

2. In the window that appears (**Figure 16.3**), choose among these options:

   Name. Type a new user name, which will appear in the Welcome screen, Start menu, and User Accounts window.

continues on next page

SETTING UP USER ACCOUNTS

437

Password. Type (and retype) a password and optional logon hint to remind you of a forgotten password (**Figures 16.4** and **16.5**). If the account already is password-protected, you can change or remove the existing password. Capitalization counts. See the "Passwords" sidebar for tips.

Picture. Change the picture associated with you in the Welcome screen, Start menu, and User Accounts window (**Figure 16.6**). (The picture doesn't appear if you're a domain member or if you use the classic Start menu.)

Account type. Change an Administrator account into a Limited account, or vice versa. See the "Account Types" sidebar and Figure 16.2.

.NET Passport. Set up a new .NET Passport or change one that's linked to your account; this option appears for only your account. See "Getting a .NET Passport" in Chapter 15.

Figure 16.4 If you provide a password hint, use one that's meaningful to only you, because...

Figure 16.5 ...everyone who uses your PC can see it. Click the ? icon on the Welcome screen to reveal your password hint.

Figure 16.6 Click Browse for More Pictures to post your own picture, automatically scaled to fit. If a camera is connected to your PC, you'll see Get a Picture from a Camera or Scanner. If you want to change only your picture, you can double-click your Start-menu picture to open this window quickly.

Welcome to the Forgotten
Password Wizard

This wizard helps you create a "password reset" disk. If you
forget the password for this user account and are unable to
log on, you can use this disk to create a new password.

Note: No matter how many times you change your
password, you only need to create this disk once.

Warning: Anyone can use this disk to reset the password,
and therefore have access to this account.

To continue, click Next.

Figure 16.7 You can have only one
password reset disk for each account.
If you make a new one, the old one
becomes unusable.

If you're worried that you'll forget your password and draw a blank on your password hint, create a *password reset disk* to recover it. You must create it now, before you actually need it. Keep the disk safe; anyone can use it to change your password. (An Administrator always can reset your forgotten password, but a reset wipes your secondary passwords; see the "Passwords" sidebar.)

To create a password reset disk:

1. In User Accounts, click your account's name or icon.

2. In the task pane at the left, click Prevent a Forgotten Password.

   The Forgotten Password Wizard opens (**Figure 16.7**).

3. Follow the onscreen instructions.

   You'll need a formatted floppy disk.

   If you mistype a password in future logons, Windows displays a Use Your Password Reset Disk link (if you're using the Welcome screen) or a Reset button (if you're not). Click the link or button to launch the Password Reset Wizard, and follow the onscreen instructions. You don't need to make a new password reset disk after you're logged on; reuse the old one.

SETTING UP USER ACCOUNTS

You, as Administrator, can delete any account that's not logged on. (Press Ctrl+Shift+Esc and click the Users tab to see who's connected if Fast User Switching is turned on.) You *can't* delete the account that you're logged on to or the last Administrator account. A deleted account is gone forever, along with its settings and secondary passwords, as described in the "Passwords" sidebar. If you create a new account with the same name and password, Windows considers it to be a different account.

To delete an account:

1. In User Accounts, click the name or icon of the account that you want to delete.

2. Click Delete This Account.

3. Click Keep Files to save the user's desktop and My Documents files on your desktop in a folder named after the deleted user (**Figure 16.8**).

   or

   Click Delete Files to erase the user's files.

4. Click Delete Account.

✔ Tips

■ For information about sharing files and folders with other users, see "Sharing Files" in Chapter 17.

■ Manage accounts through only User Accounts. If you tinker with accounts in the Documents and Settings folder, you'll create a confusing array of duplicate folders with the computer name appended (diane and diane.NILE, for example).

■ For security reasons, consider using a Limited account for routine logons and an Administrator account for special occasions. If you're logged on as a Limited user and try to install a program—which requires Administrator privileges—**Figure 16.9** appears to let you install it as an Administrator.

Figure 16.8 Windows saves only documents, not the deleted user's email, Favorites, or settings.

Figure 16.9 If this dialog box doesn't appear automatically, right-click the program's installation icon (on the CD, floppy, or your hard drive); then choose Run As.

Figure 16.10 This dialog box is more powerful and direct than Control Panel's User Accounts. You can create, edit, and delete accounts without slogging through a wizard. Click the Advanced tab for more options.

Figure 16.11 Despite its austere appearance, this tool offers power and flexibility. Double-click an account name to set advanced options, for example.

■ Windows has a built-in, hidden administrative account named Administrator, which has no password. You can use this account for emergencies: when you start your PC in Safe mode (see "Recovering After a Crash" in Chapter 19) or when no other administrative accounts exist, for example. To manage this account, use the dialog box described in the next tip.

■ Power users prefer the Windows 2000–style User Accounts dialog box to manage user accounts. It's hidden in XP. To reveal it, choose Start > Run; type `control userpasswords2` and then press Enter (**Figure 16.10**).

■ **PRO** If you're a domain member, choose Start > Control Panel > User Accounts to create and manage accounts. The dialog box that appears is almost identical to Figure 16.10, except that the Users list has an extra column named Domain. The ideas described earlier in this section apply here, with a few extras. Accounts created here are *local* accounts stored on your PC, not on the domain server. You'll want a local—not domain—Administrator account to update drivers, for example. You also can assign people to groups, as described in the next tip.

■ Upon graduation to advanced user management, you'll use the Local Users and Groups console. Choose Start > Run; type `lusrmgr.msc` and then press Enter (**Figure 16.11**). With this console, you can create and manage users and groups. *Groups* are named collections of users that transcend the standard Administrator/Limited account types and give you great flexibility in fine-tuning file and folder permissions.

Passwords

The first time that you create a password for your own account, Windows asks you whether you want to make your files and folders private (*if* you have an NTFS-formatted hard drive; see the appendix). Click Yes, Make Private to deny others access to your C:\Documents and Settings\<*your user name*> folder. (An unethical Administrator still can inspect your files by changing your password.) See also "Sharing Files" in Chapter 17.

The secondary passwords stored in your account for certain web sites, network files and folders, encrypted files, your .NET Passport, and so on *are lost* if an Administrator changes your password (but not if you change it), thus preventing someone unscrupulous from, say, cleaning out your bank account courtesy of a password memorized by your browser.

If you upgraded from Windows 9*x* with user accounts, XP set the imported accounts to Administrator and erased their passwords. XP forbids passwordless network logons, but passersby can log on. To plug this security hole, assign passwords and downgrade account types to Limited.

In most situations, it's imperative to password-protect every account. The web has good advice on how to choose (and not choose) passwords; search for *choosing a password* on Google. For starters, see www.cs.umd.edu/faq/Passwords.shtml. If you're not offended easily, search for Grady Ward's article on using "shocking nonsense" to pick a password.

Figure 16.12 Check the first option for the Welcome screen; uncheck it for the classic logon prompt. Check the second option to let more than one user be logged on at the same time. These options are related; unchecking the first turns off the second automatically.

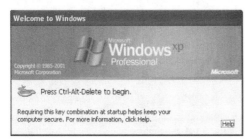

Figure 16.13 Pressing Ctrl+Alt+Delete temporarily halts any other programs running on your PC, guaranteeing an authentic logon prompt. (For this to work, the Welcome screen must be turned off in Figure 16.12.)

✔ Tip

- For added security, force users to press Ctrl+Alt+Delete to prevent user-name and password theft by Trojan-horse programs that mimic the logon screen. Choose Start > Run; type `control userpasswords2` and then press Enter. The old-style User Accounts dialog box appears (refer to Figure 16.10). Click the Advanced tab; check Require Users to Press Ctrl+Alt+Delete; then click OK. From now on, users are greeted with **Figure 16.13.**

Controlling the Logon Process

As described in "Logging On and Logging Off" in Chapter 1, Windows gives you two ways to log on (if you're not on a domain):

- The *Welcome screen* (refer to Figure 1.1) is the easiest and fastest way to log on. You simply click your name and type your password (if you have one).

- The *classic logon prompt* (see Figure 16.14 later in this chapter) is a more secure, less convenient method. You must type your user name and, if necessary, your password.

You can turn on Fast User Switching (described in Chapter 1) if:

- The Welcome screen is turned on.

- **PRO** You're not on a domain.

- **PRO** The offline-files feature is turned off. See "Making Network Files and Folders Available Offline" in Chapter 5.

To control how users log on:

1. Choose Start > Control Panel > User Accounts.

2. Click Change the Way Users Log On or Off (visible in Figure 16.1).

3. Select the logon options; then click Apply Options (**Figure 16.12**).

CONTROLLING THE LOGON PROCESS

Logging on to a Domain

If you've turned off the Welcome screen, or if you're joined to an XP Pro network domain, you'll log on via the classic logon prompt (**Figure 16.14**). Domain logon is like standard logon but requires an extra bit of information: a domain name (available from your network administrator).

Figure 16.14 The classic logon prompt usually displays the name of the previous user who logged on.

To log on to a workgroup or stand-alone computer:

1. If the dialog box in **Figure 16.15** appears, press Ctrl+Alt+Delete to display the classic logon prompt.

2. Type your user name in the User Name box.

3. If your account is password-protected, type your password in the Password box.

4. Press Enter or click OK.

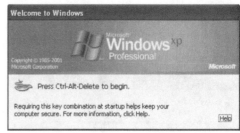

Figure 16.15 Sometimes, you must pass through this extra security checkpoint to reach the logon prompt.

PRO To log on to a domain:

1. Follow steps 1 to 3 in "To log on to a workgroup or stand-alone computer."

2. If the Log on To box doesn't appear, click Options to expand the dialog box.

3. Click the down arrow to the right of the Log on To box; then choose the correct domain name from the drop-down list.

4. Click OK to log on to Windows XP and your network domain.

✔ Tips

- **PRO** To log on to only your local PC (not a network domain), choose This Computer (or Local Computer) in the Log on To list in step 3.

- See also "Joining a Domain" in Chapter 17.

- If you're at the Welcome screen, you can press Ctrl+Alt+Delete to make the classic logon prompt appear. If you have difficulty with this keyboard shortcut, hold down Ctrl and Alt; then press Delete twice.

Figure 16.16 What you see on your desktop—the Favorites menu, Send To menu, Start menu, and so on—is a combination of what's in your user profile and what's in the All Users profile.

Managing User Profiles

A *user profile* contains an account's personal settings that Windows uses to configure the desktop each time the user logs on. Each user's desktop settings, network connections, and application settings are saved in C:\Documents and Settings*<user name>* (which also contains the user's My Documents folder). Windows also maintains the *All Users* profile to store things common to everybody. You saw in the sidebar in "Installing Programs" in Chapter 6, for example, that you can copy icons to the Programs folder in the All Users profile to make applications available to everyone. All Users contains folders similar to those in individual user profiles (**Figure 16.16**).

When you create a new account, Windows determines the new user's desktop look by using the Default User profile (a hidden folder in Documents and Settings). To change this starting point, change the desktop, Start menu, Favorites menu, and theme of a normal account (your own, perhaps) to what you want the new default to be, complete the following steps.

To change the Default User profile:

1. In Windows Explorer, choose Tools > Folder Options > View tab; select Show Hidden Files and Folders; then click OK.

2. Choose Start > Control Panel > Performance and Maintenance > System > Advanced tab > User Profiles section > Settings (**Figure 16.17**).

3. Select the account whose settings you want to copy; then click Copy To.

   The Copy To dialog box opens.

4. Click Browse, and navigate to C:\Documents and Settings\Default User.

5. Click OK in each open dialog box.

6. In Explorer, re-hide hidden files.

✔ Tip

■ **PRO** A *roaming user profile*, which your system Administrator creates, is available every time you log on to any domain computer.

Figure 16.17 The (hidden) Default User profile determines what a newly created user sees on the desktop. Use the User Profiles dialog box to change the default appearance by copying other profile settings to the Default User profile.

SETTING UP
A SMALL NETWORK

You create a *network* when you connect two or more computers to exchange data or share equipment. Cheap hardware and simpler configurations have made networks common in homes and small businesses. Setup is no longer the frustrating, complex experience it used to be, thanks to the Network Setup Wizard (but the hassle of buying and installing network hardware remains). Networks let you:

Share files. No more straying floppies and duplicate files. You can designate disks, folders, and files as shared network resources.

Share printers and devices. Any computer on the network can use a printer connected to another network computer. Ditto for backup devices, scanners, and other devices.

Share an internet connection. You can set up an internet connection on one computer and let every computer on the network share that connection.

✔ Tips

■ You must be an Administrator to perform many of the tasks in this chapter. See "Setting up User Accounts" in Chapter 16.

■ A geographically limited network that spans a small area (typically, a building or two) is called a *local area network (LAN)*.

■ **PRO** This chapter describes how to set up a simple *workgroup* network (also called a *peer-to-peer* network), appropriate for 10 or fewer computers, on XP Home and Pro editions. XP Pro (but not Home) also supports *domain* networks for large organizations. A full-time geek (or department) sets up and administers a domain, which can have thousands of users. In this chapter, I don't cover domain setup, but I do describe how to join an existing domain. Ordinary users can set up and administer their own workgroup but not a domain.

Understanding Network Types

Before you can set up Windows' network software, you must install and configure network hardware. Your choice of network depends on your budget, the proximity of the computers to be networked, and your inclination—or otherwise—to lay cable.

Ethernet

The most popular network standard, *Ethernet,* is cheap, fast, and reliable, and it imposes few limits on where the networked PCs are placed in your home or office. To create an Ethernet network, you'll need three components along with your PCs (**Figure 17.1**):

Network adapter. Each computer must have a *network adapter* (about $15 U.S.) that provides a physical connection to the network. An adapter has an *RJ-45 jack* that you connect an Ethernet cable to. If your PC didn't come with an Ethernet jack, you can buy a *network interface card,* or *NIC* (a PCI expansion card that you open your computer to install), or an external network adapter that plugs into a USB port. For laptops, plug in a PC Card (about $30) that provides an Ethernet jack. All newer NICs are Plug and Play. For installation tips, see "Connecting Devices to Your Computer" in Chapter 8.

Cable, wire, or (wireless) radio waves   *Internet*

Shared printer   *Router/hub*   *DSL or cable modem*

Figure 17.1 A typical network in which three computers share a printer and a high-speed internet connection.

Ethernet cables. The cables used in Ethernet networks are a little thicker than telephone cables, and the *RJ-45 connectors* at each end are wider than ordinary phone (RJ-11) connectors. You can buy Ethernet cables—called *10BaseT, 100BaseT, CAT5, CAT5e,* or *twisted-pair* cables—with preattached connectors ($5 to $50, depending on length). For custom lengths, you (or someone at the store) can cut the cable off a spool and attach the connectors. Or you can join two lengths by using an RJ-45 female/female coupler. A connection's length shouldn't exceed 100 meters (328 feet). If you're drilling through walls to lay cable, consider hiring a professional cable installer (or using a wireless network).

Hub. On an Ethernet network, you connect each cable from a PC's network adapter to a central connection point called a *hub* (about $30)—a small box with a row of five to eight or more jacks (called *ports*) that accept RJ-45 connectors. Small green lights on the hub glow or flicker to signal an active connection. Computers communicate through the hub, so there's no direct connection between any two PCs. One port, labeled *Uplink,* connects to a router, broadband modem, or another hub to expand the network. The other ports are numbered, but it doesn't matter which port you plug which cable into. You also can connect shared peripherals, such as printers, to the hub.

If you have an internet connection, use a *router/hub* instead of an ordinary hub to share the connection, as described in the next section.

Wireless (802.11)

Wireless networks are popular because they're versatile, don't require cables, and have dropped in price. The wireless standard is called *Wi-Fi* (short for *wireless fidelity*) or 802.11 (say *eight-oh-two-eleven*).

To set up a wireless network, install a wireless network adapter (about $60) in each PC. The adapter has a small antenna that sticks out the back of the computer to transmit and receive radio waves over a range of about 150 feet (through walls). To share a high-speed internet connection, you need a *base station* or *access point* (about $100). Turn on the password or encryption option to stop neighbors or passersby from stealing your internet bandwidth and eavesdropping.

Most wireless equipment comes in one of three flavors: 802.11*a*, 802.11*b*, or 802.11*g*. These three protocols vary by compatibility, band, range, and speed (measured in megabits per second). If you're not interested in the details, buy only *g* equipment and stop reading; otherwise, here are a few things to know about *a*, *b*, and *g* gear:

- *a* and *g* are about five times faster than *b* (54 Mbps versus 11 Mbps).

- *b* and *g* have a greater range than *a* (150 feet versus 60 feet).

- *b* and *g* work in the 2.4 GHz band and are subject to interference from pipes, weather, microwave ovens, 2.4 GHz cordless phones, and Bluetooth devices. (*a* works in the 5 GHz band.)

- *g* is backward-compatible with *b*; you can mix a *b* card with a *g* base station and vice versa.

- *a* isn't compatible with *b* or *g* unless the equipment is labeled dual-band or dual-mode/tri-mode.

◆ *a* hasn't been adopted widely because of the popularity of *b* and *g*.

◆ Faster wireless equipment doesn't make your internet connection faster (the modem is the bottleneck).

◆ A wireless network is compatible with an Apple AirPort (802.11b) or AirPort Extreme (802.11g) network.

◆ The next standard, 802.11*n*, offers greater throughput and increased range over 802.11a/b/g.

◆ The Wi-Fi Alliance (`www.wi-fi.org`) is a trade organization that tests and certifies equipment compliance with the 802.11 standards.

Telephone lines (HomePNA)

Network equipment certified by the *Home Phoneline Networking Alliance*, or *HomePNA*, uses your existing phone wires to connect computers. HomePNA networks don't interfere with other wire communications. You can use standard telephones, dial-up modems, DSL or cable modems, faxes, and answering machines simultaneously with HomePNA, because even though the devices use the same telephone wires, they occupy different frequency bands. These networks don't require a hub; instead, you plug your HomePNA network adapter (about $70) into the nearest phone jack. For more information, see `www.homepna.org`.

UNDERSTANDING NETWORK TYPES

Jumping onto a Public Wireless Network

If you've installed Service Pack 2, and your laptop has a wireless networking card (most do these days), it's easy to get fast internet access by joining a public wireless network at a café, hotel lobby, coffee shop, airport lounge, friend's house, or anywhere else that has an 802.11 base station set up.

When you try to get online, Windows hunts for a wired or wireless connection. If no Ethernet cable is plugged in, your laptop will look for a wireless hotspot and notify you automatically if it finds one. (You may have to wander a bit with your laptop.) To join the wireless network:

1. Click the Wireless Network Detected pop-up balloon when it appears in the notification area (system tray).

If the balloon disappears too fast, right-click the Wireless Network Connection icon in the notification area; then choose View Available Networks.

2. In the Wireless Network Connection window that appears, click the network's name; then click Connect.

A yellow padlock indicates a secured network that prompts you for a password; you're out of luck if you don't have it.

From now on, any time that you wander into this hotspot, Windows connects automatically without dialog boxes.

If more than one hotspot is available in the same place, choose Start > My Network Places (or open My Network Places in the Windows Explorer folders tree); right-click a wireless connection; choose Properties > Wireless Networks tab; then reorder the hotspots in the Preferred Networks list to your liking.

Electrical outlets (HomePlug)

Network equipment certified by the *HomePlug Powerline Alliance* uses the existing electrical wiring in your home to connect computers. Unlike phone jacks, power outlets are available in almost every room, ready to pull double duty as a power source and a network port. HomePlug networks are easy to set up; you plug your HomePlug network adapter (about $100) into the nearest power outlet. The network range is about 1,000 feet, including the length that the wires travel in your walls. For more information, see www.homeplug.org.

FireWire (IEEE 1394)

You can form a simple network if your computers all have FireWire jacks, which usually are used to capture video from a digital video camera. (You can buy an IEEE 1394 card to get these jacks; see "Connecting Devices to Your Computer" in Chapter 8.) Just hook together the computers with 6-pin-to-6-pin IEEE 1394 cables (about $20). There's no need to buy a hub or router. Each computer should have two free FireWire ports so that you can form a chain. The computers have to be close; FireWire cables can't be more than 15 feet (4.5 meters) long. And you can't use this arrangement to share a printer or DSL/cable modem.

Crossover cable

If your network has only two computers that are close together, you can connect them with a *crossover cable* (about $10), which runs directly between the two PCs' Ethernet jacks. This no-hassle network saves you the cost of a hub and works exactly like a "real" Ethernet network. (If you expand the network to three computers, you must buy a hub.)

✔ Tips

■ Network speeds are measured in *megabits per second (Mbps)*. 10 Mbps, called *10BaseT* or *Ethernet,* is adequate for most homes and small businesses. Most new hubs and adapters handle both 10BaseT and *100BaseT* or *Fast Ethernet* (100 Mbps) on the same network; look for the label *10/100* or *dual speed*. Pricier *Gigabit Ethernet* (1000 Mbps) equipment also is available. Wireless, HomePNA, and HomePlug speeds are comparable to 10BaseT. (Network speed doesn't affect internet-connection speed; DSL and cable modems are 10 to 20 times slower than 10BaseT.)

■ Brand-name network equipment manufacturers include 3Com, Belkin, D-Link, Linksys, Microsoft, Netgear, and SMC. No-name hardware is cheaper, but the few dollars extra that you pay for a name brand get you phone and web support, better documentation, and regularly updated drivers.

■ You can check Microsoft's Hardware Compatibility List before you buy network equipment (see "Installing Plug and Play Devices" in Chapter 8), but just because equipment is missing from the list doesn't mean it won't work.

UNDERSTANDING NETWORK TYPES

Sharing an Internet Connection

To share one internet connection with every computer on a network, you have two options:

Install a router. A *router*—called a *residential gateway* by Microsoft but by no one else on the planet—is a small box that has one jack that connects to a hub and another jack that connects to a DSL, cable, or dial-up modem. A *router/hub* (about $70) doubles as a hub, sharing the modem's bandwidth among multiple Ethernet ports that the network PCs connect to. A slightly more expensive *router/switch* gives the modem's full bandwidth to multiple computers simultaneously. In most cases, you're better off with a router than dealing with the limits of ICS (described next). A router is easy to install and configure, uses little power, lets any PC go online at any time, and has a built-in firewall. To the outside world, a router appears to be a computer, but one without programs and hard drives to attack or infect.

Use Internet Connection Sharing (ICS). ICS is a built-in Windows feature that acts like a software router. It's free but difficult to configure. You must designate one computer as the *host,* or *gateway,* PC through which all internet traffic passes. For high-speed (broadband) internet connections, the host PC must have *two* Ethernet adapters: one that connects to the DSL or cable modem and one that connects to a hub. If the host PC is turned off, the other PCs—called *clients*—can't go online. (See the sidebar in this section for more information.) Like a router, ICS works best with a high-speed internet connection, but a dial-up modem works acceptably.

ICS Checklist

Some setup and troubleshooting tips for Internet Connection Sharing:

- Make sure that the host PC can go online *before* you run the Network Setup Wizard.

- The host PC must have Windows XP installed; the other PCs can be running earlier Windows versions (except Windows 95/3.x).

- Turn on the host PC *before* turning on the client PCs.

- If your DSL service has multiple static IP addresses, you can share a connection without designating a single PC as host.

- If you're using a software firewall (Windows Firewall or ZoneAlarm, for example), turn it on for all PCs *except* the host PC. See "Securing Your Computer" in Chapter 12.

- For dial-up connections, if the host PC tries to maintain a continuous internet connection by dialing repeatedly, choose (on the host) Start > Control Panel > Network and Internet Connections > Network Connections; right-click your ISP's icon; choose Properties > Options tab; then uncheck Redial If Line Is Dropped.

- For dial-up connections, a client PC's browser or email program may report a "server/page unavailable" error before the host PC gets a chance to dial and go online. Wait a moment; then try again (that is, click Refresh or Send/Receive).

Running the Network Setup Wizard

When you've installed your network hardware according to the manufacturer's instructions, and everything's working properly, you're ready to run the Network Setup Wizard on *every* computer on the network. Windows 98/Me/2000/NT PCs can coexist peacefully with XP on the same network. If you're using Internet Connection Sharing, run the wizard on the host computer first.

Even if your network seems to be operating properly, play by the rules: Run the wizard to set workgroup names and IP addresses, configure file-sharing permissions, turn on or off Windows Firewall, and modify the registry. After the wizard finishes, you can tweak network settings manually.

To run the Network Setup Wizard:

1. Choose Start > Control Panel > Network and Internet Connections > Network Connections; then click Set up a Home or Small Office Network in the task pane at left.

   or

   Choose Start > All Programs > Accessories > Communications > Network Setup Wizard.

   or

   Choose Start > My Network Places > Network Setup Wizard.

   The wizard appears.

2. Click Next to skip the Welcome page.

3. On the Before You Continue page, click Checklist for Creating a Network for a list of the preparatory setup steps (many of which are described earlier in this chapter); then close the checklist window and click Next.

Setting up a Wireless Network

If you've installed Service Pack 2, you can use the Wireless Network Setup Wizard to set up a wireless network. Install the appropriate hardware on each computer, and run the wizard: Choose Start > All Programs > Accessories > Communications > Wireless Network Setup Wizard; then follow the onscreen instructions.

The wizard can save your network settings to a USB flash drive. You simply insert the drive first into the access point and then into each computer or device that you want to add to the network. You still can use the wizard even if you don't have a USB flash drive, but it's more of a hassle.

After running the Wireless Network Setup Wizard, you can turn on File and Printer Sharing on your new wireless network by running the Network Setup Wizard on each computer.

Figure 17.2 Select the option that best describes this computer's internet connection. Click View an Example for a pop-up illustration of a particular configuration.

4. On the Select a Connection Method page, specify how this computer connects to the internet; then click Next.

Choose one of the five following options. (To select one of the latter three options, select Other; then click Next; **Figure 17.2**).

If you're using **Internet Connection Sharing** (ICS), and this computer is the *host* PC, select This Computer Connects Directly to the Internet; The Other Computers on My Network Connect to the Internet Through This Computer.

or

If you have **a router** (residential gateway), and you're not using ICS, select This Computer Connects to the Internet Through a Residential Gateway or Through Another Computer on My Network.

(If you're using ICS, and this computer is a *client* PC, you shouldn't see this page; you should see Figure 17.6, described later.)

or

If **each PC connects to the internet** directly and independently, with no connection sharing, select This Computer Connects to The Internet Directly or Through a Network Hub; Other Computers on My Network Also Connect to the Internet Directly or Through a Hub.

or

If you have **only one computer,** select This Computer Connects Directly to the Internet; I Do Not Have a Network Yet.

or

If you have **no internet connection,** select This Computer Belongs to a Network That Does Not Have an Internet Connection.

continues on next page

5. On the Select Your Internet Connection page, if this computer has more than one internet connection, select the one that you want to use, and click Next (**Figure 17.3, top**); otherwise, skip to the next step.

6. On the Give This Computer a Description and Name page, edit this computer's description and name, if necessary; then click Next (**Figure 17.3, middle**).

   The name must be unique on the network, can be up to 15 characters long with no spaces or punctuation (except hyphens and apostrophes), and can't be the same as any user-account name.

7. On the Name Your Network page, if you don't want to use the default workgroup (network) name, *MSHOME,* change it here; then click Next (**Figure 17.3, bottom**).

   Every PC on the network must have the same workgroup name.

8. On the File and Printer Sharing page, choose whether your Shared Documents folder and shared printer (if any) will be available to everyone on the network.

9. On the Ready to Apply Network Settings page, review your settings; then click Next (**Figure 17.4**).

   The wizard displays an animation while it configures this computer.

Figure 17.3 Top: Chapter 12 describes how these connections appeared on this list. Middle: Windows remembers the name given this computer during Windows Setup. Bottom: If you change the default workgroup name on one PC, you must change it on *all* network PCs. Don't just click Next to blow through this page when you run the wizard on the other PCs.

Figure 17.4 If you're unsatisfied with your settings, click Back to change them.

Figure 17.5 Your choice here depends on the Windows version that other network PCs are running.

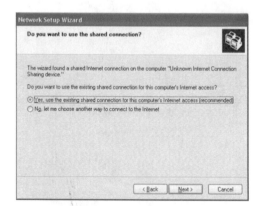

Figure 17.6 ICS users see this page when connecting to a network as a *client* PC. Select the first option for a simplified trip through the wizard.

10. On the You're Almost Done page (**Figure 17.5**), choose one of the following options, depending on the OS of the *next* network PC that you're going to run the wizard on.

    If the next PC is running XP, select Just Finish the Wizard; I Don't Need to Run the Wizard on Other Computers. After that, click Next; then click Finish.

    or

    If the next PC is running an earlier Windows version, select Create a Network Setup Disk; click Next; and follow the onscreen instructions.

    You'll need a blank, formatted floppy disk for the wizard to transfer a copy of itself to.

11. After running the wizard on the first PC, repeat the process on the other network PCs.

    If a PC is running XP, start with step 1.

    or

    If a PC has an earlier Windows version, insert the network setup disk that you created in the preceding step into the floppy drive; choose Start > My Computer; double-click 3 1/2 Floppy (A:); then double-click `netsetup.exe` to start the wizard.

    In either case, the preceding steps are the same, except that **Figure 17.6** appears instead of Figure 17.2 if you're using Internet Connection Sharing. (Also, don't create another network setup disk in step 10.)

    After you restart the computer as instructed, the PC becomes part of the network.

✔ Tips

- Test the network: Choose Start > My Network Places to see the shared folders and disks that your PC can detect on other computers on the network (**Figure 17.7**). If you're running an earlier Windows version, the icon may be called Network Neighborhood. See also "Navigating the Network" later in this chapter.

- If you're unable to see icons for other computers in My Network Places (or in Network Neighborhood), make sure that your hub or router is plugged in and turned on; also make sure that all network adapters are firmly seated and cables are firmly connected to their jacks and ports. Also, use Device Manager to make sure that each network adapter is working properly; see "Managing Device Drivers" in Chapter 8.

- To change the computer name or description quickly, choose Start > Control Panel > Performance and Maintenance > System > Computer Name tab (**Figure 17.8**). Don't rename your computer (or workgroup) when you're disconnected from the network; if you do, duplicate names might appear.

- If one of the network PCs has Windows Me, *don't* run that OS's Home Networking Wizard. Use the XP network setup disk to join the network.

- If you search Help and Support Center for *net services commands,* you'll find some useful network commands to use at the Command Prompt. Type net view at a command prompt for a list of computers on your network, for example. ping, tracert, ipconfig, and netstat also are handy.

Figure 17.7 There's not much to see at first. The top icon shows this network's router. The other icons show the shared folders on this network's two computers. (This window starts out in Details view; Tiles view appears here.)

Figure 17.8 Click Change to change the computer name without slogging through the Network Setup Wizard.

Figure 17.9 You can join a network domain during XP Pro installation or at any time afterward.

Joining a Domain

PRO If you're part of an organization that's large enough to have a domain, your network administrator probably added your PC to the domain for you. But you can join one yourself if you need to. (See also "Logging on to a Domain" in Chapter 16.)

To join a domain:

1. Choose Start > Control Panel > Performance and Maintenance > System > Computer Name tab > Network ID button.

   The Network Identification Wizard appears.

2. Click Next to skip the Welcome page.

3. Select This Computer Is Part of a Business Network; then click Next.

4. Select My Company Uses a Network Domain; then click Next.

5. Click Next to skip the Network Information page.

   This page tells you what information you'll need to know in advance to join the domain.

6. Type the user name, password, and domain name supplied by your network administrator; then click Next (**Figure 17.9**).

7. If the Active Directory domain doesn't recognize your PC, the Computer Domain page appears; consult your network administrator, and click Next.

8. Select Do Not Add a User at This Time; click Next; then click Finish.

9. You may have to restart your computer to join the domain.

Navigating the Network

After the network is running, you can explore the contents of other people's *shared* disks, folders, and files on the network. (You'll learn how to share your own items in the next section.)

To explore the network:

1. Choose Start > My Network Places (**Figure 17.10**).

2. To see icons for each network computer, click View Workgroup Computers in the task pane at left (**Figure 17.11**).

3. Double-click shared items to open them, just as though you were working in your My Computer folder (**Figure 17.12**).

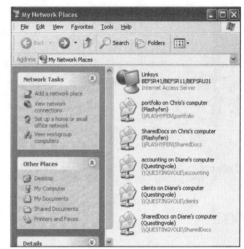

Figure 17.10 My Network Places shows shared disks and folders, including the ones on your own PC.

Figure 17.11 This view is great for crowded networks. Each network computer—instead of each shared resource—appears in this window.

Figure 17.12 If you're looking for a shared item on a specific PC, double-click that computer's icon in Figure 17.11. That PC's shared resources aren't intermingled with those of other computers, as in Figure 17.10.

NAVIGATING THE NETWORK

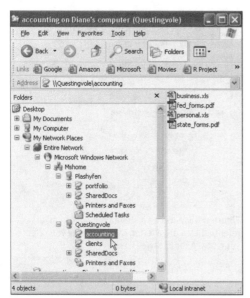

Figure 17.13 Windows Explorer offers an overview of the entire network.

✔ Tips

- In My Network Places (or Network Neighborhood), you can choose View > Arrange Icons By to sort icons by computer or network location.

- It's easy to use Windows Explorer to move and copy items between network computers (**Figure 17.13**). See "Exploring Your Computer" in Chapter 5.

- In Explorer and on the desktop, you can rename, delete, select, and manipulate shared network items just as you would items on your local drive. See Chapter 5. (Beware: If you delete a shared item on another computer, the item bypasses the Recycle Bin and disappears forever.)

- To use Search Companion to find shared network items, choose Start > Search (or press Ctrl+E in Explorer); choose Browse from the Look In drop-down list; click My Network Places; then click OK. For details, see "Searching for Files and Folders" in Chapter 5.

- In applications, shared files are available via the standard File > Open and File > Save As dialog boxes. Click My Network Places in the left-side panel or choose it from the Look In drop-down list. File > Save saves a file in its original network location; to save a local copy on your hard disk, choose File > Save As.

continues on next page

NAVIGATING THE NETWORK

- You can *map* (assign) a shared disk or folder to a drive letter so that you can access the item via My Computer or the Open or Save As dialog box. To do so, in Explorer or My Network Places, choose Tools > Map Network Drive (**Figure 17.14**); select a drive letter; browse for an item or type its Uniform Naming Convention (UNC) name; check Reconnect at Logon; then click Finish. The new "drive" appears on your Explorer tree. To kill the mapping, choose Tools > Disconnect Network Drive.

- To treat an online storage space—such as an FTP site, intranet folder, or web-based backup-service drive—as though it were connected to your network, click Add a Network Place on the task pane in My Network Places; then follow the onscreen instructions in the Add Network Place Wizard. Or if you're at a storage site in Internet Explorer, simply drag its icon from the Address bar to a local folder (typically, to My Network Places).

- **PRO** If you see a list of domains instead of a list of network computers, double-click the domain you want. You may have to type your password to gain access.

Figure 17.14 Mapping a shared network item lets you refer to it by a drive letter, the same way you refer to your local A: or C: drive.

UNC Names

The *Uniform Naming Convention (UNC)* is a system of naming network files, folders, and other shared resources so that an item's address identifies it uniquely on the network. UNC uses the following format:

`\\`*server*`\`*resource_pathname*

server is a computer name (assigned at Windows installation or in the Network Setup Wizard) or an IP address; *resource_pathname* is a standard pathname (see "Exploring Your Computer" in Chapter 5). Some example UNCs for a folder, file, and printer are:

`\\yangtze\budget\2003\qtr2`

`\\nile\books\mynovel\chap1.doc`

`\\thames\HPcolor`

To view a shared item quickly, type its UNC name in Explorer's Address bar or in the Start > Run dialog box.

NAVIGATING THE NETWORK

Figure 17.15 Oddly, this check box appears even if you're joined to a domain. No matter—checking it still won't activate Simple file sharing.

Sharing Files

Just as networked computers can share a single internet connection (as described earlier in this chapter) or network printer (see Chapter 7), they can share disks, folders, files, and devices—specific documents, MP3s, videos, CDs, or DVDs—from any net-worked PC, including yours. You in turn can access them if you're logged on to a network computer other than your usual one. File sharing abolishes "sneakernet"—transferring files by carrying floppies or CDs from one machine to another.

Windows XP offers two types of sharing: easy-to-use, slightly risky *Simple file sharing* and complex, secure *Classic file sharing*, inherited from Windows 2000. XP Home edition users have no choice: they must use Simple file sharing. Pro edition users can use either Simple or Classic file sharing unless they're joined to a domain, which *always* uses Classic file sharing.

PRO To switch between Simple and Classic file sharing:

1. In Windows Explorer, choose Tools > Folder Options > View tab.

2. Scroll to the bottom of the Advanced Settings list; then check Use Simple File Sharing (Recommended) to use Simple file sharing or uncheck it to use Classic file sharing (**Figure 17.15**).

3. Click OK (or Apply).

✔ Tip

■ If you're not on a network, you can use the techniques described here to share files with other users on the *same* PC. If they try to open a private folder or file, they see an "Access is denied" error message.

Simple file sharing

Simple file sharing is appropriate for a home or a small office where you trust *all* the other people on the network. Configuration is easy; you can share a disk or folder by checking a box. Unfortunately, it's not very safe. *Every* network user can view your shared items and, if you're collaborating, edit and delete them too. (Remember, files deleted across a network disappear instantly, bypassing the Recycle Bin.)

To share a disk or folder:

1. In Windows Explorer or My Computer, locate the disk or folder to share.

    You can share only disks and folders, not individual files. Sharing a disk or folder shares all its files, folders, and nested folders. Folder sharing is safer than disk sharing and doesn't make other users search your entire drive for a relevant folder.

2. Right-click the icon; then choose Sharing and Security (or choose Properties > Sharing tab).

    If you're sharing a disk, you'll see a warning; click If You Understand the Risk but Still Want to Share the Root of This Drive, Click Here.

3. In the Network Sharing and Security section, check Share This Folder on the Network (**Figure 17.16**).

4. In the Share Name box, type a name for the shared item.

    Other users see this name in their My Network Places windows, so use a short, descriptive name. (This network name won't change the item's name on *your* computer.)

Figure 17.16 The sharing check boxes are available only if you ran the Network Setup Wizard on this computer and unchecked Make This Folder Private.

Local Disk (C:)   DVD Drive (D:)   My Documents

Figure 17.17 A hand cradles a shared item's icon.

5. To allow *all* users to change the files in the shared folder, check Allow Network Users to Change My Files.

   Unchecking this box creates a *read-only* disk or folder. Other users can open what's inside it, but they can't edit, delete, or rename anything; neither can they add new files. They can, however, copy items *out* of the folder to their own disks.

6. Click OK.

   The shared item's icon changes (**Figure 17.17**).

✔ Tips

- In step 5, you can't determine *which* users have full access to your files; either all do, or none does. Classic file sharing remedies this problem.

- You can't share Documents and Settings, Program Files, and Windows system folders. If you're not an Administrator, you can't share folders in other users' profiles.

- Turning on a folder's sharing check boxes (refer to Figure 17.16) doesn't turn on the same check boxes for its nested folders, but those nested folders *are* shared, no matter what their check boxes say.

- To make a nested folder in a shared folder private, right-click the nested folder; choose Properties > Sharing tab; then check Make This Folder Private (refer to Figure 17.16).

- If you append a $ character to a share name in step 4 (GamblingDebts$, for example), that item is shared but *hidden;* it won't appear in anyone's My Network Places window. You and anyone else entrusted with the name can connect to the item by typing its UNC name— including the $—any place network paths are accepted, such as an Address bar or the Map Network Drive dialog box.

PRO Classic file sharing

Classic file sharing is more secure and flexible than Simple file sharing, at the cost of added complexity. You can set share permissions for individual users and groups to, say, grant some people full access, others read-only access, and others no access. (To turn on Classic file sharing, see "To switch between Simple and Classic file sharing" earlier in this section.)

Classic file sharing, roughly speaking, adds a permissions step to Simple file sharing. Unfortunately, the subtleties lurking behind that step—such as group policies, inherited permissions, and interactions with NTFS permissions—are quite complicated. I cover only the basics here. To appreciate this sharing model and use it competently, consult a book on Windows XP or 2000 network administration.

To share a disk or folder:

1. In Windows Explorer or My Computer, locate the disk or folder to share.

2. Right-click the icon; then choose Sharing and Security (or choose Properties > Sharing tab).

3. Select Share This Folder (**Figure 17.18**).

4. Accept or edit the proposed share name.

5. To avoid slowing your PC or to moderate network traffic, select Allow This Number of Users, and type the maximum number of people who can use the share at the same time.

(If you click OK now, everyone on the network gets full access.)

Figure 17.18 This dialog box is Classic file sharing's more complicated version of Figure 17.16.

SHARING FILES

Figure 17.19 The top half of this dialog box lists users or groups that you've granted or denied access permissions. The bottom shows the access levels of the selected user or group.

Figure 17.20 Spelling counts. Click Check Names to validate your "object" names before you add them.

6. Click Permissions (**Figure 17.19**).

The first time that you share a folder, the Permissions dialog box contains only Everyone in the Group or User Names list.

7. To add users or groups, click Add; type one or more user or group names separated by semicolons; then click OK (**Figure 17.20**).

8. Click the name of a person or group.

9. Select Allow, Deny, or neither for each access-control entry.

Full Control allows users to read, edit, delete, rename, and create files. In addition, users can change permissions and take file ownership (possibly locking you out of your own documents).

Change allows users to read, edit, delete, and rename files but not create new files.

Read allows users to read files but not edit, delete, or rename them.

10. Click OK in each of the open dialog boxes.

The shared item's icon changes (refer to Figure 17.17).

SHARING FILES

18

WORKING REMOTELY

Remote Connections

Windows' remote-access features come in two flavors: remote networking (direct dialing and VPN) and remote control (Remote Desktop).

Remote networking lets your local PC access remote-PC or network resources over a modem link. If you double-click a Microsoft Word file that resides on the remote PC, for example, the file is transmitted to your local PC and opens in your *local* copy of Word. If you have no copy of Word on your local PC, Word is transmitted, too—which would take days over dial-up. The moral: Avoid running programs that reside only on the remote PC, especially for slow connections.

Remote control doesn't have this problem; *all* work is done on the remote PC. If you double-click that same Word file, the remote PC's copy of Word opens. Only keystrokes, mouse gestures, and desktop images are transmitted between the two PCs. Unfortunately, refresh of a fully graphical screen over a dial-up connection is glacial.

Windows gives you several ways to connect to a computer remotely. If you're a business traveler on the road or a late sleeper working from home, for example, you can dial in from your laptop or home PC (the *local computer*) to the unattended, distant machine (the *remote computer* or *host computer*) in your office to access its files and resources. In this chapter, you'll learn three preferred remote-access techniques:

- Traditional **direct dialing** connects to a faraway PC via phone lines, probably racking up monstrous toll charges.

- **Virtual private networking (VPN)** lets you connect to a PC or network via the internet, thus avoiding long-distance charges.

- **Remote Desktop** lets you control an XP Pro-using remote computer, whose desktop appears on your local PC's screen just as though you were sitting at the remote PC's keyboard.

Dialing Direct

A direct (modem-to-modem) connection requires the remote computer to have a phone line that only it answers. (If a modem answers a voice call, the human caller gets an earful of squeal.) Before making your first call, you must set up both PCs.

To set up the remote computer:

1. Choose Start > Control Panel > Network and Internet Connections > Network Connections.

2. In the task pane at left, click Create a New Connection.
   The New Connection Wizard appears.

3. Click Next to skip the Welcome page.

4. Select Set up an Advanced Connection; then click Next.

5. Select Accept Incoming Connections; then click Next.

6. Check the box for your modem; then click Next (**Figure 18.1**).

7. Select Do Not Allow Virtual Private Connections; then click Next.

8. Check the boxes of the people who should be allowed to dial in to the remote PC; then click Next (**Figure 18.2**).

9. Confirm that all the networking software boxes are checked; then click Next.

10. Click Finish (**Figure 18.3**).
    Now the remote PC's modem answers incoming calls.

✔ Tip

■ In step 8, you can click Properties to turn on the *callback* security feature. This feature makes the remote PC hang up and call you back after you dial in, thwarting impersonators and reducing phone bills. For details, search for *callback* in Help and Support Center.

Figure 18.1 You can click Properties and check Disconnect a Call If Idle for More Than __ Mins to make the remote PC hang up automatically after an inactive period.

Figure 18.2 Don't check Guest; you'd create a security hole.

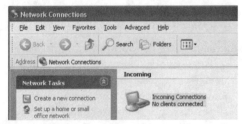

Figure 18.3 A new Incoming Connections icon appears in Network Connections when you finish the wizard. To change settings manually, right-click the icon; then choose Properties.

DIALING DIRECT

Figure 18.4 If you're a laptop user, you can add dialing codes when you actually make the call (in Figure 18.6), depending on what city you're in.

Figure 18.5 A new Dial-Up icon appears in Network Connections when you finish the wizard. To change settings manually, right-click the icon; then choose Properties.

Figure 18.6 Type your name and password exactly as you would if you were logging on to the remote PC in person.

To set up the local computer:

1. Choose Start > Control Panel > Network and Internet Connections > Network Connections.

2. In the task pane at left, click Create a New Connection.
   The New Connection Wizard appears.

3. Click Next to skip the Welcome page.

4. Select Connect to a Network at My Workplace; then click Next.

5. Select Dial-Up Connection; then click Next.

6. Type a connection name (such as *Work computer*); then click Next.

7. Type the phone number of the remote PC; then click Next (**Figure 18.4**).

8. Specify whether you want to add a connection shortcut to your desktop; then click Finish (**Figure 18.5**).
   Windows opens a Connect dialog box to call the remote PC; see the next task.

To make a call:

1. Double-click the desktop shortcut that you created in step 8 of the preceding task.
   or
   Double-click the Dial-Up icon in Network Connections (refer to Figure 18.5).

2. Type your name and password, and verify the phone number (**Figure 18.6**).

3. Click Dial to call the remote PC.
   A notification-area (system-tray) icon and pop-up balloon appear upon connection. You can check email, browse the web, open shared folders, print documents, transfer files to the local PC, and so on.

4. To hang up, right-click the notification-area icon; then choose Disconnect.

DIALING DIRECT

Connecting to a Virtual Private Network Server

A *virtual private network (VPN)* lets you connect from one PC to another securely and privately by using the internet as a conduit. Think of a VPN connection as a small steel pipe, carrying encrypted data, that links two PCs and tunnels *inside* the larger transparent pipe of the internet.

By using an internet connection (Chapter 12), you can travel worldwide and dial your ISP's *local* access number to connect to your far-off PC or network (a good reason for laptop owners to sign up with a national or international ISP). If your remote PC is rooted in place or doesn't move much, a high-speed (DSL or cable) internet connection lets you communicate faster than any dial-up modem call. Together, high-speed lines and VPNs overcome direct dialing's twin evils: slow speeds and high costs.

Setting up a local PC to connect to a VPN server is easy. Setting up a remote PC to act as a VPN server can be another story, especially if it's part of a network. (Most people use VPNs to connect to an administered network at their workplace, rather than to their home PCs.) A VPN server needs an always-on internet connection (DSL or cable) and a static IP address (see the sidebar). The local PC doesn't need these things.

To set up the remote computer as a VPN server:

1. Choose Start > Control Panel > Network and Internet Connections > Network Connections.

2. In the task pane at left, click Create a New Connection.

   The New Connection Wizard appears.

Figure 18.7 If you're using Windows Firewall, Windows changes its settings behind the scenes to allow VPN connections.

3. Click Next to skip the Welcome page.

4. Select Set up an Advanced Connection; then click Next.

5. Select Accept Incoming Connections; then click Next.

6. If the Devices for Incoming Connections page appears (refer to Figure 18.1), click Next.

   These settings don't apply to VPN servers.

7. Select Allow Virtual Private Connections; then click Next (**Figure 18.7**).

continues on next page

IP Addresses and Remote Access

An *IP address* identifies your computer uniquely on the internet for the purposes of communication. A *static* (or *fixed*) IP address is the same every time you connect; a *dynamic* IP address changes each time. An IP address is expressed as four numbers separated by dots: 127.160.0.1, for example.

Most internet connections use dynamic IP addresses. (See the "Why Dynamic IP Addresses?" sidebar in Chapter 12.) That's unfortunate, because remote PCs (but not local PCs) require static IP addresses to work with VPN and Remote Desktop. Furthermore, connecting a private network to the internet requires a *registered* IP address to prevent duplicates. Your ISP or network administrator can give you this information, or you can check yourself: Choose Start > All Programs > Accessories > Command Prompt; type `ipconfig` and then press Enter. Your IP address is *not* registered if it's in these ranges: 10.*x.x.x*, 169.254.*x.x*, 172.16.*x.x*–172.31.*x.x*, and 192.168.*x.x*.

If you don't have a registered, static IP address, your ISP may offer one for an extra fee. Otherwise, you can get a free (or cheap) unchanging alias for a dynamic IP address from a *dynamic DNS service* such as `www.dyndns.org` or `www.easydns.com`. Your chosen DNS name (*yourname*.dyndns.org, for example) is translated automatically into a numerical IP address, which communications software uses.

Another snag: VPN and Remote Desktop work fine with Windows' built-in Windows Firewall and Internet Connection Sharing, but you'll have setup pains if you've installed your own firewall (software or hardware) or router (see "Sharing an Internet Connection" in Chapter 17). All in all, setting up a VPN server or Remote Desktop may require consultation with a bona-fide geek or your router manufacturer.

8. Check the boxes of the people who should be allowed to dial in to the remote PC; then click Next (refer to Figure 18.2).

9. Confirm that all the networking software boxes are checked; then click Next.

10. Click Finish (refer to Figure 18.3).

Now the remote PC listens to the internet for incoming VPN connection requests.

To set up the local computer:

1. Choose Start > Control Panel > Network and Internet Connections > Network Connections.

2. In the task pane at left, click Create a New Connection.

The New Connection Wizard appears.

3. Click Next to skip the Welcome page.

4. Select Connect to a Network at My Workplace; then click Next.

5. Select Virtual Private Network Connection; then click Next.

6. Type a connection name (such as *Work VPN* or the VPN server name); then click Next.

The Public Network page may appear, depending on your Network Connections setup.

7. If you have a dial-up internet connection, select Automatically Dial This Initial Connection; choose the dial-up connection from the drop-down list; then click Next.

or

If you have an always-on internet connection (DSL or cable), select Do Not Dial the Initial Connection; then click Next.

8. On the VPN Server Selection page, type the host name or static IP address of the computer that you want to connect to; then click Next (**Figure 18.8**).

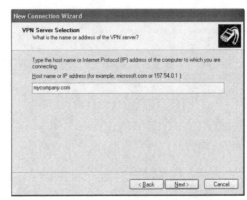

Figure 18.8 If you're connecting to a workplace network, type the host name or the IP address that your network administrator gave you. Or, if you signed up for a dynamic DNS service (see the sidebar in this section), type the host's registered DNS name.

Virtual Private Network

Work VPN
Disconnected
WAN Miniport (PPTP)

Figure 18.9 A new Virtual Private Network icon appears in Network Connections when you finish the wizard. To change settings manually, right-click the icon; then choose Properties.

Figure 18.10 If you don't already have an internet connection open, Windows offers to connect.

9. Specify whether you want to add a connection shortcut to your desktop; then click Finish (**Figure 18.9**).

Windows opens a Connect dialog box to connect to the VPN server; see the next task.

To connect to a VPN server:

1. Double-click the desktop shortcut that you created in step 9 of the preceding task.

or

Double-click the Virtual Private Network icon in Network Connections (refer to Figure 18.9).

2. Type your name and password (**Figure 18.10**).

3. Click Connect to connect to the VPN server.

A notification-area (system-tray) icon and pop-up balloon appear upon connection.

You can check email, browse the web, open shared folders, print documents, transfer files to the local PC, and so on.

4. To hang up, right-click the notification-area icon; then choose Disconnect.

CONNECTING TO A VPN

Controlling a Computer with Remote Desktop

Remote Desktop lets you connect to a remote XP Pro computer and use it as though you were sitting in front of it. Much more than a simple direct-dial or VPN connection, Remote Desktop lets you control the remote PC's full desktop, with its Start menu, taskbar, icons, documents, and programs. Programs run on the remote computer, and only the keyboard input, mouse input, and display output are transmitted over the connection. The *remote computer* is the PC that you want to control from afar. The *local*, or *client, computer* is the one that you'll be sitting at, driving the remote PC. The requirements are:

PRO **Remote computer.** An XP Pro PC with an internet or network connection, or a dial-up modem that's configured to answer incoming calls automatically. If you're connecting over the internet, a registered, static IP address is required (see the sidebar in the preceding section).

Local computer. A PC running any version of Windows since Windows 95 can control the remote PC. This PC must have access to the remote PC via a network, internet, VPN, or dial-up connection.

✔ Tips

- Remote Desktop replaces Windows 2000's Terminal Services.

- You can use Remote Desktop to let someone connect to *your* PC to give you technical help, much like Remote Assistance (Chapter 3), except that you don't have to be present at your PC to accept the connection.

- Try Ultr@VNC (free; http://ultravnc. sourceforge.net), a remote-control program that, unlike Remote Desktop, can control PCs running all Windows versions since Windows 95, not only XP Pro. You also have a few $200 commercial alternatives: Carbon Copy, Close-Up, CoSession, LapLink, and pcAnywhere. Read reviews first; these programs vary in ease of setup, connection options, and response time.

Figure 18.11 Check the bottom box to let other users control this computer remotely.

Figure 18.12 Don't add anybody you don't trust to this list. For security reasons, only users with password-protected accounts can make a Remote Desktop connection.

Your local PC running Windows XP (Home or Pro edition) won't need additional software to control the remote computer. If you use Windows 95, 98, Me, NT 4, or 2000 on the local computer, you must install Remote Desktop Connection client software from the Windows XP Pro CD.

To set up a non-XP local computer:

1. Insert the Windows XP Professional CD into the local PC's drive.

2. When the Welcome to Microsoft Windows XP window appears, click Perform Additional Tasks.

   If this window doesn't appear, open the CD in Windows Explorer; then double-click `setup.exe` in the topmost (root) folder.

3. Click Set up Remote Desktop Connection. The InstallShield Wizard for Remote Desktop Connection appears.

4. Follow the onscreen instructions.

To set up the remote computer:

1. Choose Start > Control Panel > Performance and Maintenance > System (or press Windows logo key + Break); then click the Remote tab.

2. In the Remote Desktop section, check Allow Users to Connect Remotely to This Computer (**Figure 18.11**).

3. Click Select Remote Users to change which users can connect remotely (**Figure 18.12**).

   Initially, the logged-on user and all users with Administrator accounts can connect (see "Setting up User Accounts" in Chapter 16). To add users, click Add; then type one or more user names, separated by semicolons.

continues on next page

CONTROLLING WITH REMOTE DESKTOP

4. Click OK in each of the open dialog boxes.

Now the remote computer listens for incoming Remote Desktop connection requests.

✔ Tip

■ If you're connecting over an internet connection protected by XP's Windows Firewall, take this extra step: Choose Start > Control Panel > Network and Internet Connections > Network Connections; right-click the Internet connection; choose Properties > Advanced tab > Settings button > Services tab; then check Remote Desktop.

To connect to a remote desktop:

1. Connect to the internet normally.

Skip this step if the remote PC is on your local area network.

2. Choose Start > All Programs > Accessories > Communications > Remote Desktop Connection.

The Remote Desktop dialog box appears.

3. Click Options to expand the dialog box, if necessary; then fill in the Logon Settings section (**Figure 18.13**).

Figure 18.13 In the Computer box, type the remote computer's network name, IP address, or registered DNS name. Type your name and password (and domain, if necessary) exactly as you would if you were logging on from the remote PC in person.

4. Click Connect.

Your screen goes black momentarily; then the remote PC's desktop fills the screen, hiding *your* desktop and taskbar (**Figure 18.14**).

Now you can operate the distant PC as though you were sitting in front of it. All your actions—running programs, printing, sending email, whatever— happen on the remote PC.

Anyone looking at the remote PC in person sees a Welcome screen or an Unlock Computer dialog box; that person can't see what you're doing.

Pushpin—Locks this title bar in place or makes it hide automatically

Minimize—Reduces the remote desktop to a taskbar button on your own desktop

Restore—Displays the remote desktop in a floating, resizable window on your own desktop

Close—Disconnects the remote PC but doesn't log off

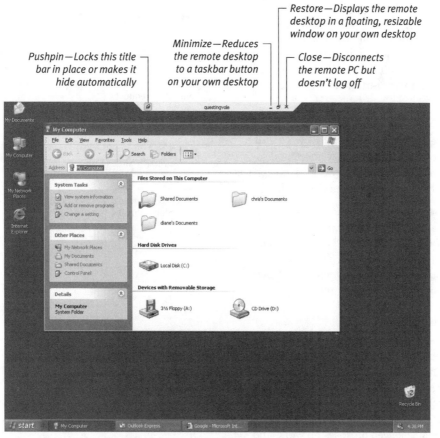

Figure 18.14 A full-screen remote desktop shows a title bar at the screen's top edge, letting you switch between your own desktop and the remote desktop. The title bar retracts from view unless you lock it or move your pointer to the top edge.

CONTROLLING WITH REMOTE DESKTOP

✔ Tips

■ Clicking Restore (refer to Figure 18.14) puts the remote desktop in a floating, resizable window on your *local* desktop (**Figure 18.15**).

■ You can use standard Cut, Copy, and Paste to transfer text, graphics, and files between the two PCs. If both desktops are visible (as in Figure 18.15), you can drag between local and remote windows.

■ Clicking Close (refer to Figure 18.14) disconnects the remote PC but doesn't log it off; it leaves your documents open and programs running, as though you had used Fast User Switching (see "Logging On and Logging Off" in Chapter 1). To pick up where you left off, reconnect via Remote Desktop or log on in person at the remote PC. To log off the remote PC, choose Log Off from *its* Start menu, not yours.

■ To shut down the remote PC, choose Start > Windows Security remotely; then use Task Manager's Shut Down menu to shut down, restart, disconnect, and so on. (The Windows Security command appears only when you're connected remotely.)

■ If someone else is already logged on to the remote PC that you're connecting to, Windows warns you that you're about to bump that person off. The message that you see depends on whether Fast User Switching is enabled on the remote PC (see "Controlling the Logon Process" in Chapter 16):

Fast User Switching is turned on. You'll see **Figure 18.16** when you try to connect. If you click Yes, the other user sees **Figure 18.17** and must respond within seconds or be disconnected without ceremony. Fortunately, that user remains logged on, loses no work, and can resume her session later as she left it, just as in Fast User Switching.

Figure 18.15 Click Restore to show your own desktop. To return to full-screen view, click Maximize in the remote window's title bar.

Figure 18.16 If someone else is logged on to the remote PC, you're given a chance to cancel your connection request.

Figure 18.17 The logged-on user can reject your attempted intrusion.

CONTROLLING WITH REMOTE DESKTOP

Figure 18.18 Clicking Yes here won't make you any friends. The other user is logged off instantly and loses all unsaved work.

Figure 18.19 This vaguely puzzling message means that someone else has logged on to the remote PC in person and disconnected your session. You don't lose your unsaved work.

Table 18.1

Keyboard Shortcuts

LOCAL DESKTOP SHORTCUT	REMOTE DESKTOP SHORTCUT	DESCRIPTION
Alt+Tab	Alt+Page Up	Switches among programs
Alt+Shift+Tab	Alt+Page Down	Switches among programs in reverse order
Alt+Esc	Alt+Insert	Cycles through programs in the order in which they were started
Ctrl+Esc	Alt+Home	Opens the Start menu
Ctrl+Alt+Delete	Ctrl+Alt+End	Displays Task Manager or, for domains, the Windows Security dialog box
N/A	Ctrl+Alt+Break	Switches the remote desktop between a window and full screen
N/A	Alt+Delete	Displays the active window's Control menu

Fast User Switching is turned off.
You'll see **Figure 18.18** when you try to connect. If you click Yes, the other user is logged off without warning and loses all unsaved work.

- If someone logs on to the remote PC in person while *you're* connected, the situation is opposite: *Your* remote session gets bumped off. If Fast User Switching is enabled on the remote PC, you'll see **Figure 18.19,** remain logged on, and lose no unsaved work; you can reconnect after the other party logs off. If Fast User Switching is turned off, you're logged off instantly, losing all unsaved work.

- If the Remote Desktop window is maximized (refer to Figure 18.14), the standard Windows keyboard shortcuts apply to the *remote* computer. Alt+Tab, for example, switches between programs on the distant PC, not your local one. But if the Remote Desktop window is active and floating on your desktop (refer to Figure 18.15), those same shortcuts apply to the *local* PC. (Alt+Tab will switch between locally running programs.) Fortunately, keyboard junkies can use the standard shortcuts in the first column of **Table 18.1** to control the *local* desktop and the second-column shortcuts to perform the equivalent function on an active, floating Remote Desktop window.

- *Before* you connect, you can configure the way Remote Desktop works by using the tabs in the Remote Desktop Connection dialog box. You may want to try a remote session or two before adjusting the default settings.

The **General** tab (refer to Figure 18.13) lets you enter or change logon or connection settings. You can have Windows save your password or all your current settings to speed future connections, which is useful if you connect to multiple PCs.

continues on next page

The **Display** tab (**Figure 18.20**) controls the remote desktop's size (screen resolution) and color depth.

The **Local Resources** tab (**Figure 18.21**) controls sound, keyboard, and local devices.

The **Programs** tab controls which, if any, programs run automatically upon connection.

The **Experience** tab (**Figure 18.22**) lets you tell Windows your connection speed so that it can turn off eye candy to improve performance. When you first used Remote Desktop, for example, you may have noticed that the remote desktop didn't display a background. This time-waster is turned off by default in this tab.

Figure 18.20 The size option is useful if the local and remote screen sizes differ.

Figure 18.21 Use this tab to specify where sounds should play, which PC responds to keyboard shortcuts, and which local devices to display on the remote desktop.

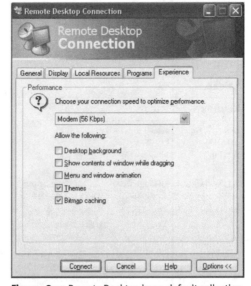

Figure 18.22 Remote Desktop has a default collection of settings for each connection speed, but you can use your own settings.

MAINTENANCE & TROUBLESHOOTING | 19

Periodic checkups and routine maintenance will keep your system running smoothly. In this chapter, you'll learn how to use Windows tools to monitor your PC's health and:

◆ Update Windows XP with the latest bug fixes from Microsoft

◆ Restore your PC to a previous working condition

◆ Keep your hard drives purring

◆ Back up your data

◆ Schedule tasks

◆ Recover from a crash

◆ View or edit the registry

✔ Tip

■ Type troubleshooting in the Help and Support Center index to see a list of Windows' troubleshooting wizards and other tools designed to identify and resolve hardware, software, and networking problems.

Updating Windows XP

Over time, Microsoft publishes patches, bug fixes, and other improvements on its web site. These changes include minor additions to the Windows feature set, upgrades to the freebie programs, and driver updates. The most important changes are those designated *critical updates* or *hotfixes,* which plug security holes or fix stability problems. Periodically, Microsoft combines many of these fixes into a package called a *Service Pack.* (As I write this chapter, Service Pack 2 is the current release.) Installing a Service Pack is equivalent to, and much less trouble than, installing its constituent fixes piecemeal. But you shouldn't wait for an SP to install critical updates, which appear with alarming regularity.

Use Control Panel's Automatic Updates program to choose how and when updates are installed on your PC. You may see pop-up messages in the notification area (system tray) that remind you to set up this feature, but you can adjust its options at any time.

With Service Pack 2, Microsoft updated Automatic Updates and set aggressive default options. Microsoft objects to any setting other than Automatic and will warn you via Security Center (see "Securing Your Computer" in Chapter 12) if you choose anything weaker.

UPDATING WINDOWS XP

Installing Service Pack 2

To see if your PC has SP2 installed, right-click My Computer in the Start menu and choose Properties; the General tab will have the phrase "Service Pack 2" (refer to Figure i.1 in the introduction). PCs purchased in the fall of 2004 or later come with SP2 preinstalled. If you have an older computer, Automatic Updates has probably offered to install SP2. If not, you can go to www.microsoft.com/windowsxp/sp2/default.mspx to download it manually or order it on a free CD (to avoid the giant download). Installation takes between 45 minutes and a few hours. Before you install:

♦ Visit Microsoft's Installing SP2 web page: http://support.microsoft.com/xpsp2getinstall.

♦ Make sure that you have at least 500 MB of free disk space.

♦ Back up your files (described later in this chapter).

♦ Remove all spyware, uninstall antivirus programs, and turn off your firewall (see "Securing Your Computer" in Chapter 12).

♦ Log off everyone but yourself if you're using Fast User Switching (see "Logging On and Logging Off" in Chapter 1).

If you're lucky, SP2's far-reaching changes won't break anything on your computer, but problems range from negligible to serious, such as not being able to start your PC. Microsoft has a few to-the-rescue articles:

♦ http://support.microsoft.com/?kbid=842242, "Some Programs Seem to Stop Working After You Install Windows XP Service Pack 2"

♦ http://support.microsoft.com/?kbid=884130, "Programs That Are Known to Experience a Loss of Functionality When They Run on a Windows XP Service Pack 2-Based Computer"

♦ http://support.microsoft.com/?kbid=885626, "Your Computer Stops Responding When You Restart to Complete the Installation of Windows XP Service Pack 2 or Windows XP Tablet PC Edition 2005"

As a last resort, you can uninstall SP2. It's listed in Control Panel's Add or Remove Programs list (see Figure 19.7 later in this chapter). Microsoft even has an article for that: http://support.microsoft.com/?kbid=875350, "How to Remove Windows XP Service Pack 2 from Your Computer."

To set up Automatic Updates:

1. Choose Start > Control Panel > Performance and Maintenance > System (or press Windows logo key+Break); then click the Automatic Updates tab (**Figure 19.1**).

   or

   Double-click Automatic Updates in Control Panel (if you use classic view).

   or

   In Security Center, click the Automatic Updates icon.

   or

   Choose Start > Run; type `wuaucpl.cpl` and then press Enter.

2. Choose one of the options described in **Table 19.1**.

3. Click OK.

Figure 19.1 Windows can download and install updates without your intervention (first option), ask for your permission (second or third options), or leave everything for you to do manually (fourth option).

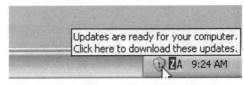

Figure 19.2 This yellow-shield-and-! icon appears when Windows finds an update. Click it to start the update process.

Table 19.1

Automatic Updates Options	
OPTION	DESCRIPTION
Automatic (Recommended)	This set-and-forget option downloads and installs all patches automatically, according to the schedule you choose. This option is appropriate if you have an always-on internet connection (DSL or cable) and you trust Microsoft not to screw up your PC with the update.
Download Updates for Me, but Let Me Choose When to Install Them	The download happens in the background, silently and without interfering with anything that you might be downloading yourself. After download, Windows shows an icon in the notification area (system tray) to get your permission to install the update (**Figure 19.2**). This option lets you research the patch before you install it; try Google or www.annoyances.org to see if it's giving people trouble.
Notify Me but Don't Automatically Download or Install Them	Windows displays a notification-area icon (refer to Figure 19.2) when it detects an update on the Microsoft web site. Click it to download the updates (**Figures 19.3** and **19.4**). When the download completes, the icon reappears, asking to be reclicked to install the updates this time. This option is a good choice for on-the-go laptop users.
Turn off Automatic Updates	No updates occur. Choose this option if you want to update Windows manually (described next) or if you're on a workplace or school network and you update from a network server rather than from Microsoft directly.

Figure 19.3 When you click the icon in Figure 19.2, you're offered a choice: You can just take what Microsoft gives you (first option) or get a description of what you're about to install (second option).

Figure 19.4 If you chose Custom Install in Figure 19.3, this dialog box appears, describing the update(s) in sometimes painful technical language. Review the list; uncheck specific updates (if you like); then click Download (or Install) to proceed.

Figure 19.5 Some updates require you to restart your computer. You don't have to right away (click Close instead of Restart Now), but the updates won't kick in until you do.

✔ Tips

■ When an update completes successfully, **Figure 19.5** appears.

■ You don't get any update notifications unless you're an Administrator (see "Setting up User Accounts" in Chapter 16).

■ If you decline to install an update and change your mind later, click Offer Updates Again That I've Previously Hidden at the bottom of the Automatic Updates tab (visible in Figure 19.1).

■ If you ignore Automatic Updates when it's ready to install an update and try to shut down, Windows shows you the Install Updates and Shut Down option as the default choice in the Shut Down Windows dialog box (**Figure 19.6**). This option ends your session, installs updates, and then shuts down Windows normally. You're still free to choose any of the other shut-down options (see "Logging On and Logging Off" in Chapter 1).

continues on next page

Figure 19.6 Microsoft won't let you escape easily from updates. This shut-down option appears on computers with Service Pack 2 installed and Automatic Updates turned on.

- To view a list of installed updates (or to uninstall an update), choose Start > Control Panel > Add or Remove Programs. The program list (**Figure 19.7**) becomes crowded with updates over time, so SP2 hides them in the Windows XP – Software Updates category. Check Show Updates at the top of the dialog box to reveal them. (See also "Removing Programs" in Chapter 6.)

If you've turned off Automatic Updates because you don't want your PC to contact the mother ship without your permission, you can use Windows Update to visit the Microsoft Update web site and update manually.

Figure 19.7 The program list in the Add or Remove Programs dialog box groups updates. Note that Service Pack 2 appears as a separate, ungrouped entry.

To update Windows manually:

1. Choose Start > All Programs > Windows Update.

    or

    In Internet Explorer, choose Tools > Windows Update.

2. Detour: If a Security Warning dialog box appears, click Yes to install the latest version of Windows Update Control; then restart your computer and begin again.

3. On the Windows Update home page, click Express Install (Recommended) to let Microsoft scan for, download, and install only the critical and security updates that your computer needs.

    or

    Click Custom Install to review all the updates on the site before downloading.

4. Follow the onscreen instructions.

    Eventually, you'll land on the Install Updates page.

5. Click Install to start the update process. You may have to accept a license agreement and restart your PC.

✔ Tips

■ Typically, you can install a critical update only by itself, separately from noncritical ones. Run Windows Update again to install the noncritical updates.

■ Windows Update works with only Internet Explorer.

■ The General tab of Control Panel's System dialog box will tell you the edition, version, and Service Pack of your Windows XP copy.

■ If you're an administrator who has to update several computers on a network, click the Administrator Options link when you first arrive at the Windows Update web page.

Updating Device Drivers

Windows Update can provide new device drivers for your PC's hardware. Unlike the other types of updates, this one should be approached skeptically, because Windows Update has a habit of recommending the wrong drivers for some hardware.

I recommend that you install Microsoft drivers for only Microsoft hardware, such as mice, keyboards, and game controllers. For other products, download drivers from the manufacturers' web sites directly. And don't be surprised if the sites don't offer an updated driver; it means only that Windows Update guessed wrong about your equipment. For details, see "Installing a New Device" in Chapter 8.

UPDATING WINDOWS XP

Getting System Information

System Information compiles and reports information about your PC's hardware, drivers, system resources, and internet settings. This overview saves you from visiting scores of Control Panel dialog boxes to see how your PC is configured. You can find information quickly to give to a techie who's trouble-shooting your system.

To display system data:

1. Choose Start > All Programs > Accessories > System Tools > System Information.

2. Use the Explorer-like tree to display information in the various categories (**Figure 19.8**):

   Hardware Resources displays hardware settings, such as IRQs and memory addresses. The Conflicts/Sharing view identifies devices that are sharing resources or are in conflict.

   Components displays Windows config- uration information for device drivers, as well as networking and multimedia software.

   Software Environment displays a snap- shot of the software loaded into computer memory. Use this information to see whether a process is still running or to check version information.

   Internet Settings displays browser- related security, connection, and version data.

Figure 19.8 To find system data, type a search phrase in the Find What box at the bottom of the window; check the appropriate search-option boxes; then click Find.

✔ Tips

- To get system information for a different computer on your network, choose View > Remote Computer.

- To save system data in a System Information file—which you can archive or email to a techie to open in his copy of System Information—choose File > Save. To save system data in a text file, choose File > Export.

- File > Print produces a 50-page printout. It makes more sense to export the data to a text file and print your choice of sec- tions in Notepad.

Figure 19.9 This tab shows all programs (including background tasks) running on your PC. Click a column header to sort by that column; this display is sorted by memory use.

Figure 19.10 This tab shows real-time graphs of the load on your CPU and virtual memory, expressed as a percentage of capacity.

Managing Tasks

Task Manager is one of the most useful tools in Windows. It displays running programs, background processes, performance statistics, network activity, and user information. It also can shut down misbehaving programs.

To start Task Manager:

1. Right-click an empty area on the taskbar; then choose Task Manager (or press Ctrl+Shift+Esc).

2. Click any of the following tabs:

   Applications for a list of foreground applications and the status of each one. See also "Killing Unresponsive Programs" in Chapter 6.

   Processes for a list of all programs running on your computer, including background programs and those shown in the Applications tab (**Figure 19.9**).

   Performance for real-time graphs and statistics that show your system's performance (**Figure 19.10**).

   Networking is similar to the Performance tab, except that it shows real-time graphs of network traffic.

   Users displays logged-on users and the status of each one. See "Logging On and Logging Off" in Chapter 1.

✔ Tips

■ Use the Options and View menus to select preferences. These menus' commands change depending on the selected tab.

■ Turn on Options > Always on Top to make Task Manager remain in front of all other windows unless it's minimized.

■ You can right-click an entry in the Applications, Processes, or Users tab for a shortcut menu.

■ The Processes tab lists filenames, not application names. Internet Explorer appears as iexplore.exe, for example.

MANAGING TASKS

491

Restoring Your System

If your system stops running correctly or becomes persistently unstable—thanks to an incompatible program, faulty driver, or bad system setting, or for no apparent reason—use System Restore to return your computer's configuration to its previous, working state without risk to personal documents, email, cookies, and Favorites. System Restore protects only Windows *system* files and settings; use Backup (described later in this chapter) to protect your personal data files and documents.

System Restore runs invisibly in the background, monitoring and taking snapshots of critical system files and registry entries. These snapshots, called *restore points,* are created the first time that you boot XP and daily thereafter; every time that you install a program through Windows Installer or InstallShield; or whenever Windows Update or Automatic Updates runs. Before you make a major change to your system or its settings, you can create a restore point manually.

To create a restore point manually:

1. Choose Start > All Programs > Accessories > System Tools > System Restore (**Figure 19.11**).

2. On the Welcome page, select Create a Restore Point; then click Next.

3. On the Create a Restore Point page, type a name for the restore point; then click Create (**Figure 19.12**).
   Windows creates a restore point and adds the current date and time to its description.

4. Click Close.

Figure 19.11 Create a restore point before you install an iffy driver or program, or change the registry.

Figure 19.12 Give the restore point a meaningful name.

✔ Tip

- You can't rely on System Restore to protect you from viruses. By the time you discover the infection, it may have spread to other files that System Restore doesn't touch, in which case rolling back does you no good. Use an antivirus program instead (see "Securing Your Computer" in Chapter 12).

Figure 19.13 By default, System Restore monitors changes to every drive on your system and reserves 12 percent of each drive to archive restore points.

Figure 19.14 Drag the slider to the left to reclaim disk space from System Restore (but reduce the number of saved restore points). In general, don't set this value below 5 percent.

System Restore is turned on by default, using up to a hefty 12 percent of each hard drive to store copies of your system configuration. That's almost 5 GB of a 40 GB drive. You can allocate less space or turn off System Restore.

To configure System Restore:

1. Choose Start > Control Panel > Performance and Maintenance > System > System Restore tab (**Figure 19.13**).

2. Adjust any of the following settings:

   To turn off System Restore, check Turn off System Restore on All Drives.

   To change the disk space allocated to restore points, click a drive in the Available Drives list; click Settings; drag the Disk Space to Use slider to change the allocation; then click OK (**Figure 19.14**).

   To turn off System Restore on a specific drive, check Turn off System Restore on This Drive in Figure 19.14. You can turn off System Restore safely for nonsystem drives that store only documents or backup files.

3. Click OK (or Apply).

✔ Tips

■ Turning off System Restore, even for an instant, erases existing restore points.

■ System Restore deletes restore points older than 90 days automatically.

■ System Restore requires at least 200 MB of free disk space. When a drive runs low on space, System Restore turns itself off automatically and silently, losing all that drive's restore points. If you receive a "low disk space" warning for a drive, check that drive's status in Figure 19.13 to see whether it's listed as Suspended. System Restore turns itself back on when you free enough space.

■ On each drive, Windows stores backup configurations in the hidden/system folder System Volume Information, which you can unhide but not move, rename, or delete.

RESTORING YOUR SYSTEM

When your PC behaves badly, you can return Windows to one of the restore points that System Restore, or you, created. But do so only as a last resort. Remember, if a driver upgrade doesn't work out, you can roll back *just* the driver rather than your entire system. See "Managing Device Drivers" in Chapter 8.

To restore your system:

1. Choose Start > Help and Support.

2. In the Pick a Task section, click Undo Changes to Your Computer with System Restore.

3. On the Welcome page, select Restore My Computer to an Earlier Time; then click Next (refer to Figure 19.11).

4. On the Select a Restore Point page, on the calendar, click the boldface date on which your computer last worked properly.

5. Click one of the restore points listed to the right of the calendar; then click Next (**Figure 19.15**).

6. Heed the warning to save your changes and close any open programs; then click Next. System Restore rewinds your system and restarts Windows automatically.

7. Click OK in the Restoration Complete window that appears after you log on (**Figure 19.16**).

✔ Tips

- If restoring the system didn't fix your problem (or made it worse), you can repeat the process and choose a restore point farther back in the past. Or you can undo the restoration: Select Undo My Last Restoration in step 2 (refer to Figure 19.11); then follow the onscreen instructions.

- If you have a severe startup problem, run System Restore in safe mode. See "Recovering After a Crash" later in this chapter.

Figure 19.15 System Restore stores several weeks of restore points, depending on how much space you've allocated to it. Boldface days indicate restore points. Click the < and > buttons to move through the months.

Figure 19.16 Success. Now check your system to see whether it's running correctly.

Figure 19.17 Disk Cleanup searches your drive and then shows you temporary files, internet cache files, and unnecessary program files that you can delete safely.

Cleaning up a Disk

Over time, your hard disk will accumulate temporary files, stale components, recycled junk, and space-wasters that you can remove safely. Use Disk Cleanup to reclaim disk space if you're running out of room.

To remove unneeded files:

1. Choose Start > All Programs > Accessories > System Tools > Disk Cleanup; select a drive (if you have more than one); then click OK.

   or

   Right-click a drive icon in My Computer; then choose Properties > General tab > Disk Cleanup.

   or

   Choose Start > Run; type cleanmgr and press Enter; select a drive; then click OK.

2. In the Disk Cleanup dialog box, check the boxes of the files that you want to delete (**Figure 19.17**).

   The right column shows how much space you can make available. The text below the list box describes the selected option.

3. Click OK.

✔ Tips

- The More Options tab contains three other cleanup tools that let you remove optional Windows components, installed programs, and all but your most recent System Restore restore point.

- Avoid deleting Downloaded Program Files, which often are useful add-ons.

- The Temporary Files option deletes only temporary files more than one week old, so the right column may show 0 KB even if your temporary folder contains many files. To clean out this folder manually, close all programs; choose Start > Run; type %temp% and press Enter; then delete the files in the folder window that appears.

- A few other disk cleaners: Empty Temp Folders (free; www.danish-shareware.dk/soft/emptemp) and DLL Archive (free; www.analogx.com/contents/download/system/dllarch.htm).

Figure 19.18 Defragmentation is a time-consuming process; don't bother for drives that are only slightly fragmented. To see the extent of the fragmentation, click View Report for a...

Figure 19.19 ...list of fragmented files and the number of pieces they're in.

Figure 19.20 For best results, do nothing during the delicate defragmentation process. If you must do something, click Pause. (A better defragmenter is Diskeeper [$30 U.S.; www.execsoft.com].)

Defragmenting a Disk

When a file grows, it won't fit back into its original disk location and becomes physically fragmented into noncontiguous pieces on the disk. As more files become fragmented, Windows has to retrieve the chopped-up pieces and reassemble them, impairing the disk's performance and reliability. Disk Defragmenter consolidates fragmented files, making both files and free space contiguous. Large blocks of available space make it less likely that new files will be fragmented.

To defragment a disk:

1. Exit all programs; turn off antivirus software; then run Disk Cleanup.

2. Choose Start > All Programs > Accessories > System Tools > Disk Defragmenter.

   or

   Right-click a drive icon in My Computer; then choose Properties > Tools tab > Defragment Now.

   or

   Choose Start > Run; type dfrg.msc and then press Enter.

3. Click a drive to defragment.

4. Click Analyze.

   The program analyzes the disk and makes a recommendation (**Figures 19.18** and **19.19**).

5. Click Defragment to start defragmentation (**Figure 19.20**).

   Colored graphs and the status bar display defragmentation progress.

6. Click Close in the dialog box that appears when defragmentation completes.

7. Choose File > Exit, or defragment other disks as necessary.

DEFRAGMENTING A DISK

497

Checking for Disk Errors

Improper Windows shutdowns—usually caused by power outages, mechanical problems, or system crashes (blue screens)—may create defects on disk surfaces. These errors can cause numerous problems, such as random crashes, data corruption, or the inability to save or open files. Check Disk, a more powerful upgrade to the Windows 9*x* ScanDisk utility, scans the disk surface for errors and fixes any that it finds.

To detect and repair disk errors:

1. Exit all programs.

2. Right-click a drive icon in My Computer; then choose Properties > Tools tab > Check Now (**Figure 19.21**).

3. Check or uncheck the following boxes:

   Automatically Fix File System Errors. Check this box to make Windows repair any errors it finds; if it's unchecked, errors are merely *reported*, not fixed. If the disk is in use, or if you're checking the system disk (the one with Windows on it), you'll see **Figure 19.22;** click Yes to defer the scan until the next time you restart your PC.

   Scan for and Attempt Recovery of Bad Sectors. Check this box to make Windows recover readable files and folders it finds in the disk's defective sections and move them elsewhere on the disk. This option fixes errors as well, even if the other option is unchecked. Unrepairable sections are locked out of available storage.

4. Click Start to begin the checking process. The progress bar indicates the phase Check Disk is in. When all phases are complete, a dialog box tells you how things turned out.

Figure 19.21 Check Disk works best for NTFS-formatted drives. See the appendix.

Figure 19.22 This message appears if the disk is in use. Check Disk runs the next time you restart your system. The disk won't be available for other tasks during the check.

✔ Tip

■ The best protection against disk dings from power fluctuation is an Uninterruptible Power Supply (UPS). See "Conserving Power" in Chapter 4.

CHECKING FOR DISK ERRORS

Figure 19.23 Drive Management is a cog in the larger machine named Computer Management, which groups many tools described elsewhere in this book. Click a tool in the left pane's console tree to open it.

Managing Disks

Disk Management is a system utility that lets you inspect and manage hard disks. You can use it to initialize a disk; create partitions; and format partitions with FAT, FAT32, or NTFS file systems on *new* hardware. Otherwise, use Disk Management to assess a disk's health, assign drive letters, format, and perform related tasks.

To open Disk Management:

1. Choose Start > Control Panel > Performance and Maintenance > Administrative Tools > Computer Management; then click Disk Management in the left pane (**Figure 19.23**).

   or

   In the Start menu, right-click My Computer; choose Manage; then click Disk Management in the left pane.

   or

   Choose Start > Run; type `diskmgmt.msc` and then press Enter.

2. Right-click any disk or partition for a list of commands, or use the View menu to specify how disks are displayed.

What's a Partition?

A *partition,* or *volume,* is a portion of a physical disk that functions as though it were a separate disk. After you create a partition, you must format it and assign it a drive letter before you can store data on it.

Every hard disk has one partition, but you can create several on one disk, mainly to:

◆ Separate files and folders from the operating system, keeping your personal documents safe if an OS upgrade turns ugly.

◆ Create dual boot systems with multiple OSes. See "Performing a Clean Install or a Dual-Boot Install" in the appendix.

Unfortunately, Disk Management is lazy and *erases* a hard disk before partitioning it, which makes it suitable—in real terms—for blank or new disks only. If you want to create or resize partitions without erasing everything, buy PartitionMagic ($70 U.S.; `www.powerquest.com/partitionmagic`).

Backing up Your Files

The love that you shower on your hard drive isn't requited. Eventually it will betray you and fail catastrophically, taking your data with it. Avoid the heartbreak by making regular backup copies of your work. Backups also protect you against accidental deletions and let you archive finished projects for remote storage.

Windows' Backup program lets you back up an entire hard disk or specified files and folders periodically. You can back up to a second local drive, a shared network folder, or a high-capacity storage device such as an external USB or tape drive. Never back up to a different partition on the same physical hard drive, because if the drive fails, all partitions go with it. The Backup or Restore Wizard walks you through the process of backing up your files or restoring backed-up files when disaster strikes.

✔ Tips

- If you store your files on a network server at work, you don't have to back up your work. Your network administrator does it for you.

- Backup won't write directly to CD recorders, but you can create a backup file and burn it on a CD.

Floppy Disks

If you use USB flash drives or CD-RWs, or if your PC is connected to a network or the internet, you probably have little use for floppy disks. They're still useful for backing up or transporting small files, however, and some programs use them to create setup or emergency disks. Most floppies come preformatted and ready for use, but you can format one manually (or erase an already-formatted one):

1. Insert a floppy into its drive.

2. In Windows Explorer or My Computer, right-click the drive's icon, labeled 3 1/2 Floppy (A:); then choose Format.

3. Choose a size from the Capacity list (usually, 1.44 MB).

4. Click Start.

To copy a floppy disk, follow the preceding steps, but choose Copy Disk from the shortcut menu in step 2; then choose where you want the copy to be made.

Figure 19.24 Windows XP Home users must install Backup manually.

Figure 19.25 Backup lets you back up or restore your files.

Backup is installed by default on XP Pro edition PCs but not on Home edition PCs.

To install Backup on a Windows XP Home edition computer:

1. Insert the Windows XP Home CD.

2. When the Welcome screen appears, click Exit.

3. Choose Start > My Computer.

4. In the My Computer window, right-click the CD drive icon; then choose Explore.

5. In the Explorer window, navigate to the folder \VALUEADD\MSFT\NTBACKUP; then double-click NTBACKUP.MSI (**Figure 19.24**).

6. Click Finish when the wizard completes the installation.

To back up files:

1. Exit all programs (because Backup can't back up open files).

2. Choose Start > All Programs > Accessories > System Tools > Backup. The Backup or Restore Wizard starts.

3. Click Next to skip the Welcome page.

4. On the Backup or Restore page, select Back up Files and Settings; then click Next (**Figure 19.25**).

continues on next page

BACKING UP YOUR FILES

5. On the What to Back Up page, specify the items to back up; then click Next.

   My Documents and Settings. Backs up your entire user profile (see "Managing User Profiles" in Chapter 16), including your My Documents folder and your desktop contents and settings.

   Everyone's Documents and Settings. Backs up everyone's user profile—in other words, the entire Documents and Settings folder.

   All Information on This Computer. Creates a monster backup of every file on the PC—including Windows XP itself, which is largely pointless for system disks, because you have those files on the Windows CD.

   Let Me Choose What to Back Up. Displays **Figure 19.26** when you click Next, letting you pick specific folders and files to back up.

6. Specify a location and name for the backup; then click Next (**Figure 19.27**).

   Unless you have an XP-compatible tape drive, the Backup Type option is File; you have no other choices.

7. Click Finish to begin the backup immediately (skip to step 11), or click Advanced to choose the additional options.

Figure 19.26 Click the plus sign in the tree to expand the list of drives and folders. Check the box of each item to back up. You can drag the vertical separator bar to resize the panels.

Figure 19.27 Backing up to floppies, the default target, is absurd given today's hard-disk sizes. Click Browse to choose a Zip, USB flash, local, network, or other drive.

Table 19.2

Advanced Backup Types	
TYPE	DESCRIPTION
Normal	Backs up all the selected files and marks them as backed up, letting subsequent Incremental and Differential backups copy only those files that have changed since their Normal backup.
Copy	Backs up all the selected files but doesn't mark them as backed up.
Incremental	Backs up only files that have changed since the last Normal backup and marks them as backed up. Incremental backups are very fast to perform but very slow to restore; you must restore your last Normal backup and each succeeding Incremental backup.
Differential	Backs up the same files as an Incremental backup but doesn't mark them as backed up. Differential backups are moderately fast to perform and to restore; you must restore your last Normal backup and only the most recent Differential backup.
Daily	Backs up files that you created or changed today but doesn't mark them as backed up. This setting is handy for copying a day's work without interfering with your regular backup schedule.

8. If you clicked Advanced in the preceding step, select one of the backup types listed in **Table 19.2**; then click Next.

9. Work your way through the rest of the wizard, selecting the desired options (described in each window).

10. On the last page, review your settings; then click Finish to start the backup.

The process takes minutes or hours, depending on the backup size and type.

11. Click Close in the Backup Progress dialog box when the backup completes.

Backup creates a .bkf file, using the name and location you specified in step 6.

✔ Tips

- In Figure 19.26, expand My Computer and click System State to back up your boot files, registry, and other system components, letting you restore the *exact* state of your PC at the time you did the backup.

- If an error message appears, click Report in the Backup Progress dialog box for a record of what went wrong.

- If you choose to run the backup at a later time (by using the advanced options in step 9), Windows can create a scheduled task that you can edit manually. See "Scheduling Tasks" later in this chapter.

BACKING UP YOUR FILES

503

To restore backed-up files:

1. Choose Start > All Programs > Accessories > System Tools > Backup. The Backup or Restore Wizard starts.

2. Click Next to skip the Welcome page.

3. Select Restore Files and Settings; then click Next (refer to Figure 19.25).

4. Select the files and folders that you want to restore; then click Next (**Figure 19.28**).

5. Click Finish to begin the restore immediately (skip to step 9), or click Advanced to choose additional options.

6. If you clicked Advanced in the preceding step, specify where to restore your backed-up files and folders; then click Next.

   Select **Original Location** if you're restoring damaged or lost files.

   Select **Alternate Location** and specify a location if you need some old files but don't want to overwrite any of the current files or folders on your disk.

   Select **Single Folder** and specify a folder if you're searching for a file and don't know its location. (This option doesn't retain the structure of the backed-up folders and files.)

Figure 19.28 Click Browse to select the source drive that contains your backup. Use the tree view to select the backed-up files and folders to restore, exactly as you did in Figure 19.26.

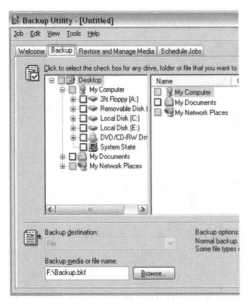

Figure 19.29 Use Backup Utility to back up and restore files without slogging through the Backup or Restore Wizard.

7. Specify whether you want Backup to overwrite existing files; then click Next.

Leave Existing Files (Recommended), the safest method, won't overwrite files already on your hard disk.

Replace Existing Files If They Are Older Than the Backup File ensures that you won't lose any changes that you've made to files since you last backed up your data.

Replace Existing Files restores *every* backed-up file on your hard drive. You'll lose any changes made to those files since your last backup.

8. Accept the default settings in the next screen (the options are quite technical); then click Next.

9. On the last page, review your settings; then click Finish to start the restore.

10. Click Close in the Restore Progress dialog box when the restore completes.

✔ Tips

■ To back up and restore without the Backup and Restore Wizard, click Advanced Mode in the wizard's opening page to make **Figure 19.29** appear.

■ If an error message appears, click Report in the Restore Progress dialog box for a record of what went wrong.

■ It's wise to restore backups regularly to a test folder to confirm that they're working properly.

BACKING UP YOUR FILES

505

Real-Life Backups

Windows' Backup program isn't adequate for orderly backups (for one thing, it can't back up to writable CDs or DVDs), so serious backer-uppers use third-party programs and have multiple backup strategies. Some popular backup schemes are:

Traditional backup. Copies selected files on a regular schedule to a target such as an external drive or network server.

Zip archives. Copies selected files to a compressed Zip file to be stored on an external drive or network server.

Online backup service. Copies selected files over an internet connection to a remote server.

Cloning. Creates an exact byte-for-byte replica of your hard drive on a different physical drive.

Disk imaging. Creates an exact snapshot of your hard drive or partition, including all programs, documents, settings, and data.

Rollback. Maintains copies of files so that you can roll back to earlier versions of drivers or other files. (See "Managing Device Drivers" in Chapter 8, for example.)

You can find backup software information and reviews on the web. For starters, read "Choosing Backup Software" at `http://db.tidbits.com/getbits.acgi?tbart=07912` (it's a Mac article, but it applies to PCs as well), and search for *backups* at `www.pcmag.com`.

Don't store your only backup on the same premises as the original, lest a fire destroy both. One tactic: Keep daily backups in a fireproof box purchased from an office-supply store; then make weekly trips to a safe-deposit box to swap your penultimate backup with the latest one.

The poor man's online backup system uses free high-capacity email accounts (a Google Gmail address has 1 GB of storage, for example). With WinZip or PKZip, create an encrypted Zip archive of backup files, and mail it to yourself. Let it sit on the server until your next backup. (If you have an iPod, you can back up to that too; it's really just a portable hard drive.)

REAL-LIFE BACKUPS

Defrag

Locates and consolidates fragmented boot files, data files, and folders on local volumes.

Syntax

defrag *volume*
defrag *volume* [**/a**]
defrag *volume* [**/a**] [**/v**]
defrag *volume* [**/v**]
defrag *volume* [**/f**]

Parameters

volume
 The drive letter or a mount point of the volume to be defragmented.

/a
 Analyzes the volume and displays a summary of the analysis report.

/v
 Displays the complete analysis and defragmentation reports.

 When used in combination with **/a**, displays only the analysis report. When used alone, displays both the analysis and defragmentation reports.

/f
 Forces defragmentation of the volume regardless of whether it needs to be defragmented.

/?
 Displays help at the command prompt.

Figure 19.30 Help and Support Center's description of the defrag command and its command-line options. The command defrag C: /f defragments your C: drive, for example

Figure 19.31 The first few times that you schedule a new task, you may want to double-click Add Scheduled Task for a wizard to walk you through the process.

Scheduling Tasks

Periodic maintenance and backups aren't useful unless they actually occur periodically—and human memory often fails here. Scheduled Tasks, which starts and runs each time you start Windows, can schedule programs to run according to a schedule that you specify.

Now things become more technical. It does you no good simply to *open* a program on schedule; you must specify the command name and command-line options that make it run to completion without your intervention. A *command name* is a program's filename as typed at a command prompt (choose Start > All Programs > Accessories > Command Prompt). Disk Defragmenter's command name is defrag, and Backup's is ntbackup, for example. *Command-line options,* or *switches,* are space-separated parameters—prefixed by a - or / character—that follow the command name and control that command's behavior. Search for *command-line reference* in Help and Support Center to find commands, their switches, and examples (**Figure 19.30**).

To schedule a new task:

1. Choose Start > All Programs > Accessories > System Tools > Scheduled Tasks.

2. Right-click an empty area in the Scheduled tasks window; then choose New > Scheduled Task (**Figure 19.31**).

3. Type a name for the task; then press Enter.

continues on next page

4. Double-click the new task.

5. On the Task tab (**Figure 19.32**), in the Run box, type the command to run as the scheduled task.

If necessary, include command-line options and a pathname (see "Exploring Your Computer" in Chapter 5). If the pathname includes spaces, type double quotation marks (") around the entire command.

If the command requires an Administrator to run, and you're not one, type an Administrator's user name in the Run As box; then click Set Password. (Blank passwords are forbidden.) If you're on an XP Pro domain, type *domain_name\user_name*.

6. On the Schedule tab (**Figure 19.33**), specify when and how often to run the task.

7. On the Settings tab (**Figure 19.34**), set the conditions under which the task will run.

8. Click OK (or Apply).

Now the task will run according to schedule, even if somebody else (or nobody) is logged on.

Figure 19.32 In this tab, specify the program that you want to run on a schedule.

Figure 19.33 Click Advanced if you want to set a task's start and end date or make it run repeatedly at specified intervals.

SCHEDULING TASKS

Figure 19.34 Don't just accept some of the nonsensical factory settings on this tab; you should stop a task if it runs for a few hours (not 72, as Microsoft suggests). The bottom section is for laptop users.

✔ Tips

- Choose View > Details to see schedule information for all tasks, including the earlier and next run times. A 0 or 0x0 in the Last Result column means that a task ran successfully; any other value represents an error.

- The Advanced menu offers some not-very-advanced commands. Use it to pause all scheduled tasks, shut down Task Scheduler, or notify you of missed tasks.

- To run a task on demand, right-click it; then choose Run.

- You can place multiple commands in a text file with a .bat extension and run this *batch file* as a single task instead of running each command individually.

- Double-click the taskbar clock to confirm that the system date and time on your computer are accurate. Scheduled Tasks relies on this information.

- At the command prompt, type a command followed by -? (or /?) to see its command-line options. Type `defrag -?`, for example.

- Command-prompt junkies can use the `at` command instead of Scheduled Tasks.

SCHEDULING TASKS

Recovering After a Crash

If you've installed a criminally faulty driver or program, and Windows won't boot—perhaps greeting you with a black screen (symbolizing thick smoke) instead of the Windows logo—you can invoke the Windows *startup menu* to recover from catastrophe. This menu takes a little fancy fingerwork to bring up.

To use the startup menu:

1. Restart your computer.

2. When the computer startup messages finish (and before the Windows XP screen appears), tap the F8 key repeatedly until the Windows Advanced Options menu appears (**Figure 19.35**).

   If you have a dual-boot system, use the arrow keys to select the OS that you need; then press Enter.

3. Use the arrow keys to select a startup option; then press Enter.

   Table 19.3 lists the most appropriate options.

```
Windows Advanced Options Menu
Please select an option:

 Safe Mode
 Safe Mode with Networking
 Safe Mode with Command Prompt

 Enable Boot Logging
 Enable VGA Mode
 Last Known Good Configuration (
 Directory Services Restore Mode
 Debugging Mode

 Start Windows Normally
 Reboot
 Return to OS Choices Menu

Use the up and down arrow keys to mo
```

Figure 19.35 If Windows won't boot, this screen gives you an excellent chance of recovering.

Table 19.3

Startup Menu Options	
OPTION	DESCRIPTION
Safe Mode	Starts Windows with only its fundamental files, drivers, and components. Only your mouse, keyboard, monitor, and disk drives will work. A generic video driver makes everything appear in jaggy 640x480 screen resolution. Safe mode lets you run most essential configuration and troubleshooting tools, including Device Manager, System Restore, Registry Editor, Backup, Services, and Help and Support. You can uninstall a program or driver that you suspect is causing the problems.
Safe Mode with Networking	Offers the same functions as safe mode, plus access to your network connections. Use this mode if you need files or drivers from another PC on the network. This mode won't work for laptops that connect via a PC Card network adapter; PC Card drivers are disabled in safe mode.
Safe Mode with Command Prompt	Loads the same set of services as safe mode but displays only the command prompt instead of the Windows graphical interface. This mode is for command-line geeks only.
Enable VGA Mode	Starts the PC with the safe-mode VGA driver but doesn't invoke any other part of safe mode. Use this option to boot past a bogus video driver.
Last Known Good Configuration	Starts the PC by using the registry information and drivers that were in effect the last time your PC was working, effectively undoing the changes that caused the problems. (This is the old Windows 2000 system rollback option; System Restore is preferable, because it restores OS system files too.)
Start Windows Normally	Starts Windows in the usual way.
Reboot	Restarts the computer.
Return to OS Choices Menu	Backs up to the screen that lets you choose the operating system. Most people have only one choice: Windows XP.

RECOVERING AFTER A CRASH

Figure 19.36 Windows stores its configuration information in a database (the registry). Registry Editor organizes the data in tree format.

Editing the Registry

Windows stores its configuration information in a large database called the *registry*, containing all user profiles and information about system hardware; programs, documents, and drivers; and property settings. Windows references this information and updates it quietly and continually. That's why Help and Support Center warns: "Incorrectly editing the registry may severely damage your system. Before making changes to the registry, you should back up any valued data on your computer."

Lots of books, magazines, web sites, and geeks, however, offer useful tips that involve registry changes. As long as you have precise instructions, editing the registry is easy— it's common even for beginners—but if you don't want to take any chances, go to http://support.microsoft.com/?kbid=256986, "Description of the Microsoft Windows Registry," and http://support.microsoft.com/?kbid=322756, "How to Back up, Edit, and Restore the Registry in Windows XP and Windows Server 2003."

To edit the registry:

1. Choose Start > Run; type regedit and then press Enter.

   Registry Editor opens.

2. In the left pane, use the Explorer-like tree to navigate to the desired folder (**Figure 19.36**).

   continues on next page

3. Double-click an entry (called a *key*) in the right pane; edit its value; then click OK (**Figure 19.37**).

✔ Tips

■ Visit www.winguides.com/registry and www.annoyances.org for registry tricks and tweaks that enhance Windows.

■ The registry replaces autoexec.bat, config.sys, and most of the initialization (.ini) files used in earlier Windows versions.

■ Over time the registry will become clogged with bad entries from misapplied tweaks, program errors, and partially uninstalled programs. You can clean the registry with SystemRegistry, part of Fix-It Utilities ($50 U.S.; www.v-com.com) or Easy Cleaner (free; http://personal. inet.fi/business/toniarts/ecleane.htm).

Figure 19.37 Double-click a registry key to edit it.

INSTALLING WINDOWS XP

If your PC came with Windows XP installed, you may be able to use it for the life of the machine without ever referring to this appendix. But if you're upgrading to XP from Windows 98, Me, 2000, or NT, this appendix will show you how to install your new operating system. Tinkerers and hobbyists will find useful information here too; a clean Windows installation is the last word in restoring the speed of a computer that has grown slow with accumulated software glitches, partially uninstalled programs, and other baggage. Read on to learn the particulars of the Windows Setup program.

Getting Ready to Install Windows XP

Before you stick that Windows XP CD into your drive, you'll need to do some planning and make a few decisions. This section describes the steps to take and information to gather before installation. (You'll need a pen to write things down.) Some steps are only for those of you upgrading from a previous Windows version.

Check system requirements

The Windows XP box lists these minimal hardware requirements:

◆ PC with 300 megahertz (MHz) or higher processor clock speed recommended, 233 MHz minimum required; Intel Pentium/Celeron family, AMD K6/Athlon/Duron family, or compatible processor recommended

◆ 64 megabytes (MB) of RAM supported, 128 MB or higher recommended

◆ 1.5 gigabytes (GB) of available hard disk space

◆ Super VGA (800x600) or higher-resolution video adapter and monitor

◆ CD-ROM or DVD drive

◆ Keyboard and Microsoft Mouse or compatible pointing device

These requirements are a tasteless joke by Microsoft's marketing department. Such a minimal machine might "run" XP, but opening the Start menu probably would take minutes. For a tolerable XPerience, your PC should have at least a 1 GHz processor and 256 MB of RAM. (Consider 1 or 2 GB of RAM if you edit digital video, do scientific calculations, or play Doom or Half-Life.) If you're upgrading a PC to run XP, don't skimp on RAM. Lots of memory and a fast hard disk can compensate for a slowish processor.

✔ **Tip**

■ Check Microsoft's Hardware Compatibility List (www.microsoft.com/whdc/hcl) before you buy equipment; see "Installing Plug and Play Devices" in Chapter 8.

Figure A.1 The Upgrade Advisor report can help you decide whether to upgrade your computer to Windows XP.

Check system compatibility

Run Upgrade Advisor to get information about potential problems that your computer may have if you upgrade to Windows XP, especially if you're using software designed for Windows 95/98/Me or older hardware. Upgrade Advisor checks the system peripherals and programs, and generates a list of items that may not work correctly with XP.

Windows Setup runs Upgrade Advisor automatically when you upgrade from a previous Windows version, but you're wise to run it manually before beginning installation.

To check system compatibility:

1. Insert the Windows XP CD.

   The Welcome window opens. (If it doesn't: Open Windows Explorer; navigate to the CD drive; then double-click setup.exe.)

2. Click Check System Compatibility.

3. Click Check My System Automatically.

4. If you have an internet connection, download the updated Setup files; then click Next.

   Update Advisor displays a list of potential problems, if any (**Figure A.1**).

5. For a full problem description and advice, click a problem in the list; then click Details.

6. To save the compatibility information in a text file, click Save As.

7. Click Finish.

✔ Tips

- To check system compatibility *before* you buy XP, download Upgrade Advisor from www.microsoft.com/windowsxp/pro/ howtobuy/upgrading/advisor.asp.

continues on next page

- *Before* installation, download updated XP-compatible drivers—particularly for graphics, audio, and multimedia devices—from manufacturers' web sites. Driver sites such as www.driverguide.com and www.windrivers.com can help.

- If you feel like being really organized, create a folder named Drivers on a USB flash drive or CD-R and a subfolder for the driver of each device. (Each driver will need its own folder because one of its files will be called setup.exe or setup.inf.) You'll be glad to have these drivers while you're installing XP and even more later, when your computer is a few years old and the drivers vanish from the web sites.

- On an older (pre-2001) PC, confirm that the *BIOS*—low-level startup software embedded in a chip on the motherboard—is compatible with XP. If you have any doubt, go to your PC manufacturer's web site, and look around for a file called "flash BIOS" or "BIOS utility," or maybe one of each. Follow the instructions on how to use this software *exactly*, because you're performing the rough equivalent of open-heart surgery.

  If your computer's BIOS is too old for XP, and no update is available, you may have to contact the manufacturer and request a newer chip.

- Never try to run obsolete, low-level system utilities on XP. Upgrade to the latest version of your virus and spyware scanners, backup program, hard-disk partitioning tool, or CD/DVD burner. (Look for the Designed for Windows XP logo.)

- If you've compressed your Windows 95/98/Me disk with the DoubleSpace or DriveSpace utility, uncompress it before installation.

Figure A.2 The dual-boot menu that appears when you turn on your PC offers you a choice of operating system. If you don't choose within 30 seconds, the computer chooses for you.

- See also "Transferring Existing Files and Settings" later in this chapter.

- To learn more about dual-boot setups, visit www.microsoft.com/windows/ multiboot.asp.

- For more information about partitions, see "Managing Disks" in Chapter 19.

Choose an installation type

If your PC is running an older version of Windows, you must choose one of three installation types (**Table A.1**). If your target PC has a blank drive, your only choice is a clean install.

✔ Tips

- The Upgrade version of Windows XP is cheaper than the Full version, but if you ever need to install the Upgrade version on a clean drive, you must first install an older (but qualifying) Windows version and *then* install XP on top of it. (This is one reason to take good care of your obsolete Windows CDs, the other one being that you *might* need a copy of an old DLL.)

Table A.1

Windows XP Installation Types

INSTALLATION	DESCRIPTION
Clean install	Installs a fresh copy of XP on your hard drive, replacing any existing operating system and erasing all files on the drive. During a clean install, you reformat or repartition your hard drive, wiping out all its accumulated crud, including outdated drivers, fragmented files, incompatible programs, and stale registry entries. A clean install has a restorative effect on a PC that's grown sluggish over time.
Upgrade	First, check Table i.3 in the introduction to see whether your current Windows version qualifies for the upgrade to XP; if not, you must perform a clean install. Upgrading to XP preserves your existing settings; installed programs; and data files, including your personal desktop elements, Favorites list, and everything in your My Documents folder. Windows Setup also attempts to upgrade device drivers to XP-compatible versions. Upgrading saves you from laborious rebuilding of preferred settings but doesn't invigorate your PC the way a clean install does. Following the upgrade, you may find that some programs run poorly on XP and need to be removed and reinstalled, possibly after being updated with a patch from the software publisher's web site.
Dual boot	If you want to preserve your existing copy of Windows and run XP, you can set up your PC to maintain both of them side by side. Each time you turn on your PC, it asks you which operating system to run (**Figure A.2**). Dual booting is useful if you have a critical piece of hardware or software that runs only on the older OS.
	Never install both OSes on the same hard-drive partition. It would be a disaster—and Microsoft Support doesn't even answer questions about such setups. Instead, take one of the following paths:
	• Buy a second hard drive, and use it for one of the two OSes.
	• Partition your existing disk—that is, divide it so that each portion functions as though it were a separate disk, with its own icon and drive letter in My Computer. Windows Setup offers a disk tool that erases as it partitions, but you may prefer to buy PartitionMagic ($70 U.S.; www.powerquest.com/ partitionmagic), a friendlier, more flexible utility that creates and manages partitions without wiping out their data.

Choose a file system

Within an operating system, a *file system* is the overall structure in which files are named, stored, and organized. Windows XP offers the choices shown in **Table A.2**.

Windows 95, 98, and Me don't recognize NTFS drives. Choose FAT or FAT32 over NTFS only if you're sharing files and folders with a Windows 95/98/Me user.

If you're unsure which file system to choose, use FAT or FAT32. You can always convert a FAT drive to NTFS, but not vice versa.

To convert a FAT drive to NTFS:

1. Choose Start > All Programs > Accessories > Command Prompt.

2. Type convert C: /FS:NTFS and then press Enter.

   (Replace *C:* with the letter of the drive that you're converting.)

   If you're converting the drive with Windows XP on it, the conversion happens when you restart your PC.

✔ Tips

■ If you plan to dual-boot between Windows 95/98/Me and Windows XP, the startup drive or partition must be FAT.

■ You can't boot an NTFS drive off a DOS floppy disk. Boot off the XP CD instead.

■ If your upgrade involves converting your system drive from FAT to FAT32, defragment the disk immediately after conversion. Your computer will run faster.

■ Some computers with older BIOS (see "Check system compatibility" earlier in this chapter) and drives upgraded to FAT32 won't be able to use XP's Hibernate feature, because they can't read the Hibernate file. The cure is a BIOS upgrade.

Table A.2

Windows XP File Systems	
FILE SYSTEM	DESCRIPTION
FAT	FAT (file allocation table, 16-bit) descends from the ancient DOS file system and still is used in Windows 95 systems. The largest disk drive (or partition) that FAT supports is 2 GB.
FAT32	FAT32 (file allocation table, 32-bit) is a more advanced version of FAT designed to overcome the 2 GB partition limit. It's used in Windows 98/Me systems.
NTFS	NTFS (NT file system), inherited from Windows 2000/NT, is a robust, secure file system that's far more reliable than FAT. NTFS also manages big hard disks more efficiently than FAT; Microsoft recommends NTFS for all 32 GB-plus drives. Some advanced features—such as automatic file compression, encryption, and file permissions—are available on NTFS but not on FAT.

Back up your data files

No matter what type of installation you choose, back up all your data files just before installation by using your usual backup medium (such as an external hard drive, CD burner, USB flash drive, Zip drive, tape backup drive, second PC, or web-based backup service). See "Backing up Your Files" in Chapter 19 and "Transferring Existing Files and Settings" later in this chapter.

Plug in and switch on devices

Make sure that peripheral devices, such as your printer or scanner, are attached to your computer and powered up, so that Windows Setup can detect them during installation.

✔ Tip

■ Some older non–Plug and Play devices may cause problems for Windows Setup. Disconnect them; then reconnect them after Setup completes. See "Installing Non–Plug and Play Hardware" in Chapter 8.

Get internet settings

If you plan to connect to the internet (Chapter 12) during installation, gather your connection settings beforehand. (You can configure your settings during setup or postpone this step until afterward.) Your ISP's web site will have necessary information, such as IP addresses and access phone numbers; Customer Service has a record of your account user name and password, if you've mislaid them. While you're at it, you may want to write down or back up your user names and passwords for web sites that you visit regularly.

Get network settings

If you plan to connect to a network (Chapter 17) during installation, gather your connection settings beforehand. (You can configure your settings during setup or postpone this step until afterward.) You will need:

◆ The name of your computer

◆ The name of the workgroup or domain

◆ **PRO** If your computer is a domain member, your domain user name and password

◆ **PRO** IP address, if your network doesn't have a DHCP or WINS server

Your Ethernet adapter and other network hardware should be connected and working properly before installation.

Turn off background programs

If you're upgrading, turn off your virus checker, lest it interpret Windows XP as a harmful infestation (ha ha). Also, turn off spyware killers, web ad blockers, non-Microsoft firewall software such as ZoneAlarm, and other utilities that load automatically.

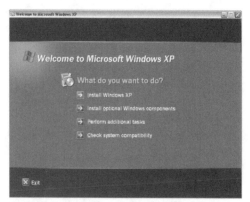

Figure A.3 This window is the starting point for installing Windows XP. Installation will take at least an hour.

Figure A.4 Use this drop-down list to choose an upgrade or clean installation.

Upgrading to Windows XP

Here's how to upgrade an older Windows version to Windows XP. If you're doing a clean install, skip to the next section.

To upgrade to Windows XP:

1. Start your computer; then insert the Windows XP CD into its drive.

   The Welcome window opens (**Figure A.3**). (If it doesn't, open Windows Explorer; navigate to the CD drive; then double-click setup.exe.)

2. Click Install Windows XP.

   The Windows Setup Wizard opens.

3. Choose Upgrade from the Installation Type drop-down list (**Figure A.4**); then click Next.

4. Review the End-User License Agreement (EULA); be mildly outraged by its terms; select I Accept This Agreement; then click Next.

5. Type the 25-character product key that appears on the back of the Windows XP folder; then click Next.

6. If you're online, select Yes to download updated Setup files; otherwise, select No to bypass this option; then click Next.

   Setup examines your system for XP potential problems and displays the Report System Compatibility page (refer to Figure A.1)—which you should have run manually before installation, as described in the preceding section.

7. Click Finish.

   Read a book while Setup copies files to your hard drive and reboots your PC. When it's done, you'll see the Welcome to Microsoft Windows screen. Proceed to "Using the Setup Wizard" later in this chapter.

Performing a Clean Install or a Dual-Boot Install

Here's how to install a clean copy of Windows on an empty disk or partition—or a nonempty disk or partition that you want to reformat and overwrite.

These instructions describe the installation of Windows XP Pro edition, which is a superset of Home edition. For Home edition, the process is the same, except that some screens either don't appear or are missing some options. (Domain settings don't pertain to Home edition, for example.) Simply ignore the steps and settings that aren't required for your installation.

To perform a clean install or a dual-boot install:

1. Start your computer from the Windows XP CD.

   Most PCs can boot up from a CD rather than a hard drive. Look for onscreen instructions when the BIOS messages appear. You may have to press a particular key (or any key). No luck? Read the PC's manual, or ask the manufacturer. Still no luck? See the Tips later in this section.

2. When the Welcome to Setup screen appears, press Enter.

   The first few screens are DOS-like text on a solid background.

3. Review the End-User License Agreement (EULA); then press F8.

4. If Setup finds a previous Windows XP installation, it asks whether you want to repair it or install a fresh (clean) copy; press Esc to install a fresh copy.

5. Press the up- or down-arrow key to select the hard-drive partition on which you want to install XP; then press Enter.

   Unless you've partitioned your drive for a dual-boot system, you probably have only one partition. For more about partitions, see "Getting Ready to Install Windows XP" earlier in this chapter.

6. If the selected partition already contains a copy of XP, Setup asks you to confirm your decision; press C to continue.

7. Press the up- or down-arrow key to select a file system (NTFS or FAT); then press Enter.

   For file-system details, see "Getting Ready to Install Windows XP" earlier in this chapter.

8. If the selected partition already contains files, Setup asks you to confirm your decision to wipe out the files; press F to format and continue.

   Setup formats the partition, copies files to it, and restarts the PC. The next few screens look like Windows, not DOS.

9. On the Regional and Language Options screen, click Next if Setup has guessed your language and country correctly; otherwise, click Customize, and choose the appropriate options.

10. On the Personalize Your Software screen, type your name and (optionally) the name of your organization; then click Next.

11. On the Your Product Key screen, type the 25-character product key that appears on the back of the Windows XP folder; then click Next.

    If your computer came with Windows XP installed, the product key may be on a sticker on the side of your PC.

12. On the Computer Name and Administrator Password screen, type a punctuation-free name for your computer; type (and retype) a password for the Administrator account; then click Next.

You can always change the computer name later; see "Running the Network Setup Wizard" in Chapter 17. For password tips, see "Setting up User Accounts" in Chapter 16.

13. If the Modem Dialing Information screen appears, specify your country, phone-system type (tone or pulse dialing), area code, and the number to dial (if any); then click Next.

14. On the Date and Time Settings screen, set the date, time, and time zone; then click Next.

If you have a network card installed, Setup detects it and displays the Network Settings screen; otherwise, skip to step 18.

15. On the Network Settings screen, select Typical Settings; then click Next.

16. On the Workgroup or Computer Domain screen, specify whether your computer is part of a workgroup or a domain; type the workgroup or domain name; then click Next.

If you're a domain member, ask your network administrator for this information.

These concepts are described in detail in Chapters 16 and 17.

17. **PRO** If you're a domain member, but your network administrator hasn't added your computer to the domain, Setup gives you the opportunity to join the domain later; click Yes to continue. (Discuss this omission with your administrator later.)

18. When Setup restarts your PC and greets you with the Welcome to Microsoft Windows screen, proceed to "Using the Setup Wizard" later in this chapter.

✔ Tips

■ If your PC can't boot from the CD in step 1, visit http://support.microsoft.com/?kbid=310994, "Obtaining Windows XP Setup Boot Disks." From there, you can download the Setup program onto six floppy disks. These disks contain the files and drivers that are required to access the CD drive and begin the Setup process.

■ If you're installing a dual-boot system, step 5 of Setup gives you the chance to delete a partition and create a new one.

PERFORMING A CLEAN OR DUAL-BOOT INSTALL

Using the Setup Wizard

All types of XP installations eventually converge at the Setup Wizard, which starts with the Welcome to Microsoft Windows screen and its animated question-mark icon, which you can click for help along the way. This wizard guides you through:

◆ Identifying and configuring your dial-up, high-speed (DSL or cable), or network internet connection. See Chapter 12.

◆ Entering IP and DNS addresses for your network connection. See Chapter 17.

◆ Activating your copy of Windows. See the next section.

◆ Registering Windows. Registration is not the same thing as activation and is optional, so click No unless you want junk email.

◆ Setting up the first five user accounts (but not their passwords), if they aren't already set up.

   If you upgraded from Windows 98/Me, XP imported existing accounts as Administrators and erased their passwords.

   To plug these security holes, add passwords immediately after you finish the wizard. See "Setting up User Accounts" in Chapter 16.

When you're done, Windows greets you with the desktop and Welcome screen. Windows XP is ready to use.

✔ Tips

■ The Setup Wizard's steps vary depending on your installed hardware, your configuration, and whether you're running Home or Pro edition.

■ You can skip many of the steps and perform them later without the Setup Wizard.

USING THE SETUP WIZARD

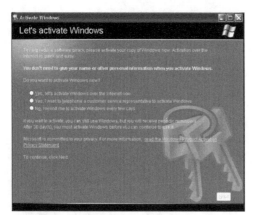

Figure A.5 You can activate Windows XP over your internet connection or over the phone. If you don't activate it within 30 days, XP stops working.

Figure A.6 If you don't have an internet connection, you can activate XP via a tedious phone call.

Activating Windows XP

Windows XP has an undesirable new feature—copy protection—that prevents you from running the same copy of Windows on more than one computer. During installation, Windows Setup examines your PC; computes a Special Secret Identifier from the exact system time plus data about key internal parts (hard drive, video card, motherboard, memory, and so on); and sends this identifier, along with your 25-character product key, over the internet to Microsoft, thereby *activating* Windows XP (**Figure A.5**).

If you don't have an internet connection, you must call a toll-free number; enter a 50-digit installation ID number on the phone's dial pad; get a 42-digit confirmation ID code back from Microsoft; then type that code in the Activate Windows screen (**Figure A.6**).

Later, if you install the same copy of Windows on another PC without uninstalling the first one, Microsoft will discover your duplicity during activation and lock you out of Windows. Unless you activate XP on the second PC, lockout occurs automatically in 30 days.

✔ Tips

- Activation is anonymous and transfers no personal information to Microsoft.

- If you skip activation during Setup, reminders pop up occasionally on the taskbar (**Figure A.7**). Click a reminder or choose Start > All Programs > Activate Windows to start the activation process.

- Bulk-purchased corporate copies of Windows XP are exempt from activation, and many new PCs come with a preactivated copy. But new retail PCs are preactivated by a method that writes to the computer's BIOS, meaning that if you flash the BIOS (see "Check system compatibility" earlier in this chapter) *after* installing XP, you may have to reactivate.

- If you replace four or more of your computer's 10 key internal parts in a four-month period, you'll have to reactivate XP.

- Windows stores its activation code in two small files, wpa.dbl and wpa.bak, in C:\Windows\System32 (or C:\WINNT\System32 if you've upgraded from Windows 2000/NT). If you replace your system drive, copy these files to a floppy and then copy them back to the new drive to keep Windows Activation happy.

- wpa.dbl and wpa.bak are *not* included in the files backed up by System Restore when you set a restore point—meaning that after you roll back your system, depending on the depth of the damage you were trying to undo, you may have to reactivate. (I suggest, again, that if these files exist on your system, you keep a backup copy, because Microsoft isn't completely straightforward about how or why they might change.)

Figure A.7 Windows nags you to activate.

Figure A.8 Use the same wizard to save your files and settings on one computer (no matter what version of Windows it runs) and reinstate them on your Windows XP computer.

Transferring Existing Files and Settings

The Files and Settings Transfer Wizard will help you move settings from one computer to another, including your personal files and info for Internet Explorer, Outlook Express, Microsoft Office, and some third-party applications (Eudora, AOL Instant Messenger, WordPerfect, Quicken, Adobe Photoshop, and Acrobat Reader, for example), as well as desktop, display, and dial-up connection settings. The XP CD contains a version of the wizard that you can run on another Windows computer—even one that's not running XP.

If you have two computers, you can transfer files and settings from the old one to the new one via a network connection, direct cable connection, floppies, CD-R, or Zip disk. If you have only one computer, run the wizard before you install XP, and save the file and settings to disk or a second hard drive.

To collect the files and settings from the old computer:

1. Insert the Windows XP CD into the drive of the computer from which you want to transfer files and settings.

   The Welcome window appears (refer to Figure A.3). (If it doesn't, open Windows Explorer; navigate to the CD drive; then double-click setup.exe.)

2. Click Perform Additional Tasks.

3. Click Transfer Files and Settings.

   The Files and Settings Transfer Wizard appears.

4. Click Next to skip the Welcome page.

5. Select Old Computer (**Figure A.8**); then click Next.

continues on next page

6. Select the transfer method that you want to use (**Figure A.9**); then click Next.

7. If you selected Direct Cable in the preceding step, follow the instructions on the Set up Your Serial Connection page that appears; then click Next.

8. Select the information that you want to transfer to the new PC (**Figure A.10**); then click Next.

9. If you checked Let Me Select a Custom List of Files and Settings When I Click Next in the preceding step, build a custom list on the Select Custom Files and Settings page that appears; then click Next.

10. The Install Programs on Your New Computer page tells you which programs are associated with the settings you've chosen; click Next.

    Install these programs on your new computer *before* you transfer the settings.

    The wizard displays its progress as it collects your files and settings.

11. If you selected Floppy Drive or Other Removable Media in step 6, Windows prompts you to insert the media (such as a floppy disk or USB flash drive).

12. Click Finish.

To transfer the files and settings to the new computer:

1. On the Windows XP computer, choose Start > All Programs > Accessories > System Tools > Files and Settings Transfer Wizard.

2. Click Next to skip the Welcome screen.

3. Select New Computer (refer to Figure A.8); then click Next.

4. Select I Don't Need the Wizard Disk; then click Next.

Figure A.9 If you back up to removable disks, keep track of the order in which you create them. You'll have to insert them into the new computer in that same order.

Figure A.10 You can transfer your settings, files, or both. Check the box if you want to create a list of *specific* files and settings to transfer.

5. Specify the location of the saved files and settings on the old computer (that is, specify the same transfer method that you chose in Figure A.9); then click Next.

6. Follow the onscreen instructions, which vary by transfer method.

   The wizard displays its transfer progress.

7. Click Finish.

   You may have to log off or restart your computer for the settings to take effect.

✔ Tips

■ Some settings may not carry over to the new computer. The wizard won't transfer old-computer settings for devices that are not available on, or incompatible with, Windows XP. On completion, the wizard lists files or folders that it couldn't restore. In particular, the wizard won't transfer third-party driver files for devices that aren't installed on the new computer and for network printers unavailable on the new computer.

■ Two superior migration programs are Alohabob PC Backup ($50 U.S.; www.eisenworld.com/pcbackup.asp) and Desktop DNA Professional ($39; http://ca.miramar.com/Products/Small_Office).

■ If you're chucking your old computer, check the phone directory or the web for recycling programs in your area (try www.eiae.org). Be sure to shred the files on all your hard drives before you disown your PC (see "Deleting Files and Folders" in Chapter 5).

TRANSFERRING EXISTING FILES AND SETTINGS

Uninstalling Windows XP

If you're unhappy with Windows XP, you can trash it and roll back to your previous version of Windows—provided that it was Windows 98 or Me. Some restrictions apply. You *can't* roll back if you upgraded from Windows 2000 or NT, converted from FAT to NTFS after upgrading, or repartitioned your drive since upgrading.

To reinstate Windows 98/Me:

1. Choose Start > Control Panel > Add or Remove Programs > Change or Remove Programs.

2. In the Currently Installed Programs list, click Windows XP Uninstall.

3. Click the Change/Remove button; then click Yes to confirm the removal.

   Windows XP uninstalls itself. Your PC restarts with your old copy of Windows 98/Me.

If you're sure that you never want to roll back to Windows 98/Me, you can delete your old copy and reclaim the hundreds of megabytes that it occupies on your hard drive.

To delete Windows 98/Me's files:

1. Choose Start > All Programs > Accessories > System Tools > Disk Cleanup.

2. If necessary, select the system drive; then click OK.

3. In the Files to Delete list, check Windows 98/Me Installation Files.

4. Click OK.

INDEX

INDEX

INDEX

INDEX